GREAT BRITAIN
Orkney Islands
Outer Hebrides
ATLANTIC
OCEAN
North
Sea
Inverness
Loch Ness
Aberdeen
Ben Nevis
Tay
SCOTLAND
Edinburgh
Glasgow
Clyde
Londonderry
Northern Ireland
Belfast
Newcastle
Carlisle
Tyne
Keswick
Lake District
Cumbria
Windermere
Kendal
Isle of Man
Yorkshire
Connemara
Irish Sea
Blackpool
Harrogate
York
Preston
Hull
REPUBLIC
Manchester
Leeds
Dublin
Liverpool
Shannon
Holyhead
Llanfair P.G.
Llandudno
Sheffield
Snowdon
OF IRELAND
ENGLAND
Limerick
Nottingham
Leicester
Peterborough
Waterford
Rosslare
Birmingham
Coventry
Dunmore East
Wales
Solihull
Severn
Fishguard
Stratford-upon-Avon
Cambridge
Ipswich
Tredegar
Gloucester
Colchester
Harwich
Oxford
Swansea
Bladon
Headington
London
Thames
Cardiff
Bristol
Gravesend
Bath
Windsor
Canterbury
Kent
Somerset
Salisbury
Dover
Folkestone
Southampton
Exeter
Bournemouth
Portsmouth
Devon
Brighton
Eastbourne
Exmouth
Weymouth
Cowes
Isle of Wight
Cornwall
Torquay
Plymouth
English Channel
Land's End

GREENWICH, LONDON

Orange **Line** 2

Herausgeber: Dr. Frank Haß

Ernst Klett Verlag
Stuttgart Düsseldorf Leipzig

Orange Line 2 für Klasse 6 an differenzierenden Schulen

Herausgeber: Dr. Frank Haß, Kirchberg
unter besonderer Mitwirkung von Harald Weisshaar, Bisingen

Autorinnen und Autoren: Jennifer Baer-Engel, Göppingen; David Lambert M.A., Cambridge; Pamela Grimes M.A., Stuttgart; Katherine A. Schmidt M.A., Stuttgart; sowie Carl Taylor M.A., Maidencombe; unter Mitwirkung von Sheila McBride, Stuttgart

Beratung: Manfred Bojes, Lohne; Anette Christiani, Dortmund; Ulf Degen, Braunschweig; Volker Pabst, Stade; Heike Parma, Halver; Annegret Preker-Franke, Bielefeld

Zusatzmaterial für Schülerinnen und Schüler zu diesem Band:

Workbook Plus Fördern mit Audio-CD und Lernsoftware	978-3-12-547626-4
Workbook mit Audio-CD und Lernsoftware	978-3-12-547625-7
Lernsoftware Einzellizenz	978-3-12-547624-0
Workbook mit Audio-CD	978-3-12-547525-0
Vokabellernheft	978-3-12-547571-7
Fit für Tests und Klassenarbeiten	978-3-12-547581-6
Action UK! Fotostory: The London Eye	978-3-12-585333-1
Action UK! Fotostory: A trip to the seaside	978-3-12-585334-8
Lektüre: The gift of the gab – A radio play from Ireland. Level 1	978-3-12-547080-4
Lektüre: OK, José – or how José saved the day. Level 2	978-3-12-547082-8
Lektüre: TOG – The TT Observer Greenwich. Level 2	978-3-12-547084-2
Lektüre: The four detectives. Level 2, mit Audio-CD	978-3-12-547081-1
Lektüre: The secret of Whispering Island. Level 3, mit Audio-CD	978-3-12-547083-5

1. Auflage **ISBN** 978-3-12-547520-5 (fester Einband) 1 13 12 11 10 9 | 2018 17 16 15 14

1. Auflage **ISBN** 978-3-12-547620-2 (flexibler Einband) 1 13 12 11 10 9 | 2018 17 16 15 14

Alle Drucke dieser Auflage sind unverändert und können im Unterricht nebeneinander verwendet werden.
Die letzte Zahl bezeichnet das Jahr des Druckes.

Redaktion: Jim Martin M.A.; Cornelia Schaller, Lektorat editoria
Herstellung: Ulrike Wursthorn

Umschlaggestaltung: Koma Amok, Stuttgart
Umschlagfoto: Kerstin Hacker, London
Illustrationen: David Norman, Meerbusch; Sabine Koch, Stuttgart; Dennis Mertz, Stuttgart; Steffen Wolff, Düsseldorf; sowie Lars Benecke, Hannover; Christian Dekelver, Weinstadt; Boris Goldammer, Berlin
Reproduktion: Meyle + Müller, Medien-Management, Pforzheim
Druck: Stürtz GmbH, Würzburg

Printed in Germany
ISBN 978-3-12-547520-5 (fester Einband)
ISBN 978-3-12-547620-2 (flexibler Einband)

9 783125 475205 9 783125 476202

Welcome back to Orange Line!

Du hast ein Jahr lang Englisch mit Orange Line 1 gelernt. Nun kommt der zweite Band, Orange Line 2. Vieles wirst du wieder erkennen:
- Die Lehrwerkscharaktere und ihre Familien sind noch dabei.
- Tom steht wieder mit Rat und Tat zur Seite.

Aber manches ist doch anders.
Diesmal geht es los mit **Zoom around Book 2**. Hier findest du Fotos von den Handlungsorten deines neuen Englischbuchs.
So lernst du nicht nur weitere Teile von Großbritannien kennen, sondern auch andere Länder, in denen Englisch gesprochen wird.

In den sieben **Units** (Kapiteln) erlebst du mit den vier Lehrwerkscharakteren und ihren Familien vieles aus deren Alltag.
Die Unit-Teile erkennst du gleich wieder. Es sind dieselben wie in Band 1. Nur zur Erinnerung:

Check-in: Neue Wörter und Landeskunde.
Language: Sprache und Grammatik.
Chats with Charlie: Die Radioseite mit DJ Charlie Black.
Story: Geschichten mit den Lehrwerks-charakteren.
Wordwise: Alles rund ums Wort!
Check-out: Prüfe, ob du alles verstanden hast.

Nach den Units gibt es eine kurze **Plus unit** mit Zusatzgrammatik.
In **Extras** findest du etwas für jeden Geschmack:
A story: Eine spannende Fortsetzungsgeschichte.
A comic: Die Kurzfassung eines Films.
A project: Poems and songs.
A play: Ein kurzes Theaterstück.
A project: Erlebnisse in Greenwich.

Nach den Extras folgen **Mediation and communication** und **Grammar** (Grammatikanhang) mit vielen Beispielen, Regeln und Tipps.
Am Ende des Buches findest du den Teil **Vocabulary** (Vokabelliste). Hier kannst du alle neuen Wörter nachschlagen und lernen.
Das **Dictionary** (Wörterbuch) listet die Vokabeln alphabetisch auf. Es ist auch zum Nachschlagen gedacht, wenn du einmal ein Wort vergessen hast.
Alles klar? Dann mache dich bereit für eine spannende Reise. Zuerst geht es nach Greenwich.

Erläuterungen:

Let's talk	Lasst uns reden
Let's listen	Lasst uns zuhören
For my folder	Für meine Sammelmappe
L1, 2 ◎	Diese Teile sind auf den Begleit-CDs (Langversion) enthalten. (Beispiel L1, 2: Lehrer-CD 1, Track 2)
(→ p. 22/ex. 19, 20)	Workbook-Verweis zu passenden Übungsaufgaben
✽	Diese Übungen sind besonders knifflig.
👥	Partnerarbeit
👥👤	Gruppenarbeit
....	Diese Übungen sind fakultativ.
▶ (orange)	Tipp zum Vokabellernen
▶ (blau)	Tipp zur Grammatik
▶ (grün)	Tipp mit Redemitteln

CAMDEN MARKET

TRADITIONAL
ENGLISH
FISH
&
CHIPS

Farmhouse
Accommodation
GREEN GROVE
FARMHOUSE B&B
2.8KM
Oifig Failte
TOURIST

GARLAND
MORGAN
BOLGER
LAHR...
HALEY...

Zoom around Book 2

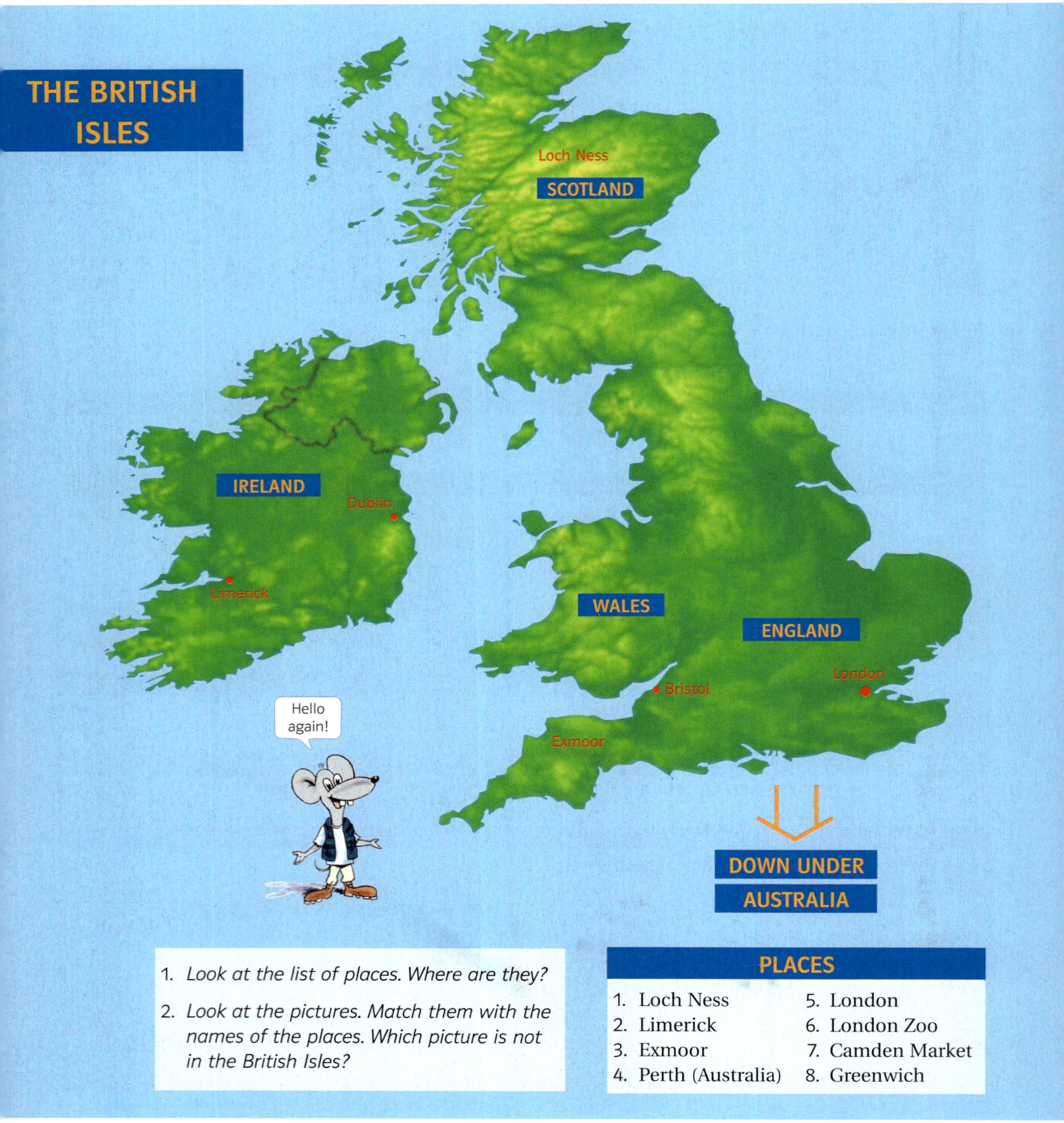

1. *Look at the list of places. Where are they?*
2. *Look at the pictures. Match them with the names of the places. Which picture is not in the British Isles?*

PLACES

1. Loch Ness
2. Limerick
3. Exmoor
4. Perth (Australia)
5. London
6. London Zoo
7. Camden Market
8. Greenwich

A

B

C

E

D

F

G

H

Zoom around Book 2 [ˌzu:m‿əˈraʊnd] – *hier: Ausblick auf Band 2*

Unit 1 Back to school

The start of term

1 I try to be at school at 8:30, but I sometimes arrive late for assembly. My friends laugh, but my class teacher gives me a dirty look!

Always wear the correct school uniform.
– Tallis T-shirt or sweatshirt
– Black trousers, skirt or shorts
– Yellow T-shirt and blue shorts for PE
C

PE is Physical Education.

Every week all pupils in Year Eight have a Drama lesson in the hall or outside. Before the lesson starts, pupils must put their bags in their lockers.
A

2 School uniform is a good idea, but I hate our PE shirts. They're yellow! Ugh!

3 I must buy a new pen before lessons start.

Pupils can use computers in History and Geography, Science and Technology, Maths, Foreign Languages, Art and Music.
B

The school shop opens every morning before school and at lunch-time. New pupils must buy their PE kit and their sweatshirts here. They can also buy pens, pencils, etc.
E

The caretaker opens the school doors at 8:00. Pupils must be in their classroom for registration or in the assembly hall before 8:35.
D

4 Drama is great! We talk about problems and do role plays. Sometimes we do drama outside.

1 Thomas Tallis School (→ p. 4/ex. 1, 2)

Match the texts A–E with the pictures 1–4.
One text hasn't got a picture. Can you find it?

2 Let's talk: Thomas Tallis and our school (→ p. 5/ex. 4)

Make two lists. What is the same?
What is different? Underline the words.

WRITING SKILLS

Notes:

Thomas Tallis	our school
start at 8:35	start at …
assembly or registration	no assembly no registration
lessons: PE, ...	lessons: PE, ...

L1, 1 3 Let's listen: Love or hate? (→ p. 4/ex. 3)

Choose the right words as answers.

1. What does Pete hate?
2. What doesn't Miss Brown like?
3. What does Mr Marco teach?
4. Who says Mr Marco is a good teacher?
5. What colour does Kate go?
6. Who is Laura with?
7. Why is she with him?

White. • Italian. • Sue's sister. • Pete. • He's really nice. • Science. • Drama. • Kate's sister. • Silly jokes. • German. • He's really cool. • Richard Black. • Red.

4 For my folder: A crazy school day

Imagine you go to school and it is different.
Your teacher isn't there, school starts late … .
Make a plan for a crazy school day.

time	crazy thing
11:00	school starts
first lesson	crazy tricks
teacher	Harry Potter
second lesson	...
teacher	...

Revision: Simple present

Sam's timetable

At T.T. we have a ten-day timetable. On Day 8 pupils can go home early because the teachers have meetings.

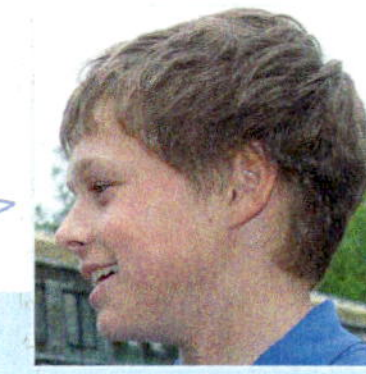

Timetable – Spencer, Sam 8 CA

Lesson		Day 1/Mon	Day 2/Tues	Day 3/Wed	Day 4/Thurs	Day 5/Fri
1	8:50 – 9:50	Drama	Italian	German	History	Science
2	9:50 – 10:50	Technology	RE	Art	English	Maths
	10:50 – 11:10	B	R	E	A	K
3	11:10 – 12:10	Technology	Music	English	Geography	Italian
4	12:10 – 13:10	Maths	PE	PE	Science	Geography
	13:10 – 14:10	lunch	lunch	lunch	lunch	lunch
5	14:10 – 15:10	History	Science	Music	German	English

Lesson		Day 6/Mon	Day 7/Tues	Day 8/Wed	Day 9/Thurs	Day 10/Fri
1	8:50 – 9:50					
2	9:50 – 10:50					
	10:50 – 11:10	B	R	E	A	K
3	11:10 – 12:10			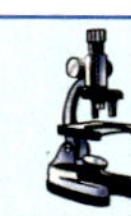		
4	12:10 – 13:10			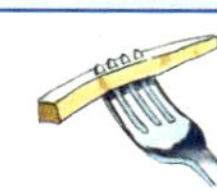		
	13:10 – 14:10			class teacher – 14:30		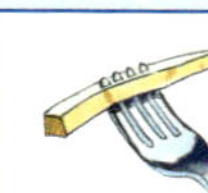
5	14:10 – 15:10					

▶ We write 13:10 and we say "ten past one."

RE is Religious Education.

1 Sam's week (→ p. 6/ex. 5, 6)

a) *Copy the timetable with times and days for Day 6 to Day 10 into your exercise book.*

b) *Look at the pictures for Day 6 to Day 10. What does Sam have on the different days and when?*

Example: On Day 6 he has **English** from **8:50 to 9:50**, RE from … .

c) *Look at Sam's timetable for Day 1 to Day 10 again and answer the questions.*

1. How many foreign languages does Sam learn?
2. What does he have on Day 8?
3. When does he have lunch on Day 1 to Day 5?
4. How many PE lessons does he have?
5. When does he have German?
6. When does he have Geography?
7. What does he have after Art on Day 10?

2 School subjects (→ p. 6/ex. 7; p. 7/ex. 8, 9)

a) *Look at the pictures. Guess where Sam is. Example:* 1. He's in his **Geography** lesson.

b) *Complete the sentences and match them with the pictures.*

Example: 1. I really love this subject, but it's difficult to draw people. – Picture 3.

1. I really … (*love/hate*) this subject, but it's difficult to draw people.
2. We always … (*take/have*) fun in this lesson. We … (*walk/talk*) about problems and … (*buy/do*) role plays.
3. I always … (*try/take*) to do the experiments, but the teacher isn't always happy.
4. My favourite subject! We … (*drink/learn*) about people in the past.
5. Here we … (*learn/like*) all about numbers.
6. We … (*speak/sing*) stupid songs in this class. I … (*write/hate*) it.
7. We … (*learn/leave*) to read maps and we … (*hear/watch*) videos about other countries.
8. I … (*try/know*) some words already like 'pizza' and 'spaghetti'.
9. We … (*wear/read*) stories and books, and then we … (*talk/eat*) about them in this class.

c) *Write about Sam's lessons.*

Example: 1. Sam really **loves Art**, but it's difficult to draw people.

▶ Sam **loves** Art.
Sam **has** … .
→ G1

3 Let's talk: A quiz

Look at the timetable on page 12.

A: What word am I thinking about? The first clue is:
We haven't got this in our school.
B: Is it lunch?
A: No, it isn't. The second clue is: The pupils do role plays.
C: Is it Drama?
A: Yes, it is. Now it's your turn. *Go on, please.*

4 For my folder: My school week

Make a timetable for your school week.

Lesson	Mon	Tues	Wed
1	Art	Maths	
2	English		
3			

Revision: Question words

L1, 2 Who's that boy?

Sam, Emma and Terry are outside the cafeteria.

Terry: Hey, who's that boy? I bet he's new.
Emma: What boy? Where?
Terry: He's over there with Mrs Carter and Mr Rose.
Emma: He has got a great suntan!
Sam: Who? Mr Rose?
Emma: No, silly! The new boy.
Mrs Carter: Good morning. This is Jake. He's in Year Eight and he's new. Can you look after him, please, Sam?
Sam: Yes, of course, Mrs Carter.
Mrs Carter: Thank you. Goodbye.
Sam: Bye, Miss. Hi, Jake! This is Emma and this is Terry.
Jake: G'day.
Terry: Hi, Jake!
Emma: Hi. I'm hungry! Let's have lunch! Which menu do you want: A, B or C?
Jake: Let's see. What tucker have they got?
Terry: 'Tucker'? We haven't got tucker on the menus today.
Emma: Oh, Terry. He means 'food'. That's what they say in Australia.
Terry: *(to Emma)* Well, why can't he speak English!? I'm having fish and chips.
Jake: Fish and chips. That's what I call tucker! I'm having that, too.
Sam: There's Lisa over there. Come on! We can sit with her.

1 Who is it? (→ p. 8/ex. 10)

1. He has got a great suntan.
2. She says "Good morning!" to Sam.
3. She's hungry.
4. He doesn't know what 'tucker' means.
5. He calls 'fish and chips' tucker.
6. The friends see her in the cafeteria.

2 Questions for Jake (→ p. 8/ex. 11, 12)

Jake has a lesson with Sam and Lisa. They ask Jake a lot of questions.
Look at his answers. Can you find their questions? Practise them with a partner.

Example: What's your family name? – My family name is Howard.

My family name is Howard.

My family **comes** from Perth in Western Australia.

We **say** "G'day" in Australia.

My favourite singer **is** Robbie Williams.

▶ **How** do you say "Hello" in Australia?
What's the best thing ... ?
→ G1

The best thing in Australia **is** the weather.

My hobbies **are** music and surfing – but not the Internet.

In Australia school **starts** at nine o'clock.

3 There's a new kid in town (→ p. 9/ex. 13)

Make a list of English questions for a new pupil.

name | house | languages | hobbies | family | music

Example: What's your name?
What are your … ?

4 That's wrong

Lisa and Sam know a lot about Jake. They tell Terry and Emma what is right.

Example: Terry: I think Jake says "Great day" to people. (Lisa: G'day)
Lisa: No, he **doesn't say** "Great day." He **says** "G'day."

Emma: I bet Jake listens to rap music. (Sam: Robbie Williams)
Terry: I'm sure Jake likes surfing the Internet. (Lisa: surfing)
Emma: I'm sure Jake's school in Perth starts at 7:00. (Lisa: 9:00)
Terry: I think Jake's dad lives in Bristol. (Sam: Perth)
Emma: I bet Jake spells his name with 'aik'. (Sam: 'ake' as in 'make')
Terry: I think Jake lives here with his dad and his brother. (Lisa: his mum and brother)

5 Let's talk: What food do you like?

Talk to a partner about food and drink.

What drinks do you like? – I like milk/… .
What food … ? – I like fish and chips/… .
What fruit … ? – I like bananas/… .
What vegetables … ? – I like carrots/… .

Which apple do you want:
the red apple or the green apple?
→ G2

6 Which food do you want? (→ p. 9/ex. 14, 15; p. 10/ex. 16)

a) At lunch Emma tries to be nice to Jake.
Look at the pictures. What does she ask him?

Example: 1. Which **food** do you want:
A, B or C?

apple | soup | food | sandwich

b) *Make up a dialogue with a partner.*

A: Which food do you want?
B: I want … .
A: Which apple … ?

Learning to learn: Grammar cards

GRAMMAR

SKILLS

A Wozu?

Du kannst eine *grammar card* vielseitig verwenden:
- als Hilfe bei Hausaufgaben,
- um bei Übungen deine Lösungen zu überprüfen,
- wenn du bei einer Aufgabe etwas nachschlagen willst,
- wenn du dich auf eine Klassenarbeit vorbereitest.

B Wie?

1. Finde eine Schachtel und stelle Kärtchen her, die dort hineinpassen. Du kannst auch ein Ringbuch verwenden.
2. Entscheide, welche Grammatik du erklären willst.
3. Schreibe Beispiele für diesen Grammatikpunkt auf deine Karte.
4. Gib nun der Karte eine Überschrift und eine Nummer.
5. Oft kann dir eine Eselsbrücke helfen, z. B. Tiere oder Menschen, die dieselben Anfangsbuchstaben haben wie der grammatische Begriff. Die kannst du dann auf die Karte zeichnen. Oder schreibe einen kurzen Reim, den du auswendig lernen kannst.
6. Lege ein Inhaltsverzeichnis an, wenn du mehrere *grammar cards* angelegt hast.

Grammar card — Nummer 1

Thema
simple present

Reim
He, she or it, (e)s geht mit.

Beispiele
You like / You don't like … .
Do you like …? / Don't you like …?
What do you like? / What don't you like?

He likes / He doesn't like … .
Does he like …? / Doesn't he like …?
What does he like? / What doesn't he like?

Eselsbrücke
simple present (SP) = Silly Pat
Silly Pat doesn't play hockey.

Zeichnung

1 Now try it! (→ p. 11/ex. 17)

a) *Make a grammar card for the 'simple present'.*

b) *Tell your partner about it. Can he/she understand it? You can now make a grammar card when you learn new grammar.*

L1, 3 1 Let's listen: Life 'down under'

a) Charlie makes notes because he wants to interview Jake about his school in Australia.

Write his notes in your exercise book and listen to the interview. He forgets to ask about two things. What are they?

Charlie's notes fo Jake Howard

pupils and teachers –
timetable –
start –
finish –
registration –
school uniform –
lunch –
after school –
school rules –

b) *Listen again: What do you learn about Jake's school in Australia? Complete the notes.*

c) *Write Charlie's questions in your exercise book. He forgets two questions. Add them to the other questions.*

Example: 1. How many **pupils and teachers** has your school in Australia got?

L1, 4 2 Sounds: [dʒ] or [g]?

Listen to the words and add them to the right list.

1. Technology
2. garden
3. gym
4. G'day
5. German
6. again
7. get
8. good
9. registration
10. joke

[dʒ]	[g]
religious	group
…	…

L1, 5 3 A poem: Down under in Australia

Down under in Australia
The world is on its head[1].
The people don't say "Hi!" to friends.
They shout "G'day" instead[2].
The water in the bathroom
Flows[3] anti-clockwise[4] down,
And birds[5] are brightly coloured[6],
Not just boring black or brown.

And all those funny animals
We only see in zoos[7]
Like wombats[8] and koalas[9]
Or jumping[10] kangaroos[11]!
But people in Australia
Are just like you and me,
And one day when I'm older
I shall[12] visit them and see.

[1]The world is on its head [… wɜːld … hed] – *Die Welt steht Kopf,* [2]instead [ɪn'sted] – *stattdessen,* [3]flow [fləʊ] – *fließen,* [4]anti-clockwise [ˌæntɪ'klɒkwaɪz] – *entgegen dem Uhrzeigersinn,* [5]bird [bɜːd] – *Vogel,* [6]brightly coloured [ˌbraɪtli 'kʌləd] – *bunt,* [7]zoo [zuː] – *Zoo,* [8]wombat ['wɒmbæt] – *Wombat,* [9]koala [kəʊ'ɑːlə] – *Koala,* [10]jumping ['dʒʌmpɪŋ] – *hüpfend,* [11]kangaroo [ˌkæŋgər'uː] – *Känguru,* [12]shall [ʃæl] – *werden*

L1, 6–8

You're boy mad, Emma!

1 Before you read

Which boy do you think Emma likes?
Why do you think this?

A It's Wednesday afternoon and Lisa and Emma are at their lockers. They are packing their bags. Jake Howard walks past. He says "Bye, girls," and leaves. Lisa smiles and says, "Bye, Jake." Emma just watches him.

"Isn't he cool?" Emma whispers to Lisa. "You're lucky. You've got Italian with him. You can sit and look at him all day!"

Lisa doesn't want to sit and look at Jake all day. She thinks Emma is boy mad.

"Maybe I can do Italian, and then I can be in your German class, too," she says.

Lisa is surprised. "But you don't like Italian, Emma!" she says. "Remember? That's why you're doing French with Terry."

Emma laughs, "Terry! Who's Terry? Jake is … well, he's just cool! I must find a way to see him after school. Maybe I can –"

"Emma!" Lisa says. "The bus leaves in ten minutes. Come on! Let's go!" The two girls go to the door of the school. Then Lisa whispers to Emma, "Don't look now, but Jake Howard is behind you."

"Oh, right," says Emma. "And Robbie Williams is with him."

"It's true," says Lisa. "He's just behind you." Emma goes red and turns round. The corridor is empty.

B Emma is really angry. She picks up her bag and runs to the bus. Lisa follows her and sits beside her. "Sorry!" she says.

Emma looks at her and the two of them laugh. The next morning they meet again on the bus. Suddenly Lisa says, "Don't look now, but Jake Howard is on the bus. I'm not joking this time. He's behind us." Emma looks round. Jake is talking to a friend. He doesn't see her. She goes red and looks very unhappy.

Lisa wants to help Emma. She sends a note to Sam in their German class. She writes:

She underlines the words 'nuts' and 'about'. She tries to pass it to Sam, but she drops it and Jake picks it up. He reads it and then gives it to Sam. "Oh no," thinks Lisa. "What can I do now?"

The girls meet on the bus after school. Emma is talking about Jake again when suddenly Emma's mobile rings.

"Hello! Yes. Oh, hi, Jake. Well, yes. That's great. See you at six o'clock! Bye!" She can't believe it! Jake wants to go to the cinema with her later. "I must go now," she says when they get off the bus. "See you tomorrow, Lisa."

C That evening Emma sends Lisa a text message:

Lisa is a bit sad, but she can always go and see Sam and Terry. On Monday morning Lisa gets onto the bus. Emma is sitting at the window with Jake.

"Hi, Lisa," Emma says. But she turns back to Jake.

In the next week Lisa only sees Emma in lessons. Emma walks home with Jake. She doesn't go on the bus with Lisa.

Two weeks later Lisa gets onto the bus at five past eight and Emma is sitting there. "Hi," says Lisa. "What are you doing here?" Emma doesn't want to talk about it.

"Lisa, I'm sorry," she says. "That thing with Jake and me –"

"Jake?" says Lisa. "Who's Jake?" And they look at each other and start to laugh.

2 Talking about the story

What do you think is the best part in the story and why?

Examples: It is where Lisa drops the note.
It is where Jake phones Emma.
It is where Emma says that she's sorry.
It is where …

3 What happens next?

Complete the sentences.

1. Jake walks past and then … .
2. The girls meet on the bus and later … .
3. Lisa writes a note to Sam and then … .
4. Emma talks on her mobile and later … .
5. Emma says "Hi, Lisa!" but after that … .
6. Lisa gets onto the bus and then … .

4 Match the two parts of the sentences

1. The girls are packing their bags 2. Emma thinks Lisa is lucky 3. Emma is doing French 4. Jake rings Emma 5. Emma sends Lisa a text message 6. Lisa doesn't see Emma on the bus 7. Two weeks later Emma is sitting there	+ because when but +	a. Lisa gets onto the bus. b. Emma gets home from the cinema. c. Jake walks past. d. Emma walks home with Jake. e. he wants to invite her to the cinema. f. she wants to do Italian to see Jake. g. Jake is in her Italian class.

5 A different ending for the story (→ p. 12/ex. 18, 19)

Look at the picture and write a different ending for the story. Write a short dialogue.

1 Definitions (→ p. 13/ex. 20)

VOCABULARY — SKILLS

Sometimes you don't know a word. Try to find a good definition!

a) *Read the definitions of the school words and match them with the correct words from the box.*

Example: They have it every morning and afternoon in schools in England. – **registration**

1. In this class, pupils do role plays about their problems.
2. Pupils do this in the gym.
3. Technology is one of thirteen of these.
4. You must wear it in Thomas Tallis.

b) *Now write your own definitions for these words:*
lunch • locker • sweatshirt • timetable

2 Schools in Germany and England (→ p. 13/ex. 21)

Choose the right verb and make sentences.

1. Pupils in Germany 2. German pupils often 3. Drama teachers in England 4. Pupils in England 5. A lot of English boys and girls	+	can needn't want to try to	+	a. do their homework in school. b. leave their books in their lockers. c. help pupils with problems. d. learn English. e. go home when it is very hot. f. wear a uniform.

3 Australia, England and Germany (→ p. 13/ex. 22)

Collect information about Australia, England and Germany. Make posters.

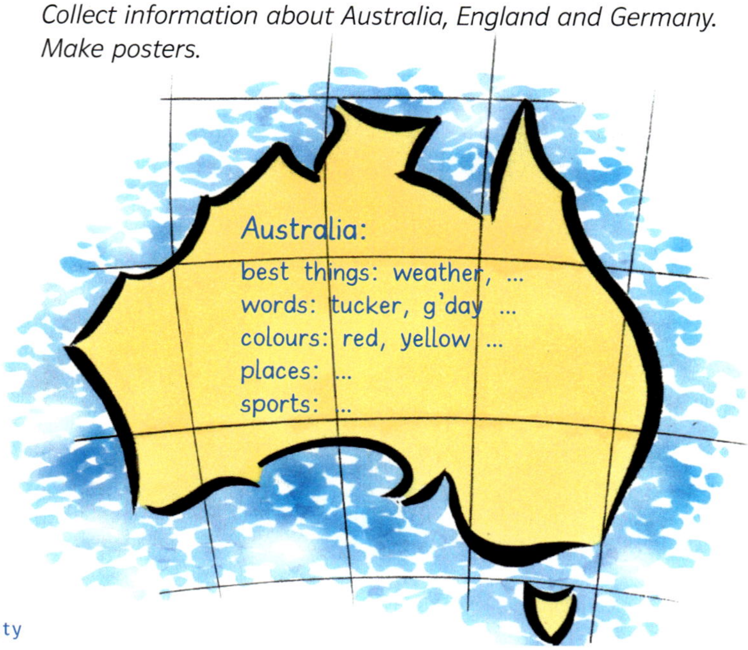

1 The new boy

(Revision of simple present → G1) (→ p. 14/ex. 23)

Emma writes to her friend in Bristol about the new boy, Jake. *Complete the text.*

Hi, how are you? And how is Bristol? I must tell you about the new boy in our year. He's really nice! His name is Jake and he … (*come*) from Australia. His dad still … (*live*) there. His mum and his brother… (*live*) near us, and he sometimes … (*take*) the bus home with me. They … (*not wear*) a uniform in his school in Australia, but they … (*get*) a lot of homework. He … (*not play*) football, he … (*play*) hockey and after school he and his friends … (*go*) surfing. He … (*say*) it's great! I want to go there next year. But I … (*not have*) the money.

2 Questions for the first day

(Questions with question words → G1) (→ p. 14/ex. 24)

Match the two parts of the questions.

1. Where do	we ask?
2. How do	we get the bus?
3. When does	we need for gym?
4. Who do	we get to the sports hall?
5. What do	he say "G'day"?
6. Why does	lunchtime finish?

3 There's a choice

(What/Which … ? → G2) (→ p. 14/ex. 25)

Choose the correct word: 'what' or 'which'.

Example: Which sports do you play: hockey, football or basketball?

1. … sports do you play: hockey, football or basketball?
2. … languages do you speak?
3. … English towns do you know?
4. … English towns are in your book: Bristol, Bath or London?
5. … languages do you learn at school: French, Italian or German?
6. … animals have you got at home: cats, dogs or fish?
7. … sports do you like?
8. … animals do you like?

DU KANNST JETZT

- ✓ Fragen über die Schule stellen. → *Stelle fünf Fragen über die Schule in einem anderen Land.*
- ✓ über deinen Stundenplan reden. → *Sage, welche Fächer du magst bzw. nicht magst.*
- ✓ deine Schule mit anderen vergleichen. → *Nenne drei Unterschiede zwischen deiner Schule und Thomas Tallis.*

Unit 2 What a week!

L1, 9 What are you doing this weekend?

1

2

Mit tomorrow *und* after school *kannst du das* present progressive *auch für Pläne verwenden.*

3

4

1 Who's going where? (→ p. 15/ex. 1, 2)

a) *Look at page 22. Example:* Terry is going to the … .
b) *Read the texts A–D and match them with the friends.*

We write:	We say:
300,000	three hundred thousand
1,000,000	a/one million

A A lot of visitors to London go to Harrods. It's a big department store, and it's expensive. At Camden Market you can buy cheap presents or clothes. It's open every day from 9:00 to 5:30.

B There are more than 300,000 things here. Young people love the Flight Lab. You can see a lot of different planes there.

C Thousands of people come to the ice rink to watch the London Knights ice hockey team. It is just 15 minutes away from the centre of London and has seats for 500 to 12,500 people.

D Every year more than 1,000,000 visitors come to see the 18,000 different animals here. Tickets for children from three to fifteen are £9.75.

2 Time and place

Put the phrases in the right place.

to the Arena • to London • every day ✓ • to the zoo • at the Science Museum • from the centre of London

Example: The market is open **every day** from 9:00 to 5:30.

1. The market is open … from 9:00 to 5:30.
2. The Arena is fifteen minutes away … .
3. The Flight Lab … is very popular.
4. More than one million visitors come … every year.
5. People come … to watch the ice hockey team.
6. A lot of visitors … go to Harrods.

L1, 10
3 Let's listen: Plans for the weekend (→ p. 15/ex. 3)

a) *Copy the grid into your exercise book. Collect information from the texts about the places.*

b) *Listen. What new information do you get?*

place	1. The Arena	2. Camden Market	3. The Science Museum	4. London Zoo
from texts	ice rink, …	…	…	…
new	concerts, …			

4 Let's talk: Things to do with friends

A: Let's go to the … tomorrow/next … .
B: No! That's boring. I'd rather go … .
A: OK. I can ask Mum for my pocket money. But I'd like to … before we go there.
B: OK. Let's meet at … o'clock at the … .

5 For my folder: Pocket money

I get pocket money every week on Saturdays. My dad gives it to me. I get … euros. I buy presents and … with it. I always put … euros in my piggy bank.

Saying where you were and how it was

L1, 11 How was your weekend?

On Monday the friends meet in the playground.

Emma: How was your weekend, Terry?
Terry: Great! The ice hockey match was cool. Sam and I were surprised – the London Knights were very good. There were thousands of people there. But I think Sam's mum was bored.
Sam: She wasn't bored, Terry. She was just cold. Don't forget she lives in Greece.
Emma: Lisa and I were cold, too, at the zoo.
Sam: The zoo? You weren't at Camden Market on Saturday then, Emma?
Emma: No! I was at the zoo with Lisa and Jade.
Terry: Was it good?
Lisa: No, it wasn't! It was terrible. After a short time Emma and I were fed up.
Terry: Why? Was Jade difficult?
Lisa: Difficult isn't the word! She was horrible!
Emma: Oh, Lisa. It wasn't that bad! There was a really sweet little elephant –
Sam: There's the bell. Let's go! You can tell us about it after school.

1 How was it? (→ p. 16/ex. 4)

Read the text and make sentences.

Example: 1. Terry's weekend **was great**. Lisa and Emma **were** … .

1. Terry's weekend 2. Lisa and Emma 3. The London Knights 4. Terry and Sam 5. Jade 6. Sam's mum 7. The zoo	+	was were	+	a. cold. b. surprised. c. fed up. d. horrible. e. very good. f. terrible. g. great.

▶ The match **was** cool.
The boys **were** surprised.
→ G3

2 Let's talk: Where were you?

▶ How **was** it?
Where **were** you?
→ G4

3 Last Saturday

Complete the sentences with 'was' or 'were'.

Last Saturday Sam and Terry … with Sam's mum in the Arena. There … an ice hockey match between the Nottingham Panthers and the London Knights. There … thousands of people at the match. Sam and Terry … happy because they … near the ice. But Sam's mum … cold. There … a sign behind them: "Café downstairs". And there … a lot of hot drinks and soups on the menu! But there … a lot of people in the café. There … one seat at a table near the window, and the game … on TV so she … happy. The Knights … really good. It … a great game, so Sam and Terry … happy. Sam's mum … happy, too, because now she … warm.

▶ There **was** a match … .
There **were** thousands of people … .
→ G3

4 Sam's dad asks about Saturday (→ p. 16/ex. 5)

Answer Mr Spencer's questions.

Example: Was your mum late this morning? – No, she **wasn't** late.
She **was** at the station before me.

1. Were you with your mum at the Science Museum, Sam?
   – No, we … at the museum. We … at the Arena.
2. Oh, was it a boring game? – No, it … boring. It … very good.
3. Was your mum happy at the game?
   – No, she … happy at the game. But later she … happy inside the warm café.
4. Were you and Terry cold near the ice? – Yes, we … cold. But we … worried.

▶ She **wasn't** late.
You **weren't** at the museum.
→ G3

5 What is right? (→ p. 16/ex. 6, 7)

Make questions and answers.

Example: **Were** Lisa and Emma happy? – **No, they weren't.**
Were they fed up? – **Yes, they were.**

▶ Was she … ?
– Yes, she **was**. / – No, she **wasn't**.
Were they … ?
– Yes, they **were**. / – No, they **weren't**.
→ G4

happy • fed up

bored • cold

difficult • horrible

terrible • good

6 For my folder: A great day

Imagine you had a great day last Saturday. Write a postcard about it to a friend.

Last Saturday was a great day. I was at the zoo with my aunt and uncle from Turkey. There were thousands of people there. It was very cold, but it was fun. The tigers and the elephants were great.

Telling a story

L1, 12 On Monday she wrote …

On Monday evening Emma wrote an e-mail to her friend in Bristol.

Hi Fiona!

Thanks for your mail. I read it half an hour ago, but supper was on the table. I was happy when the weekend came. But last Saturday was terrible, too. I went to London Zoo with Lisa. Her parents were in the café, so she had her little sister for the day. Jade is only six. We bought the tickets and went in. She was very happy – for an hour! Then she was hungry and Lisa gave her an apple. But two minutes later it fell on the ground. One of the pigs took it and ate it. She was really angry with it. Then she found a stick on the ground and threw it at the pig. A zookeeper saw her. He was very angry with her! It was so embarrassing! We saw the elephants after that. They were great. But later in the afternoon we sat down on a bridge and

Jade's hat fell in the river. It was too difficult to get it, so we left the hat there. Jade was really angry with Lisa. It was terrible. I sometimes have problems with Nasreen, but a little sister can be horrible, too. Write soon. CU, M

1 A terrible week (→ p. 17/ex. 8, 9)

Read Emma's e-mail and choose the right words.

1. Emma wasn't happy
   last Friday. • two days ago. • last week.
2. The e-mail came in
   half an hour ago. • last week. • two minutes later.
3. They took Jade to the zoo
   last week. • at the weekend. • in the afternoon.
4. Jade's hat fell in the river
   two hours ago. • yesterday. • later in the afternoon.

Past times signal words
half an hour ago
last week
two minutes later
later in the afternoon
yesterday
→ G3

2 A game: Verb dominos (→ p. 17/ex. 10; p. 18/ex. 11, 12)

Make 15 cards. Use all the irregular forms from the text. Play in groups.

see → saw
eat → ate
→ G5

GRAMMAR SKILLS

Learn past forms in a game – it's fun!
Always learn present and past together.

3 A trip to the zoo (→ p. 19/ex. 13, 14; p. 20/ex. 15)

Here are pictures of Emma's trip to the zoo. Put them in the right order and tell the story. The text on page 26 can help you.

Example: 3. Lisa **had** Jade for the day. They … .

1

be • give

2

be • leave

3

have • go

4

sit down • fall

5

find • throw

6

fall • eat

4 Later that afternoon … (→ p. 20/ex. 16, 17)

How does the story continue? Here are some ideas. Write three or four sentences.

come • go • see • have • eat • leave + zoo • burger • boys • girls • home • supper

5 Tom's lunch (→ p. 21/ex. 18)

Tell the story. Use the words in the box.

Example: Last Saturday Tom went … .

go • park

sit • wall

see • cat

sandwich • fall

cat • eat • sandwich

throw • apple

Saying what happened

L1, 13 What happened to your hair, Terry?

On Wednesday Terry arrived late for school. At break time in the playground he talked to his friends.

Sam: Hey, Terry! Where were you in Maths?
Terry: I was at home. I've got a problem. Look!
Emma: Good grief, Terry! What happened to your hair?
Terry: I dyed it! I wanted it blond.
Lisa: But it's green, Terry!
Terry: I know. I washed it six times this morning. That's why I'm late.
Lisa: But you can't go into lessons like that.
Sam: Ask your parents to give you a sick note.
Terry: I asked them, but Mum said, "No."
Sam: And your dad?
Terry: Oh, he just laughed.
Lisa: Listen, Terry. I've got an idea. We borrowed two wigs from the drama club for our play in Assembly last month. Come on, Emma! Let's find a drama teacher!

▶ Terry **wanted** … .
His dad **laughed** … .
Lisa and Emma **borrowed** … .
→ G5

1 At break (→ p. 22/ex. 19, 20)

a) *Put in the right verbs.*

Example: 1. Terry **asked** his parents for a sick note.

1. Terry … his parents for a sick note.
2. Emma … Terry about his hair.
3. Lisa and Emma … two wigs for Assembly.
4. Terry's dad just … .
5. Terry … his hair blond.
6. Terry … it six times.
7. Terry … late for school.
8. Terry … to his friends in the playground.

b) *Put the sentences in the right order.*

2 What happened next? (→ p. 22/ex. 21)

Complete the sentences.

1. Lisa and Emma … a wig.
2. They gave it to Terry and he … it.
3. They … it … OK.
4. When she saw Terry, the teacher …, "Who's your hairdresser, Terry?"
5. Terry …, "Lisa and Emma."
6. The teacher was surprised but Sam just … .

Use these verbs:

borrow • try • say • look • ask • answer • laugh

▶ He **tried** … .
They **said** … .
→ G5

1 Before you listen: Collect the names of animals

Example: In the zoo: elephant, …
At home: dog, …
On a farm: sheep, …

1, 14 ## 2 Let's listen: Charlie chats with people at the zoo

Listen and correct the sentences.

1. Charlie is talking to an old man.
2. Every month the zoo has more than ten thousand visitors.
3. Yesterday the zoo opened at eleven o'clock.
4. When the first visitors came, Steve played with them.
5. Yesterday a boy left his school bag on the wall.
6. A young elephant took it and put it in the river.
7. The boy shouted and tried to get his mobile.
8. Then the boy fell and dropped his cap.

LISTENING SKILLS

Notes:
- Read the sentences.
- Listen and write down the wrong words.
- Listen again and correct the words.

1, 15 ## 3 Let's listen: The children's zoo

Listen again. Look at the pictures of the animals. Which animals are not in the dialogue? Why not?

1

2

3

4

5

6

7

1, 16 ## 4 Sounds: [t], [d] or [ɪd] at the end?

a) *Listen to the words. Make three lists and put the words in the correct list.*

b) *Add the underlined word to the correct list.*

1. The friends walked to the elephants.
2. It happened yesterday.
3. I talked to the visitors in the morning.
4. The elephants liked the visitors.
5. A lot of people visited the zoo last month.
6. The boy shouted and dropped his mobile.
7. The elephant played with the cap.
8. They borrowed two wigs.

[t]	[d]	[ɪd]
looked	…	wanted
…	…	…

L1, 17–20 That's why Barker barked!

A On Thursday afternoon after school the four friends went to Greenwich with Barker. Terry wanted to find a hairdresser. They saw a new department store with a sign on it. It said, "Dogs must stay outside!" So Barker stayed at the door. Inside the shop Terry said, "I'd like to go to the hairdresser upstairs." But Emma wanted to look at clothes. Sam and Lisa went with her.

Soon it was six o'clock. A store detective came over to Sam and the girls. "I'm sorry," he said, "but you must leave. We're closing now."

"OK. But our friend is still in the store, I think," said Emma.

"I'm sorry. You must go now," said the store detective.

"OK. Maybe he's outside with Barker," said Lisa. The three friends walked to the doors with the store detective and he closed the doors behind them. They waited there with Barker. Ten minutes later Terry still wasn't there.

"Where is he?" asked Lisa. "It's cold and I'm hungry. I want to go home."

"Maybe he went to a different store," said Sam. "Or maybe he went home."

It was dark now. The friends started to go down the street.

B They were behind the shop when suddenly Barker stopped and listened. "He can hear a noise," said Lisa. Then he started to bark. Lisa was worried. "What's up, Barker?" she asked. He ran behind the shop and the friends followed him. Barker stopped at a high wall and looked up.

A boy shouted, "Sam!" The friends looked up and saw Terry. He was at a small window. "I'm in the toilet," he said. "I can't jump. It's too high. Can you help me?"

"Look," said Emma. "There's a big box over there. You can jump onto that." She and Sam put the box under the window. Terry climbed out of the window and jumped. "Thanks," he said.

"What happened, Terry?" asked Emma.

"When I came out of the toilets," said Terry, "the shop was closed. I waited, but no one came. So I went back into the toilet. I opened a window and shouted."

"That's why Barker barked!" said Lisa. "But let's go home now."

C Suddenly a voice said, “Stop.” It was a policeman. The store detective from the shop was with him.

“I saw this young man on the TV at my desk,” said the store detective.

“But I was in the toilet when the shop closed,” said Terry.

“Maybe that’s true, young man,” said the policeman. “But I’d like to check all your bags. Please come with us.”

The friends went to the store detective’s office and the policeman looked in their bags.

D The store detective looked at Emma. “Wait a minute,” he said. “I know you. I talked to you when I closed the shop.” Then he said to the policeman, “They wanted to look for their friend. I remember now. I think the kids are OK, Matt. I’m sure their story is true.”

“OK,” said the policeman. “You can go home now. You’ve got a good dog there. But next time watch the time, and ask a policeman or a store detective for help before you jump out of a window.”

“Thank you,” said Terry. “And thank you, Barker!”

1 Who said what? (→ p. 23/ex. 22)

Look at the story quickly and find which people said these things.
Example: 1. You can go home now. **The policeman.**

1. You can go home now.
2. It’s cold and I’m hungry.
3. We’re closing now.
4. What happened, Terry?
5. Wait a minute.
6. I was in the toilet.
7. What’s up, Barker?
8. I waited, but no one came.

2 Terry’s adventure

Match the two sentences and write one sentence. Use ‘when’, ‘because’ or ‘and’.

Example: 1. The friends were in Greenwich **when** they saw a shop with a sign on it.

1. The friends were in Greenwich.	+ when / because / and +	a. They saw a shop with a sign on it.
2. The friends wanted to look for Terry.		b. He was still in the shop.
3. The store detective closed the doors.		c. The friends waited outside.
4. Barker stopped and listened.		d. They were behind the shop.
5. Emma showed Terry the big box.		e. Terry jumped onto it.
6. The store detective saw Terry.		f. He looked at the TV in his office.
7. The policeman looked in the bags.		g. They were in the office.
8. The two men were happy.		h. The friends’ story was true.

3 The four parts of the story (→ p. 23/ex. 23)

Choose one of the parts of the story. Write a title for it and act it in your group.

L1, 21 1 Let's listen: Numbers and pounds (→ p. 24/ex. 24)

Listen to these numbers and say them. Then write the words in your exercise book.

Example: 1. Fourteen pounds, twenty-five p.

1. £14.25
2. 1,046
3. 1,500
4. 3,000,000
5. £5.15
6. 2010
7. £650,000
8. 325,000
9. £623.75
10. 16,500,000
11. 2007
12. £24,000,000

▶ 100 = one hundred
150 = one hundred and fifty
1,005 = one thousand and five
1,500 = one thousand five hundred
100,000 = one hundred thousand
1,000,000 = one million

L1, 22 2 Let's listen: Fact-file on London

a) Sam and Terry are surfing the Internet for things to do in London at the weekend. Terry finds a page of facts. *Listen and complete the grid.*

b) *Make a fact-file for a town which you know.*

fact	number
people in London	7,000,000
languages in London	…
people on buses	
visitors every year	
child's ticket	
group ticket	
street markets	

3 Word stars

Make word stars for these places:

animals

trees

…

…

…

…

…

…

4 Where were they? (→ p. 24/ex. 25–27)

Use 'in', 'at' or 'on'.

1. **in** a café
2. … a bike
3. … the market
4. … a department store
5. … the DLR
6. … the museum
7. … the bathroom
8. … the bus
9. … the ice rink
10. … a horse
11. … a zoo
12. … the playground

1 Jade's story (*Simple past: was/were, wasn't/weren't* → G3) (→ p. 25/ex. 28)

Jade tells a friend about the zoo, but Lisa corrects her. What does Lisa say?

Example: Our parents *were at home*. – No, they weren't, Jade. They **were in the café**.

1. The zookeeper was really *happy*.
2. I was very happy *all day* at the zoo.
3. I wasn't really hungry *all day*.
4. The elephants were *boring*.
5. It was *easy* to get my hat.
6. *Lisa* was very angry with the pig.

2 Barker's story (*Simple past: regular and irregular forms* → G5) (→ p. 25/ex. 29)

Complete the sentences in Barker's story.

I (*wait*) outside with the other dogs. People (*stop*) and (*play*) with us. One man (*give*) me his sandwich! A little boy (*talk*) to me for fifteen minutes, but then he (*go*) inside. When the store (*close*) and Lisa (*come*) out, I (*be*) really happy. I (*jump*) up on her and then she and her friends (*follow*) me. I (*walk*) behind the store and (*find*) Terry.

3 Telling a story (*Simple past: be + regular and irregular forms* → G3/G5) (→ p. 25/ex. 30)

Look at the pictures and tell the story. Use these words:
Start like this: **Last Saturday** Tom **watched** TV.
He **saw** Supermouse. **The next day** … .

last Saturday • the next day • later • after that • then • an hour later • that evening

watch • see — go • buy — look at • put on

dye • say — find • be — shout • wash

DU KANNST JETZT

- ✓ bis zu einer Million zählen. → *Zähle von 999.900 bis 1.000.000.*
- ✓ sagen, wo du warst und wie etwas war. → *Sage, wo du gestern warst und wie es war.*
- ✓ sagen, was du gemacht hast. → *Erzähle, was du gestern gemacht hast.*
- ✓ eine Geschichte erzählen. → *Erzähle eine kurze Geschichte aus der Unit nach oder erfinde eine eigene Geschichte.*

1 Dave's free morning (*Simple present* → G1 *and present progressive* → Band 1)

Dave works on a farm. He often has a lot of things to do. But he has a free morning.
What does he often do? What is he doing this morning?

1. 6:00 – feed the cows
2. 8:00 – take vegetables to market
3. 9:30 – feed dogs
4. 10:00 – collect eggs
5. 10:30 – check sheep
6. 11:00 – help farmer with pigs

▶ I'm working.
He's sleeping.
They're playing.
→ Band 1

Example: 1. At 6:00 Dave often **feeds** the cows. At 6:00 this morning **he is sleeping.**

1

6:00 sleep

2

8:00 listen

3

9:30 have

4

10:00 check

5

10:30 read

6

11:00 phone

2 A boring day (*Simple present* → G1 *or present progressive* → Band 1)

Look for signal words. Put in the right verb form. (→ p. 26/ex. 1)

▶ **simple present**
always / sometimes / often / never

present progressive
at the moment / now / today

Example: Emma and Lisa **sometimes go** to the park on Sundays.
But **today** they **are sitting** in Lisa's room.

1. They often (*take*) Barker out in the afternoon but it (*rain*) now.
2. It is June but at the moment Emma (*wear*) a warm sweatshirt. She never (*wear*) a sweatshirt in June but it (*be*) cold today.
3. At the weekend the two girls sometimes (*meet*) Terry and Sam in Terry's shed. They often (*play*) computer games there.
4. But at the moment Terry (*visit*) his cousins. They (*have*) a party today.
5. Mr Taylor always (*make*) scones or a cake on Sundays. He (*make*) scones in the kitchen at the moment.
6. Barker (*want*) to go outside but the girls (*want*) to stay at home.
7. So now Mr Taylor (*take*) him to the park and Lisa and Emma (*make*) scones.
8. Lisa never (*make*) scones. She (*hate*) cooking. But today she (*have*) fun.

3 It was terrible
(*Simple past of 'be'* → G3) (→ p. 26/ex. 2)

Use the correct form of 'was'/'wasn't' or 'were'/'weren't' in the dialogue.

Sam: How … your weekend, Terry?
Terry: Don't ask. It … terrible!
Sam: But … you in Bristol?
Terry: No, Sam, we … in Bristol. We … in Bath.
Sam: So what … so terrible?
Terry: Dad and I … at a football match on Saturday afternoon.
The Greenwich players … very good.
I … really angry. What about you? … you out with Lisa and Emma?
Sam: No, I … . I … with my dad. The girls … at Lisa's house and I … at his fishing club.
Terry: Oh! … that a bit boring?
Sam: Yes, it … .
Terry: That … the bell. Come on!

4 Super Barker!
(*Question words with 'was'/'were'* → G4)

Who? How? What? Why? Where?

Barker helped a store detective. A reporter interviewed Lisa. Complete his questions.

Example: 1. **Where was** your dog on Thursday afternoon? – Barker **was** in my mum's café. He … .

1. … … your dog on Thursday afternoon? – Barker … in my mum's cafe. He … at the window.
2. … … with Barker in the café? – My mum … there. But she … busy.
3. … time … it? – It … half past four.
4. … … the two men? – They … outside the music shop.
5. … … Barker excited? – The men … very strange. They … small but their jackets … very big.
6. … … under their jackets? – There … a lot of CDs.
7. … … the store detective? – She … there, too. She … with one of the men.
8. … … the other man? – He … under Barker.
9. … … Barker when he got his new bed? – He … very happy. Now he has got two beds.

5 A letter from home
(*Simple present and simple past* → G1/G5)

Jake gets an e-mail from his cousin Chris in Australia. Find the right form of the verbs.

Hi, Jake!
How (*be*) you and how (*be*) Greenwich? We often (*talk*) about you and your family here in Perth. I (*start*) my new school last week and (*meet*) my new teachers. Mrs Peters (*be*) our class teacher. Guess what she (*do*) on the very first day! She (*give*) us homework. It (*be*) Maths and the questions (*be*) very difficult. In class I (*sit*) next to this girl. Her name (*be*) Sophie. Last month she and her family (*come*) here from Germany. She (*think*) that all Australians are good at surfing. I (*ask*) her, 'Do all Germans (*wear*) Lederhosen?' She (*laugh*). How (*be*) you? Please write and tell us.

Unit 3 We all need friends!

Problem page

Last month Susan wrote:

The kids in my new school don't want to play with me at lunchtime and they laugh at my Scottish accent. I often cry. What can I do?

Here are your answers:

Dear Susan,
Two horrible boys in my last school tried to take my pocket money. They bullied other kids, too. One day they even pushed me off my bike. My dad told the teacher. She talked to the boys and their parents. After that they stopped. Yours, Jake

Hey Susan!
Once I had a problem with bullies in my class. I'm very small. But last year my cousin Todd from America visited me. He's really tall. When the bullies saw him with me, they were very suprised.
They never laughed at me again!
Roger

Hi Susan!
A horrible girl in our hockey team, Debbie, hated me because I was so good at hockey. One day she hit me on the head in a game. She visited me in hospital and we talked for a long time. After that we were best friends.
Nicole

1 Match the sentences (→ p. 27/ex. 1, 2)

1. The bullies in the class 2. Debbie 3. Two horrible boys 4. The kids at school	+	bullied	+	Susan Nicole Roger Jake	+	because	+	she has got a Scottish accent. he is small. they wanted his money. she was good at hockey.

2 An answer to the problem (→ p. 28/ex. 4)

In groups find a good answer to Susan's problem. Write a letter to the problem page. Compare your answer with the other groups' answers.

WRITING SKILLS

How to write a letter:
Start with: Dear ... ,
What ... (The first word has a capital letter.)
Finish with: Yours, (your name)

L1, 23

3 Let's listen: 'Friends' last night (→ p. 28/ex. 3)

Lisa and Emma are talking about 'Friends'. Their names are Phoebe, Monica, Rachel, Ross, Joey and Chandler.

Listen to the text. Then say who's who.

Example: Number 1 must be Phoebe because she's ... .
Number 2 must be ... .

4 Let's talk: A good friend

Tell the class about your friend. Answer their questions.

5 For my folder: My best friend

Who is your best friend? Write your own text about him or her.

Talking about past events

L1, 24 I'm sorry

Last Friday at six o'clock Terry sent a text message to Jake: "meet u at the youth club at 7." Terry went to the club, but Jake didn't come. The next day he went to Jake's house. Jake opened the door and took Terry to his room.

Terry: What's up, Jake? You didn't answer my message. Did you go out with your family last night?
Jake: No, I didn't, Terry. I'm sorry. I was tired. Did you go to the club?
Terry: Of course, I did. Where were you? Did you go out with a girl?
Jake: No, I didn't. I was with – Lisa.
Terry: Lisa? Did she invite you to supper?
Jake: Yes, she did. But it isn't what you think, Terry. We're just good friends.
Terry: So you went and had supper at her house and that was all? And you didn't get home before ten!?
Jake: Erm! No. We – we did my Maths homework.
Terry: You what?
Jake: Terry, don't tell the others, please! I have a real problem with Maths.

1 Find the questions (→ p. 29/ex. 5)

How does Terry ask about
1. Jake?
2. last night?
3. a girl?
4. supper?

▶ **Did** you … last night?
Did she … ?
→ G7

▶ **Did** he send … ?
– Yes, he **did**.
– No, he **didn't**.
→ G7

2 Did they do that? (→ p. 29/ex. 6, 7)

a) *Sort these questions. Then answer them.*

1. Did • Jake? • visit • Terry
2. do • they • Jake's homework? • Did
3. Terry and Jake • TV? • Did • watch
4. they • Did • play • computer games?
5. Lisa? • phone • Did • they
6. to Jake's house? • go • Did • Lisa

b) *Make dialogues with these sentences.*

Example:
A: **Did** Jake go to Lisa's house?
B: Yes, he **did**. **Did** Terry … ? *Go on, please.*

1. Jake went to Lisa's house.
2. Terry sent a postcard to Jake.
3. Lisa helped Jake with his homework.
4. Terry went over to Jake's house.
5. Lisa invited Terry for supper.
6. Terry went to the club.

3 A plan: To do or not to do? (→ p. 30/ex. 8)

Emma had a lot of plans for last weekend.
What did she do? What didn't she do?

Example: She **didn't send** a present to Fiona.

▶ Emma **didn't send** a present to Fiona.
→ G6

Saturday
- *send a present to Fiona* ✗
- *do English homework* ✗
- *learn my lines for the play* ✓
- *visit Terry* ✗

Sunday
- *finish Geography project* ✗
- *go shopping with Lisa* ✓
- *learn words for German* ✗
- *call Sam* ✗

4 A survey: Last week

a) *Think of five activities for the people in your group. Make a grid. Ask questions with 'did' and find out what they did last week.*

Example:
You: Gabi, did you watch TV last week?
Gabi: Yes, I did.
You: Did you go to a youth club?
Gabi: No, I didn't.
You: Did you … ? *Go on, please.*

b) *Use your grid. Tell the class about activities in your group.*

Example: In our group four pupils **watched** TV. Six pupils **went** to … .

Activities last week	Gabi	Linda	…
1. watch TV	☺		
2. go to a youth club	☹		
3. …			
4. …			
5. …			

5 Let's talk: Your teacher

Ask your teacher what he/she did when he/she was 16 years old.

▶ Did you go to discos?
… eat at burger bars?
… have a girlfriend?
… wear strange clothes?
… have long hair?

6 For my folder: I'm sorry about last week

Write a polite letter to your teacher.
Say why you didn't do your homework.

Dear …,
I'm sorry I … .
I was … .
Yours, …

Asking questions about the past with a question word

L1, 25 How did you do that? (→ p. 30/ex. 9)

a. On Saturday Sam borrowed his dad's bike. He tried a trick in the park, but he fell off. He hurt his arm and his face. He phoned his friend, Terry.

b. Sam was worried. The chain was off and it wasn't easy to put it back. Terry helped him. Then the boys went to Terry's house.

c. The boys cleaned the bike, but there were still black marks on it. Terry found some yellow paint and soon the bike looked like new.

d. Sam's dad took him to the doctor. She told him a lot of jokes. Then she checked his eyes, his ears and his arm. His arm wasn't broken and his head was OK.

e. Later, Sam's dad rode his bike. He came home and Grandma saw a terrible yellow mark on his new blue trousers. Sam felt terrible!

f. He told his dad about the paint. "But, Sam," said his dad, "there were marks on the bike when I bought it. That's why it was so cheap."

1 What does 'that' mean? (→ p. 30/ex. 10)

Look at the pictures.

Example: In picture 1 'that' means 'fall off the bike'.

▶ **What did** Sam **do?**
How **did** Sam **feel?**
→ G7

fall off the bike ✔ • hurt your arm • yellow paint • put marks on the bike • paint the bike • a yellow mark on his trousers

2 Questions about the accident (→ p. 31/ex. 11)

Make questions with 'what', 'where', 'when', 'why' and 'how', and ask your partner the questions.

L1, 26

3 Let's listen: Parts of the body (→ p. 32/ex. 12, 13)

a) *Listen to the words.*
Match the words and the numbers.

Example: Number 1 is 'eye'.

b) *Make dialogues.*

A: What did you hurt?
B: I hurt number 2.
A: Ah! You hurt your … . *Go on, please.*

finger | elbow | nose | knee | toe | hand | stomach | leg | eye | back | mouth | ear

4 A joke a day[1] keeps the doctor away[2]

Here are some of the doctor's jokes. Match the two parts.

Example: Why did the chicken[3] cross[4] the road?
– To get to the other side[5].

Questions

1. Why did the chicken cross the road?
2. Why did the fox[6] cross the road?
3. Where did the sheep go in the break?
4. Why did the elephant wear red trousers?
5. What did the mouse say to the camera[7]?
6. Why did the farmer buy a brown cow?
7. Why did the Maths book look unhappy?
8. Where did the sheep go on holiday[9]?

Answers

a. His white trousers had a mark on them.
b. Cheese!
c. To Baaaaaath.
d. To the baaaaaathroom.
e. To get to the other side.
f. Because it had a lot of problems[8].
g. He wanted that chicken!
h. Because he wanted chocolate milk.

[1]a day [deɪ] – *täglich,* [2]keep away [ˌkiːp əˈweɪ] – *fernhalten,* [3]chicken [ˈtʃɪkɪn] – *Huhn,* [4]cross [krɒs] – *überqueren,* [5]side [saɪd] – *Seite,* [6]fox [fɒks] – *Fuchs,* [7]camera [ˈkæmrə] – *Fotoapparat,* [8]problem [ˈprɒbləm] – *hier: Matheaufgabe,* [9]go on holiday [ˌgəʊ ɒn ˈhɒlədeɪ] – *Urlaub machen*

Defining people and things with 'who' and 'which'

Books which you can read

Two friends who came from Australia

Mrs Carter's class is doing a project about these books.

1 Book titles (→ p. 33/ex. 14, 15)

The bully who cried

The accident which changed my life

Animals which live in town

a) *Which title goes with which book?*

b) *Make one sentence from two. Use 'who' or 'which'.*

Example: This is the story of a kid. He has problems at home.
This is the story of a kid **who** has problems at home.

▶ person – who; thing – which → G8

1. This book is about animals. They live in town.
2. In this story we read about young people. They come from Australia.
3. Under the title you can see an accident. It happened in the street.
4. This is a story about a school. It has a lot of difficult pupils.
5. In this book there are animals. They hide in the park.
6. This story is about a girl. She did tricks on her bike in the street.

c) *Match your sentences from a) with the book titles.*

Example: This is the story of a kid who has problems at home.
– That's *The bully who cried.*

d) *Write a book title about bullies or friends. Make a cover for your book.*

2 People and things in a crossword puzzle

Use 'who' or 'which' and make clues for the words in the puzzle.

Example:
1 across: A person who hurts other people.
1 down: A thing which you can read.
2 down: A thing … .
Go on, please.

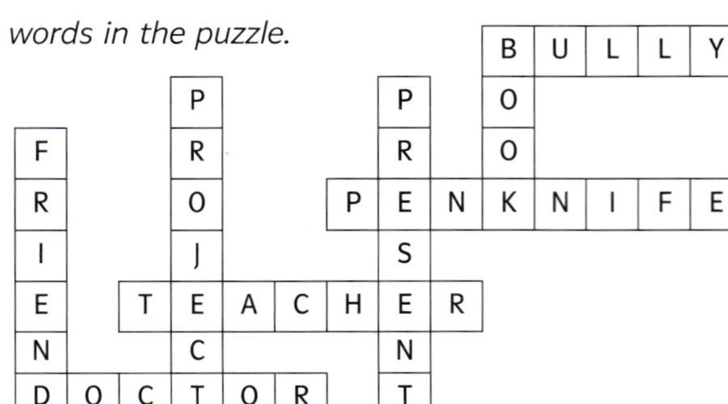

Chats with Charlie

L1, 27 **1 Let's listen: Friends and enemies**

Today Charlie is talking to two young people about a film.
Find the following information:

1. The title of the film.
2. The hero.
3. His enemy.
4. His friend.

The President lives in the White House.

L1, 28 **2 Let's listen: What's the film about?**

Listen again. Write five sentences about the film.
You can use these words:

magazine | kitchen | the President | lemonade | the White House

L1, 29 **3 Sounds: Same sound, different spelling**

a) *Listen to the sentences. Which spelling is right?*

1. write or right
2. ours or hours
3. "Bye!" or buy
4. eight or ate
5. their or there
6. road or rode
7. knew or new
8. high or "Hi!"

b) *Find more words with the same sound but a different spelling. Ask your partner to spell them.*

A: How do you spell the word '[haɪ]'?
B: You can spell it 'H I' or 'H I G H'.
A: Right! Now it's your turn.
B: How do you spell … ? *Go on, please.*

too or … • they're or … • know or … • hear or … • where or … • … or …

L1, 30 **4 A song: You've got a friend in me**

(Text: Randy Newman © Walt Disney Music)

You've got a friend in me (2x)
When the road looks rough[1] ahead[2]
And you're miles and miles
From your nice warm bed
You just remember what your old pal[3] said
Boy, you've got a friend in me
You've got a friend in me (2x)
If you've got troubles, I've got 'em[4] too
There isn't anything[5] I wouldn't[6] do for you
We stick together[7] and can see it through[8]
Cause[9] you've got a friend in me
You've got a friend in me

[1]rough [rʌf] – *rau,* [2]ahead [ə'hed] – *voraus,* [3]pal [pæl] – *Kumpel,* [4]'em [əm] – *Kurzform von „them",* [5]not … anything ['eniθɪŋ] – *nichts,* [6]would [wʊd] – *würde,* [7]stick together [stɪk] – *zusammenhalten,* [8]through [θru:] – *durch,* [9]cause [kɔ:z] – *Kurzform von „because"*

L1, 31–34

We're watching you!

1 Before you read

Are there bullies in your school? What do they do?

A On Monday Lisa's class had a Maths test. In the break the pupils talked about it. "How did you find the test, Jake?" asked Terry. "I found it difficult."

"It wasn't easy," said Jake. "Did you know all the answers, Lisa?"

"No, I didn't know all of them," she said. "But I think I got most of them right."

On Friday they got their marks and Lisa was very happy because she only got two questions wrong. Later at home Emma said, "Let's go into town."

"OK," said Lisa. "But I must tell my mum." Lisa took her mobile phone from her bag. "Wait, I've got a message," she said. She looked at it.

"Who's it from?" asked Emma. Lisa didn't want to say. Emma thought it must be a boy.

B Lisa sent a message to her mum and then the two girls walked into town. Half an hour later Lisa got another message on her phone. She was upset.

"What's up?" asked Emma. But Lisa still didn't want to say. Then they saw Sam and Terry in Burger Bonanza. "Let's go in here," Emma said. Lisa and Emma sat down next to the two boys. Lisa started to talk to them, but then she got another text message. Emma looked at Lisa. "Is it another message?" she asked.

"Yes," said Lisa. She was really upset now. "I want to go home."

"Why, Lisa? What does it say?" asked Emma. Lisa didn't answer. "Tell me." Lisa showed the message to Emma. It said, "We know where you are."

C Sam and Terry read the message, too. "Who's it from?" asked Terry.

"I don't know," said Lisa.

"When did this start?" asked Emma.

"Today," said Lisa. "After last lesson. This is the third message in two hours."

"Maybe it's a joke," said Sam.

"Maybe," said Lisa, but she wasn't sure. They left the burger bar at half past four. They wanted to look in the music shop, but then the next message came. It said, "We're watching you."

"I don't know what I can do," said Lisa. "I'm scared. Maybe they're here."

D On Monday the four friends talked to Mrs Richards before school. She listened to their story.

"Can I have your phone, please, Lisa?" she asked. Mrs Richards read all the messages. "Do you know why you got these messages?"

"No, but maybe it's because I'm good at Maths. We got our marks on Friday and then the messages started. Maybe some kids are jealous."

"OK, thank you, Lisa," said Mrs Richards. "You did the right thing. This is not a joke."

2 Some questions about the story (→ p. 34/ex. 16)

1. When did the pupils talk about the test?
   a. after school
   b. in the break
   c. at lunchtime
2. Where did Lisa and Emma go after school?
   a. to the park
   b. into town
   c. to the zoo
3. Where did they meet Sam and Terry?
   a. at the jazz café
   b. in the cafeteria
   c. at the burger bar
4. What did the four friends do on Monday?
   a. talked to Mrs Richards
   b. phoned Mr Rose
   c. looked for the caretaker

3 How does the story end? (→ p. 34/ex. 17)

What do you think happened next? What did the bullies do next? What did the teacher do then? What did the friends do then? Did they catch the bullies? Write an ending.

WRITING SKILLS

Before you write:
- Read the story again.
- Answer the questions.
- What do you think happened?

4 The bullies say they are sorry

Imagine the bullies are writing a note to Lisa. They want to say they are sorry. Finish the e-mail.

Hi Lisa,
On Friday we got our Maths marks. My friends and I are bad at Maths, but you are so good.
We ... .

Some more ideas:

be jealous • have some fun • didn't want to worry you • I'm sorry

1 Guessing words

Look at the baby kangaroo's face. Guess what "I feel sick." means.

2 Using a dictionary (→ p. 35/ex. 18; p. 36/ex. 19, 20)

If you can't guess a word, you can look it up in a dictionary.

LOOKING UP WORDS — SKILLS

a) The words are in alphabetical order. For example, you don't know the word 'sick'. *Look under the letter 's' first. Now look under 'si'. The word 'sick' comes between 'shy' and 'side'.*

s
sa-
sc-
se-
sh- sha- … shy
si- **sick** … side

sick [sɪk] ❶ krank (**with** vor); **be sick** krank sein; (*bei Übelkeit*) sich erbrechen; **fall** [*oder* **be taken**] **sick** krank werden; **I feel sick** mir ist übel ❷ (*übertragen*) **be sick [to death] of something** etwas satt haben; **I'm getting sick and tired of it** es hängt mir zum Hals heraus; **it makes me sick** das macht mich ganz krank ❸ (*umgangsspr*) *Witz*: geschmacklos, makaber; *Mensch*: abartig ❹ **I'm worried sick about it** ich bin darüber höchst beunruhigt **sick bag** Spucktüte **sick bay** Krankenrevier **sick·en·ing** ['sɪkənɪŋ] ❶ Ekel erregend ❷ (*übertragen*) entsetzlich, widerlich, ekelhaft **sick leave** ['sɪkliːv] **be on sick leave** krankgeschrieben sein **sick·ness** ['sɪk nɪs] ❶ Krankheit ❷ Übelkeit, Erbrechen **sickness benefit** Krankengeld **sick·pay** Lohn im Krankheitsfall

PONS express Wörterbuch Englisch

b) *When you look up a word it often has different meanings.*
Check the six meanings of 'sick'.
Which meaning is right for which sentence?

1. The sick child needed a doctor.
2. They are sick of life in the big city.
3. They were worried sick about the boys.
4. Can I go to the toilet, please? I feel sick.
5. Terry, that's a really sick joke.
6. The baby was sick on her new jacket.

3 More meanings

Translate these sentences into German.

1. It makes him sick when he sees fish in a supermarket.
2. She always has a sick bag when they go to Scotland by car.
3. The school has a sick bay for kids who are sick.
4. When you are sick and can't work, you get sick pay.

1 Grandma got it wrong (*Negatives in the past* → G6) (→ p. 37/ex. 21)

What did Sam say?

fell off | yellow | terrible | doctor | new | trousers | trick

Example: Grandma: Sam borrowed his dad's old bike.
Sam: I didn't borrow his ***old*** bike. I borrowed his ***new*** bike.

1. Sam tried a new game in the park.
2. Some boys pushed him off the bike.
3. He and Terry put black paint on the bike.
4. Sam's dad took him to the school nurse.
5. I saw a horrible mark on his T-shirt.
6. Sam felt really happy.

2 Sam's accident (*Questions and short answers in the past* → G7) (→ p. 37/ex. 22)

Complete the dialogue.

No, we didn't. | No, he didn't. | Yes, I did. | No, I didn't.

Example: Emma: **Did you see** Terry yesterday?
Sam: **Yes, I did.**

Emma: … to the park?
Sam: … . Terry had homework.
Emma: … your bike?
Sam: … . I took my dad's bike.
Emma: … it to you?
Sam: … . I borrowed it.

Emma: … some tricks?
Sam: … . But I fell off.
Emma: Oh! … your arm?
Sam: … . But it still hurts.
Emma: … to the doctor.
Sam: … . I'm OK.

Did you break …
Did you do …
Did you see …
Did you go …
Did you two go …
Did you take …
Did he give …

3 Guess who or what it is (*Using 'who' and 'which'* → G8) (→ p. 37/ex. 23)

Make sentences with the information and guess the word.

Example: name of a tunnel/ it goes under the Thames.
It's the name of a tunnel which goes under the Thames. – The Foot Tunnel.

1. a person / works in a hospital at night
2. a game / begins with the letter 'h'
3. a place in London / has got a lot of animals
4. a very famous woman / lives in Buckingham Palace
5. a part of your arm / is between elbow and fingers

DU KANNST JETZT

- ✓ fragen, was Freunde in letzter Zeit zusammen gemacht haben. → *Stelle einem Partner/einer Partnerin drei Fragen über gestern.*
- ✓ über *bullies* reden. → *Nenne drei Dinge, die 'bullies' tun.*
- ✓ über Freundschaft reden. → *Schreibe einen kurzen Brief an einen Freund/eine Freundin.*
- ✓ Körperteile benennen. → *Erstelle einen 'word star' zum menschlichen Körper.*
- ✓ Personen und Sachen beschreiben. → *Beschreibe drei Personen oder Sachen mit 'who' oder 'which'.*

Unit 4 You are what you eat!

Takeaways in Greenwich

Sam and Emma are looking at these takeaway menus.

1 Takeaway menus (→ p. 38/ex. 1, 2)

a) *Match the words in the lists with the pictures opposite.*

Example: Spicy lamb curry is on the menu from the Taj Mahal.

b) *Copy the lists from part a) and add more menu words to them.*

Main courses	Starters and desserts	Drinks
pizza with ham and cheese		
spicy lamb curry	minestrone soup	lassi
sweet and sour pork	Indian bread	tea
sausage and chips	rice	mineral water
chicken and chips	salad	lemonade
fish and chips	rice pudding	coke
spaghetti		

2 Let's talk: What food do you like?

Talk to your group about food.
What's the favourite food in your group?

I like … .
I don't like … .
I hate … .

L2, 1 3 Let's listen: What's for supper? (→ p. 38/ex. 3)

1. Which food does Sam hate?
   a. soup b. spaghetti c. fish d. chips
2. What can't Grandma eat now?
   a. Indian food b. fish and chips
   c. Italian food d. Chinese food
3. What doesn't Mr Spencer order?
   a. soup b. salad c. spaghetti d. sandwiches
4. Where do they order their takeaway?
   a. Taj Mahal b. Greenwich Supper Bar
   c. Ching Ming d. La Caverna

4 For my folder: A menu

a) *Make a menu with your favourite food and drinks on it. You can draw pictures or use photos from magazines.*

b) *Tell the class about your menu.*
Example: My favourite food is Turkish. On my menu there is a dessert. It's … .

My favourite food: Turkish
Tea and 'baklava'

Comparing things and people

L2, 2 Fast food

Sam and Emma are setting the table. The bell rings.

Emma: That's what I call 'fast food'.
Sam: I think Ching Ming is faster.
Emma: Yes, but the food at La Caverna is better.
Sam: Well, Ching Ming can't be worse than school lunches.
Emma: School food isn't bad. The rice pudding is the best. The worst place is the Supper Bar. Everything is with chips!
Mr Spencer: Supper is ready! The soup is Grandma's and the salad is for me. Hands off!
Sam: Salad? No thanks, Dad. Nothing is more boring than salad.
Mr Spencer: Or healthier? Salad is healthy!
Emma: It's maybe the healthiest food, but it's also the most boring. Pizza is tastier. But this pizza is bigger than I thought.
Sam: Don't worry. We can help you!

1 Comparing

a) *What do Sam, Emma and Mr Spencer think about salad?*

b) *Look at the text. Copy the grid and complete it.*

c) *Make a grammar rule for comparing adjectives.*

d) *Check your rule on page 134.*

GRAMMAR SKILLS

Making a grammar rule:
1. Find examples in the text and add them to your grid.
2. How do you make the comparative of adjectives like 'fast', 'big' and 'healthy'?
3. How do you make the superlative of these adjectives?

adjective	fast	...	...
comparative	faster	bigger	...
superlative	...	...	(the) healthiest

2 Different kinds of food (→ p. 39/ex. 4)

Compare the food.

Example: sweet A banana is **sweet**. Cake is **sweeter than** a banana. But chocolate is **the sweetest**.

1. healthy cheese • fish • vegetables
2. big German burgers • American burgers • Australian burgers
3. hot soup • tea with milk • tea without milk
4. nice apple cake • chocolate cake • birthday cake

3 I think pizza is the best! (→ p. 39/ex. 5)

good → **better** → (the) **best**
bad → **worse** → (the) **worst**
→ G9

a) *Compare the things in the pictures.*

Example:

I think chicken is good. It's **better than** … .
But … is **the best**.

food ✔ • seasons • tests • days • accidents

1.

2.

3.
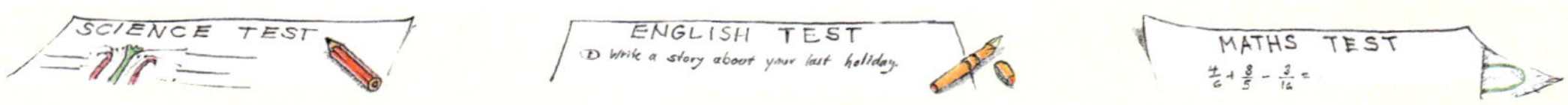

4.

b) *Draw more things and compare them.*

4 Comparing food (→ p. 40/ex. 6, 7)

Choose an adjective and compare the things.

Example: I think Italian food is interesting, but Chinese food is **more** interesting. Indian food is **the most** interesting.

interesting → **more** interesting → (the) **most** interesting
→ G9

1. Italian food • Indian food • Chinese food
2. green salad • old vegetables • cold soup
3. old cheese • fish • cat food
4. school food • fast food • baby food
5. party food • food at home • food in a restaurant
6. the recipe for pizza • the recipe for scones • the recipe for chocolate cake

exciting | boring | interesting | expensive | terrible | difficult

5 A group opinion: Food

a) *Collect superlatives about food from your group.*

Example: The most interesting is Indian food.
The cheapest is … . The best is … .

b) *Tell the class about your group's opinions. Make a class chart.*

WRITING SKILLS
Reporting on opinions:
1. Make notes and use them.
2. Start with "We think …"

6 Let's talk: People in our group

Find the three smallest/tallest/fastest/… in your group and compare them.

Example: Derek is tall. But Daniel is taller than Derek.
Robert is the tallest boy in our group.

small • tall • fast • old • young • heavy • funny

Giving advice or instructions, making suggestions

Should I go on a diet?

L2, 3

Mr Jackson isn't as fit as he would like to be. When he was younger he could run fast. But now he feels tired and his trousers are too small.

Mr Jackson: Wow! I need to lose a few pounds. I must go on a diet!
Terry: Dad, we're learning about food in Science at the moment. Dr Bell came to our lesson and talked about diets. He gave us these tips.
Mr Jackson: These tips look good, Terry. Let's go jogging in the park together!

DR BELL'S TIPS

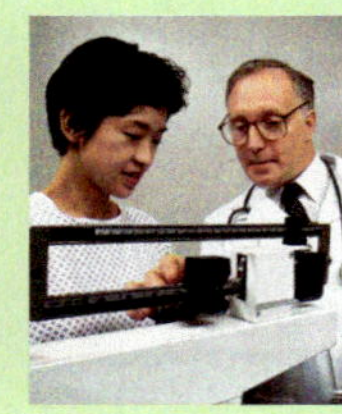

1. You must watch what you eat, but you needn't go on a diet, and you mustn't stop eating.
2. You must plan your day. You mustn't go without a meal. Don't forget breakfast!
3. You needn't go without your favourite food, but you should eat a salad and fruit and vegetables every day.
4. You shouldn't eat between meals. But you should drink a lot of water.
5. You should exercise 3 or 4 times a week, but you needn't exercise for hours. Thirty minutes is OK.
6. Go to a doctor before you go on a diet or start to exercise.

1 How to get fit (→ p. 41/ex. 8–10)

a) *Which tip do you think is most important? Why?*

b) *What advice does Dr Bell give to Terry's class? Match up the parts of the sentences.*

Example: You **must** see a doctor before you go on a diet.

You **must** watch … .
You **mustn't** stop … .
You **needn't** go on … .
→ G10

You **must** You **mustn't** You **needn't**	eat more salads and vegetables. • feel hungry. • exercise. • eat more fruit. • do sports every evening. • go without breakfast. • watch what you eat. • plan your day.

2 You mustn't do that here!

Make lists: What must/mustn't you do at home/at school?
What needn't you do at home/at school?

At home I must …	At school I must …
At home I mustn't …	At school I mustn't …
At home I needn't …	At school I needn't …
…	…

3 Terry's suggestions (→ p. 42/ex. 11, 12)

What are Terry's suggestions for his dad? Match and make sentences.
Example:
Mr Jackson: I'm on a diet and I'm always hungry.
Terry: You **shouldn't** go on diets! You **should** eat small meals.

▶ You **should** eat more fruit.
You **shouldn't** eat a lot of sweets.
→ G10

1. I'm on a diet and I'm always hungry. ✓
2. I get tired and red in the face when I run a lot.
3. I'm not fit, but I can't do sport every day.
4. I like fast food and hate boring salads.
5. I need sweet things when I'm tired.
6. I never eat breakfast; I don't have time.

a. eat a lot of fast food • try different salads
b. go without a meal • always eat breakfast
c. run • exercise every day
d. go on diets • eat small meals ✓
e. do sport every day • exercise every week
f. eat sweet things • eat fruit

4 What do you eat?

a) *Do this quiz. How many points do you get?*

1. How many times did you eat vegetables last week?
   7 or more = 10 points 6–4 = 5 points fewer than 4 = 0 points
2. Did you have breakfast before school today?
   yes = 10 points no = 0 points
3. How much milk did you drink yesterday?
   two glasses = 10 points one glass = 5 points none = 0 points
4. How many apples did you eat last week?
   five or more = 10 points 2–4 = 5 points 0–1 = 0 points
5. How many times did you eat sweets last week?
   0–1 = 10 points two or three = 5 points more than three = 0 points
6. How many times did you eat chips last week?
   0–1 = 10 points two or three = 5 points more than three = 0 points

0–20: You don't eat the right food. Ask your parents or friends about healthy food.
21–35: Think more about what you eat. Don't eat between meals.
36–50: Not bad. You usually eat the right things. Don't forget a good breakfast!
more than 50: Very good. You always eat the right things.

b) *Compare your answers with your partners' answers. What can/must/needn't you change?*

5 Let's talk: My own questionnaire (→ p. 43/ex. 13, 14)

Make your own questionnaire. Use other words for the words in colour in exercise 4 a). Use your list of foods and drinks. Ask the people in your group and tell the class about the answers.

6 For my folder: Healthy or unhealthy?

Imagine your mum or dad wants to go on a diet.
Make a list of healthy and unhealthy foods and drinks.

Healthy foods	Unhealthy foods
salad, apples, ...	crisps ...

Healthy drinks	Unhealthy drinks
water, ...	coke ...

Using 'some' and 'any'

L2, 4 At the market

1 'Some' or 'any'? (→ p. 45/ex. 15)

Look at the picture of the stall at Greenwich Market and then make sentences.

Example: The stall holder has got **some** …, but he hasn't got **any** … .

► + = some
– = any
? = any
→ G11

2 Grandma makes supper

'Some' or 'any'? Choose the right word.

Sam: Can we have a fruit salad? We've got (*some*/*any*) apples and pears.
Grandma: I can't make a fruit salad. There aren't (*some*/*any*) bananas.
I'd like to make a salad, but we haven't got (*some*/*any*) tomatoes.
Have we got (*some*/*any*) lettuce?
Sam: Yes, I found (*some*/*any*) nice lettuce at the market.
Grandma: How about a green salad? And we can have peas and carrots with the chicken.
You bought (*some*/*any*) really nice food at the market today, Sam.

3 Let's talk: A shopping dialogue (→ p. 45/ex. 16)

Look at Sam's list and at the picture. Finish his shopping. One of you is the stall holder.

A: Have you got any carrots?
B: Yes. I've got some nice carrots today.
A: How much are they?
B: They're … .
A: Have you got any oranges?
B: No, I'm sorry, I haven't. *Go on, please.*

beans
carrots
potatoes
tomatoes
lettuce
oranges
pears
bananas
peas

1 Before you listen: Healthy food

You want to get fit. What should or shouldn't you eat?

L2, 5 2 Let's listen: Charlie's diet

Charlie is having a break today. Burt Brown phones him but he doesn't tell Charlie that he is on the air.

Use the listening skills and find the right answers.

1. Charlie wants to lose
   a. 10 pounds.
   b. 30 pounds.
   c. 20 pounds.
2. He is having
   a. lunch.
   b. breakfast.
   c. a snack.
3. Tracy and Todd are
   a. his doctors.
   b. his children.
   c. two young people.
4. Charlie orders
   a. a big green salad.
   b. rice pudding.
   c. spicy chicken.

LISTENING SKILLS

1. Before you listen:
   - Write down some words about the topic.
   - Read the title of the text and make sure you understand it.
   - Read the introduction.
2. When you listen the first time:
   - Don't take any notes.
   - Try to find out who is talking, where and about what.
3. Before you listen the second time:
   - Read the questions. Make sure you understand them.
   - Write down the answers which you already know.
4. When you listen the second time:
   - Write down the answers which you now know.
5. When you listen the third time:
   - Check your notes. Are they correct?

3 Let's listen: At the café
L2, 6

Listen and answer the questions.

1. What would the parents like?
2. What do they order as a dessert?
3. How much change do they give the waiter?

L2, 7 4 Let's listen: Tongue twisters

a) *Listen and try to say:*

1. My favourite foods are fish and fresh vegetables.
2. When I eat vegetables and drink water, I feel very fit.

b) *Make up your own tongue twister with [v] and [f] sounds.*

5 Let's talk: At the restaurant

Imagine you are in a restaurant.
Make dialogues with a partner.
One of you is the waiter.

Good afternoon. What can I bring you?
Would you like to order now?
Would you like a starter/dessert/drink/... ?
We'd like ..., please.
May we have the bill, please?
Here's ... . Keep the change.
Thank you very much. Have a nice day.

L2, 8–10

Sport can be dangerous!

1 Before you read: *What dangerous sports do you know?*

A It was six o'clock on Tuesday evening, and Mr and Mrs Jackson were in the living room. Terry came in. "Hey, Dad, we aren't having supper until a quarter to seven. Let's go jogging," said Terry.

"Oh, Terry, I'm so tired," said Mr Jackson. "I had a very busy day at work. And now it's dark. I don't like jogging when it's dark. It can be dangerous."

"Oh, Dad, don't be silly," said Terry. "It isn't dangerous. There are two of us. And don't forget, the doctor said you need to get more exercise."

"Yes, Terry is right," said Mrs Jackson. "He said you need to do something like jogging or swimming. It's cold now, so I think jogging is a better idea than swimming."

"OK, OK, you two," said Mr Jackson. "Let's go jogging. But tell me first what we're having for supper. I'm getting hungry."

"It's fish and a salad for you," said Mrs Jackson.

"Should I buy some chips?" asked Mr Jackson.

"No, you shouldn't," said Mrs Jackson. "We don't need any tonight."

B The paths in the park were dark because there were a lot of big, old trees along them.

"Terry, it's so cold and dark, and I don't see any other people who are jogging," said Mr Jackson. "Let's go and look in the department store next to the park. It's nice and warm there."

"Dad!" said Terry. "Come on, let's run!" Terry and his father didn't see the young man in front of them. He had a CD player with headphones and he ran into Mr Jackson.

"Oh, I'm sorry," said the young man. "You know, it's so dark here under the trees."

"It's OK," said Mr. Jackson. Terry and Mr Jackson started jogging again. After a minute Mr Jackson said, "Terry, stop. My wallet isn't in my right back pocket. I think that young man has got it." They ran after him.

"Hey, you, give me my wallet," Mr Jackson shouted at the young man.

"What?" said the young man. "What wallet?"

"It's in your pocket!" shouted Mr Jackson. The young man was scared.

"OK," he said. "No problem." He took the wallet from his pocket and threw it to Mr Jackson. Then he ran away.

"That was cool, Dad," said Terry.

"It wasn't cool," said Mr Jackson. "I was really scared. Let's go home now."

C Back at home, Terry and his father went into the kitchen. “Hi there. How was your run through the park?” asked Mrs Jackson.

“Mum, a man stole Dad’s wallet!” said Terry. “But then Dad ran after him, and he got the wallet back.”

“His wallet?” said Mrs Jackson. “What do you mean? It’s here on the kitchen table.”

Terry and his dad looked at the table. There was a wallet on it. Then Mr Jackson pulled the wallet out of his back pocket.

“This isn’t my wallet,” said Mr Jackson. “Oh no! What should I do now?”

“I can’t believe this! Look inside,” said Terry. “The man’s name must be in there somewhere. We can look up his phone number and call him right away.”

2 First impressions

Do you think the title is good? Did you laugh at the end? Did you want to know what happened next?

3 What happened first?

Look at the sentences and put them in the right order.

Example: 1. – “Let’s go jogging,” said Terry.

- Mr Jackson and Terry ran after the young man.
- “This isn’t my wallet,” said Mr Jackson.
- “Terry, it’s so cold and dark, and I don’t see any other people who are jogging,” said Mr Jackson.
- “Let’s go jogging,” said Terry.
- “It’s here on the kitchen table.”
- “Oh, Terry, I’m so tired,” said Mr Jackson.
- He took the wallet from his pocket and threw it to Mr Jackson.

4 Mr Jackson’s phone call (→ p. 46/ex. 17)

What does Mr Jackson say to the young man when he phones him? What does the young man say? What do they want to do? Write a short dialogue and act it.

Mr Jackson: Hello! This is … . Is that … ?
Young man: Yes, it is.
Mr Jackson: We just met in the park. I’m very sorry, but … . *Go on, please.*

Hello / Good evening / … .
This is … . / My name is … .
Is that … ? / Are you … ?
We’ve just met … . / I was in the park … .
I’m very sorry, but … / You won’t believe it, but … .
I don’t know how to tell you this, but … .

L2, 11 1 Let's listen: A picture rhyme (→ p. 47/ex. 18)

VOCABULARY SKILLS

Pictures and rhymes can help you to remember words.

a) *Look at the pictures and say the words.*

I don't like stupid vegetables like ,  and .

I never eat  but I always like some .

I sometimes eat an  or an  or some .

But I never eat  and there's nothing worse than .

You can always give me 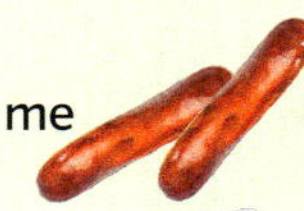 or  legs with .

And I sometimes like a  with a  and  – that's nice!

But my favourite food's  and I don't care what you say;

With a  and  I can eat it every day!

b) *Listen and check. Have you got the right words?*

c) *Rewrite the last two lines. Use different food words.*

2 Time for a rhyme

Start a list of rhyming words.
Add more rhyming words to your list.

peas	ham	tea	rice
cheese	lamb	me	nice
trees	...	...	...
...			

3 A food quiz (→ p. 47/ex. 19, 20)

1. Where can you find the spiciest food?
2. Where can you get the healthiest food?
3. Where can you buy the cheapest food?
4. Where can you eat the nicest food?

café • Indian restaurant • fish and chips shop
cake shop • burger bar • salad bar
restaurant • burger bar • school cafeteria
at home • at school • in a burger bar

1 Comparing things *(-er, -est/more, most → G9)* (→ p. 48/ex. 21)

Fill in the right form of the adjectives.

Example: Soup must be … . It should be … than spaghetti, but tea should be … . (*hot*)
Soup must be **hot**. It should be **hotter** than spaghetti but tea should be **the hottest.**

1. The vegetable curry is … . It is … than the fish curry but the lamb curry is … . (*spicy*)
2. The ham sandwiches are … . They are … than the cheese sandwiches. But the fish sandwiches are … . (*expensive*)
3. Fish and chips are not … food. Are they … than cake? Salads and vegetables are … food. (*healthy*)
4. Sam thinks salad is … food. It's even … than soup. But vegetables are … food. (*boring*)
5. The doctor thinks walking is … . But jogging is … and swimming is … sport. (*good*)
6. Terry's teacher says cakes are … for you. Are they … than sausages? She says burgers are … food for you. (*bad*)

2 In town *(must/shouldn't → G10)* (→ p. 48/ex. 22)

What do these signs mean? Match them with the instructions.

1

2

3

4

5

a. You shouldn't give bread to the birds.
b. You must turn off your mobile.
c. You shouldn't eat ice-cream on the bus.
d. You mustn't go right.
e. You shouldn't ride your bike here.

3 Have we got any tomatoes? *(Using 'some' and 'any' → G11)* (→ p. 48/ex. 23)

Complete the sentences. Then put them in the right order.
What do Terry and his dad have for lunch?

Mr Jackson: Oh, no! I must eat … vegetables today.
Mr Jackson: I want to make … lunch for us, Terry. Have we got … tomatoes or … lettuce?
Terry: Well, we've got … carrots and … beans. You can make … vegetable burgers.
Terry: No, we haven't got … salad things.
Terry: No, you're right. But there's … rice in the cupboard.
Mr Jackson: But we haven't got … potatoes. I can't eat just burgers!

DU KANNST JETZT

- ✓ Dinge vergleichen. → *Vergleiche zwei Städte.*
- ✓ einen Rat geben/Vorschläge machen. → *Nenne zwei Sachen, die du (nicht) machen musst, um fit zu bleiben.*
- ✓ Essen bestellen. → *Spiel eine Bestellung in einem Café nach.*
- ✓ Anweisungen geben. → *Nenne zwei Verkehrsverbote.*

1 Did you see Jake yesterday? *(Questions/negative forms in the simple past → G6/G7)* (→ p. 49/ex. 1)

Complete the following dialogue with 'did' or 'didn't'.

Sam: … you see Jake yesterday after school, Terry?
Terry: No, I … . But … he go to the club with you and Emma?
Emma: No, he … . And he … leave a message on my mobile.
Terry: I think he was at Lisa's house in the evening. … he tell you, Sam?
Sam: No, he … . … Lisa invite him for supper?
Terry: Yes, she … .
Emma: Lisa … tell me about it. … Jake phone you this morning, Terry?
Terry: Yes, he … But he … want to talk about it.
Sam: Well, let's ask them. There they are at the lockers!

2 A phone call from Mum! *(Questions in the simple past → G7)*

a) *Sam's mum phoned him from Greece to hear how his week was. What were her questions?*

Example: … in History class? (*What/do?*) – **What did you do** in History class?

1. … late for school on Wednesday? (*Why/be*)
2. … at the ice rink? (*Who/meet*)
3. … at the weekend? (*What/do*)
4. … your computer game? (*Where/find*)
5. … the football match? (*How/be*)
6. … in English this week? (*What/write*)

b) *Match the sentences with the questions in part a).*

a Emma and Lisa.
b. Terrible! Our team lost.
c. Stories about our best friends.
d. Terry and I went to a football match.
e. My bike chain fell off, so I walked to school.
f. Under my bed!

3 A new plan *(Negatives in the simple past → G6)*

Some teachers weren't at school last week. The school made a new plan.
What didn't the pupils do? What did they do? Choose the right verb form.

Week 6

Monday	– *English : interview the teacher*
	– *Maths : learn about money*
Tuesday	– *PE : play football*
Wednesday	– *Science : do experiments*
	– *History : finish project*
Thursday	– *German : go on class trip*
	– *French : start Unit 4*
Friday	– *Drama : talk about problems*

Week 6 – new

Monday	– read a book
	– play computer games
Tuesday	– jog in the park
Wednesday	– make a poster
	– watch a video
Thursday	– tell stories
	– do exercises on worksheet
Friday	– act role plays

Example: They **didn't interview** the teacher on Monday. They **read** a book.

4 Pupils get fit (Comparatives with '-er'/'-est' and 'more'/'most' → G9)

Thomas Tallis School magazine did a survey on the after-school activities of pupils.
What did the reporter write? Find the correct words.

Did you know that pupils at Thomas Tallis are mad about sport? We talked to fifty pupils at the school. Eight out of[1] ten think the (*more/most*) interesting activities after school or at the weekend are sport or exercise. They find these activities (*more/most*) exciting than soaps on TV! Only two out of ten think TV is the (*good/better/best*) activity of all.

First we talked to the teachers. They told us that pupils who played in a team are not just (*healthy/healthier/healthiest*) than other kids. They are also (*good/better/best*) in lessons than kids who watch a lot of TV.

Then we talked to the pupils. Some are (*more/most*) interested in sport than in exercise. We asked them, "What is the (*good/better/best*) thing of all about team sports?" They said, "It is (*more/most*) fun to play in a team than to do exercise."

Others don't like team sports. "It's just so much (*cool/cooler/coolest*) to take my skateboard out to the park than to run around[2] a football field," said Robert Fisher. "The (*bad/worse/worst*) thing is when it rains. Then we must find something that's (*good/better/best*) than TV."

Some pupils said they do a sport or exercise because they think they are not (*fit/fitter/fittest*). "It's much (*easy/easier/easiest*) to go on a diet if you also go jogging or swimming two or three times a week," said Sue Brown. And what about TV?

"TV isn't so (*bad/worse/worst*). But you must know where to find good programmes," said Paul Hunter. "You can learn a lot from some shows, and it can't be (*bad/worse/worst*) than playing computer games. I watched a (*good/better/best*) film about Australia just last night. Did you know that the (*big/bigger/biggest*) crocodiles[3] live in Australia?"

[1]out of [□□a□t͜□v] – *von*, [2]run around [□r□n͜□□ra□nd] – *herumrennen*, [3]crocodile [□□kr□k□daɪl] – *Krokodil*

5 Happy birthday! ('Some' and 'any' → G11)

Lisa and her mum are planning Lisa's birthday party later in the week.
Complete the dialogue with 'some' or 'any'.

Example: Mrs Taylor: Do you want **any** burgers. Lisa?
Lisa: No, I don't want **any** burgers this year. I'd rather have **some** Italian food.

Mrs Taylor: Can you give me … ideas then?
Lisa: Yes, Mum. I'd like … pizzas, … salads and … fruit. I don't want … chips and please don't buy … biscuits because … of my friends are on a diet.
Mrs Taylor: Don't you want … cake at the party then?
Lisa: Oh, yes, we need … cake, and … ice-cream, too.
Mrs Taylor: Umh!! Funny diet! Do you want … coke? Or would you rather have … milk?
Lisa: Milk? No, thanks. I don't want … milk, just … coke. Have we got … more of that nice fruit tea?
Mrs Taylor: No, we haven't got … fruit tea. But I can get … green tea at the Indian shop.

Unit 5 Media: Music and more!

1 Who were they? (→ p. 52/ex. 1, 2)

Match the names with the facts.

Example: Napoleon was French.

… was French. ✓ | … wrote great music. | … wrote famous plays. | … was Queen of England.

Shakespeare | Elizabeth I | Beethoven | Napoleon ✓

2 Busy people

Match the activities with the famous people and say what they are doing.

Example: Napoleon is taking pictures with his digital camera.

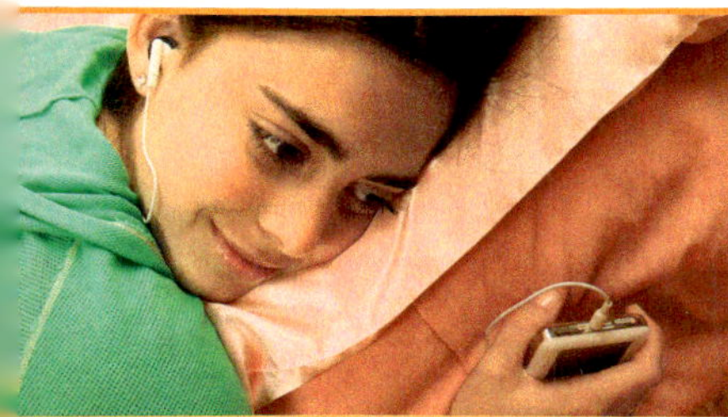

3 Other uses

What else can you do with the things in the poster?

Example: A digital camera: You can copy pictures onto your PC or laptop. You can also delete pictures which … . *Go on, please.*

▶ Take/copy/delete pictures/… .
Surf the Internet/download …/… .
Send a text message/an e-mail/… .
Record/watch/… DVDs … .
Download/listen to music/… .
Play games/do homework/… .

4 Let's talk: My media

PC
digital camera
mobile phone

Have you got a … ?
Yes, I have.
Can you … with it?

laptop
MP3 player
DVD player
…

L2, 12

5 Let's listen: Terry's new webcam (→ p. 52/ex. 3)

Sam and Terry are sending pictures of Terry's room to Sam's cousin, Phil, in New York.
Listen and look at the pictures. Are these pictures of Terry's room? Why or why not?

Example: Number 1 **is** a picture of Terry's room. There is a poster on the door. Number 2 **isn't** … .

1

2

3

4

5

6

6 For my folder: Our favourite music

a) *Ask the people in your group about their favourite songs. Make a list for your group. Compare it with the other groups' lists.*

b) *Put a photo of your favourite star in your folder.*

favourite songs:
1. …
2. …
3. …
4. …

Saying what you have (just) done

L2, 13

I've found something for you, Terry!

At 4:00 on Friday afternoon Sam arrives at Terry's house. They have decided to make a CD.

A

1

Sam and Terry are making a CD for Phil for his birthday. Sam is downloading music and Terry is taking pictures of Sam for the cover.

B

1

They have just finished. Sam has copied ten songs, and Terry has already printed the cover. He has taken some good photos for it.

A

2

Sam is surfing the Internet. He is looking for things to do this weekend. He is clicking on Greenwich Youth Club's address.

B

2

Sam has found a text about an audition for *The Wizard of Oz* on their website. Terry and Emma have already acted in it at school.

A

3

Terry wants to go to the audition with Emma. She is going to Bristol today. Maybe she's still at home. Sam phones her to explain.

B

3

Emma has gone to Bristol. She has already left with her parents. She has lost her mobile phone.

A

4

Terry and Sam are filling in two forms. They have to send them in today. They are writing Emma's e-mail address on one form.

B

4

Terry has already filled in the forms and sent them. He couldn't tell Emma about the audition. But he can see her tomorrow.

1 A CD for Phil (→ p. 53/ex. 4, 5)

Make sentences about the pictures 1 A + 1 B.

Example: Sam **has** arrived at Terry's house. Sam and Terry **have already** decided … .

▶ Sam **has arrived** … .
Sam and Terry **have already decided** … .
→ G12

Sam Terry Sam and Terry	+	has have	+	(just) (already)	+	arrived at Terry's house. decided to make a CD for Phil. downloaded some music. copied ten songs. printed the cover. finished the CD for Phil.

2 An interesting website (→ p. 54/ex. 6)

Make sentences about other pictures (2–4).

Example: Sam **has just found** an interesting website.

▶ Sam **has just found** … .
Emma and her parents **have already left.**
→ G12

1. Sam • just • find an interesting website
2. Terry and Emma • already • act in it
3. Terry • decide to go to the audition
4. Sam • just • phone Emma
5. Emma and her parents • already • leave
6. Emma • go to Bristol
7. Emma • lose her mobile phone
8. Terry • fill in two forms

3 At the end of the evening (→ p. 54/ex. 7; p. 55/ex. 8, 9)

What can you say about the Taylors at the end of the evening?

Example: Ben **has made** spaghetti for supper.

1. Ben • make spaghetti for supper
2. The Taylors • eat supper
3. Mr and Mrs Taylor • go to the café
4. Lisa • do her homework
5. Lisa and Jade • take Barker to the park
6. Barker • lose his ball
7. Jade • leave her cap in the park
8. Ben • find the cap again

▶ leave → has/have left
find → has/have found
do → has/have done
take → has/have taken
lose → has/have lost
go → has/have gone
make → has/have made
eat → has/have eaten
→ G12

4 Let's talk: Things to do

WRITING SKILLS

Making a list:
– Write the things like this.
– Tick what you have already done.
do my homework
clean my shoes ✔
send a card to Grandma ✔
phone …

Questions and short answers

L2, 14 Have you two gone bananas? (→ p. 56/ex. 10)

It's Saturday evening. Emma has just come back from Bristol. She hasn't phoned Lisa yet. First she reads her e-mails. Then the doorbell rings.

> Dear Wizard of Oz fan,
> I have just read your e-mail about the audition. It's on Sunday evening at six o'clock in the hall at Greenwich Youth Club. Have you been to our youth club yet? Have you ever acted in a play?
> Have you ever seen the film? Has your mum or dad signed the form yet? Please call me before Sunday.
> Steve Jones

Emma: Hi, Lisa! Come in. Look at this. A 'Steve Jones' has sent me an e-mail about *The Wizard of Oz*.

Lisa: Who's Steve Jones? I've never heard of him. Have you ever been to Greenwich Youth Club?

Emma: No, I haven't.

Lisa: Maybe Mrs Carter gave him your name. Has she sent you an e-mail, too?

Emma: Let's look. Hmm … No, she hasn't. Wait, that was the doorbell.

Sam: Hi, Emma! Hi, Lisa!

Terry: Hi, Emma. Have you got an e-mail from Steve Jones?

Emma: Yes!?

Terry: Don't be mad. I can explain. Sam and I sent in two forms to Steve Jones at Greenwich Youth Club.

Emma: So it was you! Have you two gone bananas? An audition tomorrow? OK, we've already acted parts of *The Wizard of Oz*, but we haven't done it outside school.

Lisa: But you and Terry have sung and danced before. And you're really good.

Sam: Oh, come on, Emma. It's Saturday. You can practise tomorrow.

Emma: But I haven't done the plan for my story for English yet.

Lisa: I can help you, Emma. I've done it. It's really easy.

1 Questions about the audition (→ p. 56/ex. 11)

Make questions.

Example: gone • Have • bananas? • you two – **Have you two gone bananas?**

1. too? • an e-mail • has • sent • she
2. in • ever • you • have • a play? • acted
3. your mum or dad • signed • the form? • has
4. two forms? • have • sent in • Sam and Terry
5. practised? • have • yet • Emma and Terry
6. her English homework? • has • done • Lisa

▶ **Have** you two **gone** … ?
Has she **sent** … ?
→ G13

2 Things they haven't done yet

Make sentences.

Example: Terry/close/door/yet – Terry **hasn't closed** the door of his shed yet.

1. Emma/phone/Lisa/yet
2. The girls/make/cake/yet
3. Ben/put on/jacket/yet
4. Barker/eat/food/yet
5. Emma's parents/sign/form/yet
6. Sam/do/homework/yet

▶ He **hasn't closed** … **yet.**
→ G14

3 Has Emma ever … ? (→ p. 56/ex. 12; p. 57/ex. 13)

a) *Ask your partner questions about Emma.*

act in a play in school | act outside school | hear of Steve Jones | sing and dance | go to Bristol | …

Example:
A: **Has** Emma **ever** acted in a play in school?
B: Yes, **she has**.
A: Has she ever … ? *Go on, please*

b) *Have you ever done these things?*

▶ Have you ever … ?
– Yes, **I have.** / No, **I haven't.**
Has she ever … ?
– Yes, **she has.** / No, **she hasn't.**
→ G13

4 Mr Brook's shop assistant (→ p. 58/ex. 14)

Alison is Mr Brook's new shop assistant. She wants to go home, but she still has a lot of things to do.

Look at the picture and her 'to-do' list. Say what she has done and what she hasn't done yet.

Example: She **hasn't closed** the window **yet**.

5 Let's talk: A class survey

A: Have you ever acted in a play?
B: Yes, I have. What about you?
Have you ever … ?
Go on, please.

▶ go to a play • make music • see the *Wizard of Oz* • cook supper for friends • work in a shop • …

Asking questions with question words

What have you done to your hair?

L2, 15

It's five o'clock on Sunday, an hour before the audition. Emma and Terry have practised their song and they are now getting ready. Sam and Lisa are helping them.

Emma: Where have I put my red shoes? I can't play Dorothy without them. Maybe I've left them in the car.
Sam: Who has taken the CD player? It was here five minutes ago.
Lisa: I have. I've just put it in Terry's bag. Oh, Terry! What have you done to your hair?
Terry: Don't worry. It's only a wig!
Lisa: Whose wig is it?
Terry: I don't know. I found it in the cupboard.

1 Five o'clock

1. What have Emma and Terry done?
2. Where has Emma left her shoes?
3. Where has Lisa put the CD player?
4. What has Terry found?

> **What have** they **done** … ?
> **Where has** she **put** … ?
> → G15

2 An hour before the audition

Make questions. Example: Terry • done • his hair? • to • has • What
– What **has** Terry **done** to his hair?

1. What • happened • has • to the CD player?
2. my • taken • camera? • Who • has
3. put • Where • Lisa • her • has • jacket?
4. What • Mum • with • done • my wig? • has
5. forms? • parents • Where • put • have • your • the
6. has • my • stolen • MP3 player? • Who

3 'Where?', 'Who?' and 'What?' (→ p. 58/ex. 15; p. 59/ex. 16)

Complete the questions. Example: Lisa asks, "Who … (*break*) … ?" – "**Who has broken** Barker's bowl?"

1. The boy has lost his hat. He asks, "Where … (*leave*) … ?"
2. The girl's shoes aren't there. She asks, "Who … (*take*) … ?"
3. The man can't find his glass. He asks, "Where … (*put*) … ?"
4. The child feels sick. Her mum asks, "What … (*eat*)?"
5. Sam comes late. Lisa asks, "Where … (*be*)?"
6. Emma leaves for a party. Mum asks her, "Who … (*invite*) … ?"
7. Lisa starts crying. Emma asks, "What … (*happen*)?"

4 Let's talk: Today

Ask your partner about today.

> What have you done?
> Where have you been?
> Who have you seen?

L2, 16

1 Let's listen: The evening of the audition

a) Charlie is talking to Steve Jones from Greenwich Youth Club about their play, *The Wizard of Oz*. *Find the answers.*

1. The youth club is in … .
2. Steve and Charlie are in Steve's … .
3. Steve has been in the club for … months.
4. The bullies were … .
5. They have a … every week.
6. The wizard lives in … .
7. The auditions are this … .
8. A name for Australia.

b) *Now write down the first letter of your answers in part a). Sort the letters and finish this sentence:*

Dorothy must find the wizard because she wants … .

L2, 17

2 Sounds: Which word was it?

Listen to the sentences. Look at the words and write down the words which you hear.

1. free/three/tree
2. bed/bad/bet
3. big/pig/pick
4. plays/place/please
5. cats/kits/kids
6. Oz/does/ours

L2, 18

3 A song: We're off to see the wizard

(Text: E. Y. Harburg © Leo Feist Inc.)

Follow the Yellow Brick[1] Road.
Follow the Yellow Brick Road.
Follow, follow, follow, follow,
follow the Yellow Brick Road.
Follow the Yellow Brick, follow the Yellow Brick,
Follow the Yellow Brick Road!
You're (we're) off to see the wizard, the wonderful[2] Wizard of Oz.
You'll find he is a whiz[3] of a wiz[4] if ever a wiz there was.
If ever, oh ever, a wiz there was,
the Wizard of Oz is one because,
Because, because, because, because, because –
Because of the wonderful things he does!
You're (we're) off to see the wizard, the Wonderful Wizard of Oz!

[1]brick [brɪk] – *Backstein*, [2]wonderful ['wʌndəfl] – *wunderbar*,
[3]whiz [wɪz] – *Genie*, [4]wiz [wɪz] – *Kurzform von „wizard"*

L2, 19–21 ◎
Where's my bag?

1 Before you read

Have you ever seen an audition? Where? What happened?

A It's 6:30 on Sunday evening. The auditions have already started. Terry and Emma have practised all day. Sam has helped them with the music. Now they have changed their clothes. Terry has just gone to the toilet for the third time. Lisa is waiting outside the hall with Emma.

Emma: Is my make-up OK, Lisa? What about my hair? And my shoes?
Lisa: Yes, Emma. You've asked me four times now. They're still fine. Don't worry. You look great. It's only an audition.
Emma: I know but –
Lisa: Here's Terry. Wow, you look like a really fierce lion, Terry. Have you bought a new jacket?
Terry: No, I haven't. It's my dad's. I've only borrowed it for the audition.
Sam: Come on, you're on.

B Ten minutes later it's all over.

Sam: That was wicked, you two. Here, I've brought you some water.
Lisa: You were brilliant. I can't wait to hear what the judges have decided. I'm sure you've got the parts.
Emma: I don't know, Lisa. Steve Jones didn't look very happy. Did you take some photos?
Lisa: Yes, I did. I got a great picture of Terry on his knees.
Emma: I must phone my mum. Where have you put my bag, Lisa?
Lisa: It's on that shelf over there with the other bags. Above the table.
Emma: OK, thanks. I'll go and get it.
Lisa: What's wrong, Emma?
Emma: My bag isn't there, Lisa! Someone has taken it. And my mobile phone is in it.
Lisa: OK, don't panic. Let's all look for it.

C The friends look everywhere – in the toilets, in the room where they changed their clothes, in the cafeteria. But they can't find Emma's bag. They decide to ask Steve Jones to help them. When they go back into the hall the auditions have stopped. Then they hear a voice at the microphone. It's Steve Jones.

Steve: Can you all listen please? Someone found this bag on the floor, and they gave it to me. There's a mobile phone in it, but the owner hasn't turned it off. It rings every few minutes, and it's driving us all crazy. Can the owner please come and collect it and turn it off?
Terry: Well, now we know where your bag is, Emma!
Emma: Steve, I can explain everything.

2 What has just happened?

Look at the three pictures. What has just happened?

Example: Picture 1: Emma and Terry have just changed … .

3 Impressions (→ p. 60/ex. 17)

a) *What can you say about the people in the story? How do you think they feel? Match the names with the adjectives.*

Example: I think Terry feels **nervous**.

Terry ✓ | Steve Jones | Emma | Lisa | Sam

worried | nervous ✓ | helpful | excited | angry

b) *There are clues in the story which tell you that the people feel like this. Write sentences.*

Example: I think Terry feels **nervous**. He has just gone to the toilet for the third time.

4 Emma's e-mail (→ p. 60/ex. 18)

a) *Terry lost his e-mail about the auditions, so he wrote some notes from Emma's e-mail. Finish his notes.*

Auditions
The auditions start at 6 o'clock on Sunday. The doors are open from 4 o'clock. When you arrive, go to the room behind the hall and change there. Then put on your make-up in the toilets. Please bring a drink and sandwiches or fruit with you.

Notes:
start: 6:00 Sun
open: 4:00
change: room behind hall.
make-up: ...
bring: ...

WRITING SKILLS

Finding facts:
Write down what you need to know.
- the time
- the place
- the date
- …

Use short forms of words, e.g. Sun = Sunday

b) *Write notes about one part of the story. Use your notes and tell this part of the story to your partner.*

VOCABULARY S K I L L S

1 Things you can make, do and take (→ p. 61/ex. 19)

a) *Use the words in the box and make three lists under 'make', 'do' and 'take'.*

a cake • a mistake • my dog to the park • your homework • exercise • scones • a lot of noise • different things • a photo • notes • a wallet • a role play • a CD • a list • the bus

make	do	take
a list	different things	a photo
different things	...	...
...	...	...

b) *Add more words to your lists.*

c) *Which of the things on your lists have you done this week?*
Which things haven't you done?
Example: I have taken my dog to the park, but I haven't done my homework.

2 The odd one out (→ p. 61/ex. 20)

Look at the things on the magazine covers.
What is the odd one out and why?

watch DVDs | phone your friends | listen to music ✓ | send an e-mail

Example: 1. In the first magazine, the odd one out is the digital camera.
You can't listen to music with it.

1 

2 

3 

4 

3 A picture story (→ p. 61/ex. 21)

Look at the pictures, find the missing words and read the story.

Terry has just made a  . He's  the Internet. He pushes some 

off his 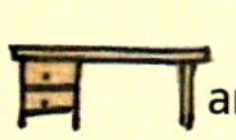 and then he can't find his  . He's looking behind a  when Sam comes in. Sam thinks his friend has gone  . "Can I help you?" asks Sam.

"No!" says Terry. "I'm looking for my 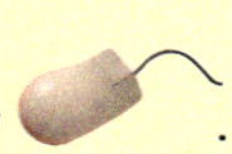 . I think I dropped it behind this  ."

"Well, maybe Tiger can help. All  can catch  ."

1 Saturday morning at the Taylors' house (*Present perfect* → G12) (→ p. 62/ex. 22)

Look at the pictures. What can you see? What have they all done?

Example: 1. Barker's bowl is empty. He has just eaten his food.

1

empty • eat food

2

clean • wash

3

he pful • set the table

4

hungry • jog in the park

5

late • turn off the alarm clock

6

happy • get a new sweatshirt

2 On the phone (Fragen im *present perfect* → G13/G14)

Complete the questions and answers with 'has'/'hasn't' or 'have'/'haven't'.

Emma: Hi, Lisa. … you had breakfast yet?
Lisa: No, I … . But Dad … just told me it's ready.
Emma: … he made breakfast this morning?
Lisa: Yes, he … . Mum … gone to the park.
Emma: … she started her diet yet?
Lisa: No, she … . She wants to start tomorrow.
Emma: Oh, … you asked your mum and dad about this evening yet?
Lisa: Yes, I … . It's OK. We can go to the cinema. But they … given me my pocket money yet.
Emma: Don't worry. Mum … just given me ten pounds.
Lisa: Great! I must go, Emma. Mum … just come in.

3 Steve's questions (*Wh*-Fragen im *present perfect* → G15) (→ p. 62/ex. 23)

Steve isn't happy. *What does he ask?*

1. He can't find his shoes. (*Who/take*)
2. He is looking for his book. (*Where/leave*)
3. His sandwich looks funny. (*What/put*)
4. He needs the manager. (*Where/go*)
5. His water glass is empty. (*Who/drink*)
6. He can't read a message. (*What/write*)

DU KANNST JETZT

- ✓ sagen, was du gerade erledigt hast. → *Sage, was du heute erledigt hast.*
- ✓ Fragen stellen über das, was andere gemacht haben. → *Frage einen Partner/eine Partnerin, was er/sie heute erledigt hat.*
- ✓ Notizen machen. → *Mache Notizen über Steves E-Mail von Seite 66.*

Unit 6 It's our world!

L2, 22 A trip to Exmoor (→ p. 63/ex. 1)

Terry's class is doing a project on water. They have learnt about the weather, flash floods, water power and rivers. They want to find out more about these things on Exmoor.

A TRIP TO EXMOOR

YOU CAN

- learn about water power.
- ride ponies.
- walk on the moor.
- learn about the environment.
- study our plants and trees.
- fish in our rivers.
- sleep and eat at our school centre.

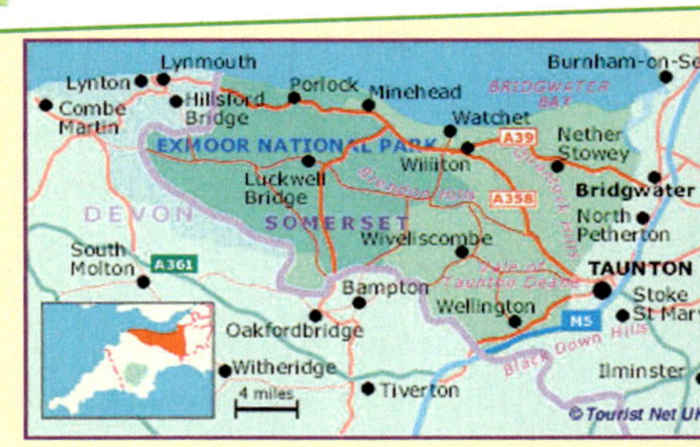

1 Important things

What is important for the friends?

1. Sam is thinking about … .
2. Emma is worried about … .
3. Terry is mad because … .
4. Lisa wants … .

L2, 23

2 Let's listen: A week before the trip

a) *Listen and find the missing words.*

1. … asks about his laptop.
2. Sam hasn't got any … … .
3. It can be very wet on Exmoor in … and May.
4. Mr Rose tells them a bit about the … .
5. Lisa! … in big trouble.
6. The day room has got a lot of … and games.
7. The centre is not a fast food … .
8. The trip is … for pupils in Year Seven.
9. The showers aren't very … .
10. The centre is not … the road.

b) *Why does Terry want to stay in Greenwich?*
Write down the first letter of the words from part a) and find the answer.

3 Let's talk: Let's go on a day trip!

Plan a class trip. What should you take? What shouldn't you take? What can you do? Collect ideas with a partner and talk about the trip.

Take	Don't take	Do:
rubber boots	MP3 player	go swimming
…	…	…

Let's plan a day trip. • Where can we go? • We can go to … . • What can we do there? • We can visit the museum/go swimming/… . • What should/shouldn't we take?

4 For my folder: A class trip (→ p. 63/ex. 2)

Imagine your class went on a trip. Write about it.

Where to?
What did you do?
How was the trip?
What happened?

Offering help and making promises

L2, 24

I'll give them ten minutes!

1 Just before they leave (→ p. 64/ex. 3, 4)

Make correct sentences. Example: 1. It won't fit inside.

1. It 2. The boys 3. You 4. He 5. Peter and I 6. They 7. I 8. We	+	'll won't will	+	a. check the weather on the Internet. b. miss Barker. c. give them ten minutes. d. fit inside. e. help you, Emma. f. wait for them this time. g. be late for their own funeral. h. be fine.

▶ **I'll give** … .
He'll be … .
The boys **will** … .
We won't … .
→ G16

2 Let's help!

Match the sentences and make dialogues.
Example: 1. I'm bringing my MP3 player with me. – **Don't worry. I won't tell the teacher.**

1. I'm bringing my MP3 player with me. 2. Look, there's Sam! 3. Look! That dog likes your sandwich. 4. I don't have any ideas for a project. 5. I have the best idea for a project: rivers. 6. Oh, no. I forgot my alarm clock. 7. Have you got a pen? 8. My bag is too heavy.	+	Don't worry. That's OK. Wait.	+	a. I'll wake you up. b. I'll tell Mrs Carter. c. I won't tell the teacher. d. He won't eat it. e. I'll help you think of some. f. I'll help you to carry it. g. I won't steal your idea. h. I'll look in my bag.

3 What can you say? (→ p. 65/ex. 5)

1

close

2

get

3
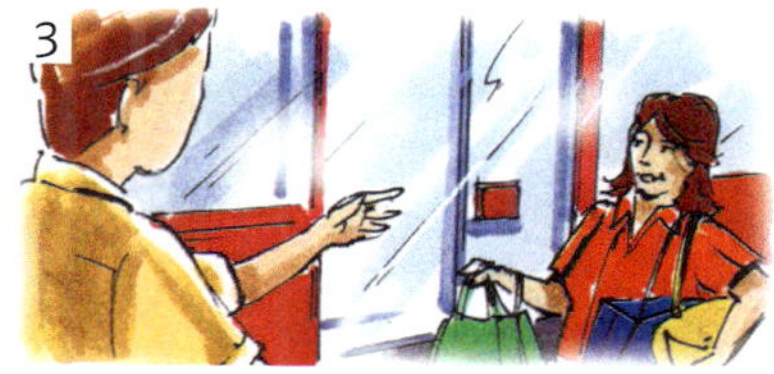
open

4

feed

5

help

6

carry

4 Promises, promises (→ p. 65/ex. 6; p. 66/ex. 7)

What do they promise?

Example: 1. Terry: I promise I won't forget to phone.
2. Sam: I promise I'll … .

1. Terry: not forget to phone
2. Sam: wake up early
3. Mrs Taylor: take Barker to the park
4. Barker: take Jade to the park
5. Tiger: not sleep on the roof
6. Mr Rose: not drive too fast

5 Let's talk: I'll help you!

Your partner tells you about a problem which he or she has. You offer some help.

- finish German homework
- write to Grandma
- wash the car
- do the shopping
- walk the dog
- get you some food

Forecasting: Asking questions about forecasts with and without question words

L2, 25

What will the weather be like? (→ p. 66/ex. 8; p. 67/ex. 9)

>Home >Weather >Europe >UK

Search Southwest GO **Devon, Cornwall and the Scilly Isles**

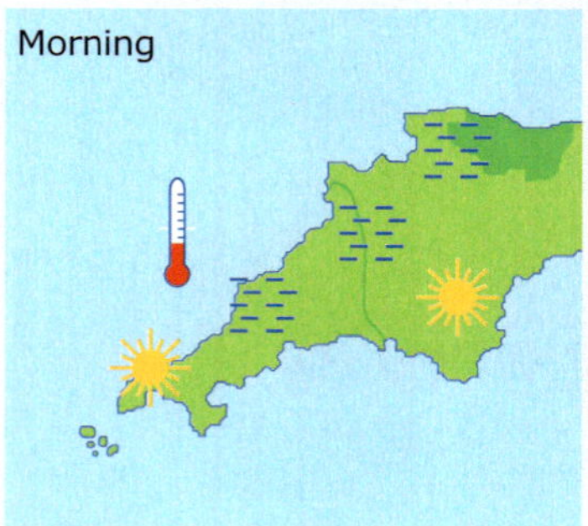

Forecast: On Friday it will be foggy and cold in the early part of the morning in the far west and on Exmoor. Later it will be warm and sunny there. Temperatures will rise to 15°–18° C. In the early evening rain will move in from the southwest and it will be cloudy and stormy. By midnight there will be rain over most of Devon and Cornwall. On the Scilly Isles it will be hot most of the day. There will be some rain in the late evening.

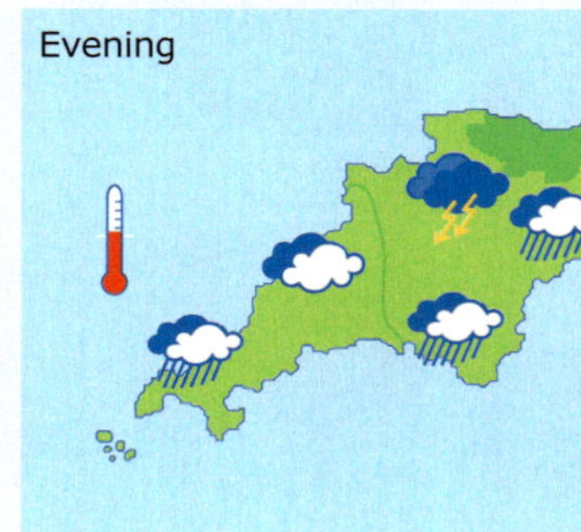

Mr Jones from North Devon asks, "What will the weather be like in the Southwest at the weekend? Will I still need heating at the weekend?"
Our answer: *Well, you will need heating on Exmoor and in North Devon. It will be windy and rainy there. You can escape to the Scilly Isles. It will be hot and sunny there. South Devon and Cornwall will be cloudy but warm with temperatures around 20°C.*

1 Weather maps (→ p. 67/ex. 10)

What do the symbols on the maps mean?

sunny • rainy • cloudy • stormy • foggy

2 The weather in England (→ p. 68/ex. 11)

a) *Ask your partner.*
1. Will it be cold in Devon on Friday morning?
2. Will temperatures rise to 20°?
3. Will there be fog on Exmoor?

b) *Make a dialogue about the forecast.*

▶ **Will** it be cold? – Yes, **it will.** / No, **it won't.**
Will temperatures reach … ?
– Yes, **they will.** / No, **they won't.**
Will there be … ?
– Yes, **there will.** / No, **there won't.**
→ G17

3 Questions for the weatherman (→ p. 68/ex. 12; p. 69/ex. 13)

Look at the forecast and answer the questions.

▶ **Where will** it be hot?
When will be a good time … ?
→ G17

1. Where will it be hot on Friday afternoon?
2. What time on Friday will be a good time to go to Exmoor?
3. What will the weather be like on Exmoor at the weekend?
4. What will it be like for my garden party in North Devon on Sunday?
5. When will it be rainy on the Scilly Isles?
6. Where will the best weather be at the weekend in the Southwest?

4 A card game: Weather forecasts

a) *Make 40 cards with words on them (ten for each colour):*

b) *Shuffle the cards. Each pupil gets five cards and tries to make a sentence with four of them.*

Example: A: It will be foggy on Rügen tomorrow.
B: It won't rain in Berlin at the weekend.

c) *Sometimes you won't have the cards which you need. Then you can take a new card and miss a turn. The person who makes the most sentences wins.*

5 Let's talk: The weather in Germany

a) *Write a weather forecast for next week in your area.*

b) *Draw a map with symbols.*

c) *Present your weather forecast in class.*

GRAMMAR SKILLS

Presenting a forecast

1. Use will/won't for forecasts.
2. Your symbols must match your forecast.
3. Say what you are forecasting.
4. Leave time for questions.

6 From CO_2[1] to flash floods

Match the pictures with the forecasts. What will happen?
Start like this: 1. → e. Cars, planes and heating will produce[2] more CO_2.

1

2

3
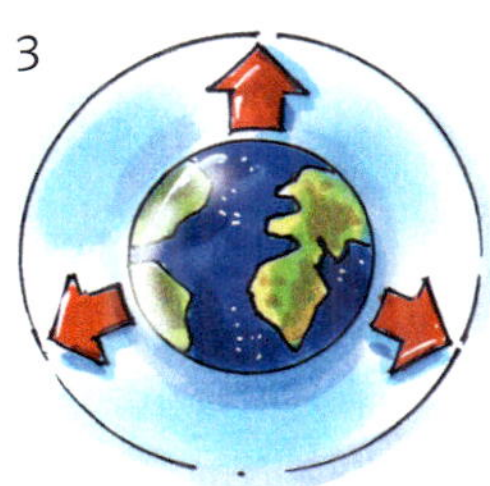

4
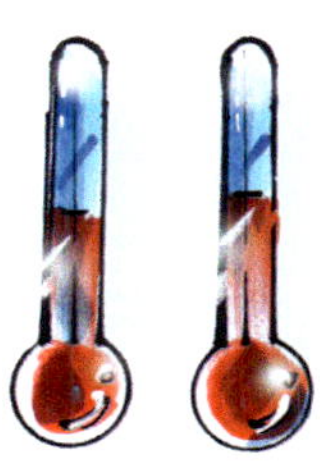

5

6

a. The heat[3] won't escape from the earth[4].

b. CO_2 will form[5] a blanket around the earth.

c. The temperature will rise.

d. We will have more floods.

e. Cars, planes and heating will produce more CO_2.

f. There will be more storms[6] and rain.

[1]CO_2 [ˌsiːəʊˈtuː] – *Kohlendioxid,* [2]produce [prəˈdjuːs] – *erzeugen,* [3]heat [hiːt] – *Wärme,* [4]earth [ɜːθ] – *Erde,* [5]form [fɔːm] – *bilden,* [6]storm [stɔːm] – *Sturm*

Making predictions

L2, 26

TEEN HOROSCOPES

AQUARIUS: Be careful! You won't be bored in the next few days. You will have a big adventure. Water will play an important role. Something frightening will happen. But stay calm and use your head. You won't find the answers to the problems at first. Some people don't know how important you are and will laugh at you. Don't worry. Your friends will see you as a leader in the end. You will save the day!

1 Emma's horoscope (→ p. 69/ex. 14, 15)

Emma tells Lisa about her horoscope in the bus. What does she say?

1. It says I should	a. won't find the answers to their problems at first.
2. Aquarius people	b. will happen.
3. Some of us	c. be careful.
4. Water	d. won't be bored in the next few days.
5. Something frightening	e. will see me as a leader in the end.
6. I	f. will have a big adventure.
7. Some people	g. will laugh at me.
8. My friends	h. will play an important role.

▶ **You will** have an adventure.
You won't be bored.
→ G16

2 For my folder: A horoscope

Write a horoscope for a person in your group. Write about two of these things:

money | family | friends | job | love | adventure

Example: You will have a good job which you enjoy. You will have a lot of … .

L2, 27

3 Let's listen: The signs of the zodiac

a) *Look at the names of the signs and listen. What dates are they?*

Example: Leo is from 23rd July to 22nd August.

b) *What is your sign? What do you know about it?*

zodiac [□z□□dɪ□k] – *Tierkreis*

Leo ['li:əʊ]	Libra ['li:brə]
Scorpio ['skɔ:piəʊ]	Aries ['eə,ri:z]
Pisces ['paɪsi:z]	Aquarius [ə'kweəriəs]
Cancer ['k□ntsə]	Sagittarius [□s□dʒɪ'teəriəs]
Gemini ['dʒemɪnaɪ]	Virgo ['vɜ:gəʊ]
Capricorn ['k□prɪkɔ:n]	Taurus ['tɔ:rəs]

L2, 28 ## 1 Let's listen: A school project (→ p. 70/ex. 16)

Listen. What can you say about …

1. … the weather today in London?
2. … changes in the weather?
3. … the weather project at T.T.?
4. … how a lot of the pupils get to school?
5. … how they were careful in the school?
6. … the garden?
7. … their plans for the garden?

a. There are floods more often now.
b. They walk or go by bike.
c. It's rainy and cold.
d. They closed doors and windows.
e. It has got plants, flowers and trees.
f. They want to buy umbrellas and tables.
g. They call it "Stop the rain".

L2, 29 ## 2 Let's listen: More rain will fall

Listen and find the missing words.

1. Charlie has just chatted to … .
2. Let's talk to their … teacher Mr Rose.
3. We have all heard about … .
4. We are … in a big greenhouse.
5. We must … or the temperature will rise.
6. And then we will get more storms and bad … .
7. More rain will fall and we will have … .

L2, 30 ## 3 Let's listen: Mr Rose's tongue twister

Whether[1] the weather be fine or whether the weather be not.
Whether the weather be cold or whether the weather be hot.
Whatever[2] the weather we'll weather[3] the weather whether we like it or not.

[1]whether ['weðə] – *ob*, [2]whatever [wɒt'evə] – *egal welches*,
[3]to weather ['weðə] – *aushalten, überstehen*

L2, 31 ## 4 Sounds: Which letter is missing?

1. *b or p?* _lane, _roject, _oots, Su_ertram_, ex_lain, im_ortant, _onies, esca_e, _lanket
2. *t or d?* Lon_on, momen_, aske_, star_ed, _ried, ri_e, use_, gar_en, a lo_ of, save_

L2, 32 ## 5 A song: It's raining again

It's raining again. Oh no, my love's at an end.
Oh no, it's raining again
and you know it's hard to pretend[1].
Oh no, it's raining again
Too bad I'm losing a friend.
Oh no, it's raining again
Oh, will my heart ever mend[2]?
Oh no, it's raining again

[1]pretend [prɪ'tend] – *sich etwas vormachen*, [2]mend [mend] – *heilen*

L2, 33

The Rescue

1 Before you read (→ p. 71/ex. 17, 18)

What do you already know about Exmoor? What can you do and see there?

EXMOOR NATIONAL PARK

In April Emma's class went to a centre in Exmoor National Park. They wanted to do a project on the rivers and streams there.

"It isn't raining at the moment," said Mr Rose. "But the radio says it will be wet and windy today, so make sure you've got your anoraks and rubber boots. And don't forget your bottles, your worksheets and your pens."

Terry, Emma, Sam and Lisa were in a group with two other boys, Peter and Martin.

"I've got my digital camera in my bag," said Peter. "So we'll get some good pictures for our project."

"Please be back here at Tarr Steps at one o'clock," said Mrs Carter. "And stay together in your groups."

"There's a path over there," said Terry. "We can try that."

Five minutes later it started to rain.

"Hey, wait for me," said Emma. She stopped and opened her pink umbrella.

Sam laughed. "Just the thing for a field trip! Emma, what else have you got in your bag?"

"Oh, just some things," said Emma. "An extra sweatshirt and some lip balm because it'll be windy on the moor, my mobile … ."

"Lip balm? We're doing a project on rivers, Emma," said Terry, "not on fashion! Ha-ha! Come on now!"

Soon they found a good place on the river. There were large stones in the water and a small island with a big tree on it. They walked over to the island on the stones. They took out their bottles, worksheets and pens and left their bags under a tree. There they took pictures of the different plants and collected water in bottles from the stream. It started to rain harder, so they sat down under the tree to do their worksheets. An hour later, Emma jumped up.

"Oh, my God!" she said.

"What is it now, Emma?" laughed Terry. "Have you lost your lip balm?"

2 What has Emma seen?

Look at the two pictures of the island.

(→ p. 71/ex. 18)

"Look!" she shouted. "The stones have disappeared." The others looked at Emma. The stream was now a very fast river.

"It's a flash flood," said Terry. "We learnt about it in Geography." Peter was very excited.

"This will be a great picture," he said.

"How can you take pictures at a time like this?" asked Emma. "We're trapped on this island! How will we get back?"

"I can't swim." said Martin. He was really frightened.

Sam tried to stay calm. "Let's shout," he said. "Maybe the others will hear us." They all started to shout. "Help! Help!" They waited.

"Don't worry," said Lisa. "I'm sure the teachers will come and rescue us." But no teachers came. Terry called Mr Rose on his mobile and told him where they were.

"Don't worry," said Mr Rose. "I'll call the Rescue Services. They'll send a helicopter."

"They'll be too late," said Peter "The water is getting higher! Look over there! The trees are half under water. And it's raining really hard. I'm sure they won't see us here under this tree."

"What'll we do?" asked Martin.

"I've got an idea," said Emma. "I hope it'll work!" She jumped onto a stone next to the tree and waved her pink umbrella. The others shouted.

3 Finding evidence (→ p. 71/ex. 19)

a) *What have all the kids got with them on their trip? What has Emma got? How does she use it to save the day?*

b) *Complete these sentences.*

1. The radio says … .
2. The pupils want to do a project on … .
3. Emma opened her umbrella because … .
4. When it started to rain harder … .

4 Peter's photo

Look at Peter's photo. What happened before he took it?

▶ … found an island • … under a tree • … started to rain • … it was very fast • … shouted • … called Mr Rose • … waved her umbrella • … rescued us

Start like this: On the way to the river it started to rain. We found an … .

1 A trip to Exmoor

a) *Sort the words from the list and put them in the grid.*

an anorak • an umbrella • an MP3 player • rubber boots • a football • a torch • a worksheet • trousers • a sweatshirt • some flowers • a blanket • a pen • an alarm clock • a helicopter • …

	You will need	You won't need
Projects	a worksheet, …	an alarm clock, …
Activities	…	…
Clothes	…	…

b) *Add five more things to your grid which you will/won't need.*

2 Weather photos (→ p. 72/ex. 20)

a) *What do these weather photos show?*

1

2

3

b) *Draw your own pictures for: stormy, hot, cold, sunny and foggy.*
Can your partner guess what it is?

3 A word puzzle (→ p. 72/ex. 21)

Find the letters and then the word. The pictures can help you.

My first is in project and promise and phone.
My second is always in pony and own.
My third is in weather but isn't in rain.
My fourth is in ticket but isn't in train.
My fifth you can find at the end of a shower.

Now look at the pictures – the word must be … .

4 Words with two meanings

Find words with two meanings and use them in sentences.

Examples: 1. Do they have **showers** at the centre?
There were **showers** on Exmoor today.
2. She dropped her **soap** in the shower.

1 Girls will be girls ('ll, will or won't → G 16) (→ p. 73/ex. 22, 23)

When they get back to Greenwich, Lisa phones Emma with a problem

Lisa: Hi, Emma. Have you got this week's "Star" magazine?
Emma: No, Nasreen has got it at the moment. I … go and get it from her.
Lisa: No, wait. I … read something to you. It's my horoscope for next week.
Emma: OK, just a minute. I … close the door, so Nasreen … hear. OK. What does it say?
Lisa: It says, "Be really careful! Things … go wrong for you at the weekend. You … meet a new friend but he … be very nice to you. You … be very happy on Saturday."
Emma: So what's the big problem? Just don't go out with a boy on Saturday and you … be happy.
Lisa: But I want to go to *Spiderman III* with Peter tomorrow.
Emma: Lisa, it … be OK. Peter isn't a new friend. You've known him for weeks. And Martin and I … be there, too. But you … tell Jake, I hope.
Lisa: Who? Me? I … say a word. But what's all this with Martin?
Emma: I … tell you later. Bye!

2 European weather (Will → G 16)

Look at the countries. What will the weather be like in Italy, Poland and Ireland next week?

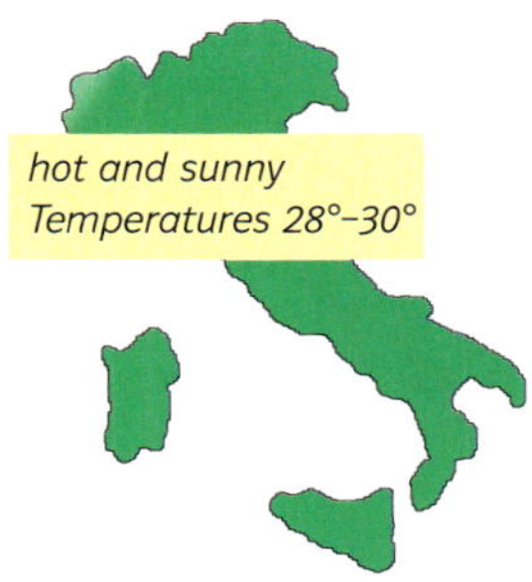

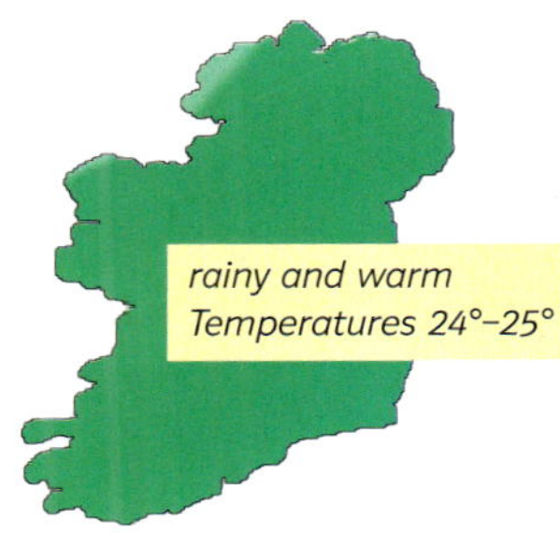

3 Was the note right? (Will, won't → G 16)

On holiday Tina got a note. Read what the note said and look at the picture. Was it right?

Go to the café at the station. An old mouse will come to your table. He won't order anything. He will give you a big book. There will be some money with it. He won't smile, but he will ask you a question.

DU KANNST JETZT

- ✓ Hilfe spontan anbieten. → *Biete Hilfe in 3 Situationen an.*
- ✓ Wettervorhersagen lesen und verstehen. → *Informiere dich über das Wetter nächste Woche in London.*
- ✓ über die Zukunft reden. → *Sage 5 Sachen voraus, die eventuell diese Woche passieren werden.*

1 Things have changed (*Present perfect: statements* → G12) (→ p. 74/ex. 1)

Complete the following text. Use forms of the present perfect.

Sam's grandma (*live*) in Greenwich for more than sixty years. She (*see*) a lot of changes in that time. Some of her school friends (*move*) to other towns or they (*leave*) England. Two friends (*go*) to America. The streets (*change*), too. They (*take*) away the old cinema and (*put*) a new shopping centre there. The little café near the station (*change*), too. It is now a burger bar. The shops in the old town (*go*). That is where the market is now. An American (*buy*) the ice rink. He (*invite*) teams from America to play here. The old hospital (*disappear*), too. There is a really nice new hospital near the river now. The street market (*go*) and a lot of people (*forget*) where it was. They (*close*) the little church school and the youth club uses it now. "Times (*change*)," says Grandma. "And some things are really better."

2 Have they done it yet? (*Present perfect: questions + short answers, negatives* → G13/G14)

a) *Mrs Taylor has left a list for her children. She phones to check what they have done. Lisa answers. What do they say?*

Example: Lisa, has Ben finished his homework yet? – No, he hasn't.

Ben, finish your homework! ✗
Lisa and Ben, make the beds! ✓
Lisa and Jade, take Barker out to the park! ✗
Lisa, turn off the computer! ✓
Jade, put your games back in the cupboard! ✗
All of you, eat your supper! ✓
Barker, find my car keys! ✗

b) *Make sentences about the children.*
Example: Ben hasn't finished … .

3 Help! (*Present perfect: signal words* → G12) (→ p. 74/ex. 2)

Emma calls Fiona. Complete the dialogue.

yet | already | never | just | ever | still

Emma: Have you … sent the e-mail, Fiona?
Fiona: Yes! Hasn't it arrived … ?
Emma: No, it hasn't arrived … . Have you … had problems with your PC before?
Fiona: Well, it has been slow sometimes, but it has … taken[1] longer than thirty minutes.
Emma: Can you send it again?
Fiona: I've … sent it three times. But I'll try again. Bye!
Mrs Brook: Hurry up, Emma. Supper is ready. I have … put it on the table.
Emma: I'm … waiting for Fiona's mail. She has … sent it three times, but I … haven't got it.

[1]take [teɪk] – *hier: dauern*

4 Visitors to Greenwich (*'will'-future* → G16)

a) *Look at the forecast for next week and answer the questions.*

Example: What days will be good for a trip to the museum?
– Monday and Friday because it will rain.

1. What will it be like at the weekend?
2. When will it rain in Greenwich this week?
3. When will it be sunny?
4. What will it be like on Friday?
5. Will I need an umbrella on Thursday?
6. Will Tuesday be a good day for photos?

b) *Write a weather forecast for next week in Greenwich.*

Start like this: On Monday it will be cloudy and there will be … .

5 Lisa's horoscope (*'will'-future* → G16)

Look at the picture. What will happen to Lisa? What will the weather be like?

Example: It will be a beautiful, sunny day.

I can see …
… a beautiful, sunny day.
… you with a young man in the park.
… two boys arrive.
… they have a football.
… one boy kicks the ball.
… it goes into the river.
… you run and get it.

6 Wait! I'll help you (*'will'-future* → G16)

What can you say? Match the sentences.

1. Your dad wants to clean the windows.
2. It is starting to rain.
3. You see a boy doing tricks on his bike.
4. You are saying goodbye to a friend at a station.
5. Your sister is going to Italy for a week.
6. Your friend has just bought some trousers.

a. I won't see you for a month.
b. Stop! You'll fall and break your arm.
c. I hope you'll have good weather.
d. I'll get the water for you.
e. They'll look great with your pink T-shirt.
f. Wait, we'll get our umbrellas.

Unit 7 A holiday in Ireland

L3, 1 Swapping houses (→ p. 75/ex. 1)

The O'Briens live with their children Patrick and Helen in an old farmhouse on the west coast of Ireland, not far from Limerick. Last year in Dublin they met a German family from Berlin and this year they want to swap houses with them.

The Lehmanns live in a flat in Berlin. They want to visit the Republic of Ireland in the summer holidays. Mrs Lehmann comes from Dublin and her children Hannah and Christoph speak English and German, of course.

1 Two different worlds

Helen and Christoph have different ideas about the west coast of Ireland. What are they? Use these words:

clean air | lots to do | ghost | peace and quiet | play room | old castles

2 Let's talk: Swapping houses (→ p. 75/ex. 2)

Because:
I like big cities.
The sea is calm near … .
I want to visit … and it's near … .
I like … food/music/ … .
I have friends/family/ … there.

L3, 2 ## 3 Let's listen: What's wrong? (→ p. 75/ex. 3)

Christoph and Hannah are in the kitchen. Mrs Lehmann has just put down the phone. Listen and correct the sentences.

1. Everything is OK for the house swap this month.
2. They'll give us the keys to their flat and their car.
3. He's worrying about the airport in Ireland.
4. I'd like to spend the weekend with my friends, too.
5. They can't all be over 40.
6. I'm sure they've got lots of friends.

4 For my folder: A project on Ireland

Imagine you and your family want to go to Ireland. Find out more about Ireland. Collect pictures, draw a map and make a poster.

Ireland has two parts,
Northern Ireland and … .
people?
rivers?

Saying how people do things

L3, 3

That's a good idea!

It's the evening before the Lehmanns leave for Ireland. Mr Lehmann is ironing happily in the kitchen. Mrs Lehmann is in her bedroom. She's busily packing a bag for the journey and Christoph is quietly surfing the Internet. Hannah is worried. She's looking for her anorak. "I must find it," she says worriedly.

"If you can't find it," says her brother helpfully, "I'll lend you my green coat. Maybe they'll think you're a leprechaun."

Hannah looks at him. "What's a leprechaun?" she asks.

"An Irish goblin," says Christoph. "He makes shoes and guards a pot of gold." The phone in the kitchen rings.

Mrs O'Brien: Hello, Erich. I'm just calling you quickly to say that there's a problem with our meeting tomorrow. They've changed our flight time to 12 o'clock. Your plane arrives at 10:30. Is that right?

Mr Lehmann: Yes, that's right. But we'll need to collect our luggage and get through customs.

Mrs O'Brien: OK. Let's say 11:15. If you come to the departures desk near gate 10 by 11.15, I'll give you the car keys and the map. If you aren't there, I'll leave the keys in an envelope at the information desk. I'll write your name on it clearly, so there shouldn't be any problem. I'll leave the house key with the neighbours. Just one more thing, we've got a new burglar alarm. We'll set it before we leave. If you ask the neighbours they will show you how it works.

Mr Lehmann: Thank you, Mary. …

1 Getting ready (→ p. 76/ex. 4)

a) *What are the people doing?*

Example: Christoph is surfing.

b) We use adverbs of manner to say how people do things. Most adverbs of manner end in -ly. *Find examples in the text.*

▶ **happily**
quietly
→ G18

c) *How are the people doing the things in part a)?*

Example: Christoph is quietly surfing the Internet.

2 How did they do it?

(→ p. 76/ex. 5)

sing • walk • smile • watch • write • drive

a) *Example:* 1. She **sang loudly**.

1

2

3

careful
clear
happy
worried
slow
loud

4

5

6

Adjectives	**Adverbs**
slow	slow**ly**
happy	happ**i**ly

b) *How do you or your parents do these things?*

3 If you have any problems …

(→ p. 77/ex. 6, 7)

Mrs O'Brien leaves some notes for the Lehmanns.
Match the parts.

Example: 1. If you have any problems, my sister will help you.

If you go to …, they **will** … .

→ G19

1. If you have any problems,
2. If you go to the neighbours' house
3. If you want a German magazine,
4. If you need more milk,
5. If you leave the gate open,
6. If you don't turn off the alarm,
7. If you ask the neighbours,
8. If you walk our dog, Rover, every day,
9. If you want fresh vegetables,

a. the farmer's brother will bring it.
b. sheep will come into the garden.
c. it will make a terrible noise.
d. they will give you the door key.
e. the farmer will bring them.
f. he will be happy.
g. my sister will help you.
h. the newsagent will order it for you.
i. they will show you how it works.

4 The 'if' game

(→ p. 77/ex. 8)

Write 10 different wishes on cards. Shuffle the cards. Each person in the group takes a card and says what he or she will do if the wish comes true.

A: If I win 1000 Euros, I will fly to … .
B: Why? What will you do/see/visit there?
A: I will … . What about you?
C: If I meet …, I will … .

win 1000 Euros
see a ghost
meet a leprechaun
get a … for my birthday
…

'Reading' pictures

Germany or Ireland?

1

2

5

3

4

6

7

8

1 Where is it? (→ p. 78/ex. 9; p. 79/ex. 10)

GETTING INFORMATION FROM PICTURES — SKILLS

Before you start:
1. Answer these questions:
   - Are there any words in the picture?
   - Are there any signs?
   - Do you know the things or places in the picture?
2. Look carefully at the small things in the picture.

Look at each picture and find out:
1. *Is it in Germany? Why?*
2. *Is it in Ireland? Why?*
3. *Some pictures are difficult. You can't say where they are: Which pictures are they?*

▶ I think it looks like … because … .
I think this pictures is of a place/town/street/ … in … because … .
I'm not sure about this picture.
The … looks German and Irish.

Chats with Charlie

L3, 4 ## 1 Let's listen: On holiday in Ireland

Where are Laura, Malik and Christoph? What can they do there?

The Cliffs of Moher
The River Shannon
Kilkenny Castle

1

2

3

L3, 5 ## 2 A song: Molly Malone

In Dublin's fair[1] city where the girls are so pretty[2]
I first set my eyes on[3] sweet Molly Malone
As she wheeled[4] her wheel barrow[5] through
streets broad[6] and narrow[7]
Crying cockles[8] and mussels[9] alive[10] alive-o.

Chorus[11]: Alive alive-o, alive alive-o
Crying cockles and mussels alive alive-o.

She was a fishmonger[12], sure it was no wonder[13]
For so were her mother[14] and father[15] before
And they both wheeled their barrow
through streets broad and narrow
Crying cockles and mussels alive alive-o. Chorus

She died[16] of a fever[17] and no one could save her
And that was the end of sweet Molly Malone
But her ghost wheels her barrow
through streets broad and narrow
Crying cockles and mussels alive alive-o. Chorus

[1]fair [feə] – *schön*, [2]pretty ['prɪti] – *hübsch*, [3]set my eyes on [ˌset ˌmaɪ 'aɪz‿ɒn] – *erblickte*, [4]to wheel [wi:l] – *schieben*, [5](wheel) barrow ['bærəʊ] – *Schubkarren*, [6]broad [brɔ:d] – *breit*, [7]narrow ['nærəʊ] – *eng*, [8]cockles [kɒkls] – *Herzmuscheln*, [9]mussels ['mʌsls] – *Miesmuscheln*, [10]alive [ə'laɪv] – *lebendig*, [11]chorus ['kɔ:rəs] – *Refrain*, [12]fishmonger ['fɪʃˌmʌŋgə] – *Fischhändler(in)*, [13]no wonder [ˌnəʊ 'wʌndə] – *kein Wunder*, [14]mother ['mʌðə] – *Mutter*, [15]father ['fɑ:ðə] – *Vater*, [16]died [daɪd] – *starb*, [17]of a fever [ˌəv‿ə 'fi:və] – *am Fieber*

3 Two poems: Limericks

Limericks have five lines. The last word in lines 1, 2 and 5 rhymes[18].
The last word in lines 3 and 4 rhymes.

a) *Read the Limerick.*

There was a young lady of **Wilts**
Who walked up to Scotland on **stilts**[19]
When they said it was **shocking**[20]
To show so much **stocking**[21]
She answered, "Well, what about **kilts**[22]?"

b) *Put in the missing words:*

There once was a hungry old ...
Which lived in a place near the ...
But it always came ...
When the breakfast was ...
And it ate all the butter and ...

here
toast
coast
near
ghost

[18]rhyme [raɪm] – *sich reimen*, [19]stilts [stɪlts] – *Stelzen*, [20]shocking ['ʃɒkɪŋ] – *entsetzlich*, [21]stocking [stɒkɪŋ] – *Strumpf*, [22]kilts [kɪlts] – *Schottenröcke*

L3, 6 Things that go bump in the night!

1 Before you read

What do you know about the house where the Lehmanns are staying? Look at the picture for help.

It was the second week of their holiday in Ireland and the Lehmanns were all in bed asleep. It was a bit windy and there were a few clouds in the sky. Somewhere downstairs a window banged, then again and again. Christoph woke up. He turned over in bed and listened. A barn owl hooted somewhere not far from the house. He got out of bed and went to the window. All was quiet again but the light on the wall of the barn was on. Someone or something was in the garden.

Suddenly the light went out again and all was dark. Christoph opened the window and leaned out. He thought he saw a figure near the big tree. But it was difficult to see because the moon was behind some clouds. "Maybe Patrick and Helen's grandad was right," he thought. "There **is** a ghost! I must wake Hannah and tell her." He walked to the door of his room and opened it. The floors creaked in the old farmhouse. In fact everything creaked so he walked slowly and carefully to Hannah's bedroom.

"Hannah! Hannah!" he said softly. "Did you hear that noise?"

"You mean my door?" asked Hannah sleepily. "**That** woke me up!"

"Oh, sorry. I saw something outside in the garden. Do you remember what the O'Brien kids told us about the ghost?" asked Christoph.

"Yes!" said Hannah. "But I hope you don't believe that rubbish."

"Of course not! But there's something or someone in the garden. Maybe it's a burglar. Mrs O'Brien told us that there are burglars in the area. Let's wake Mum and Dad."

"Let's look from the bathroom window first. We can see more from there. If it **is** a burglar we'll tell them at once."

"Wait," said Christoph. "I'll get my camera."

They walked quietly past their parents' room to the bathroom. From the small window there, they could see the garden, with the big tree and the barn. They waited for ten minutes. The moon came out from behind a cloud. The figure was still there.

"Did you see that?" Hannah asked her brother.

"What?" said Christoph.

"Look!" said Hannah. There was a flash of white between the tree and the barn. "It's white, like a …"

"Ghost?" asked Christoph.

"Rubbish," said Hannah. "Take some pictures!"

Christoph tried to get a good picture, but when he pressed the button nothing happened. "Oh, no! I've forgotten to put in a new battery," he said.

"OK," said Hannah. "If it **is** a burglar, he'll try to get into the house."

"If he opens a door or window, he'll set off the alarm." said Christoph. "And he'll wake Mum and Dad," said Hannah.

"So let's wake them first! Come on!"

2 Feelings

How do you feel about the story?
Choose some phrases from the list.

Example: This story is … .

This story is interesting/scary/boring/ … .
The kids must be scared/worried/ … .
Their parents … .

3 All about stories (→ p. 80/ex. 11; p. 81/ex. 12)

a) *Who is in this story? When is it? Where are the people?*
b) *Things happen in the middle part of a story. What happens in this story? Think about the garden, the figure and the camera.*
c) *This story doesn't have an ending. What do you think will happen next? Here are some ideas. Choose a good ending and draw a picture.*

1. The burglar alarm goes off and the kids run to their parents' bedroom.
2. Christoph and Hannah go down into the garden with a torch. The 'ghost' is a big white sheep!
3. Christoph wakes up. It was a dream.

WRITING SKILLS

Finding the parts of a story:

Every story has got a beginning, a middle and an ending.

1. Where? When? and Who?
The beginning tells you where it happens, when it happens and who is in the story.

2. What?
The middle tells you what happens. There is often a problem or a question in it.

3. Why?
The ending gives you an answer to the problem or question.

4 A good ending (→ p. 81/ex. 13, 14)

Choose a good ending from Exercise 3c) and write a short text.
Who or what do you think the white figure was?

5 Let's talk: If I ever …

1 Adjectives (→ p. 82/ex. 16)

VOCABULARY SKILLS

Some adjectives have two forms: an *-ing* form and an *-ed* form.
Compare: The film was **exciting**. – The kids were **excited**.

a) *Find the correct form in these sentences.*

1. Kevin is … in ghosts. He finds them very … . (*interesting/interested*)
2. Hannah thinks ghosts are very … . She was … in the garden. (*frightening/frightened*)
3. Some people think farms are … . They are … in the country. (*boring/bored*)
4. The Lehmanns were … . when they saw the house. It was … how many rooms it had. (*surprising/surprised*)
5. Trips are … . The dog was … when they arrived. (*exciting/excited*)

b) *Collect more adjectives like these. You can look in your vocabulary list at the back of your book.*

2 An adjectives poster (→ p. 82/ex. 15)

a) *Say how the people in the pictures are feeling.*

1 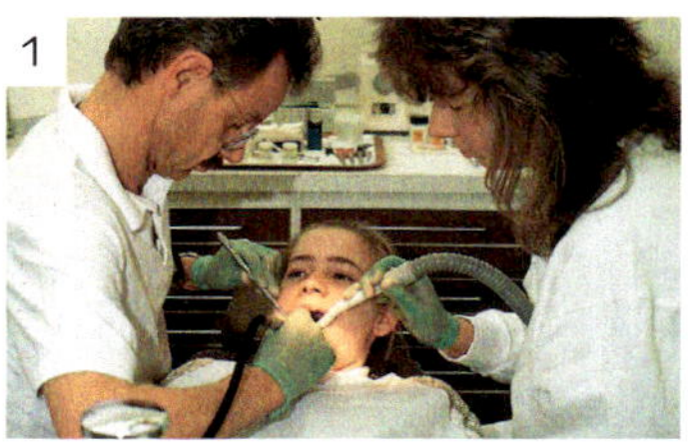

2 

3 

b) *Collect more adjectives and find pictures for them. You can use old magazines or draw them.*

3 Technical things

Match the things in the pictures with the verbs.

Example: 1. You can turn off an alarm.

turn off ✓ | press | set | change | wave | use | put in

1 

2 

3 

4 

5 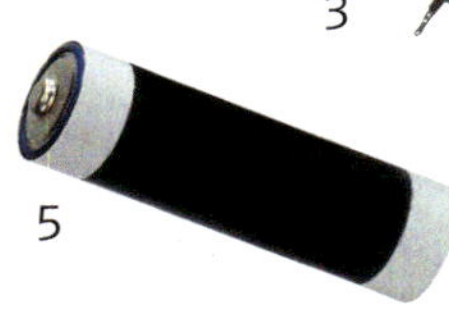

6 

1 In town (*Adverbs of manner* → G 18)

Put in the correct adverb in the sentences.

slowly · carefully · correctly · quietly · crazily · loudly

1. You should always drive … when the roads are wet.
2. If you ride your bike …, there will be an accident.
3. Ring your bell … before you go past people in the park.
4. Skate … when you are near old people.
5. You can play music … in the bus.
6. Give a sign … before you turn left or right.

2 Tom's week (*Adverbs of manner* → G18) (→ p. 83/ex. 17, 18)

a) *Copy the grids and complete them.*

adjective	adverb of manner
angry	angrily
bad	…
beautiful	
correct	
quick	

adjective	adverb of manner
excited	…
healthy	
hungry	
nervous	
soft	

b) *Use the adverbs with these verbs and say how Tom acted.*

shout ✓ • run • sing • cook • dance • wait • watch • write • whisper • eat

Example: 1. Tom shouted angrily.

1 

2 

3 

4 

5 

6 

7 

8 

9 

10 

3 Finish the sentences (*'If'-clauses* → G 19)

Example: If it rains tomorrow, I (*take/umbrella*).
If it rains tomorrow, I **will take my umbrella**.

1. If it is sunny tomorrow, we (*go swimming/river*).
2. If the plane is late, they (*wait/café*).
3. If sheep come into the garden, the dog (*bark*).
4. If you go to Ireland, I hope you (*send/postcard*).

DU KANNST JETZT

✓ beschreiben, wie du etwas machst. → *Beschreibe, wie du 5 Dinge in der Schule oder zu Hause machst.*

✓ eine Geschichte einteilen. → *Teile die Geschichte auf Seite 82/83 ein.*

Talking about plans

L3, 7 Old junk[1]

Mr Jackson: I'm going[2] to need some help this morning.

Terry: Why? What are you going to do?

Mr Jackson: I want to clear out[3] the garage[4]. There's so much old junk in it.

Terry: Oh, I can help you with that. Come on. Let's see what we can find!

They go into the garage together.

Terry: Great! Here's an old skateboard! It hasn't got any wheels[5], but –

Mr Jackson: No, Terry! Throw it away. Put it outside with that old bath[6] and all the other things.

Terry: OK, OK. Don't worry. I'm not going to keep it. – Hey, I think that girl wants to talk to us.

Girl: Are you going to throw these things away?

Terry: Yes, we are. We can't sell them. People aren't going to buy junk.

Girl: Can I have that kite[7], please?

Mr Jackson: Yes, of course. Just take it.

Girl: Thanks a lot.

Terry: But what are you going to do with it? There's a hole[8] in it, so you can't fly[9] it.

Girl: That's OK. It's for my little brother. It's going to be a funny face. I can draw the eyes and the nose – and the hole can be the mouth!

I'm going to … .
He's/She's going to … .
They're going to … .

1 Make sentences

1. Mr Jackson 2. Terry and his dad 3. Terry 4. People 5. The kite 6. The girl	+	is is not are are not	+	going to	+	clear out the garage together. buy old junk. be a funny face. need some help this morning. fly the kite. keep the old skateboard.

2 What are you going to do with it?

A: What are you going to do with that old bath?
B: I'm going to wash my dog in it.

old box | skateboard with no wheels | old alarm clock | … | make a shelf with it | wake my brother up! | clean it | …

[1]junk [dʒʌŋk] – *Ramsch*, [2]I'm going to ['gəʊɪŋ ˌtə] – *ich werde*, [3]clear out [klɪər̩'aʊt] – *aufräumen*, [4]garage [gə'rɑ:ʒ] – *Garage*, [5]wheel [wi:l] – *Rad*, [6]bath [bɑ:θ] – *Badewanne*, [7]kite [kaɪt] – *Drachen*, [8]hole [həʊl] – *Loch*, [9]fly [flaɪ] – *hier: steigen lassen*

3 Summer fun

Make the correct 'going to' forms with the verbs on the right.

not buy | fall | miss | be | rain | not win

Example: 1. Oh, no! Look, it's going to rain soon.

4 Terry's plans for next week

Ask and answer questions about Terry's plans for next week. You can ask questions with and without question words.

Examples:

A: When is he going to visit the zoo?
B: He's going to do that on Friday.

A: Is he going to eat lunch with Tiger?
B: No, he isn't. He's going to eat with his dad.

When is he going to … ?

Where is he going to … ?

What is he going to do on … ?

Is he going to … ?
– Yes, he is.
– No, he isn't.

Monday:
get birthday present for Tiger
Tuesday:
play basketball
Wednesday:
clear out shed
Thursday:
eat lunch with Dad
Friday:
visit the zoo
Saturday:
look for new poster for shed
Sunday:
meet Lisa – 2 o'clock

5 Let's talk: What are you going to do?

Talk about what you are going to do …

… after school today.
… next weekend.
… on your next birthday.
… in the holidays.

Example:

A: What are you going to do this evening?
B: Not much. I'm just going to listen to music.
C: I'm going to watch TV.
D: Me, too! What are you going to watch?

[1]competition [ˌkɒmpəˈtɪʃən] – *Wettbewerb*, [2]swimming pool [ˈswɪmɪŋ ˌpuːl] – *Schwimmbecken*

Reading skills

READING SKILLS

VOR DEM LESEN:

Tipp Nr. 1: Relax! Stelle dich innerlich darauf ein, dass du gleich eine Geschichte lesen wirst. Suche dir einen bequemen und angenehmen Leseort, wo du nicht gestört wirst. Entspanne dich und freue dich auf ein spannendes Leseerlebnis.

Tipp Nr. 2: Relate! Schau dir den Umschlag des Buchs an. Dann lies auch den Titel der Geschichte. Überlege, worum es in der Geschichte gehen könnte. Schau dir auch die Bilder an. Vielleicht hast du ja eine ähnliche Geschichte schon einmal gelesen?

Tipp Nr. 3: Regulate! Nimm dir nicht zu viel auf einmal vor. Wenn du häufiger ein kurzes Stück liest, macht das Lesen mehr Spaß und strengt nicht so sehr an.

READING

WÄHREND DU LIEST:

Tipp Nr. 4: Read! Bemühe dich immer die Hauptgedanken der Geschichte zu verstehen. Ignoriere unbekannte Wörter, wenn sie für das Verständnis nicht wirklich wichtig sind. Wichtige unbekannte Wörter kannst du in deinem Wörterverzeichnis nachschlagen.

Tipp Nr. 5: Recognize! Versuche immer, dir das Gelesene bildlich vorzustellen. Denke dich in die Situation hinein. Was siehst du? Was riechst du? Was hörst du? Wie findest du die Menschen, denen du begegnest? Frage dich, ob du etwas Ähnliches schon einmal erlebt hast.

Tipp Nr. 6: Recall! Mache während des Lesens immer mal wieder eine Pause und fasse für dich den Abschnitt, den du gerade gelesen hast, in eigenen Worten zusammen.

READING

NACH DEM LESEN:

Tipp Nr. 7: Reconstruct! Nachdem du mit dem Lesen fertig bist, fasse alles, was du gelesen hast, noch einmal zusammen. Frage dich immer

- wer
- wo
- was
- mit wem
- wann
- warum erlebt hat.

Tipp Nr. 8: Repeat! Vielleicht hast du das Gefühl nicht alles richtig verstanden zu haben und du möchtest den Abschnitt ein zweites Mal lesen. Finde heraus, ob du beim zweiten Lesedurchgang mehr verstehst.

Tipp Nr. 9: Reflect! Überlege, wie dir das Gelesene gefallen hat und was es für dich persönlich bedeutet. Was hast du Neues erfahren und was hast du aus dem Gelesenen gelernt?

Also dann viel Spaß beim Schmökern.
PS: Wenn du jetzt häufiger längere englische Geschichten liest, ist es eine gute Idee ein Lesetagebuch zu führen.

The mystery[1] of Loch Ness

Before you read

1. *Find Scotland on the map in the front of this book. Where is it?*
2. *What do you know about Scotland?*

My family and I live in the most beautiful place in Scotland. From my bedroom window I can see Urquhart Castle and Britain's largest lake[2], Loch Ness. A 'loch' is what we call a lake in Scotland.

We McArthurs haven't always lived here. We lived in the big city of Glasgow until last year. Dad worked in a factory[3] and Mum cleaned other people's houses. When they got home, they were always dog-tired. My younger brother Douglas and I got up really early every morning to catch the bus to our big school in the city.

But two summers ago we came here on holiday. We went for walks[4] in the green hills[5], walked along the blue waters[6] of Loch Ness, and visited Urquhart Castle. We had a great holiday. No one wanted to go home to Glasgow. Mum and Dad liked Loch Ness so much, they decided to leave their work in the city.

We came back to Loch Ness to live, and we opened a bed and breakfast[7] near the castle. Now, Mum and Dad don't go out to work. Our new school is really small and it's just down the road, so we can walk there.

Our first summer there it rained a lot. Not many guests[8] came to stay at our B & B. Mum and Dad worried a lot. They didn't want to close it and go back to Glasgow.

"Oh, I hope more tourists[9] come," said Mum. "But it's always raining. We're a new B & B, no one knows us. How will we live?"

"Don't worry, love[10]," said Dad. "There'll always be lots of tourists at McArthur's B & B because of the mystery of Loch Ness."

[1]mystery ['mɪstri] – *Geheimnis; Rätsel,* [2]lake [leɪk] – *der See,* [3]factory ['fæktri] – *Fabrik,* [4]walk [wɔ:k] – *Wanderung,* [5]hill [hɪl] – *Hügel,* [6]waters [wɑ:təz] – *Gewässer,* [7]bed and breakfast (B & B) [ˌbed n 'brekfəst] – *Pension,* [8]guest [gest] – *Gast,* [9]tourist ['tʊərɪst] – *Tourist(in),* [10]love [lʌv] – *here: Schatz*

Maybe I should explain. For more than a thousand years, people have told stories about something strange in the Loch. In one story, a big fish came out of the water and ate a fisherman[1] and his boat[2]! In another story, some kids saw a strange creature[3] 15 metres long! It came out of the Loch and walked on land. People who saw the creature called it a dinosaur[4].

Is this the creature in Loch Ness?

Others said it looked more like an elephant. I saw an old picture in the newspaper[5] of something in the water in front of Urquhart Castle, but it wasn't very clear. The newspaper called it 'The Loch Ness Monster[6]!' A lot of people call it Nessie. But no one really knows. It's a mystery.

One Saturday evening, our family went to a concert at Urquhart Castle. We heard some great Scottish bagpipe[7] music.

After the concert, old Mr Muir came to talk to us. He's the really nice caretaker at the castle. "Well, did the young McArthurs like the concert?" he asked Douglas and me.

"It was great," I said. "I love the bagpipes."

"And I love the drums," said Douglas.

"Ay[8], they all like the castle concerts," Mr Muir laughed. "There were more than three hundred people here tonight. Well, I must start to put these chairs away. We keep them down in the old dungeons[9], you know."

"The dungeons?" said Douglas. "I didn't know the castle had dungeons."

"Oh, yes, there are dungeons, my boy. Deep[10] under the castle. In the old days[11] they put prisoners[12] there. But today we only use them as the castle storerooms[13]." Mr Muir started to walk away.

"Can I help you, Angus?" asked Dad.

"No, no, thank you, Tom, I have my workmen[14]. And there's a lift[15] down to the castle storerooms. It's old and slow like me, but it works."

Douglas and I watched the workmen put some chairs into the big lift. Mr Muir was right. It was old and slow. And it made a terrible noise.

[1]fisherman ['fɪʃəmən] – *Fischer,* [2]boat [bəʊt] – *Boot,* [3]creature ['kri:tʃə] – *Lebewesen,* [4]dinosaur ['daɪnəsɔ:] – *Dinosaurier,* [5]newspaper ['nju:speɪpa] – *Zeitung,* [6]monster ['mɒnstə] – *Monster,* [7]bagpipe ['bægpaɪp] – *Dudelsack,* [8]ay [aɪ] – *ja,* [9]dungeon ['dʌndʒən] – *Verlies,* [10]deep [di:p] – *tief,* [11]in the old days – *früher,* [12]prisoner ['prɪzənə] – *Gefangene(r),* [13]storeroom ['stɔ:rʊm] – *Lagerraum,* [14]workman ['wɜ:kmən] – *Arbeiter, Helfer,* [15]lift [lɪft] – *Aufzug*

When we got home, there was an old black van outside our B & B. There were a lot of boxes on its roof, but they didn't look like the normal things that tourists take on holiday. The van had no windows so we couldn't see inside, but there were strange white letters on the doors: S.A.M.

"S.A.M. What does that mean?" asked Douglas.

"It means we've got guests!" said Dad. Mum and Dad were always happy when new guests arrived.

A woman and a man were waiting[1] in front of our house. The woman was very tall with small crocodile[2] eyes and red lipstick[3]. She was carrying a strange black bag and was wearing a big black winter coat. The man was short and had short grey[4] hair. He didn't speak and he never even smiled.

"Two rooms on the east side of the house," the woman said. "We want to see the Loch." She did not say "please".

"Oh, yes, the Loch is beautiful in the morning," said Mum. "Breakfast is from seven until nine o'clock. Here are your keys."

The woman took the keys, but she did not say "thank you".

Dad asked, "Are you going fishing?"

The woman looked at Dad with her crocodile eyes. "Fishing?"

"Yes, all those things in your van. I hope you catch something."

The woman smiled for the first time, but it was not a nice smile[5]. "If there is something to catch in the Loch, Mr McArthur, we will catch it. You can be sure!"

They went upstairs and we did not see them again until the next morning.

"That van is weird[6], Stella," said Douglas.

"Our new guests are weird, too," I said.

"You can say that again! What does S.A.M. mean? It's on the van doors."

"I've got no idea," I said. "I'd like to know what's inside. And look at those things on the roof. That looks like part of a telescope[7]."

"Yeah, and what's this? A microphone?" Douglas asked.

"I don't know, but they don't look like fishing things," I said. It was true. They looked more like the things we use in science class. "Those two are not normal tourists," I said.

"You're right. Come on, Stella. Let's find out who our guests really are."

[1]were waiting [wɜː ˈweɪtɪŋ] – *warteten,* [2]crocodile [ˈkrɒkədaɪl] – *Krokodil,* [3]lipstick [ˈlɪpstɪk] – *Lippenstift,* [4]grey [greɪ] – *grau,* [5]smile [smaɪl] – *Lächeln,* [6]weird [ˈwɪəd] – *seltsam,* [7]telescope [ˈtelɪskəʊp] – *Teleskop*

The next morning, the woman and the man were sitting in the breakfast room. They weren't eating breakfast. They were just drinking cup[1] after cup of coffee. Black coffee. Mum and Dad were telling them about nice places to visit, like Urquhart Castle and the gardens. "You can hear great concerts in the castle," said Mum. "Last night we heard Scottish bagpipes." But our guests weren't really listening. They only listened when we told them about Loch Ness.

"It's the deepest lake in Britain, and the largest, too," said Douglas. "A lot of people come here just to try and see Nessie."

The woman put down her coffee cup. She looked at Douglas. "Nessie?"

"You know," laughed Dad, "Nessie, the Loch Ness Monster. That's what they call the creature in the Loch."

"That's right," said Mum. "Tourists come here from all over[2] the world to try to see her. But no one knows if there really is a creature in there. It's a mystery."

"Well, the Loch is really deep," I said. "They say there are deep caves[3] under the water where a monster could[4] hide."

"Yes," said Douglas. "I've seen pictures of a strange creature like a dinosaur. Some people say they've heard strange noises from the Loch at night. Once it ate a fisherman and his boat!"

The woman and the man looked at us with big eyes.

"Now, Douglas and Stella. You're scaring[5] our guests," laughed Mum. "They're going fishing on the Loch today, remember?"

"Oh, yes," said Dad. "What do you have in your van? A fishing boat?"

The woman looked at her partner. "Yes," she said. "That's right, a fishing boat."

"What fish do you want to catch?"

"Oh … fish. Just fish." The man and the woman got up suddenly. "We must go now."

"I love to go fishing" said Dad. "Maybe I could come with you and show –"

The woman was going out the door. She turned round and said, "No!" Then she said, "Em, sorry, our boat is too small. There's only room for two."

Douglas and I went into the living room so Mum and Dad could not hear us.

"Stella, those two aren't normal tourists," said Douglas. "They didn't listen to a word Dad and Mum said about Urquhart Castle or going for walks in the hills."

"But they listened when we told them about Nessie," I said.

"Why didn't they want Dad to go fishing with them?" asked Douglas.

"Because they aren't going fishing!"

"Well, where do you think they're going, Stella?"

[1]cup [kʌp] – *Tasse,* [2]all over [ɔ:l‿'əʊvə] – *überall,* [3]cave [keɪv] – *Höhle,* [4]could [kʊd] – *könnte,* [5]scare [skeə] – *Angst machen*

"I've no idea," I said. "But there's only one way to find out."

Douglas and I ran and got our bikes, but the black van was not there. "I think they've gone to the Loch!" I said. We took a short-cut[1] to the Loch through the castle gardens. Outside the castle, we passed[2] the caretaker and his workmen.

"Hi, you two. We're just having a break," said Mr Muir. "We're still taking the chairs from the lawn[3] down to the storeroom. It's a long way down." Mr Muir wanted to talk, but we were in a hurry. "If you've got some time now, I'll show you the dungeons deep under the castle. Would you like that?"

"Wow!" said Douglas. I knew Douglas really wanted to see the dungeons. But this was not the time for a visit to the dungeons. We needed to find out what the strange pair was doing! We didn't want to lose them.

"Thanks, Mr Muir," I said. "Maybe another time. We're in a hurry just now."

"But it's the holidays," said Mr Muir. "Kids today are always in a hurry."

"You see," I said. "We've got new guests at our B & B, and ... Mum needs bacon[4] and eggs ... for breakfast. We must go now. Good bye, Mr Muir! Come on, Douglas!"

Douglas really wanted to stay, but he came with me. "Breakfast?" we heard Mr Muir say as we rode away. "It's already 11 o'clock!"

When we got to the road, we couldn't see the black van. "We've lost them!" I said.

"Now we don't know where they're going!"

"Or what they're doing!" said Douglas. "Oh, well. Hey! Let's just go back and ask Mr Muir if we can visit the castle dungeons."

"Douglas!" I said. "Don't you want to

[1]shortcut ['ʃɔ:tkʌt] – *Abkürzung,* [2]pass [pɑ:s] – *vorbeifahren,* [3]lawn [lɔ:n] – *Rasen,* [4]bacon ['beɪkn] – *Frühstücksspeck,* [5]turn down ['tɜ:n daʊn] – *abbiegen in,* [6]mini-submarine [ˌmɪni ˌsʌbmər'i:n] – *kleines U-Boot*

find out what those two are doing? And what S.A.M. means?" Just then we saw the black van! It was turning down[5] a little road to the Loch. "There they are!" I said. "Come on! After them!" We followed the van down a quiet road. It stopped by the Loch where there were no people. Douglas and I put our bikes down and hid behind a tree. The man and woman got out of the van.

"W-What are they doing?" said Douglas.

"Shh!" I said. "They mustn't see us!" We saw them open the back doors of the van. Together they took out a strange boat. It wasn't a fishing boat. It looked more like a mini-submarine[6]!

"Quick, put the underwater[1] microphones in the sub[2]," the woman said to the man.

"Yes, Professor[3]," he said. It was the first time we heard him speak.

"Don't forget the infrared[4] camera. We'll show them! There's no monster in Loch Ness. Nessie is a fake[5]! The fake in the lake[6]! Ha-ha! Science Against Monsters will show them! Let's go!"

Douglas and I watched them put the little submarine in the water. Then they got into the sub and closed the doors. "Look! It's going under!" said Douglas. We rode home on our bikes as fast as we could to tell Mum and Dad.

"What!?" said Mum. "Science Against Monsters?"

"Yes, she's a professor," I said. "They're calling Nessie 'The Fake in the Lake'."

"And they've got this cool submarine," said Douglas. "But they want to prove[5] that there's no creature in the Loch."

"Oh, no!" said Dad. "This is the end! Now we must go back to live in Glasgow –"

"B-But why?" we asked. "We love it here!"

"Dad and I love it here, too," said Mum. "But when people hear that there's nothing in the Loch, we'll have no guests. And without guests, how can we live?"

"Your mother's right," said Dad. "We must sell McArthur's B & B. I must go back to work in the factory again and Mum must clean other people's houses. And you two must go back to the big city school."

"No more playing at the Loch," I said.

"No more bike rides[6] and walks[7] in the hills," said Douglas.

"No more concerts in the castle," said Mum. We were all very sad. Suddenly the door opened. The strange pair ran into the breakfast room. They looked really scared.

"Quick!" shouted the woman. "We're leaving! We've just come back to get our things!" They ran upstairs and then came down again with their bags and got into the van.

"Run for your life[8]!" they shouted to us and ran out the door.

The next day the phone rang all morning. "More guests!" Mum said every time she answered it.

[1]underwater [ˌʌndəˈwɔːtə] – *unterwasser*, [2]sub [sʌb] – *U-Boot*, [3]professor [prəˈʃesə] – *Professor(in)*, [4]infrared [ˌɪnfrəˈred] – *infrarot*, [5]fake [feɪk] – *Schwindel*, [6]lake [leɪk] – *See*, [7]prove [pruːv] – *beweisen*, [8]bike ride [ˈbaɪk ˌraɪd] – *Fahrradtour*, [9]walk [wɔːk] – *Spaziergang*, [10]life, lives [laɪf, laɪvz] – *Leben*

Suddenly, a lot of guests wanted to stay at McArthur's B & B. "I just can't understand it," said Dad.

When the newspaper arrived later in the morning, this is what we read:

Scientists[1] hear monster noises in Loch Ness

Scientists from London came back from a visit to the famous Loch Ness in Scotland yesterday. Professor Gruntle and Dr Bland used a special[2] submarine with infrared cameras and underwater microphones in the Loch just beside Urquhart Castle.

"We heard some very scary noises under the water. Terrible noises!" the Professor said. "It's no mystery! We are sure a terrible monster is hiding in the deep caves under Loch Ness! And this monster is big!"

"Now we know why so many people are calling our B & B," I said.

"Does this mean we don't have to go back to the city?" asked Douglas. "Can we stay here?"

"Yes, maybe," said Dad. "But what made those terrible noises? Maybe there really is something in the Loch."

That afternoon, Douglas and I were walking in the castle gardens. We saw the caretaker. "Hi, kids," called Mr Muir. "Are you too busy to see the dungeons today?"

"No, we aren't!" said Douglas.

Mr Muir took us into the castle. There were a lot of visitors there. But Mr Muir still took the two of us down into the dungeons. We got in the lift and closed the door. It started to go down. It was really loud in the old lift so we couldn't talk. When we got to the bottom[3], Mr Muir opened the door. It was dark and very cold down there. When we spoke, there was a loud echo[4].

[1]scientist ['saɪəntɪst] – *Wissenschaftler(in)*, [2]special ['speʃl] – *speziell*, [3]bottom ['bɒtəm] – *Boden, Grund*, [4]echo ['ekəʊ] – *Echo*

"This is so cool!" we said. "Thanks, Mr Muir. We've never been in a castle dungeon before."

"Well, we're right under the castle here, and we're under the water of the Loch, too."

It was really scary. When it was time to take the lift back up, Mr Muir asked us, "Why were you two in a hurry the other day?"

"We were following some weird guests who stayed at the B & B. They said they were going fishing, but we saw them put a mini-submarine in the Loch. Now it's in all the newspapers."

"Really?" said Mr Muir. "Well, I haven't got time for newspapers. What happened?"

"They wanted to prove that Nessie is a fake," I told him.

"Nessie a fake?" said Mr Muir. "Pah! Well, what did they find?"

"They went under water and they heard some terrible noises … just like a monster! They were really scared! They told us to run for our lives!"

Mr Muir just laughed.

"Do you think there really is a creature in the Loch, Mr Muir?" we asked.

"I don't know, kids. But I think I know what those scientists heard."

Mr Muir pressed a button and the lift started to come down with a lot of noise.

It made a terrible echo in the dungeons. "Do you hear that?" he asked. "If you're in a submarine under the Loch, I'm sure it sounds[1] just like a terrible monster!"

"Wow!" we said. "You mean that's all it was? Your old lift?"

"It's just an idea," smiled Mr Muir. "Maybe there is a creature in the Loch. Who can say?"

After the story

1. *What was the best part of the story for you? Why?*
2. *How did it make you feel?*
3. *Would you like to have a holiday in a place like Loch Ness? What could you do there?*

[1]sound [saʊnd] – *klingen*

L3, 8

Robin Hood and his merry band[1]

Robin Hood
Maid Marian
Dicken
Will Scarlet
Little John
Friar[2] Tuck

A poor[3] farmer
His wife[4]
His son[5]

The Sheriff[6] of Nottingham
The Sheriff's men

Scene 1 Robin Hood's camp[8] in Sherwood Forest[9].

Robin Hood: Look at this poster, everyone[10]. The Sheriff of Nottingham and his men are coming to Sherwood Forest to collect taxes[11].
Maid Marian: It's terrible, Robin! They come to people's doors and ask for money.
Dicken: And poor people don't have any money to give them!
Will Scarlet: If you can't pay[12] the taxes, the Sheriff takes your animals, your cows or horses.
Little John: Or he puts you in jail[13]!
Friar Tuck: That Sheriff of Nottingham is a cruel[14], cruel man.
Dicken: What does he do with all the taxes that he collects?
Robin Hood: He gives them to cruel King[15] John.
Dicken: When is the Sheriff coming to Sherwood Forest?
Robin Hood: On Monday.
Friar Tuck: B-But that's today, Robin!
Robin Hood: You're right. Listen to this: The cruel Sheriff of Nottingham is in the forest today. He's collecting taxes. He's even collecting taxes from the poor.
Merry band: Down with the Sheriff! Down with King John!
Robin Hood: We must stop them!

[1]merry band ['meri ˌbænd] – *lustige Bande,* [2]friar [fraɪə] – *Mönch,* [3]poor [pɔː] – *arm,* [4]wife [waɪf] – *Ehefrau,* [5]son [sʌn] – *Sohn,* [6]sheriff ['ʃerɪf] – *Sheriff,* [7]storyteller ['stɔːrɪtelə] – *Erzähler(in),* [8]camp [kæmp] – *Lager,* [9]forest ['fɒrɪst] – *Wald,* [10]everyone ['evrɪwʌn] – *jeder,* [11]collect taxes [ˌkɒlekt 'tæksɪz] – *Steuern erheben,* [12]pay [peɪ] – *(be)zahlen,* [13]jail [dʒeɪl] – *Gefängnis,* [14]cruel ['kruːəl] – *grausam,* [15]king [kɪŋ] – *König*

All the merry band:
We're Robin Hood and his merry band!
We live in Sherwood Forest and
We take from the rich[1] to give to the poor[2]!
So when the Sheriff knocks[3] on your door,
Don't be scared, that does no good!
Give a call to Robin Hood!
He's the man they're talking about!
He's the man who can sort it out!

Maid Marian: How can we sort it out Robin?
Robin Hood: Er … I don't know … er … . That's why I called you.
Maid Marian: I have a plan!

L3, 9

Scene 2 The Sheriff visits the poor farmer.

Storyteller: *The Sheriff of Nottingham and his men arrive in the forest. His first man knocks on the door of a poor farmer's home.*
Poor farmer: Who's there?
Sheriff: It's the Sheriff of Nottingham! It's time to pay taxes to your King! Open the door!
Poor farmer: G-Good day, Sheriff of Nottingham.
Wife: H-How do you do?

Son: *(from behind his mother)*: Good morning, Mr Sheriff.
Sheriff: How many people live in this house?
Poor farmer: J-Just me and my wife.
Sheriff: But I heard three voices!
Wife: No, really! Only we two live here!
Sheriff: Hmm. Taxes from two people. That's … one pound!
Wife: One pound!
Poor farmer: We don't have money like that!
Sheriff: No money, eh? *(to his men)* Take these two! It's jail for you! Ha-ha-ha!
Storyteller: *They take the farmer and his wife and they all leave. Then the boy runs out of the house and looks around. He runs off the other way.*
Poor boy: Only one man can help us!

[1]the rich [ðə 'rɪtʃ] – *die Reichen* [2]the poor [ðə 'pɔː] – *die Armen*, [3]knock [nɒk] – *(an)klopfen*

L3, 10 Scene 3 The boy asks for help.

Poor boy: Robin Hood, Robin Hood! The Sheriff and his men are taking my mum and dad to jail! Just because we can't pay taxes to cruel King John!
Merry band: Down with the Sheriff! Down with King John!
Poor boy: My dad said that you take from the rich and give to the poor! You must help us, Robin Hood!
Robin Hood: Don't worry, my boy. Take us to the Sheriff and his men. I have a plan –

L3, 11 Scene 4 The Sheriff's men want to sleep.

First man: It's too late to go back to Nottingham, Boss[1].
Second man: Yeah, Boss. I'm dog-tired. Let's sleep here for the night.
Third man: Sleep in Sherwood Forest? It's too windy.
Fourth man: A-And Robin Hood could find us!
First man: Or Maid Marian. She has all the ideas!
Second Man: They take from the rich to give to the poor!
Sheriff: I'm not afraid of Robin Hood! Or Maid Marian! I'm the Sheriff of Nottingham! *(He looks around.)* But you're right. We can't sleep here.

Storyteller: *The boy comes out from behind a tree. His parents see him, but he puts his finger to his mouth to tell them not to say anything.*
Poor farmer: *(to his wife)* Look, it's our son!
Wife: Ooh, my baby!
Sheriff: *(to the parents)* What did you say?
Poor farmer: N-Nothing, Sheriff!
Poor Boy: Good evening, sirs[2]! Excuse me, can I help you?
First man: Yes. We're looking for a good place to sleep.
Poor boy: Oh, I know the perfect[3] place to sleep in the forest, Sir. It's out of the wind. Follow me!

[1]Boss ['bɒs] – *Chef(in),* [2]sir [sɜː] – *Herr,* [3]perfect ['pɜːfɪkt] – *perfekt*

3, 12 Scene 5 They find a place to sleep.

Storyteller: *The Sheriff and his men, the farmer and his wife arrive. There are lots of green trees which are moving in the wind.*
Poor boy: This is the perfect place to spend the night, Sheriff. The wind isn't so bad under these trees.
Sheriff: Ha! And Robin Hood can never find us here. Or Maid Marian. Tomorrow we go to Nottingham to give King John all this lovely[1], lovely money!
Storyteller: *The boy leaves. They all lie down[2] to sleep. The trees are moving, but they are strange trees. They are Robin Hood and his merry band! They are wearing green and brown and have tree branches[3] in their hands. When the Sheriff and his men are sleeping, Robin and his merry band take the bag of taxes, free[4] the poor farmer and his wife, and tiptoe[5] away.*

3, 13 Scene 6 Robin helps the poor people.

Storyteller: *Robin and his band come back to the camp with the poor farmer and his wife. The boy runs to his parents.*
Poor boy: Mum! Dad!
Wife: Our baby!
Robin: Ha-ha-ha! The Sheriff is cruel, but he's stupid, too!
Maid Marian: We tricked[6] him and his men!
All: Down with the Sheriff! Down with King John!
Robin Hood: Here you are. Here's some money. Now you aren't so poor!
Poor farmer: Oh! Thank you, Robin Hood! Thank you all!
Robin Hood: You're welcome!

All the merry band:
We're Robin Hood and his merry band
We live in Sherwood Forest and
We take from the rich to give to the poor!
So when the Sheriff knocks on your door,
Don't be scared! That does no good.
Give a call to Robin Hood.
He's the man they're talking about.
He's the man who can sort it out.
We hope you liked our little play.
Come back and see us soon one day!

[1]lovely [ˈlʌvli] – *schön,* [2]lie down [laɪ ˈdaʊn] – *sich hinlegen,* [3]branch [brɑntʃ] – *Ast,* [4]free [friː] – *befreien,* [5]tiptoe [ˈtɪptəʊ] – *auf Zehenspitzen gehen,* [6]trick [trɪk] – *täuschen*

The Wizard of Oz

L3, 14

Dorothy lived on a farm in Kansas with her Aunt Em and Uncle Henry. They always had a lot of work to do. Her dog Toto was her only[1] friend.

Dorothy was very unhappy. She wanted to run away, but a big twister[3] came and she got worried. She went back to the house in a hurry.

Dorothy went into the house. Suddenly a window flew open and hit her on the head. Then the house flew through the sky.

After the house landed[4], Dorothy went to look outside and saw that she was not in Kansas any more[5].

[1]only ['əʊnli] – *einzig*, [2]wicked ['wɪkɪd] – *böse*, [3]twister ['twɪstə] – *Wirbelsturm*, [4]land [lænd] – *landen*, [5]not … any more [nɒt … ˌeni 'mɔː] – *nicht mehr*, [6]kill [kɪl] – *umbringen*, [7]grateful ['greɪtfl] – *dankbar*

L3, 15 Glinda gave the dead[1] witch's magic[2] shoes to Dorothy. Suddenly the Wicked Witch of the West appeared[3]. She was angry with Dorothy because her house killed the witch's sister.

Dorothy was scared of the witch. She wanted to go back to Kansas. But how? Glinda told her where to get help.

On the way, Dorothy made three friends: Scarecrow[8], Tin[9] Man, and Cowardly[10] Lion. They all needed help.

Dorothy told her friends about the Wizard of Oz. She invited them to go with her to see him.

[1]dead [ded] – *tot,* [2]magic ['mædʒɪk] – *Zauber-,* [3]appear [ə'pɪə] – *erscheinen,* [4]be alive [ə'laɪv] – *leben,* [5]my pretty [ˌmaɪ 'prɪti] – *Schätzchen,* [6]Emerald ['emərəld] – *Smaragd,* [7]brick [brɪk] – *Backstein,* [8]scarecrow ['skeəkrəʊ] – *Vogelscheuche,* [9]tin [tɪn] – *Blech,* [10]cowardly ['kaʊədli] – *feige,* [11]heart [hɑːt] – *Herz,* [12]brain [breɪn] – *Gehirn,* [13]courage ['kʌrɪdʒ] – *Mut,* [14]wonderful ['wʌndəfl] – *wunderbar*

L3, 16 After a long trip, they arrived at the Emerald City. They asked the wizard for help.

On their way to the witch's castle, the witch captured[2] Dorothy and Toto.

Dorothy's friends wanted to rescue her. As they started to leave the castle, the witch set fire to[3] Scarecrow.

Dorothy threw water on the fire. It saved Scarecrow, and it killed the witch. Everyone thanked Dorothy.

[1]broomstick ['bru:mstɪk] – *Besen*, [2]capture ['kæptʃə] – *gefangen nehmen*, [3]set fire to [set 'faɪə tə] – *in Brand stecken*

L3, 17 The friends took the broomstick to the wizard, but he was not a real wizard. He tried to help them with a diploma[1], a ticking[2] heart and a medal[3].

The wizard's hot-air balloon[5] left Oz without Dorothy. But Glinda told her how to get home all by herself[6].

When Dorothy opened her eyes, she was back in Kansas. She was very happy to see her family and friends again. She told them about her trip.

[1]diploma [dɪˈpləʊmə] – *Diplom, Zeugnis,* [2]ticking [ˈtɪkɪŋ] – *tickend,* [3]medal [ˈmedəl] – *Medaille, Orden,* [4]fake [feɪk] – *Hochstapler(in),* [5]hot-air balloon [hɒt ˈeə bəˌluːn] – *Heißluftballon,* [6]all by herself [ɔːl ˌbaɪ həˈself] – *ganz alleine* [7]tap [tæp] – *leicht schlagen,* [8]to yourself [ˌtə jɔːˈself] – *bei dir (selbst)*

Six situations[1] in Greenwich

Work in groups. Choose a dialogue and act it. You can change what happens in the dialogue. The phrases can help you.

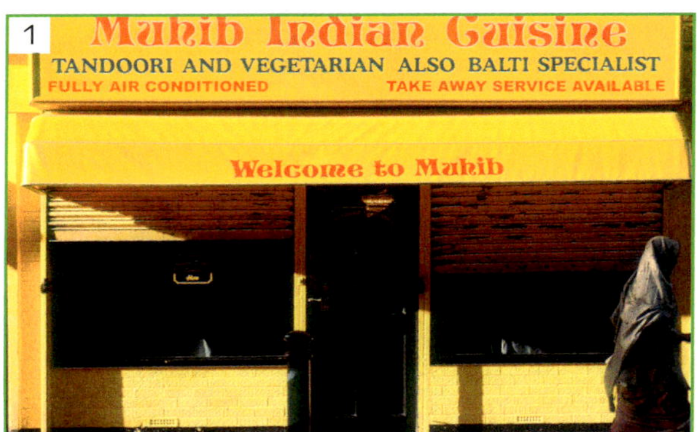

You are on holiday[2] in London and want to buy something from a takeaway for lunch. Choose two dishes[3] and order them.

Is this where the queue[4] starts?
I'd like a chicken curry and a lamb curry with rice, please.
How much is a bottle of water, please?
That's £6.25 altogether[5], please.
(Check pages 15 and 49 for more phrases.)

You go to the doctor because you don't feel well[6]. Tell the doctor what's wrong.

I've got a very sore[7] throat[8].
I think I've got a temperature[9].
I'll give you a prescription[10] for some tablets[11].
Go to bed and drink a lot of tea and water.
(Check page 41 for more phrases.)

[1]situation [ˌsɪtju'eɪʃn] – *Situation*, [2]on holiday [ɒn 'hɒlədeɪ] – *im Urlaub*, [3]dish [dɪʃ] – *hier: Gericht*, [4]queue [kju:] – *Schlange*, [5]altogether [ˌɔ:ltə'geðə] – *insgesamt*, [6]feel well [ˌfi:l 'wel] – *sich wohl fühlen*, [7]I've got a very sore … . [sɔ:] – *Mir tut der/die/das … weh.*, [8]throat [θrəʊt] – *Hals*, [9]temperature ['temprətʃə] – *hier: Fieber*, [10]prescription [prɪ'skrɪpʃn] – *Rezept*, [11]tablet ['tæblət] – *Tablette*

3

You are in a café. You order a drink and some sandwiches. You want to go to the toilet but the door is locked[12].

Have you got any sandwiches without meat[13]?
May I have the key to the toilet, please?
Yes, of course. But please bring it back to me.
(Check page 55 for more phrases.)

4

You go to the market to buy things for a party. Tell the stall holder what you want to make and buy the things you need.

Have you got any new potatoes?
I'd like some fruit for a fruit salad, please.
How much are the grapes[14]?
(Check page 54 for more phrases.)

5

You are in a clothes shop. You want to buy a T-shirt. You have found something, but it's the wrong size[15] or colour. You ask the shop assistant for help before you buy it.

Excuse me, have you got this in pink, please?
Can I exchange[16] it if it's too small?
Yes, if you have the receipt[17].

6

You meet your neighbour in the park and offer to look after her dog for 5 minutes. She wants to run to the bakery[18]. It's a nice dog and you are very happy.

Could you look after him for 5 minutes, please?
Sure. It's no trouble!
Good dog, Bonzo[19]! Sit!
Oh, dear[20]. Where did he go?

[12]locked [lɒkt] – *verschlossen,* [13]meat [mi:t] – *Fleisch,*
[14]grape [greɪp] – *Traube,* [15]size [saɪz] – *Größe,*
[16]exchange [ɪks'tʃeɪndʒ] – *tauschen,* [17]receipt [rɪ'si:t] – *Quittung,*
[18]bakery ['beɪkri] – *Bäckerei,* [19]Bonzo ['bɒnzeʊ] – *Hundename,*
[20]Oh dear [əʊ 'dɪə] – *Oje*

Poems and songs

A diamond[1] poem: School

School
Busy, loud
Speaking, listening, learning,
Teacher, classroom, evening, homework,
Watching TV, eating, playing
Quiet, tired
Home

My letter poem: A

I am an "**A**"
I live in **Australia**,
with my **aunt**,
I don't like **alarm clocks**.
I like **animals**
and **adventures**,
And in **autumn**
I eat a lot of **apples**
and wear an **anorak**
I am an "**A**".

GROUP SKILLS

- Jeder in der Gruppe soll bei dem Projekt eine Aufgabe übernehmen. Entscheidet, wer was machen soll. Es gibt viele verschiedene Aufgaben: das Gedicht soll schön geschrieben und schön gestaltet werden, einer kann vorstellen, wer was lesen wird, und ihr könnt die Gedichte sogar zu zweit oder zu dritt vortragen. Überlegt euch auch, ob die Klasse an einigen Stellen mitmachen soll.
- Macht eine Liste von Themen, die ihr interessant findet, und die ihr gut kennt. Dann einigt euch auf ein Thema.
- Wo findet ihr weitere Informationen, Bilder und andere Dinge zu eurem Thema? Sucht in eurem Englischbuch, in anderen Büchern, in Zeitschriften, in eurer Bibliothek oder im Internet. Entscheidet, wer wo suchen soll.
- Schaut euch dann alles, was ihr gefunden habt, gemeinsam an. Macht Listen und *mind maps*.

Step 1: Prepare your project

1. *Work in groups of three to six pupils.*
2. *Read and act the four poems.*
   Which poems do you like? Why?

Step 2: Collect ideas for your project

1. *Find an idea for a poem or song.*
2. *Collect words, pictures, music or other things you need for your poem or song.*

Step 3: Write your poem or song

1. *Write two or three poems in your group.*
2. *Use your dictionary to help you. Ask your teacher for help.*
3. *Now read your poems again. Are you happy with them?*
   Can you make them more interesting?

An action poem: Barny, the ghost

Say the poem and do the actions, too.

It's midnight	(close your eyes)
Barny, wake up!	(open your eyes)
Barny, fly around!	(wave your arms)
Barny, make a sound!	(clap your hands)
Barny, laugh madly!	(laugh)
Barny, sing sadly!	(sing)
Barny, dance!	(dance)
Barny, whisper!	(whisper)
Oh, no! It's morning!	(look worried)
Barny, disappear!	(hide under your desk)

A chant: Cats and dogs

You need two groups for this song, group A and group B.

A: Dogs
B: Cats
A: Dogs
B: Cats
A: We like dogs – they're very, very nice!
B: We like cats – they find a lot of mice!
A: Woof!
B: Meow!
A: Woof!
B: Meow!
A & B: Dogs and cats.

Step 4: Present your poem or song

1. *You can make a poster, use your computer, say it as a rap, say it with music, act it, …*
2. *Decide who will read which poem or chant and practise them. Read them to the other people in your group.*
3. *Now have a project party. Read your poems and sing your songs to your class.*

PRESENTATION SKILLS

- Übt das Gedicht vor einem Spiegel zu Hause und vor eurer Gruppe in der Schule.
- Fragt eure Gruppenmitglieder oder euren Lehrer / eure Lehrerin, ob eure Aussprache so in Ordnung ist.
- Habt ihr alles, was ihr braucht? Überlegt euch, ob ihr Bilder, Plakate, Masken, Kostüme, Musik, Instrumente oder andere Dinge benötigt.
- Wenn ihr euer Gedicht vortragt, lest nicht nur vom Blatt ab, sondern versucht auch, eure Zuhörer anzuschauen.
- Sprecht langsam und deutlich und laut genug, so dass man euch auch ganz hinten im Klassenzimmer gut verstehen kann.

Step 5: How good is your poem?

1. *Now talk to your teacher and the other pupils in your class. Which three poems are the best?*
2. *Which poems do you like? Why?*

▶ I like the poem / song about … .
The poem about … is good because … .
I like / the pictures / the actions / the music / …
I think … is good.

Mediation and communication

Unit 1 School rules

COMMUNICATION SKILLS

Es gibt Situationen, in denen du englische Regeln verstehen oder deutsche Regeln anderen Leuten auf Englisch erklären musst. Das kannst du gut mit *must* und *don't* tun. Übertrage nur die wichtigsten inhaltlichen Angaben. Versuche nicht, Wort für Wort zu übersetzen.

Situation: Stell dir vor, du solltest einem englischen Austauschschüler diese Schulregeln erklären, weil er noch nicht so gut Deutsch kann. Das kannst du mit deinen eigenen Worten tun. Aber denke daran: Regeln beinhalten oft Empfehlungen, Verbote oder Anweisungen. Dafür sind Imperative gut geeignet.

Schulordnung:

1. Nach jeder Stunde muss die Tafel geputzt werden.
2. Handys müssen im Unterricht ausgeschaltet werden.
3. Fußball spielen in den Gängen ist verboten.
4. Keine Straßenschuhe in der Turnhalle.
5. Das Schulgelände darf während der Pausen nicht verlassen werden.
6. Rauchen auf dem Schulgelände ist verboten.
7. Die Essensausgabe ist in der Cafeteria; Klassen 5–7 ab 12 Uhr, Klassen 8–10 ab 13 Uhr.

Unit 2 An exciting story

COMMUNICATION SKILLS

Wenn englische Gesprächspartner dir etwas erzählen, musst du dich meistens sehr konzentrieren, um ihrer Rede folgen zu können. Sie reden meist recht schnell und außerdem verwenden sie auch oft Wörter, die du noch nicht kennst. Hierbei gibt es zwei wichtige Regeln:

1. Halte nicht an jedem Einzelwort fest, sondern versuche, aus dem großen Zusammenhang wichtige Wörter – Schlüsselwörter – zu erkennen, die dir helfen, den Inhalt zu erschließen. Nutze das, was du verstehst, und dein sonstiges Wissen über die Zusammenhänge, um das Gesagte zu enträtseln.
2. Wenn du damit nicht erfolgreich bist, frag doch einfach nach!

Situation: Deine neue englische Freundin Alison erzählt dir eine höchst amüsante Geschichte aus ihrem letzten Urlaub – in Englisch natürlich. Deine Familie will auch mitlachen, aber leider klappt es mit dem Englischen nicht mehr so gut. Hilf ihnen. Frage zunächst nach den Wörtern, die du nicht verstehst. Verwende dafür die angegebenen Sätze und Fragen. Achte auf das Beispiel.

Alison: We were on holiday in the West of Scotland. We were camping in a really **isolated** place.
You: Isolated? What does that mean?
Alison: Well, there weren't other people or houses. OK. My parents were in the caravan and my sister and I were in our tent. I was **fast asleep**.
You: ...
Alison: I slept very well. Suddenly Katy woke me up. She was **frightened**.
You: ...
Alison: She was scared. There was someone outside the tent. At first we thought it was a **poacher**.
You: ...
Alison: That's a man who kills animals to sell or eat them. Then we heard strange noises. It was an animal – maybe a wild cat or a dog. We were **terrified**.
You: ...
Alison: We were really scared. After ten minutes the noises **got softer**.
You: ...
Alison: We didn't hear the noises. I took my torch and opened the tent. But all we saw was a big horse. It was eating grass!

What does ... mean?

Can you say that again?

What is ... ?

What is a ... ? What does he/she do?

Sorry, I don't understand.

Unit 3 Letters

COMMUNICATION SKILLS

Leserbriefe sind oft sehr interessant. Wenn du jemandem erzählen willst, worum es darin geht, brauchst du nicht wörtlich zu übersetzen.
Aus der Anrede und der Briefunterschrift erfährst du meist bereits, wer hier wem schreibt. Manchmal steht noch dabei, wie alt der Schreiber ist und woher er/sie stammt.
Meist steht in den ersten Sätzen, um was es geht. In den Folgesätzen steht oft etwas über die Meinung des Schreibers dazu oder über Hilfe, die er/sie erwartet.

Situation: Deine kleine Schwester hat diese beiden Leserbriefe gesehen und möchte wissen, was Holly und Dean erlebt haben. Beantworte ihre Fragen:

1. „Wo ist denn Devon? Und was hat Holly dort gemacht?"
2. „Und wer ist dieser Steve? Ist er Hollys Bruder?"
3. „Was hat Dean in Wales gemacht? War er dort schwimmen?"
4. „Und wer ist jetzt dieser Mr Roberts? Ist er ein Lehrer?"

My best holiday was last year. I went to Devon with my friend Kerry and her mum and dad. We stayed in a holiday flat with a fantastic garden and a swimming pool. It was sunny every day and we met some really nice kids on the beach. I still write e-mails to one of them. His name is Steve and he lives in London. Maybe he can visit me in the holidays.

Holly

I went to Wales with my class for a week in May. We stayed in tents and did different activities every day. One day we went rowing. I don't usually like water, but that was great! And we had a karaoke competition. Mr Roberts, my teacher, got the prize (his song was "My way"). Mr Roberts is always strict at school, but that week he was really cool.

Dean

Unit 4 A fast food menu

COMMUNICATION SKILLS

Unbekannte Wörter kann man häufig leichter erschließen, wenn man sie bestimmten Sachgruppen (Ober- oder Untergruppen) zuordnen kann. Auch die Schreibung einzelner Wörter bietet oft Anhaltspunkte zum Deutschen und lässt Schlussfolgerungen für die Bedeutung zu. Sei mutig – versuche es doch einmal!

Situation: Du bist mit David, einem englischen Gastschüler an einer Imbissbude. Weil die Speisekarte nur auf Deutsch ist, musst du für ihn übersetzen.

David: OK, what can I eat? What's number two?
You: (*übersetze, was 2. ist*)
David: Hm. I'd like something with meat. Is number three with meat?
You: (*verneine und übersetze, was 3. ist*)
David: Interesting. *'Gulaschsuppe'* looks funny, too. Is that with meat?
You: (*bejahe und füge hinzu, dass es sehr scharf ist*)
David: I don't like spicy food. Is there anything else with meat?
You: (*sage, welche Nummern mit Fleisch sind*)
David: Number eight? Really? But what does *'Salat'* mean?
You: (*sage, dass es dasselbe ist wie in Englisch und erkläre, dass Wurstsalat ein Salat mit Fleisch ist*)
David: Wow! Can I have '*Wurstsalat*', please?

Ingos Imbiss

1. Hähnchen mit Pommes	3,20
2. Pommes frites	1,30
3. Portion Kartoffelsalat	1,50
4. Belegtes Brötchen mit Wurst	1,80
5. Belegtes Brötchen mit Käse	1,80
6. Fischbrötchen	2,00
7. Gulaschsuppe – scharf!	2,80
8. Portion Wurstsalat	2,50
Getränke:	
Cola (0,33 l)	1,00
Fanta (0,33 l)	1,00
Wasser (0,33 l)	1,00

Unit 5 Reading about your favourite stars

COMMUNICATION SKILLS

In Klasse 5 hast du bereits gelernt, wie man einen unbekannten Text aus einer Broschüre erschließen kann, dass du nämlich auf die Überschrift, Eigennamen, die Aufmachung des Textes und die Abbildungen besonders achten musst. Internettexte kannst du so ähnlich bearbeiten und ins Deutsche übertragen. Achte bei diesen Portraits besonders auf Länder- und Städtenamen im Zusammenhang mit Jahresangaben, auf Zahlenangaben und Daten im Zusammenhang mit bestimmten Tätigkeiten. Manchmal geben dir auch Bilder im Zusammenspiel mit einzelnen Schlüsselwörtern aus dem Text weitere Informationen.

Situation: Etwas über seine „Lieblinge“ zu erfahren, ist für alle Jugendlichen ein beliebtes Hobby. Das Internet ist eine unerschöpfliche Quelle, aber vieles findet man dort nur in Englisch. Aber das ist ja kein Problem für dich. Schließlich geht es nicht um eine wörtliche Übersetzung sondern um die wichtigsten Zahlen, Daten und Fakten über deinen Favoriten. Da freut sich auch deine Familie über solche nützlichen Fähigkeiten, die du ihnen auch gern weitervermitteln kannst.

The best!

David Beckham has played football for Manchester United and England since 1995 and for Real Madrid since 2003. Is he the best football player in the world?

Queen Elizabeth lives in Buckingham Palace in London. But she's also got four more castles in Scotland and England. She loves dogs.

Bill Gates liked computers when he was a boy. When he was 20, he had his own software company. Now he's one of the richest people in the world.

Halle Berry is an exciting actress, who has been in over 20 films. She was the first black actress to win an Oscar.

Your grandma doesn't speak English but she'd like to know more about these famous people. Act dialogues in German with a partner.

Grandma: Was ist denn an David Beckham so besonders?
You: (…)
Grandma: Und diese Halle Berry?
You: (…)
Grandma: Bill Gates hat etwas mit Computern zu tun, stimmt's?
You: (…)
Grandma: Und die Queen, die kennt man ja. Aber ich weiß eigentlich nicht wirklich etwas über sie.
You: (…)

Unit 6 What can they say?

COMMUNICATION SKILLS

Unbekannte Redewendungen haben oft eine ganz spezielle Bedeutung, so dass man sie nicht einfach wörtlich übersetzen kann. Aber durch Unterstützung von Bildern wird ihre Bedeutung schnell klar.

Situation: Diese Wendungen kennst du noch nicht, aber einzelne Wörter daraus sind dir bereits bekannt. Schau dir die Bilder an. Sicherlich wird es dir nicht schwer fallen herauszufinden, wann die einzelnen Ausdrücke gebraucht werden und was sie bedeuten.

1

2

3

4

5

6

Dad will go up the wall!

She'll go a long way!

Wait! I'll give you a hand!

I won't be a minute.

That'll teach you!

He feels on top of the world.

Unit 7 A joke

COMMUNICATION SKILLS

Bilder sind nicht nur als Dekoration oder Ergänzung einer Textseite gedacht. Sie liefern häufig auch vorab wichtige Informationen zu einem Thema und helfen, die Gedanken vor dem Lesen bereits in die richtigen Bahnen zu lenken und dadurch anschließend genauer zu lesen. Oft liefern sie auch Informationen, die uns beim Lesen helfen, schwierige Textstellen zu „knacken".

Situation: Bei dem folgenden Text handelt es sich um einen Witz. Das Bild liefert dir vorab schon wichtige Informationen, die dir das Verstehen erleichtern werden.

a) Überlege vor dem Lesen:
  1. Was ist abgebildet?
  2. Was weißt du darüber? Tausche mit deinem Nachbarn eure Informationen aus.
  3. Welche englischen Wörter fallen dir dazu ein?
  4. Welche Informationen gibt dir das Bild noch?

A violinist was standing in the jungle with his violin. He was playing so beautifully that all the animals came and sat down to listen to him. Then a very old lion came out of the jungle, went up to the violinist, opened his mouth and ate him and his violin. The other animals were absolutely shocked.
"Why did you do that?" asked a gorilla. "He was playing so nicely! We were all enjoying his music."
The old lion held his paw to his ear and said, "What?"

b) Nach dem Lesen:
   Hast du den Witz verstanden? Was hat der Löwe gemacht und warum?
   Erzähle den Witz deinem Partner/deiner Partnerin auf Deutsch.

L3, 18
Unit 7 At the airport

Situation: Du wartest auf deinen Flug in der Abflughalle eines Londoner Flughafens. Der Passagier, der neben dir sitzt, kann nur Deutsch und bittet dich bei den Durchsagen um Hilfe.

Listen to the three different announcements and give the passenger the information in German.

1. Das war eine Durchsage für einen Passagier mit dem Namen … .
   Er … . *Go on, please.*
2. …
3. …

Lies die Grammatikpunkte (G1–G19). Sie sagen dir,
- um welche grammatische Erscheinung es sich handelt (Was?).
- wie sie gebildet wird (Wie?).
- was man **damit** in der englischen Sprache ausdrücken kann (Wozu?).
- wie sie ins Deutsche übersetzt wird.

Achte dabei auf unterstrichene oder fettgedruckte Wörter, die dir anzeigen, was besonders wichtig ist.

Weiterhin solltest du unbedingt auf dieses Symbol achten:

Vorsicht Falle!

Hier wird immer auf besondere Schwierigkeiten hingewiesen. Aber keine Angst, ich werde dir natürlich auch mit Rat und Tat zur Seite stehen!
Wenn du trotzdem einmal einen Begriff nicht mehr weißt, kannst du einfach auf der Seite 139 nachschlagen. Dort findest du eine Übersicht der wichtigsten grammatischen Begriffe mit einem Beispiel dazu und der Angabe, in welchem Grammatikpunkt du mehr darüber lesen kannst.

GRAMMAR SKILLS

1. Es ist hilfreich, wenn du deinem Nachbarn die Regel mit deinen eigenen Worten erklärst und ihr dann gemeinsam die Beispiele durchgeht.

2. Du kannst für deine *grammar cards* bzw. deinen *folder* auch Symbole oder Formeln verwenden, z. B.
   Verneinung *simple past* = ***didn't*** + **Verb**
   Fragebildung *simple past* = ***Did/Didn't*** + Sub(jekt) **+ V(erb)**
   Fragewort + ***did/didn't*** + Sub(jekt) + **V(erb)**

   I will go to London.
   Will I go to London?

3. Wenn du ein Pensum wiederholen möchtest, kannst du auch selbstständig im Grammatischen Anhang nachschauen.

4. Wie war das doch gleich mit *mustn't* und *needn't*? Schreibe wichtige grammatische Regeln oder Wörter auf Kärtchen und hänge sie irgendwo zu Hause hin, wo du sie regelmäßig anschauen kannst, z. B. an den Badezimmerspiegel oder über dein Bett.

5. Du hast jetzt schon viele Zeiten gelernt. Manche kannst du dir gut bildlich merken:

Unit 1

G1 Wiederholung: Die einfache Gegenwart — *Revision: The simple present*

Mit dem ***simple present*** drückst du aus, was **regelmäßig passiert** oder was jemand **regelmäßig tut.** Du kannst damit auch **Tatsachen** ausdrücken.

Aussagen

I **go** to Thomas Tallis School.	*Ich gehe in die TT Schule.*
She **likes** music.	*Sie mag Musik.*
Sam **does** his homework.	*Sam macht seine Hausaufgaben.*
They **live** in Greenwich.	*Sie leben in Greenwich.*

Verneinung

I **don't live** in Greenwich.	*Ich lebe nicht in Greenwich.*
School **doesn't start** at 9 o'clock.	*Die Schule fängt nicht um 9 Uhr an.*
We **don't speak** French.	*Wir sprechen kein Französisch.*

Entscheidungfragen und Kurzantworten

Does he **go** to school by bike?	*Fährt er mit dem Rad zur Schule?*
– Yes, he **does.**/No, he **doesn't.**	*– Ja./Nein.*
Do you **like** History?	*Magst du Geschichte?*
– Yes, I **do.**/No, I **don't.**	*– Ja./Nein.*

Fragen mit Fragewörtern

What do you like? – I like cheese.	*– Was magst du? – Ich mag Käse.*
Where do you live? – In Australia.	*– Wo wohnst du? – In Australien.*
How do you get to school? – On foot.	*– Wie kommst du zur Schule? – Zu Fuß.*
When do you have PE? – On Monday.	*– Wann hast du Sport? – Montags.*
Why do you go surfing? – Because I don't like football.	*– Warum surfst du? – Weil ich Fußball nicht mag.*

Bei *be* und *have got* ist alles anders: Hier benötigst du das Hilfsverb *do* nicht.
Beispiele: – *Are* you at home? – No, I'*m not.*
– *Where* are you? – I'*m* at school.
– *Have* you *got* an apple? – No, I *haven't.*
– *What* have you got? – I'*ve got* a cheese sandwich.

G 2 Fragen mit *What …?* und *Which …?* *Questions with 'What …?' and 'Which …?'*

Mit ***What …?*** fragst du nach **etwas,** das du **nicht weißt** oder **nicht kennst** (Was für ein …?).
Mit ***Which …?*** fragst du nach **etwas,** das zwischen zwei oder mehreren **Dingen zur Auswahl** steht (Welche/r/s?).

What languages do you know?
– English, French and Italian.
Which language do you speak – English or French?
– English.

Welche Sprachen kennst du?
– Englisch, Französisch und Italienisch.
Welche Sprache sprichst du – Englisch oder Französisch?
– Englisch.

Unit 2

G 3 Die einfache Vergangenheit von *be* *The simple past of 'be'*

Du verwendest das ***simple past,*** um von Ereignissen zu erzählen, die in der **Vergangenheit** passiert sind. Dabei werden *am* und *is* zu ***was,*** *are* wird zu ***were.***
Die **Verneinung** wird ähnlich wie beim *simple present* gebildet, indem man ***not*** an *was/were* anfügt *(was not, were not).* Es werden aber meist die Kurzformen ***wasn't/weren't*** verwendet.
Es gibt so genannte **Signalwörter,** die uns zeigen, dass eine Handlung in der Vergangenheit stattgefunden hat und deshalb das *simple past* verwendet werden muss, z. B. *yesterday, last week, two hours ago.*

Yesterday **Last Monday** **A month ago**	I he she	**was/was not/wasn't**	in France. at the cinema. at home.
	we you they	**were/were not/weren't**	

G 4 *Be:* Die einfache Vergangenheit – Fragen *'Be': The simple past – Questions*

Die Fragebildung funktioniert im *simple past* genauso wie im *simple present.*
Bei den **Entscheidungsfragen** steht *Was* oder *Were* am Anfang. Die Antwort gibst du wie im *simple present* als **Kurzantwort.**
Bei **Fragen mit Fragewörtern** folgt nach dem Fragewort direkt *was* oder *were.*

Entscheidungsfragen und Kurzantworten

Was I late? | *Bin ich zu spät gekommen?*
– Yes, you **were.**/No, you **weren't.** | *– Ja./Nein.*
Was the CD expensive? | *War die CD teuer?*
– Yes, it **was.**/No, it **wasn't.** | *– Ja./Nein.*
Were we good? | *Waren wir gut?*
– Yes, you **were.**/No, you **weren't.** | *– Ja./Nein.*
Were you in the playground? | *Wart ihr auf dem Schulhof?*
– Yes, we **were.**/No, we **weren't.** | *– Ja./Nein.*

Fragen mit Fragewörtern

How was school? – OK. | *Wie war die Schule? – OK.*
Where were you? – In the park. | *Wo wart ihr? – Im Park.*
What was so funny? – Tom's joke. | *Was war so lustig? – Toms Witz.*
Who was at the café? – My friends. | *Wer war im Café? – Meine Freunde.*
When were you at home? – At 10 o'clock. | *Wann warst du zu Hause? – Um zehn.*
Why was Dad angry? – Because I was late. | *Warum war Papa böse? – Weil ich zu spät kam.*

G 5 Die einfache Vergangenheit: Aussagen — *The simple past: Statements*

Alle Verben – nicht nur *be* – haben eigene Vergangenheitsformen. Viele davon bilden das *simple past* durch Anhängen der Endung ***-ed.*** Sie heißen deshalb **regelmäßige** Verben. Andere Verben bilden ganz neue Formen, die du auswendig lernen musst. Sie heißen deshalb **unregelmäßige** Verben (→ G3).

Regelmäßige Verben

The London Knights play**ed** last night.	*Die London Knights spielten gestern Abend.*
Sam's mum visit**ed** him.	*Sams Mutter besuchte ihn.*
Terry tri**ed** a new hair colour.	*Terry probierte ein neue Haarfarbe aus.*

Unregelmäßige Verben

Sam and Terry **went** to the game.	*Sam und Terry gingen zu dem Spiel.*
Jade's hat **fell** into the water.	*Jades Hut fiel ins Wasser.*
Lisa **bought** Jade an ice-cream.	*Lisa kaufte Jade ein Eis.*

Schau dir die Liste der **unregelmäßigen Verben** auf S. 203 an.

to read → read [red]
to come → came
to take → took

to have → had
to give → gave
to say → said

G 6 Die einfache Vergangenheit: Verneinung — *The simple past: Negation*

Für die **Verneinung** des *simple past* verwendest du ***didn't*** *(did+not)*. Dann folgt die **Grundform** des Verbs.

Regelmäßige Verben

The London Knights **didn't play** last week.	*Die London Knights haben letzte Woche nicht gespielt (spielten letzte Woche nicht).*
Terry's mum **didn't laugh.**	*Terrys Mutter hat nicht gelacht (lachte nicht).*
Sam's uncle **didn't visit** him.	*Sams Onkel hat ihn nicht besucht (besuchte ihn nicht).*

Unregelmäßige Verben

Lisa and Emma **didn't go** to the game.	*Lisa und Emma sind nicht zu dem Spiel gegangen (gingen nicht zu dem Spiel).*
Sam's cap **didn't fall** into the water.	*Sams Mütze fiel nicht ins Wasser.*
Terry **didn't buy** Jade an ice-cream.	*Terry kaufte Jade kein Eis.*

Immer schön daran denken: *Did* ist die Vergangenheitsform von *do*.
Deshalb steht nach *didn't* das Verb natürlich wieder in der Grundform.
Beispiel: He **went** to the game. *Aber:* He **didn't go** to the game.

Unit 3

G 7 Die einfache Vergangenheit: Fragen und Kurzantworten — *The simple past: Questions and short answers*

Wenn du im *simple past* eine Frage stellen willst, setzt du das Hilfsverb ***did*** (Entscheidungsfragen) oder **Fragewort + *did*** (Fragen nach etwas Bestimmtem) an den Satzanfang. Mit *did* verwendest du das Verb in der **Grundform.** In den **Kurzantworten** verwendest du ebenfalls ***did*** oder die verneinte Form ***didn't.***

Entscheidungsfragen und Fragen mit Fragewörtern

	Did	you **go** home after the game?	*Seid ihr nach dem Spiel nach Hause gegangen?*
When	did	you **go** to the zoo?	*Wann seid ihr in den Zoo gegangen?*
How	did	she **like** the elephants?	*Wie haben ihr die Elefanten gefallen?*
What	did	you **do** then?	*Was habt ihr dann gemacht?*
Where	did	you **buy** your new hats?	*Wo habt ihr eure neuen Hüte gekauft?*
Who	did	you **meet** there?	*Wen habt ihr dort getroffen?*

Kurzantworten

Yes, I **did.**		No, I **didn't.**	
Yes, you **did.**		No, you **didn't.**	
Yes, he **did.**		No, he **didn't.**	
Yes, she **did.**	*Ja!*	No, she **didn't.**	*Nein!*
Yes, it **did.**		No, it **didn't.**	
Yes, we **did.**		No, we **didn't.**	
Yes, you **did.**		No, you **didn't.**	
Yes, they **did.**		No, they **didn't.**	

G 8 Die Relativpronomen *who* und *which* — *The relative pronouns 'who' and 'which'*

Notwendige Relativsätze werden durch ein Relativpronomen eingeleitet. ***Who*** bezieht sich nur auf **Personen**, ***which*** nur auf **Dinge**. Beide werden sowohl für den Singular als auch für den Plural gebraucht und beide können **Subjekt** und **Objekt** im Relativsatz sein.

Subjekt

It was Sam **who** broke the bike.	*Es war Sam,* ***der*** *das Fahrrad kaputtmachte.*
It was his left arm **which** hurt.	*Es war sein linker Arm,* ***der*** *wehtat.*
It was the boys **who** cleaned the bike.	*Es waren die Jungs,* ***die*** *das Fahrrad putzten.*

Objekt

That's the bike **which** he broke.	*Das ist das Fahrrad,* ***das*** *er kaputtmachte.*
His dad took him to a doctor **who** he knew.	*Sein Vater brachte ihn zu einer Ärztin,* ***die*** *er kannte.*
The marks **which** she saw were yellow.	*Die Flecken,* ***die*** *sie sah, waren gelb.*

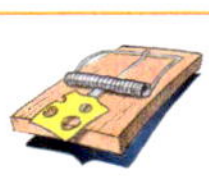

Im Englischen wird der Relativsatz nicht durch ein Komma vom Hauptsatz abgetrennt. Beim Sprechen macht man keine Pause zwischen Haupt- und Relativsatz.

Unit 4

G 9 Die Steigerung der Adjektive — *The comparison of adjectives*

Wenn du Personen, Tiere oder Dinge näher beschreiben willst, verwendest du häufig Adjektive. Sie drücken Eigenschaften aus, z. B. Meine Katze ist **dick.** Wenn du Eigenschaften miteinander vergleichst, benötigst du die Steigerungsformen der Adjektive, z. B. Deine Katze ist **dicker.** Es gibt zwei Arten Adjektive zu steigern.

Einsilbige Adjektive

small – small**er** – (**the**) small**est** — *klein – kleiner – am kleinsten*
nice – nic**er** – (**the**) nic**est** — *nett – netter – am nettesten*
big – bigg**er** – (**the**) bigg**est** — *groß – größer – am größten*

Zweisilbige Adjektive auf -*y*

healthy – health**ier** – (**the**) health**iest** — *gesund – gesünder – am gesündesten*
tasty – tast**ier** – (**the**) tast**iest** — *schmackhaft – schmackhafter – am schmackhaftesten*

Zwei- und mehrsilbige Adjektive

boring – **more** boring – (**the**) **most** boring — *langweilig – langweiliger – am langweiligsten*
difficult – **more** difficult – (**the**) **most** difficult — *schwierig – schwieriger – am schwierigsten*

Wenn du die Unterschiedlichkeit der beiden Dinge oder Personen stärker hervorheben möchtest, kannst du dies tun, indem du die Vergleichsgröße mit *than* anfügst. Im Deutschen benutzen wir hierfür das Wort „als". Die Gleichheit von Personen oder Dingen drückst du mit *as … as* aus.

He's older **than** my brother. — *Er ist älter **als** mein Bruder.*
I think French is **as** difficult **as** English. — *Ich finde Französisch ist **genauso** schwer **wie** Englisch.*

Beachte: *Than* (**als**) wird mit 'a' geschrieben.
Nicht verwechseln mit *then* (**dann**)!
Hier eine kleine Eselsbrücke: *When? – then*
als – than

good und *bad* werden unregelmäßig gesteigert. Ihre Formen musst du lernen.
good – better – (the) best
bad – worse – (the) worst

G10 Die Modalen Hilfsverben *must, mustn't needn't, should and shouldn't* — *The modal verbs 'must', 'mustn't', 'needn't', 'should' and 'shouldn't'*

Die Bezeichnung „Hilfsverben" sagt uns, dass diese Verben immer zusammen mit einem Vollverb in der Grundform stehen müssen, z. B. *I* ***must go.*** – Ich **muss gehen.**
Die Hilfsverben drücken eine **Verpflichtung** *(must)*, ein **Verbot** *(mustn't)* oder eine **Empfehlung** *(needn't, should, shouldn't)* aus. Sie sind für alle Personen gleich und können nur im *simple present* verwendet werden.

You **must eat** fruit every day. It's healthy.	*Du musst jeden Tag Obst essen. Das ist gesund.*
He **mustn't eat** chips. They're unhealthy.	*Er darf keine Pommes essen. Sie sind ungesund.*
We **needn't go** jogging every day. Every second day is OK.	*Wir müssen nicht jeden Tag joggen gehen. Jeder zweite Tag reicht.*
You **should drink** more.	*Ihr solltet mehr trinken.*
They **shouldn't think** about food too often.	*Sie sollten nicht zu oft über das Essen nachdenken.*
Must we go on a diet? – No, you **needn't.**	*Müssen wir eine Diät machen? – Nein.*
What needn't we do today?	*Was brauchen wir heute nicht zu machen?*

Verwechsle nicht *mustn't* und *needn't*.
mustn't heißt „nicht dürfen".
needn't heißt „nicht müssen".

G11 *some* und *any* — *'some' and 'any'*

Mit *some* und *any* drückst du eine **unbestimmte Menge** oder Anzahl aus: „einige", „etwas", „ein paar".
In **Aussagen** verwendest du ***some***, in **Fragen** und **Verneinungen** meist ***any***. Im Deutschen werden *some* und *any* oft nicht übersetzt.

– I'd like **some** milk and **some** biscuits. Have you got **any** chocolate biscuits?	– *Ich hätte gerne (etwas) Milch und (ein paar) Kekse. Hast du (ein paar) Schokoladenkekse?*
– I have**n't** got **any** milk and I have**n't** got **any** chocolate biscuits. I have only got **some** lemonade and **some** sweets.	– *Ich habe keine Milch und keine Schokoladenkekse. Ich habe nur (etwas) Limonade und (einige) Süßigkeiten.*

Hier eine kleine Eselsbrücke zum Einprägen!

	A										S					
N	E	G	A	T	I	V	E		P	O	S	I	T	I	V	E
	Y										M					
											E					

1. Vergiss nicht ***not (n't)***, wenn du mit ***any*** verneinst.
Beispiel: We have not (have**n't**) got any more time. *Wir haben keine Zeit mehr.*
2. Bei Fragen mit *can* und bei Angeboten mit ***would you like*** verwendest du *some*.
Beispiel: **Can** I have **some** cake, Mom? – **Would you like some** cake, too?

Unit 5

G12 Das Perfekt — *The present perfect*

Du verwendest das *present perfect*, wenn etwas in der Vergangenheit geschehen ist, das **Auswirkungen auf die Gegenwart** hat bzw. von dem ein **Ergebnis** vorliegt. Schau dir die beiden Bilder an. In der Vergangenheit war Toms Zimmer nicht sehr schön (Bild 1). Dann hat er renoviert und jetzt ist das Zimmer wie neu. Dieses Ergebnis kannst du in Bild 2 sehen. Deshalb steht hier das *present perfect*. Im Deutschen verwenden wir ebenfalls das Perfekt.

I **have painted** the walls. — *Ich habe die Wände gestrichen.*
I **have put** the books on the shelf. — *Ich habe die Bücher ins Regal gestellt.*
I **have cleaned** the window. — *Ich habe das Fenster geputzt.*
I **have broken** the bed. — *Ich habe das Bett kaputt gemacht.*
My hair **has gone** pink. — *Meine Haare sind pink geworden.*

Bei unregelmäßigen Verben wird das *present perfect* mit ***have*** oder ***has*** und der **dritten Form des Verbs** gebildet. An die **regelmäßigen Verben** wird ***-ed*** angehängt. Die Form von *have* kann im Deutschen mit „haben" oder „sein" übersetzt werden (***habe** gesehen*, ***bin** gelaufen*).
Es gibt **Signalwörter,** die anzeigen, dass eine solche Handlung aus der Vergangenheit mit einem sichtbaren Ergebnis vorliegt, z. B. ***just, already*** und ***never.*** Sie stehen zwischen *have/has* und dem Verb.

He has **just** washed his hair. — *Er hat **gerade** seine Haare gewaschen.*
He has **already** put his clothes in the wardrobe. — *Er hat seine Kleider **schon** in den Schrank geräumt.*
He has **never** painted the walls **before**. — *Er hat die Wände **vorher noch nie** gestrichen.*

Sollen *already, never* und *just* richtig passen, musst du sie zwischen den Verbteilen lassen!

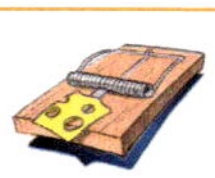

Hier musst du gleich mehrere Dinge beachten:
1. Bei *he, she, it* musst du *has* verwenden. Auch hier gilt also:
He, she, it, das *-s* muss mit.
2. Im Deutschen steht das Objekt zwischen den beiden Teilen des Prädikats (Ich **habe** die Wände **gestrichen**). Im Englischen steht das Objekt immer hinter den beiden Teilen des Prädikats *(I **have painted** the walls).*

G 13 Das Perfekt: Entscheidungsfragen und Kurzantworten — *The present perfect: Questions and short answers*

Die Fragebildung ist ganz einfach – ***have*** oder ***has*** wandert an den **Satzanfang**. ***Ever*** und ***yet*** sind typische **Signalwörter** für Fragen im *present perfect*. In der Kurzantwort verwendest du ebenfalls *has* oder *have*.

Have we **told** you about the show **yet**? – Yes, you **have.** / No, you **haven't.**	*Haben wir euch schon von der Show erzählt?* *– Ja./Nein.*
Have you **ever made** a web site? – Yes, I **have.** / No, I **haven't.**	*Hast du (schon) jemals eine Website gemacht?* *– Ja./Nein.*
Has she **ever surfed** the Internet? – Yes, she **has.** / No, she **hasn't.**	*Hat sie (schon) jemals im Internet gesurft?* *– Ja./Nein.*

Du verwendest *already* meist in Aussagen, *(not ...) yet* in Fragen und Verneinungen. *Beispiel:* Have we told you about the show **yet**? – Yes, you have **already** told us about it. But we have**n't** seen it **yet**. *Haben wir euch schon von der Show erzählt? – Ja, aber wir haben sie noch nicht gesehen.*

G 14 Das Perfekt: Verneinung — *The present perfect: Negation*

Wenn du einen Satz im *present perfect* **verneinen** willst, setzt du einfach ***not*** hinter *have* oder *has*. Dabei verwendet man meist die **Kurzform.** Oft steht ***yet*** am Satzende.

You **haven't answered** my question.	*Du hast meine Frage noch nicht beantwortet.*
The shop **hasn't closed yet.**	*Der Laden hat noch nicht geschlossen.*
They **haven't read** our letter **yet.**	*Sie haben unseren Brief noch nicht gelesen.*

G15 Das Perfekt: Fragen mit Fragewort — *The present perfect: Questions with question words*

Das Fragewort steht immer ganz am Anfang. ***Have*** oder ***has*** **folgt direkt** auf das Fragewort.

What **has** Terry **done** to his hair?	*Was hat Terry mit seinen Haaren gemacht?*
– It's not his hair, it's only a wig.	*– Es sind nicht seine Haare, es ist nur eine Perücke.*
Where **have** you **put** my bag?	*Wo hast du meine Tasche hingelegt?*
– On the table.	*– Auf den Tisch.*
Why **have** you **changed** your hair?	*Warum hast du dir die Haare anders gemacht?*
– Because I didn't like it.	*– Weil ich sie nicht gut fand.*
Who **has** ever **been** to England?	*Wer war schon mal in England?*
– I have.	*– Ich.*

Who heißt „wer", manchmal auch „wen" oder „wem".
Beispiel: **Who** has Emma seen? ***Wen*** *hat Emma gesehen?*
Who has Sam helped? ***Wem*** *hat Sam geholfen?*

Unit 6

G16 Das *will*-Futur: Aussagen und Verneinung — *The 'will'-future: Statements and negation*

Wenn du etwas voraussagen willst, z. B. das Wetter, oder ein Horoskop erstellen willst, verwendest du das ***will-future.*** Du benutzt es auch, wenn du dich spontan für etwas entscheidest, z. B.: *I'll do it.* Dazu setzt du ***will*** oder die Kurzform ***'ll*** vor die Grundform des Verbs. Die **Verneinung** *will not* wird meist als Kurzform ***won't*** verwendet. Das *will-future* wird häufig mit *I think, I promise, I hope, I'm sure* und *maybe* verwendet.

I		miss Barker.	*Ich werde Barker (nicht) vermissen.*
You		have an adventure.	*Du wirst ein/kein Abenteuer erleben.*
He	'll	help her.	*Er wird ihr (nicht) helfen.*
She	will	eat it.	*Sie wird es (nicht) essen.*
It	won't	rain.	*Es wird nicht regnen.*
We		wait for them.	*Wir werden (nicht) auf sie warten.*
They		be late.	*Sie werden (nicht) zu spät kommen.*

G 17 Das *will*-Futur: Fragen und Kurzantworten — *The 'will'-future: Questions and short answers*

Wenn du eine **Frage** im *will-future* stellen willst, steht ***Will*** oder ein **Fragewort + *will*** am Anfang.
In der **Kurzantwort** verwendest du ***will*** oder ***won't***.

Entscheidungsfragen und Kurzantworten

Will you **help** me?	*Wirst du mir helfen?*
– Yes, I **will.** / No, I **won't.**	*– Ja./Nein.*
Will it **be** rainy?	*Wird es regnerisch sein?*
– Yes, it **will.** / No, it **won't.**	*– Ja./Nein.*
Will they **wait** for us?	*Werden sie auf uns warten?*
– Yes, they **will.** / No, they **won't.**	*– Ja./Nein.*

Fragen mit Fragewort

What will happen tomorrow?	*Was wird morgen geschehen?*
Where will it rain?	*Wo wird es regnen?*
When will the rain stop?	*Wann wird der Regen aufhören?*
Who will help me?	*Wer wird mir helfen?*
How will the weather be?	*Wie wird das Wetter sein?*

Unit 7

G 18 Adverbien der Art und Weise — *Adverbs of manner*

Adverbien erklären, **wie** du eine Sache machst, z. B. Ich mache meine Hausaufgaben sorgfältig.
Im Englischen hängst du dazu einfach *-ly* an das Adjektiv an, z. B. *quiet* → *quietly.* Bei Adjektiven, die auf *-y* enden, wird das *y* zu einem *i*, z. B. *happy* → *happ**i**ly.*

quick → quickly
helpful → helpfully
happy → happily
busy → busily

He's late. He's walking **quickly**.	*Er ist spät dran. Er geht schnell.*
Mrs Lehmann has got a lot of work. She's walking around **busily**.	*Frau Lehmann hat viel zu tun. Sie läuft geschäftig umher.*

Im Deutschen sind Adjektiv und Adverb in ihrer Form gleich.
Beispiel: He's **quick.** He walks **quickly.** *Er ist **schnell.** Er geht **schnell.***

G19 Bedingungssätze *'If'-clauses*

Bedingungssätze bestehen aus zwei Teilen: dem Nebensatz mit *if* und dem Hauptsatz.
Mit dem *if*-Satz drückst du eine **Bedingung** aus, mit dem Hauptsatz, was passiert, wenn diese Bedingung erfüllt wird. Steht der ***if*-Satz** im ***simple present,*** verwendest du im **Hauptsatz** meist ***will-future.*** Der *if*-Satz kann am Anfang oder am Ende des Satzes stehen.

If-Satz	Hauptsatz	
If you **go** by car,	you **will** arrive late.	*Wenn du mit dem Auto fährst, wirst du spät ankommen.*
If you **arrive** late,	you **won't** have supper.	*Wenn du spät ankommst, wirst du nicht zu Abend essen.*

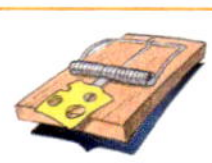

Im *if*-Satz steht niemals *will* oder *won't*!

Wortstellung

Die Wortstellung im Aussagesatz ist Subjekt – Verb – Objekt (**S – V – O**). Dabei bilden Verb und Objekt (V + O) eine feste Einheit; man darf keine anderen Satzteile dazwischen stellen.

Subjekt (S)	Verb (V)	Objekt (O)
The pupils	wear	school uniform.
Tom	has got	a big family.

Orts- und Zeitangaben stehen in der Regel am Ende des Satzes. Es gilt: Ort vor Zeit. Will man die Zeitangaben stärker betonen, stellt man sie an den Satzanfang.

Zeit	S	V	O	Ort	Zeit
	Tom	plays	with his friends	in the park	every day.
Every Sunday	Tom	visits	his grandma.		

In Fragen bleibt die Wortstellung unverändert. Es wird nur das Hilfsverb ***Do/Does*** (im *simple present*) oder ***Did*** (im *simple past*) bzw. das **Fragewort** + *do/does/did* an den **Satzanfang** gestellt.

Fragewort	Hilfsverb	S	V	O
	Does	Lisa	like	dogs?
Where	do	the Brooks	have	a computer shop?
	Did	you	like	the film?

Grammatical terms

(Lateinisch) / Deutsch	Englisch	Englisches Beispiel
Adjektiv / Eigenschaftswort G8, G17	adjective	quick, small, nice, old
Adverb / Umstandswort	adverb	always, often, sometimes, never
Adverb der Art und Weise G17	adverb of manner	quickly, softly, loudly
Apostroph	apostrophe	I'm, you're, here's
Bedingungssätze G18	'if'-clauses	If it is sunny, I'll go swimming.
Besitzangaben mit *have got/has got*	have got/has got	You've got a cool T-shirt.
Besitzangaben mit *-'s*	possessive form with -'s	Emma's sister, the Taylors' house
Demonstrativpronomen / hinweisende Fürwörter	demonstrative pronouns	this, that, these, those
Entscheidungsfragen G1, G4, G7, G13, G16	'yes/no'-questions	Do you like computers?
Frage G1, G2, G10	question	What's your name?
Fragewort G1, G4, G7, G14, G16	question word	Who? What? When? Where? Why? How?
Futur / Zukunft G15, G16, G18	'will'-future	It will be sunny at the weekend.
Häufigkeitsadverb	adverb of frequency	always, often, sometimes, never
Hilfsverb	auxiliary	be, have got, do, can
Imperativ / Befehlsform	imperative	Don't talk! Listen, please.
Infinitiv / Grundform des Verbs G6, G7, G9, G15	infinitive	to do, to go, to see
Konsonant / Mitlaut	consonant	b, d, k, l, r, n
Kurzantwort G1, G4, G7, G13, G16	short answer	Yes, I did. No, he won't.
Kurzform G12, G15	short form	I'm, we're, I've got, we won't
Langform	long form	I am, we are, I have got, he will not
Mengenangaben G10	expressions of quantity	a lot of, much, many, a bottle of
modales Hilfsverb G9	modal verb	must, mustn't, needn't, should, shouldn't
Objektpronomen	object pronoun	me, you, him, her, it, us, them
Perfekt G11–14	present perfect	Tom has painted the walls.
Personalpronomen / persönliches Fürwort	personal pronoun	I, you, he, she, it, we, you, they
Plural / Mehrzahl	plural	girls, children, babies
Possessivbegleiter / besitzanzeigendes Fürwort	possessive pronoun	my, your, his, her, its, our, your, their
Präsens / einfache Gegenwart G1, G18	simple present	I live in Greenwich.
Präteritum / einfache Vergangenheit G3–7	simple past	I watched TV yesterday.
Relativpronomen G8	relative pronoun	Sam is the boy who I like.
Signalwort G3, G11, G13	signal word	last, ago, yesterday, ever, yet
Singular / Einzahl	singular	a girl, a boy, an apple
Steigerung von Adjektiven G8	comparison of adjectives	old - older - (the) oldest, good - better - (the) best
Substantiv / Hauptwort	noun	book, dog, sandwich
Verb / Tätigkeitswort	verb	to be, to go, to do, to write
Verlaufsform der Gegenwart	present progressive	We are having a party.
Verneinung G1, G3, G6, G10, G12, G15	negation	I didn't listen. She hasn't taken the picture.
Vokal / Selbstlaut	vowel	a, e, i, o, u
Vollverb G9	verb	to go, to do, to write

Vocabulary

Auf den folgenden Seiten findest du alle neuen englischen Wörter und Ausdrücke. Sie stehen in der Reihenfolge, wie sie im Buch vorkommen.
Diese Wortliste ist in drei Spalten aufgeteilt:

- Links stehen die englischen Wörter und Sätze.
- In der Mitte werden sie übersetzt.
- Rechts findest du Beispiele, Erklärungen und Tipps, die dir beim Lernen helfen.

Die fett gedruckten Wörter musst du lernen. Normal gedruckte Wörter solltest du wiedererkennen, wenn du sie hörst oder liest.
Gleich nach jedem neuen englischen Wort steht die Lautschrift in eckigen Klammern. Sie zeigt dir, wie das neue Wort ausgesprochen wird. Wie du diese Lautzeichen liest, siehst du unten.

Englische Laute

Mitlaute

[b]	bed	[p]	picture
[d]	day	[r]	red
[ð]	the	[s]	six
[f]	family	[ʃ]	she
[g]	go	[t]	ten
[ŋ]	morning	[tʃ]	lunch
[h]	house	[v]	video
[j]	you	[w]	we, one
[k]	can, milk	[z]	easy
[l]	letter	[ʒ]	revision
[m]	man	[dʒ]	page
[n]	no	[θ]	thank you

Selbstlaute

[ɑː]	car
[æ]	apple
[e]	pen
[ə]	again
[ɜː]	girl
[ʌ]	but
[ɪ]	it
[i]	happy
[iː]	teacher
[ɒ]	dog
[ɔː]	ball
[ʊ]	book
[u]	January
[uː]	too, two

Doppellaute

[aɪ]	I, my
[aʊ]	now, mouse
[eɪ]	name, they
[eə]	there, pair
[ɪə]	here, idea
[əʊ]	hello
[ɔɪ]	boy
[ʊə]	sure

[ː] der vorangehende Laut ist lang, z. B. *you* [juː]

[ˈ] die folgende Silbe wird betont, z. B. *hello* [heˈləʊ]

Tipps zum Vokabellernen findest du in den Kästen zu Beginn jeder *unit* sowie auf den *wordwise*-Seiten.
Am Ende der *units* kannst du nützliche Ausdrücke für deinen *folder* sammeln, mit denen du dich auf Englisch verständigen kannst.
Es gibt auch noch *word games*. Dies sind kleine Aufgaben, Rätsel und Wortspiele, in denen du die neuen Wörter üben kannst.

Auf das *vocabulary* folgt das *dictionary*, eine alphabetische Wortliste aller englischen Wörter in dem Buch. Wenn du ein Wort nicht verstehst, kannst du es hier nachschlagen.

Abkürzungen und Zeichen

pl	Plural, Mehrzahl	!	Achtung!
sing	Singular, Einzahl	↔	ist das Gegenteil von
10	Auf dieser Seite kommen die Wörter vor.	→	ist verwandt mit
		=	entspricht

! *Homework* hat keine Mehrzahl.
old ↔ new
teach → teacher
Dear Sam = Lieber Sam

Unit 1 Back to school

Erinnerst du dich an die Tipps vom letzten Schuljahr?

Auch im neuen Schuljahr kannst du diese Tipps gebrauchen:
- Lerne weiterhin möglichst immer am gleichen Arbeitsplatz.
- Führe deine Vokabelkartei fort.
- Lerne neue Wörter dreimal fünf Minuten lang.
- Wiederhole die Vokabeln immer wieder mit einen Partner/einer Partnerin zusammen. Dabei könnt ihr auch Lernspiele spielen.
- Schreibe schwierige Wörter auf kleine Zettel. Auf die Rückseite kommt in einer anderen Farbe die deutsche Bedeutung. Lege die Zettel mit der deutschen Seite nach oben vor dich hin. Wenn du die englische Bedeutung kennst, darfst du den Zettel einsammeln. Wenn nicht, legst du ihn zurück.
- Problemwörter kannst du auf Zettel schreiben oder malen, die du zu Hause an Stellen anbringst, die du oft siehst.
- Lerne neue Wörter möglichst im Zusammenhang. Dazu kannst du *word stars* machen oder dir die Beispielsätze in der dritten Spalte gut durchlesen.

10	**start** [stɑːt]	Anfang, Beginn, Start	
	term [tɜːm]	Trimester *(Einteilung des englischen Schuljahrs)*	
	to **try** [traɪ]	versuchen, probieren	
	assembly [əˈsembli]	Versammlung, Morgenappell →	A lot of English schools have *assembly* in the morning.
	to **give ... a dirty look** [ˌɡɪv‿ə dɜːti ˈlʊk]	einen vernichtenden Blick zuwerfen	
	dirty [ˈdɜːti]	schmutzig	
	look [lʊk]	Blick, Aussehen →	look
	correct [kəˈrekt]	richtig, korrekt →	to correct → *correct*
	sweatshirt [ˈswetʃɜːt]	Sweatshirt	
	trousers *(pl)* [ˈtraʊzəz]	Hose	
	skirt [skɜːt]	Rock →	Emma's new *skirt* is very nice.
	shorts *(pl)* [ʃɔːts]	Shorts, kurze Hose →	! Die Wörter *trousers* und *shorts* stehen immer im Plural.
	Physical Education (PE) [ˌfɪzɪkl‿edʒʊˈkeɪʃn]	Sport *(Schulfach)* →	PE [ˌpiː‿ˈiː] is short for *physical education*.
	physical [ˈfɪzɪkl]	physisch, körperlich	
	education [edʒʊˈkeɪʃn]	Erziehung, Bildung	
	locker [ˈlɒkə]	Schließfach →	 Sam is putting his things into his *locker*.
	History [ˈhɪstəri]	Geschichte →	
	Geography [dʒiˈɒɡrəfi]	Geografie, Erdkunde →	! Schulfächer werden meistens groß geschrieben.
	Science [ˈsaɪənts]	Wissenschaft, Naturwissenschaft →	Achtung Aussprache!
	Technology [tekˈnɒlədʒi]	Technik →	Achtung Aussprache!
	Maths [mæθs]	Mathematik →	Robert isn't good at *Maths*.
	foreign [ˈfɒrɪn]	fremd, ausländisch →	! *foreign* language = Fremdsprache
	Art [ɑːt]	Kunst	
	(to) **hate** [heɪt]	hassen; Hass →	*hate* ↔ love

	PE kit [ˌpiː‿ˈiː kɪt]	Sportzeug	
	etc. [ɪtˈsetrə]	usw., et cetera →	You can also buy pens, pencils, *etc.*
	registration [ˌredʒɪˈstreɪʃn]	Registrierung, Erfassung →	Pupils must be in their classroom for *registration*.
	role [rəʊl]	Rolle →	We do *role* plays in the drama club.
11	same [seɪm]	derselbe/dieselbe/dasselbe	
	to underline [ˌʌndəˈlaɪn]	unterstreichen	
	skill [skɪl]	Fertigkeit; Geschick	
	note [nəʊt]	Notiz, Anmerkung	
	as [æz; əz]	als, wie	
	to **go red** [ɡəʊ ˈred]	rot werden →	Emma *goes red*.
	with [wɪð]	bei →	! *'With'* kann „mit" und „bei" heißen. Der Textzusammenhang zeigt dir die richtige Bedeutung.

	silly [ˈsɪli]	dumm; Dummkopf →	
	to imagine [ɪˈmædʒɪn]	sich (etwas) vorstellen	

Language

12	**timetable** [ˈtaɪmteɪbl]	Stundenplan, Fahrplan	
	meeting [ˈmiːtɪŋ]	Treffen, Besprechung →	to meet → *meeting*
	Religious Education (RE) [rɪˌlɪdʒəs‿edʒʊˈkeɪʃn]	Religionsunterricht	
	religious [rɪˈlɪdʒəs]	religiös	
	break [breɪk]	Pause	
	past [pɑːst]	nach *(Uhrzeit)*	
13	**subject** [ˈsʌbdʒɪkt]	Schulfach; Thema →	

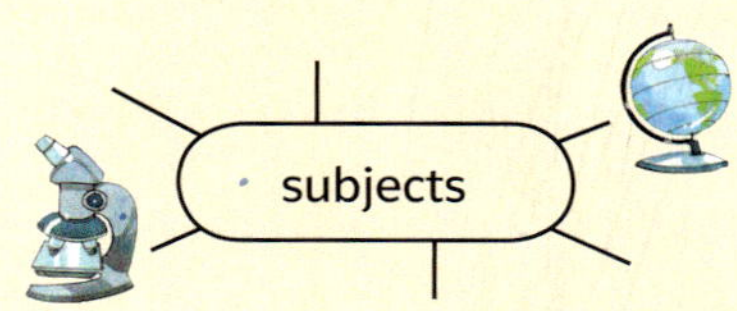

	difficult [ˈdɪfɪklt]	schwierig →	easy ↔ *difficult*
	experiment [ɪkˈsperɪmənt]	Experiment, Versuch →	Achtung Aussprache!
	past [pɑːst]	Vergangenheit →	What do you know about the *past*?
	some [sʌm]	einige; etwas →	Not all. *Some* girls wear skirts, *some* boys wear shirts.
	spaghetti [spəˈɡeti]	Spaghetti	
	clue [kluː]	Hinweis	
	It's your turn. [ɪts jɔː ˈtɜːn]	Du bist dran. →	Is it *your turn* now?
14	to **bet** [bet]	wetten →	! I *bet* he likes pizza. = Wetten, dass er Pizza mag?
	suntan [ˈsʌntæn]	Sonnenbräune →	! He has got a great *suntan*. = Er ist braun gebrannt.
	to **look after** [lʊk‿ˈɑːftə]	sich kümmern um, aufpassen auf →	

	g'day [ɡəˈdeɪ]	Tag, hallo *(australische Begrüßung)*	
	hungry [ˈhʌŋɡri]	hungrig →	! I'm *hungry*. = Ich habe Hunger.
	which [wɪtʃ]	welche/welcher/welches	
	menu [ˈmenjuː]	Speisekarte, Menü	
	tucker [ˈtʌkə]	Essen *(australischer Ausdruck)*	
	I'm having .... [aɪm ˈhævɪŋ]	Ich nehme .... →	*I'm having* pizza.

chips *(pl)* [tʃɪps]	Pommes frites →	! Pommes frites = *chips*; Chips = *crisps*
That's what I call .... [ˌðæts wɒt‿'aɪ ˌkɔ:l]	Das nenne ich .... →	*That's what I call* good food.
to practise ['præktɪs]	üben, proben, praktizieren	
singer ['sɪŋə]	Sänger/Sängerin →	to sing → *singer*
best [best]	beste/bester/bestes	
weather ['weðə]	Wetter →	The *weather* is sunny today.
surfing ['sɜ:fɪŋ]	Wellenreiten, Surfen →	My hobbies are music and *surfing*.
to **surf the Internet** [ˌsɜ:f ði‿'ɪntənet]	im Internet surfen	
to **surf** [sɜ:f]	surfen, windsurfen	
Internet ['ɪntənet]	Internet	
15 **a lot** [ə 'lɒt]	viel	
to talk to ['tɔ:k tə]	sprechen mit, reden mit	
fruit [fru:t]	Obst, Frucht →	
banana [bə'nɑ:nə]	Banane	
vegetable ['vedʒtəbl]	Gemüse	
carrot ['kærət]	Karotte, Mohrrübe	
soup [su:p]	Suppe	
16 grammar ['græmə]	Grammatik	
hockey ['hɒki]	Hockey →	I play basketball and *hockey*.
to understand [ˌʌndə'stænd]	verstehen →	Sorry, I can't *understand* you. I don't speak French.

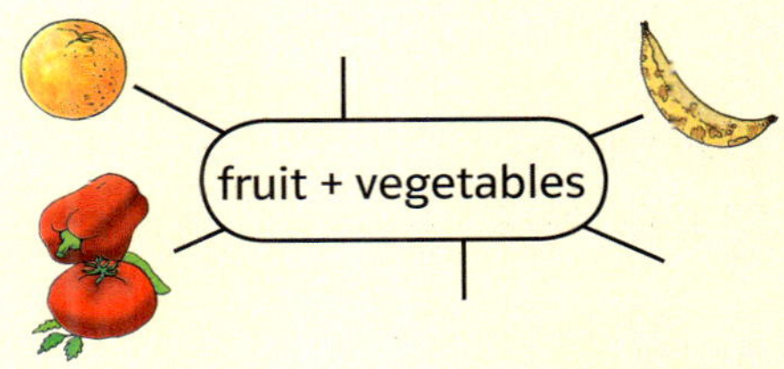

Chats with Charlie

17 life, lives *(pl)* [laɪf; laɪvz]	Leben	
down under [daʊn‿'ʌndə]	in Australien	
(to) **interview** ['ɪntəvju:]	interviewen; Interview →	Charlie *interviews* Jake about his school.

Verb und Nomen

Im Englischen sehen einige Nomen und Verben gleich oder sehr ähnlich aus. In der folgenden Liste findest du verschiedene Beispiele. Manche kennst du schon, andere kommen in dieser Unit neu vor.

work	arbeiten, Arbeit	*start*	anfangen, Anfang	*plan, planner*	planen, Planer
hate	hassen, Hass	*answer*	antworten, Antwort	*teach, teacher*	lehren, Lehrer/Lehrerin
call	anrufen, Anruf	*visit*	besuchen, Besuch	*sing, singer*	singen, Sänger/Sängerin
help	helfen, Hilfe	*interview*	interviewen, Interview	*run, runner*	laufen, Läufer/Läuferin
love	lieben, Liebe	*look*	aussehen, Aussehen	*meet, meeting*	treffen, Treffen

to learn [lɜ:n]	erfahren	

Story

18 to **leave** [li:v]	(weg)gehen	
to **whisper** ['wɪspə]	flüstern, zuflüstern →	The kids are *whispering*.
mad [mæd]	verrückt; wütend →	! You're boy *mad*! = Du bist verrückt nach Jungs!
class [klɑ:s]	Kurs, Unterricht →	*classes* = lessons

surprised [sə'praɪzd]	überrascht, erstaunt	
that's why ['ðæts ˌwaɪ]	deshalb →	*That's why* I'm asking.
French [frentʃ]	französisch →	Tim is learning *French* at school now.
true [tru:]	wahr →	
to **turn round** [tɜ:n 'raʊnd]	(sich) umdrehen	
empty ['empti]	leer →	The bottle is *empty*.
angry ['æŋgri]	verärgert, böse →	The teacher is *angry* with the children.
to **pick up** [pɪk‿'ʌp]	aufheben, abholen →	There is a pen on the floor, please *pick* it *up*.
beside [bɪ'saɪd]	neben, außer →	She sits *beside* her.
the next morning [ðə ˌnekst 'mɔ:nɪŋ]	am nächsten Morgen →	*The next morning*/evening/day they meet again.
on the bus [ˌɒn ðə 'bʌs]	im Bus →	He's *on the bus*/on the train.
time [taɪm]	Mal →	I help you, but it's the last *time*!
to **look round** [lʊk 'raʊnd]	sich umsehen	
to **be nuts about** [bi: ˌnʌts‿ə'baʊt]	verrückt nach … sein →	Emma *is nuts about* Jake. Lisa *is nuts about* football.
interested ['ɪntrəstɪd]	interessiert	
to **underline** [ˌʌndə'laɪn]	unterstreichen	
to **pass** [pɑ:s]	weitergeben, herüberreichen →	Can you *pass* me the butter, please?
to **drop** [drɒp]	fallen, fallen lassen →	*to drop* ↔ to pick up
to **believe** [bɪ'li:v]	glauben →	She can't *believe* it!
cinema ['sɪnəmə]	Kino	
tomorrow [tə'mɒrəʊ]	morgen →	*Tomorrow* is Saturday! Great, no school!
19 **that evening** [ˌðæt‿'i:vnɪŋ]	an diesem Abend →	*That evening*/morning/day she writes a letter.
sad [sæd]	traurig, bedauerlich →	*sad* ↔ happy
to **see** [si:]	besuchen →	*to see* = to visit
to **get onto** [get‿'ɒntə]	einsteigen *(Bus)*	
onto ['ɒntu:; 'ɒntə]	auf … hinauf →	on + to = *onto*
to **turn back** [tɜ:n 'bæk]	umkehren, zurückgehen	
each other [ˌi:tʃ‿'ʌðə]	sich gegenseitig →	They look at *each other*.

Text messages

Wenn du diese SMS von Seite 19 laut vorliest, kannst du die Bedeutung der Zeichen leicht erraten:

*Jake is **4** me. I really ♥ him. He wants me **2** meet his mum **2**morrow.*
***CU** on Monday.*

***4** = for*
♥ = love
***2** = to*
***CU** = See you.*

next [nekst]	als Nächstes →	after that, then
ending ['endɪŋ]	Ende, Schluss *(einer Geschichte)*	
20 **definition** [ˌdefɪ'nɪʃn]	Definition	
vocabulary [vəʊ'kæbjəlri]	Wortschatz, Vokabular	
own [əʊn]	eigener/eigene/eigenes	
verb [vɜ:b]	Verb	

21	**still** [stɪl]	noch, immer noch →	They are *still* friends.
	to **need** [ni:d]	brauchen, benötigen, müssen	
	choice ['tʃɔɪs]	Auswahl, Wahl	

For my folder: I love/hate …

Schreibe alle Ausdrücke (*phrases*), mit denen du Gefühle ausdrücken kannst, auf ein Blatt Papier. Lege es in deinem *English folder* ab. Lass dahinter Platz für weitere *phrases*, damit du deine Redemittelsammlung im Laufe des Schuljahres ergänzen kannst.
So kannst du anfangen. Schreibe noch mehr Ausdrücke dazu.

Gefühle
I love/hate … because … .
She's boy mad.
He goes red.
You're nuts about … .
…

Word game

Schreibe deinen Freunden/Freundinnen eine englische SMS. Verwende dabei die folgenden Kürzel. Kennst du noch andere Kürzel?

CU	*see you*	tlk	*talk*
GR8	*great*	THX	*thanks (= thank you)*
FYI	*for your information*	2	*to*
PLS	*please*	2MORO	*tomorrow*
PCM	*please call me*	U	*you*
RUOK	*Are you OK?*		

Unit 2 What a week!

Lerntipp: Nutze deine Stärken.

Sicher hast du schon bemerkt, welche Stärken und Schwächen du beim Vokabellernen hast. Lernst du neue Wörter besser durch Lesen, Hören, Schreiben oder Malen? Sprich mit anderen in deiner Klasse darüber und versuche herauszufinden, welche Methode dir am besten hilft. Wende sie dann gezielt an.

Bestimmte Schwächen bekommst du leichter in den Griff, wenn du sie in deiner Vokabelkartei oder deinem Vokabelheft farbig markierst.

- gelber Punkt heißt: Die Aussprache fällt mir schwer.
- blauer Punkt heißt: Die Rechtschreibung bereitet mir Schwierigkeiten.
- roter Punkt heißt: Die Bedeutung kann ich mir schlecht merken. Du kannst dir einen kleinen Beispielsatz als Merkhilfe zu dem Wort schreiben und versuchen, ihn auswendig zu lernen.

So siehst du sofort, was du besonders üben musst. Wende dabei auch die Lernmethode an, die dir am besten hilft.

22	**What a week!** [ˌwɒt‿ə 'wi:k]	Was für eine Woche!	
	knight [naɪt]	Ritter	
	arena [ə'ri:nə]	Arena, Stadion →	

I'd rather [aɪd 'rɑːðə]	ich würde lieber →	
zoo [zuː]	Zoo, Tierpark →	
pocket money ['pɒkɪt ˌmʌni]	Taschengeld →	
pocket ['pɒkɪt]	Hosen-/Jackentasche →	
I'd like to [ˌaɪd 'laɪk tə]	ich würde gern →	
market ['mɑːkɪt]	Markt →	
23 **hundred** ['hʌndrəd]	hundert	
thousand ['θaʊznd]	tausend	
million ['mɪlɪən]	Million	

I'd rather watch TV, but she wants to play cards.
There are lots of animals in a *zoo*.
Don't spend all your *pocket money*.
Sarah has got 50p in her *pocket*.
I'd like to go to the zoo this afternoon.
You can buy a lot of things at a *market*.

Numbers 101–1,000,000

101	**one hundred and one** [wʌn ˌhʌndrəd‿ənd 'wʌn]	1000	**one thousand** [wʌn 'θaʊznd]
102	**one hundred and two** [wʌn ˌhʌndrəd‿ənd 'tuː]	2000	**two thousand** [tuː 'θaʊznd]
110	**one hundred and ten** [wʌn ˌhʌndrəd‿ənd 'ten]	10,000	**ten thousand** [ten 'θaʊznd]
200	**two hundred** [tuː 'hʌndrəd]	100,000	**one hundred thousand** [wʌn hʌndrəd 'θaʊznd]
300	**three hundred** [θriː 'hʌndrəd]	200,000	**two hundred thousand** [tuː hʌndrəd 'θaʊznd]
451	**four hundred and fifty-one** [fɔː hʌndrəd‿ənd 'fɪftiwʌn]	1,000,000	**one million** [wʌn 'mɪljən]

clothes *(pl)* [kləʊθs]	Kleider, Kleidung →	
open ['əʊpn]	offen, geöffnet	
flight [flaɪt]	Flug	
lab(oratory) [læb; lə'bɒrətri]	Labor	
plane [pleɪn]	Flugzeug	
ice rink ['aɪs rɪŋk]	Eis-/Schlittschuhbahn	
ice hockey ['aɪs ˌhɒki]	Eishockey	
ice [aɪs]	Eis	
team [tiːm]	Mannschaft, Team →	
seat [siːt]	Sitz, Sitzplatz →	
popular ['pɒpjələ]	populär, beliebt →	
concert ['kɒnsət]	Konzert →	
piggy bank ['pɪgi bæŋk]	Sparschwein	

! Das englische Wort *clothes* steht immer im Plural: Emma's *clothes* **are** nice.

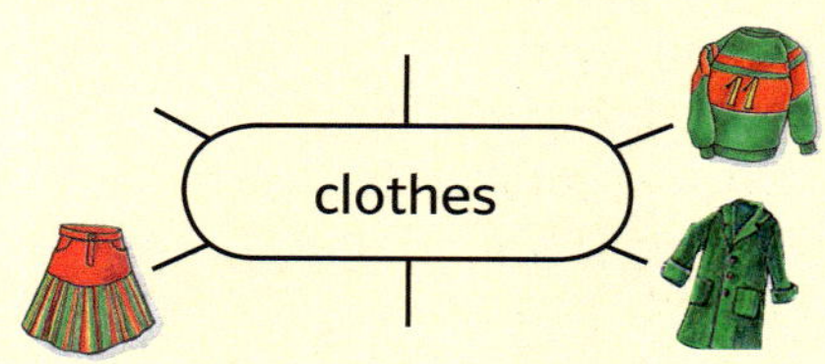

There are six people in an ice hockey *team*.
The ice rink has *seats* for 12,500 people.
All my friends like her – she's really *popular*.
Let's go to the *concert* next Saturday!

Present progressive für Pläne

*Tomorrow the Knights **are playing** at the Arena.* — Morgen **spielen** die Knights in der Arena.
*Sam's mum **is coming** after school.* — Sams Mutter **kommt** nach der Schule.
Wie im Deutschen drückt die Gegenwart hier etwas aus, das für die nahe Zukunft geplant ist.

Language

24 **was** [wɒz]	war →	
match [mætʃ]	Spiel, Wettkampf →	
were [wɜː]	warst/wart/waren →	
bored [bɔːd]	gelangweilt →	

How *was* your weekend?
Can we watch the *match* this evening?
We *were* fed up.
! to be boring = langweilig sein
to be *bored* = gelangweilt sein

	to **be cold** [biː 'kəʊld]	frieren →	She *was cold*.
	horrible ['hɒrəbl]	schrecklich, furchtbar	
	that (bad) ['ðæt bæd]	so (schlimm)	
	bell [bel]	Glocke, Klingel →	*bells* 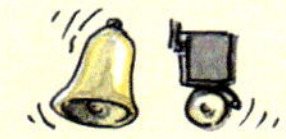
25	**panther** ['pæntθə]	Panter	
	warm [wɔːm]	warm →	! She *was warm*. = Ihr war warm.
26	**thanks** [θæŋks]	danke	
	half an hour [ˌhɑːf ən ˈaʊə]	eine halbe Stunde	
	ago [ə'gəʊ]	vor (*zeitlich*) →	I read your e-mail half an hour *ago*.
	to **go in** [gəʊ 'ɪn]	hineingehen	
	to **fall, fell** [fɔːl, fel]	fallen, herunterfallen, hinfallen →	! Die Vergangenheitsform musst du mitlernen. Weitere unregelmäßige Verben findest du weiter unten.
	ground [graʊnd]	Boden	
	to **be angry with** [biː 'æŋgri wɪð]	böse sein auf →	She *was angry with* her little sister.
	stick [stɪk]	Stock	
	zookeeper ['zuːkiːpə]	Tierpfleger/Tierpflegerin, Wärter/Wärterin →	zoo → *zookeeper* 
	embarrassing [ɪm'bærəsɪŋ]	peinlich	
	hat [hæt]	Hut →	This *hat* looks nice.
	to **get, got** [get, gɒt]	holen	
	signal ['sɪgnl]	Signal	
	yesterday ['jestədeɪ]	gestern →	*yesterday* – today – tomorrow
	domino ['dɒmɪnəʊ]	Dominospiel	
	irregular [ɪ'regjələ]	unregelmäßig	
	present ['preznt]	Gegenwart, Präsens	

Unregelmäßige Verben in *Unit 2*

to write, wrote	schreiben, schrieb	*to eat, ate*	essen, aß
to read, read	lesen, las	*to find, found*	finden, fand
to come, came	kommen, kam	*to throw, threw*	werfen, warf
to go, went	gehen, ging	*to see, saw*	sehen, sah
to have, had	haben, hatte	*to sit, sat*	sitzen, saß
to buy, bought	kaufen, kaufte	*to leave, left*	(ver-)lassen, (ver-)ließ
to give, gave	geben, gab	*to put, put*	legen, legte
to fall, fell	fallen, fiel	*to run, ran*	rennen, rannte
to take, took	nehmen, nahm	*to say, said*	sagen, sagte

27	to continue [kən'tɪnjuː]	weitergehen, weitermachen	
28	**hair** [heə]	Haar, Haare →	! Ihre Haare **sind** lang. = Her *hair* **is** long. 
	to **talk to** ['tɔːk tə]	sprechen mit, reden mit →	Terry is *talking to* Lisa.
	Good grief! [gʊd 'griːf]	Du liebe Zeit!	
	to **dye** [daɪ]	färben →	I want to *dye* my hair.
	blond [blɒnd]	blond →	He has got *blond* hair.
	sick note ['sɪk ˌnəʊt]	Krankmeldung	
	wig [wɪg]	Perücke	
	hairdresser ['heəˌdresə]	Friseur/Friseurin →	! the *hairdresser's* = der Friseursalon

Chats with Charlie

29	to mark [mɑːk]	markieren →	*Mark* the short forms, please.

Story

30	**It said ….** [ɪt 'sed]	Es lautete … .	
	store detective ['stɔː dɪˌtektɪv]	Kaufhausdetektiv/Kaufhausdetektivin	
	store [stɔː]	Kaufhaus, Geschäft, Laden →	*store* → department store
	detective [dɪ'tektɪv]	Detektiv/Detektivin →	Achtung Aussprache!
	to **go down** [gəʊ 'daʊn]	hinuntergehen, entlanggehen	
	down [daʊn]	(nach) unten, herunter, hinunter, nieder →	*down* → downstairs
	high [haɪ]	hoch, groß →	I can't look over the wall, it's too *high*.
	to **look up** [lʊk‿'ʌp]	(hin)aufschauen; nachschlagen	
	up [ʌp]	auf, hinauf, oben →	*up* ↔ down
	to **jump** [dʒʌmp]	springen →	
	to **climb** ['klaɪm]	klettern, steigen, besteigen →	He *climbed* out of the window.
	no one ['nəʊwʌn]	niemand	
31	**voice** [vɔɪs]	Stimme	
	policeman, policemen *(pl)* [pə'liːsmən; pə'liːsmen]	Polizist →	There are also policewomen.
	office ['ɒfɪs]	Büro	
	to **watch** [wɒtʃ]	achten auf →	*Watch* the time!
	quickly ['kwɪkli]	schnell	
	adventure [əd'ventʃə]	Abenteuer	
32	fact-file (on) ['fæktˌfaɪl]	Datei mit Informationen (über)	
	fact [fækt]	Fakt, Tatsache	

For my folder: Times

Du kennst jetzt schon eine Menge Ausdrücke, mit denen du Zeitangaben machen kannst. Schreibe sie auf ein Blatt Papier für deinen *folder* und bilde Sätze damit. Du kannst auch versuchen, mit diesen Ausdrücken einen Tagebucheintrag zu schreiben.

Zeitangaben
last week/month/ …
yesterday/today/ …
(later) in the morning/ …
…

Word game

Bilde lustige Sätze mit den Buchstaben folgender Wörter. Denk dir weitere Wörter und Sätze aus. Du kannst auch mit einem Freund/einer Freundin um die Wette Sätze bilden. Versuche auch, Sätze aus den Buchstaben deines Namens zu bilden.

W here	**H**	**T**	…
A re	**A**	**E**	
R ed	**I**	**A**	
M ice?	**R**	**M**	

T erry's
O ld
M obile
O ften
R ings
R ob
O n
W ednesdays.

Unit 3 We all need friends.

Lerntipp: Konzentriere dich auf einen bestimmten Bereich.

Beim Vokabellernen hilft es dir oft, wenn du dich auf nur einen Bereich konzentrierst. Nimm dir eine Unit vor und schreibe z. B. alle Wendungen mit Präpositionen heraus. Dies sind in Unit 1:
*to look **after**, to smile **at**, to pick **up**, **on** the **bus*** etc.
Danach kannst du für jede Präposition eine Karteikarte anfertigen, z. B. für ***up***: *to pick up, to get up, to wake up, to put up* etc.
Du siehst, dass viele der Ausdrücke ganz leicht zu lernen sind, weil sie wie im Deutschen sind. So bekommst du den Kopf frei für die wenigen wirklich schwierigen Wendungen.

36	to **laugh at** ['lɑ:f‿ət]	auslachen, sich lustig machen über	
	Scottish ['skɒtɪʃ]	schottisch	
	accent ['æksnt]	Akzent →	The kids laugh at Susan's Scottish *accent*.
	to **cry** [kraɪ]	weinen; schreien, rufen	
	once [wʌnts]	einmal, einst →	At a time in the past.
	(to) **bully** ['bʊli]	tyrannisieren; Rabauke, jemand, der andere tyrannisiert	
	tall [tɔ:l]	groß, hoch	
	Dear [dɪə]	Lieber .../Liebe ... *(Anrede in Briefen)*	
	one day [wʌn 'deɪ]	eines Tages	
	to **push** [pʊʃ]	stoßen, schieben, drücken →	
	off [ɒf]	herunter, ab, weg von →	They pushed me *off* my bike.
	Yours [jɔ:z]	Dein .../Deine .../Euer .../Eure ... *(in Briefen)*	
	to **hit, hit** [hɪt, hɪt]	schlagen, treffen	
	head [hed]	Kopf →	
	hospital ['hɒspɪtl]	Krankenhaus	
37	how to ... ['haʊ tə]	wie man ...	
	capital letter [ˌkæpɪtl 'letə]	Großbuchstabe	
	last night [lɑ:st 'naɪt]	gestern Abend/Nacht	

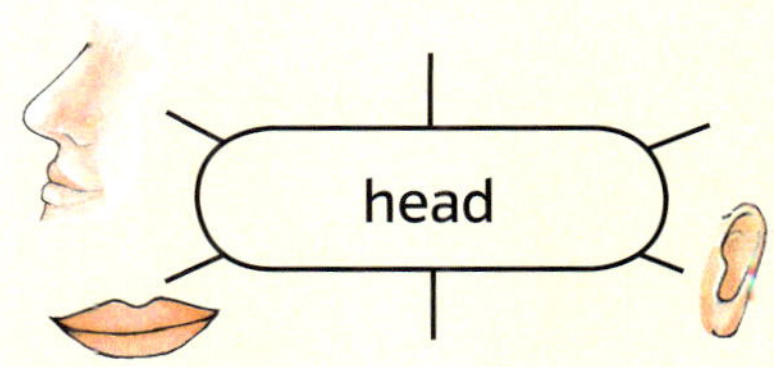

Language

38	**youth** [ju:θ]	Jugend →	Is there a *youth* club in your town?
	message ['mesɪdʒ]	Nachricht →	Achtung Schreibung!
	to **go out** [gəʊ‿'aʊt]	(hin)ausgehen, erlöschen	
	tired ['taɪəd]	müde →	I don't want to watch TV. I'm *tired*.
	real [rɪəl]	echt, richtig, wirklich →	Do you want a *real* English breakfast?
	to **go over** [gəʊ‿'əʊvə]	hinübergehen →	Let's *go over to* Sam's house.
	for supper [fə 'sʌpə]	zum Abendessen →	She invited me *for supper*/lunch/ ...

Präpositionen

Je nachdem, mit welchem Wort Präpositionen zusammenstehen, können sie völlig unterschiedliche Übersetzungen haben.

for tea	zum Tee	***with a pen***	mit einem Füller	***go to school***	zur Schule gehen
for me	für mich	***I'm with Lisa.***	Ich bin bei Lisa.	***talk to***	sprechen mit
for my birthday	zu meinem Geburtstag			***a visit to the doctor***	ein Besuch beim Arzt

39	to think of ['θɪŋk‿əv]	denken an	
	girlfriend ['gɜ:lfrend]	Freundin *(in einer Paarbeziehung)* →	He's angry with his *girlfriend*. 
	I'm sorry about … . [aɪm 'sɒri‿əˌbaʊt]	Es tut mir Leid wegen … .	
	polite [pə'laɪt]	höflich	
40	to **fall off** [fɔ:l 'ɒf]	herunterfallen	
	to **hurt, hurt** [hɜ:t, hɜ:t]	verletzen, weh tun →	I *hurt* my foot last week. It still *hurts*.
	arm [ɑ:m]	Arm	
	chain [tʃeɪn]	Kette	
	to **clean** [kli:n]	säubern, reinigen →	*Clean* the board, please.
	paint [peɪnt]	Farbe →	to paint → some *paint*
	doctor ['dɒktə]	Arzt/Ärztin →	! 'Dr' is short for *'doctor'*.
	ear [ɪə]	Ohr	
	to **feel, felt** [fi:l, felt]	(sich) fühlen →	How do you *feel*?

Unregelmäßige Verben in *Unit 3*

*to **hurt, hurt***	verletzen, verletzte	*to **ride, rode***	fahren, fuhr; reiten, ritt
*to **tell, told***	erzählen, erzählte	*to **feel, felt***	fühlen, fühlte
*to **hit, hit***	schlagen, schlug	*to **get, got***	(be-)kommen, (be-)kam
*to **send, sent***	schicken, schickte	*to **think, thought***	denken, dachte
*to **do, did***	tun, tat	*to **begin, began***	beginnen, begann

41	**accident** ['æksɪdnt]	Unfall →	
	body ['bɒdi]	Körper	
	nose [nəʊz]	Nase	
	mouth [maʊθ]	Mund →	Before you can speak, you must open your *mouth*.
	hand [hænd]	Hand →	Clap your *hands*.
	finger ['fɪŋgə]	Finger →	! Achtung Aussprache: das *g* wird mitgesprochen!
	back [bæk]	Rücken	
	elbow ['elbəʊ]	Ellbogen	
	stomach ['stʌmək]	Magen, Bauch	
	leg [leg]	Bein	
	knee [ni:]	Knie	
	toe [təʊ]	Zeh	
42	**who** [hu:]	der/dem/den/die *(Relativpronomen)* →	Emma is the girl *who* comes from Bristol.
	which [wɪtʃ]	der/dem/den/die/das *(Relativpronomen)* →	I like the house *which* you can see over there.
	person ['pɜ:sn]	Person	

	to **change** [tʃeɪndʒ]	(ver)ändern, tauschen, wechseln →	*Change* places with your partner.
	life, lives *(pl)* [laɪf; laɪvz]	Leben →	to live [lɪv] → *life* [laɪf]
	title ['taɪtl]	Titel, Überschrift →	Do you like the *title* of the book?
	cover ['kʌvə]	Einband, Titelseite	
	across [ə'krɒs]	waagerecht *(im Kreuzworträtsel)*	
	down	senkrecht *(im Kreuzworträtsel)*	

Chats with Charlie

43	**enemy** ['enəmi]	Feind/Feindin →	friend ↔ *enemy*
	film [fɪlm]	Film →	a *film* 
	following ['fɒləʊɪŋ]	folgende/folgender/folgendes	
	hero, heroes *(pl)* ['hɪərəʊ; 'hɪərəʊz]	Held	
	What's the film about? [wɒts ðə 'fɪlm‿əˌbaʊt]	Wovon handelt der Film?	
	president ['prezɪdnt]	Präsident/Präsidentin →	! *President* schreibst du groß, wenn es sich um eine bekannte Person handelt.
	spelling ['spelɪŋ]	Orthographie, Rechtschreibung	

Story

44	**test** [test]	Test, Klassenarbeit →	We had a Maths *test* last Monday.
	to **get ... right/wrong** [get ... 'raɪt/rɒŋ]	richtig/falsch machen →	How many questions did you *get right*?
	mark [mɑːk]	Note *(in der Schule)*	
	another [ə'nʌðə]	noch ein/eine, ein anderer/eine andere/ein anderes →	These cakes are fantastic. Can I have *another* cake, please?
	to **be upset** [biː ʌp'set]	aufgeregt sein, bestürzt sein	
	What does it say? [ˌwɒt dʌz‿ɪt 'seɪ]	Was steht da?	
	I'm scared. [aɪm 'skeəd]	Ich habe Angst. →	
45	**jealous** (of) ['dʒeləs]	eifersüchtig, neidisch (auf) →	Are you *jealous of* other pupils?
	jazz [dʒæz]	Jazz	
	to catch, caught [kætʃk, kɔːt]	fangen	
	The bullies say they are sorry. [ðə ˌbʊliz seɪ ðeɪ ə 'sɒri]	Die Rabauken sagen, dass es ihnen Leid tut.	
	to **worry** ['wʌri]	ängstigen, beunruhigen →	Sorry, I didn't want to *worry* you.
46	kangaroo [ˌkæŋgər'uː]	Känguru	
	to **feel sick** [fiːl 'sɪk]	Übelkeit verspüren →	! I *feel sick*. = Mir ist schlecht.
	sick [sɪk]	krank →	Yesterday I was cold and today I'm *sick*.
	dictionary ['dɪkʃnri]	Wörterbuch	
	if [ɪf]	wenn, falls	
	shy [ʃaɪ]	schüchtern	
	side [saɪd]	Seite →	Do you sleep on your back or on your *side*?

	city ['sɪti]	Stadt, Großstadt	
47	to get … wrong [get … 'rɒŋ]	falsch verstehen	
	at night [ət 'naɪt]	nachts →	*At night* you need a torch.
	to **begin, began** [bɪ'gɪn, bɪ'gæn]	beginnen, anfangen →	In England school *begins* with registration.
	part [pɑ:t]	Teil	

For my folder: People

Du hast schon eine Menge Adjektive und Ausdrücke gelernt, die du zur Beschreibung einer Person verwenden kannst.
Mache ein Liste dieser Wörter für deinen *folder* und beschreibe deinen besten Freund oder deine beste Freundin.

is from, parents are, …
☺ *nice, good at, …*
☹ *strange, stupid, …*

Word game

Das Relativsatz-Rennen spielt ihr zu viert. Einer fängt an mit einem Satz wie: *This is the man*. Die nächsten, die an der Reihe sind, hängen immer einen neuen Satz mit *who* oder *which* an, z. B.:
This is the man – ***who** took the bag* – ***which** I put on the table* – …
Dieses Spiel könnt ihr auch als Gruppenwettstreit spielen. Jede Gruppe muss abwechselnd einen neuen Relativsatz hinzufügen.

*Are you the pupils **who** played the game **which** I saw in the shop **which** …*

Unit 4 You are what you eat!

Lerntipp: Vokabellernen im Zusammenhang

Wörter behältst du besser, wenn du sie nicht einzeln lernst, sondern z. B. in einer Wortfamilie. Diese wird oft in der dritten Spalte des *vocabulary* angezeigt (z. B. in Unit 3: *to bully* → *a bully*). Bei einem neuen Wort kannst du dir immer die Frage stellen: Welches Wort kenne ich aus dieser Wortfamilie noch?
Außerdem kannst du ein neues Wort auch in Verbindung mit seinem Gegenteil (z. B. *friend* ↔ *enemy*) oder mit einem Wort oder Ausdruck mit gleicher Bedeutung (z. B. *Do you have?* = *Have you got?*) lernen.

48	**takeaway** ['teɪkəweɪ]	Restaurant mit Straßenverkauf; Essen zum Mitnehmen →	Let's get a *takeaway* from the new *takeaway* in town.
49	opposite ['ɒpəzɪt]	gegenüber	
	main [meɪn]	Haupt-	
	course [kɔ:s]	Gang *(Menü)* →	I'd like fish and chips for the *main course*, please.
	ham [hæm]	Schinken	
	spicy ['spaɪsi]	würzig, pikant	
	lamb [læm]	Lamm, Lammfleisch →	Achtung Aussprache! Das *b* bleibt stumm.
	curry ['kʌri]	Curry *(Gewürz oder Gericht)* →	Do you like lamb *curry*?
	sour ['saʊə]	sauer	
	pork [pɔ:k]	Schweinefleisch →	Pig is the animal. *Pork* is the name for what we eat.

sausage ['sɒsɪdʒ]	Wurst, Würstchen →	*sausages* 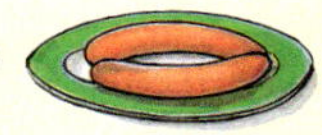
chicken ['tʃɪkɪn]	Huhn, Hähnchen	
starter ['stɑ:tə]	Vorspeise →	to start → *starter*
dessert [dɪ'zɜ:t]	Dessert, Nachtisch →	Achtung Aussprache!
minestrone [ˌmɪnɪ'strəʊni]	Minestrone →	A soup from Italy.
Indian ['ɪndiən]	indisch	
bread [bred]	Brot	
rice [raɪs]	Reis	
salad ['sæləd]	Salat →	Kein Kopfsalat!
pudding ['pʊdɪŋ]	Pudding; Nachtisch →	! Nachtisch heißt auf Englisch *'pudding'* oder 'dessert'.
lassi ['lasɪ]	Lassi *(Jogurtgetränk)*	
mineral ['mɪnərəl]	Mineral- →	In the morning I always drink *mineral* water.
coke [kəʊk]	Cola	
Chinese [tʃaɪ'ni:z]	chinesisch	
to **order** ['ɔ:də]	bestellen →	Let's *order* a pizza.

Language

50 fast food [ˌfɑ:st 'fu:d]	Schnellimbiss →	Hamburgers are *fast food*.
plate [pleɪt]	Teller →	A *plate* for a pizza must be big.
bowl [bəʊl]	Schüssel →	You eat soup from a *bowl*.
knife, knives *(pl)* [naɪf; naɪvz]	Messer →	Achtung Aussprache!
fork [fɔ:k]	Gabel	
spoon [spu:n]	Löffel →	You can't eat your pizza with a *spoon*.
glass [glɑ:s]	Glas →	Can I have a *glass* of coke, please?
to **set the table** [ˌset ðə 'teɪbl]	Tisch decken →	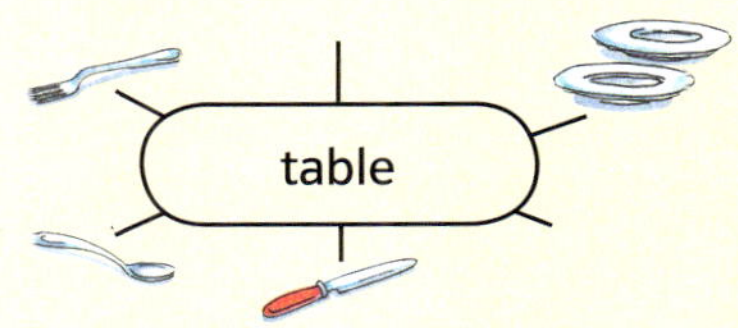
The bell rings. [ðə 'bel rɪŋz]	Es klingelt.	
fast [fɑ:st]	schnell	
to **think, thought** [θɪŋk, θɔ:t]	glauben	
better ['betə]	besser	
worse [wɜ:s]	schlimmer, schlechter	
worst [wɜ:st]	schlimmste/schlimmster/ schlimmstes, schlechteste/schlechtester/ schlechtestes	

Adjektive und ihre Steigerungen

small – smaller – smallest
nice – nicer – nicest
*big – bi**gg**er – bi**gg**est*
*funny – funn**i**er – funn**i**est*
...

beautiful – more beautiful – most beautiful
boring – more boring – most boring
expensive – more expensive – most expensive
...

good – better – best
bad – worse – worst

everything ['evriθɪŋ]	alles →	*Everything* is OK.
ready ['redi]	fertig, bereit	
Hands off! [hændz‿'ɒf]	Hände weg!	
nothing ['nʌθɪŋ]	nichts	

	healthy ['helθi]	gesund →	Fruit and vegetables are *healthy*.
	tasty ['teɪsti]	schmackhaft →	to taste → *tasty*
	Pizza is tastier. ['piːtsə ɪz ˌteɪstɪə]	Pizza schmeckt besser. →	
	comparative [kəm'pærətɪv]	Komparativ	
	superlative [suː'pɜːlətɪv]	Superlativ	
	kind [kaɪnd]	Art, Sorte	
	American [ə'merɪkən]	amerikanisch; Amerikaner/ Amerikanerin →	Is Jake *American*?
	Australian [ɒs'treɪliən]	australisch; Australier/ Australierin	
51	**interesting** ['ɪntrəstɪŋ]	interessant →	You can see *interesting* things in a museum.
	exciting [ɪk'saɪtɪŋ]	spannend, aufregend →	I am excited. → This is *exciting*. I am bored. → This is boring.
	opinion [ə'pɪnjən]	Meinung	
	to report [rɪ'pɔːt]	berichten	
	chart [tʃɑːt]	Schaubild, Diagramm →	a *chart* 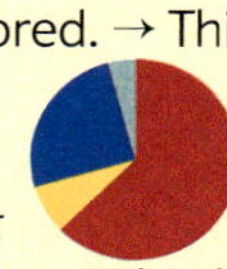
	heavy ['hevi]	schwer →	I can't carry this box – it's *heavy*.
52	**should** [ʃʊd]	sollte/sollten	
	diet ['daɪət]	Diät →	Why don't you eat? Are you on a *diet*?
	to **go on a diet** [ˌgəʊ‿ɒn‿ə 'daɪət]	eine Diät machen	

Ausdrücke mit *to go* and *to get*

*to **go** to school*	zur Schule gehen	*to **get** into*	einsteigen
*to **go** down*	hinuntergehen	*to **get** lost*	sich verirren
*to **go** shopping*	Einkaufen gehen	*to **get** off*	aussteigen
*to **go** on*	weitermachen	*to **get** up*	aufstehen
*to **go** on a diet*	eine Diät machen	*to **get** to school*	zur Schule kommen

as ... as [æz ... æz; əz ... əz]	so ... wie ...	
as [æz; əz]	als, wie	
fit [fɪt]	fit	
would like [wʊd 'laɪk]	hätte gern, möchte gern	
could [kʊd]	konnte/konnten →	I *couldn't* do it yesterday and I can't do it now.
to **lose, lost** [luːz, lɒst]	verlieren →	Here's a new pencil. Don't *lose* it!
a few [ə 'fjuː]	einige, ein paar	
pound (lb) [paʊnd]	Pfund *(Gewicht)*	I can give you *tips* for your trip to England. 
tip [tɪp]	Tipp →	
to **go + -ing** [gəʊ]	... gehen →	You can *go jogging*.
to **jog** [dʒɒg]	joggen	You can *go swimming*.
mustn't ['mʌsnt]	nicht dürfen →	! You must. – Du musst. You *mustn't*. – Du darfst nicht.
to **stop + -ing** [stɒp]	aufhören etw. zu tun →	*Stop making* that noise!
to **plan** [plæn]	planen →	To make a plan.
to **go without** [ˌgəʊ wɪ'ðaʊt]	ohne ... auskommen →	I can't *go without* chocolate!
meal [miːl]	Mahlzeit →	The three *meals* are breakfast, lunch and supper (or tea).

to **exercise** ['eksəsaɪz]	üben, Sport machen	
a week [ə 'wiːk]	pro Woche, in der Woche →	We have English four times *a week*.
for hours [fər‿'aʊəz]	stundenlang	
advice [əd'vaɪs]	Rat, Ratschlag	
to match up ['mætʃ‿ʌp]	zusammenfügen	
to **see a doctor** [siː ə 'dɒktə]	zum Arzt gehen	
53 suggestion [sə'dʒestʃn]	Vorschlag, Anregung	 *sweets*
sweet [swiːt]	Bonbon, Süßigkeit →	
point [pɔɪnt]	Punkt →	That's right. One *point* for you.
usually ['juːʒli]	normalerweise, gewöhnlich	
questionnaire [ˌkwestʃə'neə]	Fragebogen →	question → *questionnaire*
unhealthy [ʌn'helθi]	ungesund →	un + healthy = *unhealthy* un + happy = unhappy un + fit = unfit
54 **any** ['eni]	irgendein, irgendwelche →	Have you got *any* apples?
left [left]	übrig →	I'm hungry. Is there any pizza *left*?
nice [naɪs]	schön	
lettuce ['letɪs]	Kopfsalat	
fresh [freʃ]	frisch →	Can you make some *fresh* tea, please?
pear [peə]	Birne	
pea [piː]	Erbse	
orange ['ɒrɪndʒ]	Orange →	*Oranges* are orange.
bean [biːn]	Bohne	
potato, potatoes *(pl)* [pə'teɪtəʊ, pə'teɪtəʊz]	Kartoffel →	…ke *potatoes*?" …ke chips."
kilo (kg) ['kɪləʊ]	Kilo(gramm)	

Maße und Gewichte

1 **mile** (m) = 1,609 km
1 **foot** (ft) = 30.48 cm
1 **kilo** (kg) = 1,000 g
1 **pound** (lb) = 453.59 g

stall holder ['stɔːl ˌhəʊldə]	Standbesitzer/ Standbesitzerin	

Chats with Charlie

55 to get [get]	werden	
on the air [ˌɒn ði‿'eə]	auf Sendung	
air [eə]	Luft →	The *air* ist often dirty in towns.
snack [snæk]	Imbiss, Snack	
to make sure [meɪk 'ʃʊə]	sichergehen	
introduction [ˌɪntrə'dʌkʃn]	Einleitung	
to take notes [teɪk 'nəʊts]	sich Notizen machen	
change [tʃeɪndʒ]	Wechselgeld; Änderung →	to change → a *change*
waiter ['weɪtə]	Kellner, Bedienung →	The *waiter* brings you your food in a restaurant.
tongue twister ['tʌŋ ˌtwɪstə]	Zungenbrecher	
restaurant ['restrɒnt]	Restaurant →	Achtung Aussprache!
may [meɪ]	kann/könnte(n) vielleicht →	I *may* be late. = Ich komme vielleicht zu spät.

	bill [bɪl]	Rechnung	
	to **keep, kept** [ki:p, kept]	(be)halten →	Can I *keep* the CD for another day, please?
	Have a nice day. [ˌhæv‿ə naɪs 'deɪ]	Einen schönen Tag (noch).	

Story

56	**dangerous** ['deɪndʒrəs]	gefährlich →	Don't go so fast – it's *dangerous*.
	until [ʌn'tɪl; n'tɪl]	bis →	We can stay in bed *until* 10.
	to **be right** [bi: 'raɪt]	Recht haben	
	something ['sʌmθɪŋ]	etwas	
	to **get hungry** [get 'hʌŋgri]	Hunger bekommen →	I always *get hungry* after the second lesson.
	path [pɑ:θ]	Pfad, Weg	
	CD player [ˌsi:'di: ˌpleɪə]	CD-Player	
	headphones *(pl)* ['hedfəʊnz]	Kopfhörer	
	wallet ['wɒlɪt]	Brieftasche, Geldbeutel →	
	back [bæk]	Hinter-, rückwärtig	
57	**run** [rʌn]	Lauf	
	through [θru:]	durch	
	to **steal, stole** [sti:l, stəʊl]	stehlen	
	to **pull** [pʊl]	ziehen →	to push ↔ *to pull*
	somewhere ['sʌmweə]	irgendwo →	some – something – *somewhere*
	right away [raɪt‿ə'weɪ]	sofort, gleich →	Please call your parents *right away*.
	impression [ɪm'preʃn]	Eindruck	
	end [end]	Ende, Schluss →	to end → an *end*
	phone call ['fəʊn kɔ:l]	Anruf	
58	**I don't care.** [aɪ dəʊnt 'keə]	Es ist mir egal.	
	to rewrite, rewrote [ˌri:'raɪt, ˌri:'rəʊt]	noch einmal schreiben	
	rhyming ['raɪmɪŋ]	(sich) reimend	
59	instruction [ɪn'strʌkʃn]	Instruktion, Anweisung	
	bird [bɜ:d]	Vogel →	The *bird* is eating my sandwich. 

For my folder: At the restaurant

Du kannst jetzt in einem Restaurant Essen und Getränke bestellen. Schreibe alle Ausdrücke in deinen *folder*, wie du etwas bestellst oder was der Kellner/die Kellnerin antworten könnte. Vergiss Begrüßung und Verabschiedung nicht. Schreibe auch alle Vorspeisen, Hauptgerichte und Nachspeisen auf, die du kennst.

What can I bring you?
I'd like/We'd like …
What about …?
…

Word game

a) Bilde Reimpaare aus den nebenstehenden Wörtern und mache Verse daraus, z. B.: *Let's **make** a **cake***.

b) Finde Reimwörter zu folgenden Wörtern, und versuche, auch damit Verse zu machen. Du kannst dir auch selber weitere Reime überlegen.

mouse | **head** | **park** | **to clean** | **thing** | **white** | **ball** | **ear**

TEA
MAKE
SEND
ME
FRIEND
CAKE

Unit 5 Media: Music and more!

Lerntipp: Wortfelder

Von den *Wordwise*-Seiten und aus der dritten Spalte des *vocabulary* kennst du *word stars*, mit denen du Wörter im Zusammenhang eines Wortfelds lernst. Ausgehend von einem zentralen Begriff sammelst du drum herum möglichst viele andere Wörter, die etwas mit ihm zu tun haben,
z. B. ***media***: *music, TV, radio, magazine, Internet* etc.
Du kannst die Wortfelder als Liste aufschreiben oder *word stars* malen.
Noch besser behältst du die Wörter, wenn du Sätze damit bildest:
My favourite **music** is … . I often watch soaps on **TV**. You can surf the **Internet** for interviews in sports **magazines**. …
Viele Beispielsätze findest du in der dritten Spalte des vocabulary.

62	media *(pl)* ['mi:diə]	Medien →	Books, e-mails and the cinema are all *media*.
	to update [ʌp'deɪt]	aktualisieren	
	to **take pictures** [teɪk 'pɪktʃəz]	fotografieren, Fotos machen	
	digital ['dɪdʒɪtl]	digital	
	camera ['kæmrə]	Kamera, Fotoapparat →	Sam took a lot of pictures of Greenwich with his *camera*.
	MP3 [empi:'θri:]	MP3	
	MP3 player [empi:'θri: ˌpleɪə]	MP3-Player	
	DVD [di:vi:'di:]	DVD	
	DVD player [di:vi:'di: 'pleɪə]	DVD-Player	
	queen [kwi:n]	Königin →	a *queen* 
63	use [ju:s]	Verwendung, Nutzung	
	to **copy** ['kɒpi]	abschreiben, kopieren	
	PC [ˌpi:'si:]	PC	
	to **delete** [dɪ'li:t]	löschen *(Text)* →	Where's my text? Oh no, you've *deleted* it!
	to **download** [ˌdaʊn'ləʊd]	herunterladen →	I often *download* music from the Internet.
	to **record** [rɪ'kɔ:d]	aufnehmen, aufzeichnen	
	webcam ['webkæm]	Webcam	
	star [stɑ:]	Star; Stern	

Language

64	to **decide** [dɪ'saɪd]	entscheiden →	"Lemonade or coke?" – "I don't know. I can't *decide*."
	cover ['kʌvə]	Einband, Titelseite →	Last week Robbie Williams was on the *cover* of the youth magazine.
	to **print** [prɪnt]	drucken	
	photo ['fəʊtəʊ]	Foto, Fotografie →	That's a *photo* of our house. 
	to **click** [klɪk]	klicken	
	audition [ɔ:'dɪʃn]	Vorsprechen, Vorsingen, Vortanzen	
	website ['websaɪt]	Website, Internetauftritt →	You can find the Thomas Tallis *website* on the Internet.

to **explain** [ɪk'spleɪn]	erklären, erläutern →	Can you *explain* the rules of ice hockey to me?

Sprechen …

… neutral		**… auf eine bestimmte Art**	
to ask	fragen	*to call*	rufen
to answer	antworten, beantworten	*to cry*	schreien, weinen, rufen
to say	sagen	*to laugh*	lachen
to speak	sprechen	*to shout*	schreien, rufen
to talk	reden, sprechen		
to tell	sagen, erzählen		

… und gleichzeitig handeln

to agree	zustimmen	*to interview*	interviewen
to explain	erklären	*to invite*	einladen
to ask for	bitten um	*to offer*	anbieten

to **fill in** [fɪl͜'ɪn]	ausfüllen →	*to fill in* = to complete
form [fɔ:m]	Formular, Form	
to **have to** ['hæv tə]	müssen →	You *have to* practise before you go to an audition.
to **send in** [send͜'ɪn]	einschicken	

Ausdrücke mit *to do* und *to make*

to ***do*** *your homework*	Hausaufgaben machen	*to* ***make*** *sandwiches*	Sandwiches machen
to ***do*** *a project*	ein Projekt durchführen	*to* ***make*** *lunch*	Mittagessen machen
to ***do*** *a play*	ein Theaterstück aufführen	*to* ***make*** *noise*	Lärm machen
to ***do*** *sports*	Sport treiben	*to* ***make*** *a list*	eine Liste machen
to ***do*** *the shopping*	einkaufen	*to* ***make*** *your bed*	dein Bett machen
What are you ***doing****?*	Was machst du?	*to* ***make*** *a poster*	ein Poster machen

65	to tick [tɪk]	abhaken →	*Tick*! ✓
66	to **go bananas** [ˌɡəʊ bə'nɑ:nəz]	verrückt werden, durchdrehen	
	not … yet [jet]	noch nicht →	Have you chosen a dessert? No, *not yet*.
	doorbell ['dɔ:bel]	Türklingel	
	fan [fæn]	Fan →	He's a real football *fan*.
	to **sign** [saɪn]	unterschreiben	
	ever ['evə]	jemals	
	to **practise** ['præktɪs]	üben, proben, praktizieren	
	plan [plæn]	Plan →	Draw a *plan* of your house, please.
67	**shop assistant** ['ʃɒp͜əˌsɪstnt]	Verkäufer/Verkäuferin	
	key [ki:]	Schlüssel	
68	to **get ready** [get 'redi]	sich vorbereiten →	*Get ready*! I can see the school bus coming.
	whose [hu:z]	wessen →	*Whose* CD is this? – It's Sam's.
	lion ['laɪən]	Löwe	

	to **break**, **broke**, **broken** [breɪk, brəʊk, 'brəʊkn]	(zer)brechen; kaputtmachen →	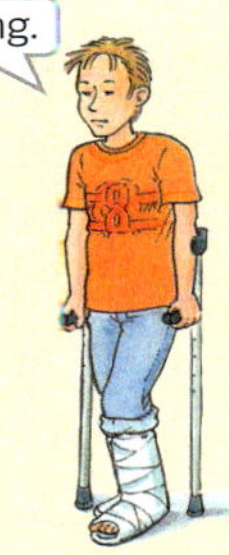

Chats with Charlie

69	**for** [fɔː]	seit	
	wizard ['wɪzəd]	Zauberer →	 a *wizard*

Story

70	**fierce** [fɪəs]	bösartig	
	to **be on** [biː‿'ɒn]	an der Reihe sein; im Gange sein, laufen →	The race *is on*.
	over ['əʊvə]	vorbei, vorüber	
	wicked ['wɪkɪd]	großartig	
	brilliant ['brɪljənt]	toll, prima; leuchtend →	I like this game. It's *brilliant*.
	judge [dʒʌdʒ]	Richter, Kampfrichter	
	part [pɑːt]	Rolle →	What *part* did you play in the musical?
	above [ə'bʌv]	oben, über, oberhalb	
	someone ['sʌmwʌn]	jemand	
	to **panic** ['pænɪk]	paniken, sich aufregen	
71	**everywhere** ['evriweə]	überall →	I've looked *everywhere*, but I can't find my keys.
	microphone ['maɪkrəfəʊn]	Mikrofon →	! Achte auf die Betonung! [' -] 
	floor [flɔː]	Fußboden →	The book is on the *floor*.
	owner ['əʊnə]	Besitzer/Besitzerin	
	few [fjuː]	wenige →	! He's got *few* friends. = … wenige Freunde. It rings every *few* minutes. = … alle paar Minuten.
	to **drive crazy** [draɪv 'kreɪzi]	verrückt machen	
	to **collect** [kə'lekt]	abholen →	Please *collect* your mobile from your teacher.
	nervous ['nɜːvəs]	nervös, aufgeregt	
	helpful ['helpfəl]	hilfreich	
	to **put on** [pʊt‿'ɒn]	auftragen *(Make-up)* →	*Put on* your make-up.
72	**odd one out** [ɒd wʌn‿'aʊt]	das nicht dazu passende (Wort)	

For my folder: Media

Ein Computer mit Internetanschluss bietet uns viele Möglichkeiten mit Medien umzugehen, die wir ohne ihn nicht hätten. Sammle in deinem *folder* die Wörter und Ausdrücke für alles, was du damit tun kannst.

pictures: take, copy, delete
music: listen, record, download
e-mails: read, save, write, send
…

Word game

Schreibe die folgenden Wörter auf und markiere die Buchstaben, die nicht gesprochen werden, z. B. *Greenwich*.
Kannst du noch mehr solche Wörter finden?

walk	***penknife***
write	***know***
listen	***chocolate***
answer	***fruit***
white	***ghost***
right	***cupboard***
evening	***lamb***

Unit 6 It's our world!

Lerntipp: Unregelmäßige Verben

Selbst bei unregelmäßigen Verben kannst du Regelmäßigkeiten erkennen. In Gruppe I sind die zweite und dritte Form jeweils gleich. In Gruppe II sind sich die erste und dritte Form sehr ähnlich.

Gruppe I

to leave	*left*	*left*
to find	*found*	*found*
to send	*sent*	*sent*
to make	*made*	*made*
to read	*read*	*read*
to get	*got*	*got*
to meet	*met*	*met*

Gruppe II

to do	*did*	*done*
to go	*went*	*gone*
to come	*came*	*come*
to be	*was*	*been*
to give	*gave*	*given*
to take	*took*	*taken*
to eat	*ate*	*eaten*

Probiere doch mal diese Spiele aus:

1. Schreibe alle unregelmäßigen Verbformen auf kleine Zettel. Breite sie auf dem Tisch aus. Versuche nun, die drei zusammengehörigen Formen so schnell wie möglich wieder zueinander zu bringen. Du kannst auch gegen einen Partner/eine Partnerin spielen.
2. Stecke die Zettel in eine Tüte. Ziehe eine Form heraus und sage die beiden anderen Formen dazu. Auch dieses Spiel macht zu zweit noch mehr Spaß. Überprüfe deine Antworten mit der Liste der unregelmäßigen Verben am Ende dieses Buchs.

74	world [wɜːld]	Welt
	flood [flʌd]	Überschwemmung, Hochwasser
	flash flood [ˈflæʃ ˌflʌd]	flutartige Überschwemmung, Sintflut
	power [ˈpaʊə]	Kraft, Stärke, Macht
	pony [ˈpəʊni]	Pony
	moor [mɔː]	Hochmoor
	environment [ɪnˈvaɪərnmənt]	Umwelt, Umgebung →
	to **study** [ˈstʌdi]	studieren; lernen →
	plant [plɑːnt]	Pflanze

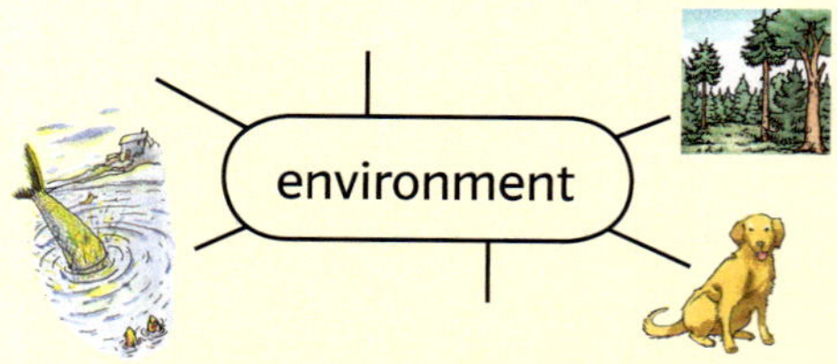

If you *study* a subject, you learn much about it.

mile [maɪl]	Meile *(brit. Längenmaß)* →	1,609 m
wet blanket [wet ˈblæŋkɪt]	Miesmacher/Miesmacherin	
wet [wet]	nass	
blanket [ˈblæŋkɪt]	(Woll-)Decke →	Our dog's bed is a box with a *blanket* in it.
important [ɪmˈpɔːtnt]	wichtig; einflussreich →	This letter is *important*, Sam. You must take it to school tomorrow.
shower [ˈʃaʊə]	Regenguss; Dusche	
rubber boots *(pl)* [ˌrʌbə ˈbuːts]	Gummistiefel →	*rubber boots* 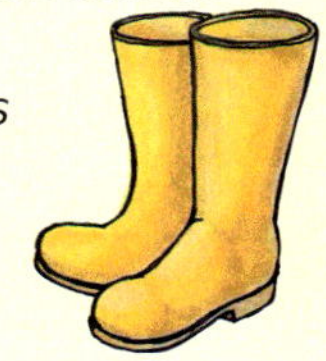

Language

76	**will ('ll), won't** [wɪl; wəʊnt]	werden *(futurisch)* →	*won't = will not*

When?

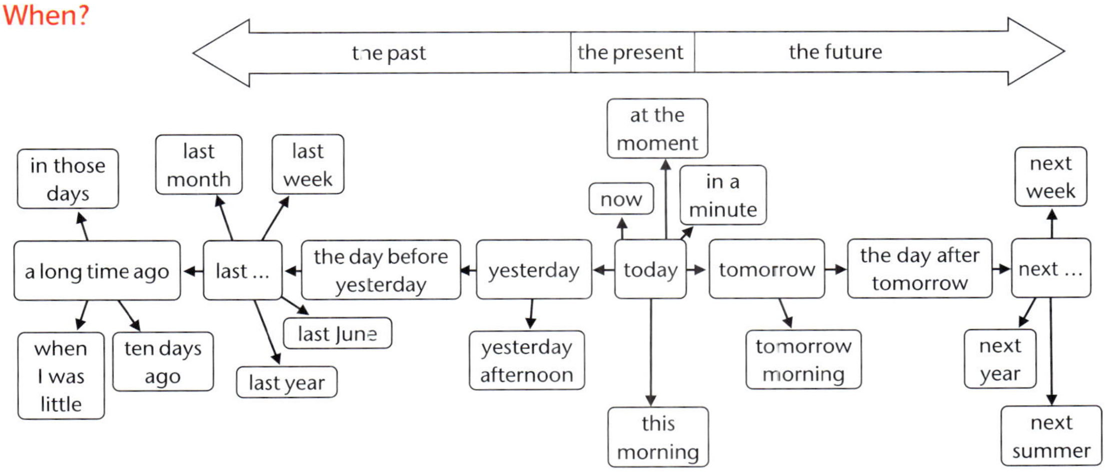

	own [əʊn]	eigener/eigene/eigenes →	! Verwende *own* nie ohne *my/your/his/her* etc.: Have you got *your own* room?
	funeral [ˈfjuːnrəl]	Beerdigung	
	to **fit** [fɪt]	passen	
	to **miss** [mɪs]	vermissen, fehlen; verpassen →	I'll *miss* you. = Du wirst mir fehlen.
77	promise [ˈprɒmɪs]	Versprechen	
	to **promise** [ˈprɒmɪs]	versprechen →	to give a promise = *to promise*
	to offer [ˈɒfə]	anbieten →	Can I *offer* you a drink? = Would you like a drink?
78	**southwest** [ˌsaʊθˈwest]	Südwesten	
	forecast [ˈfɔːkɑːst]	Vorhersage *(Wetter)* →	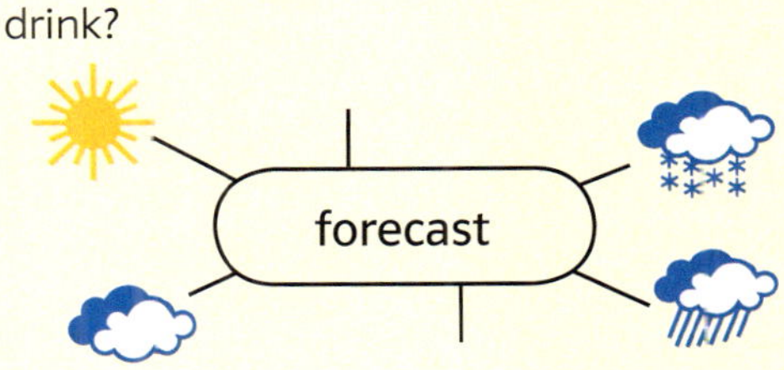
	far [fɑː]	weit	
	temperature [ˈtemprətʃə]	Temperatur	
	to **rise, rose, risen** [raɪz, rəʊz, rɪzn]	steigen, wachsen, zunehmen	
	degree (°) [dɪˈgriː]	Grad	
	Celsius (C) [ˈselsiəs]	Celsius →	Today the temperature will rise to 25 °C.

	rain [reɪn]	Regen →	to rain → the *rain*
	to **move** [mu:v]	(sich) bewegen; umziehen →	Please don't *move*! 
	cloudy ['klaʊdi]	wolkig	
	stormy ['stɔ:mi]	stürmisch	
	by [baɪ]	bis	
	midnight ['mɪdnaɪt]	Mitternacht →	Let's have a *midnight* party!
	heating ['hi:tɪŋ]	Heizung	
	to **escape** [ɪ'skeɪp]	flüchten, entkommen →	The Sheriff didn't catch Robin Hood. He *escaped* at the last minute.
	around [ə'raʊnd]	um … herum, umher	
	symbol ['sɪmbl]	Symbol	
	fog [fɒg]	Nebel →	foggy → *fog*
	to **reach** [ri:tʃ]	(er)reichen →	I'm too small. I can't *reach* the books on the shelf.
	weatherman, weathermen *(pl)* ['weðəmæn; 'weðəmen]	Meteorologe	
79	(to) **snow** [snəʊ]	schneien; Schnee →	*to snow* → *snow* → snowy
	to shuffle ['ʃʌfl]	mischen	
	to miss a turn [mɪs ə 'tɜ:n]	einmal aussetzen	
	to win [wɪn]	gewinnen, siegen	
	area ['eəriə]	Gebiet; Fläche	
	to present [prɪ'zent]	präsentieren →	! Die Betonung unterscheidet dieses Verb vom gleich geschriebenen Nomen.
	to forecast ['fɔ:kɑ:st]	vorhersagen *(Wetter)* →	forecast → *to forecast*
80	**teen** [ti:n]	Jugendlicher/Jugendliche →	*Teens* are between 13 and 19 years old.
	horoscope ['hɒrəskəʊp]	Horoskop	
	Aquarius [ə'kweəriəs]	Wassermann	
	careful ['keəfl]	vorsichtig; sorgfältig →	It's dangerous. Be *careful*!
	adventure [əd'ventʃə]	Abenteuer	
	frightening ['fraɪtnɪŋ]	schrecklich, furchtbar	
	calm [kɑ:m]	ruhig	
	at first [ət 'fɜ:st]	zuerst, zunächst →	I didn't like the book *at first*, but it got really interesting later.
	leader ['li:də]	Führer/Führerin, Anführer/Anführerin →	The group has to follow the *leader*.
	in the end [ɪn ði:‿'end]	schließlich, zum Schluss	
	to **save** [seɪv]	retten; sparen	
	job [dʒɒb]	Arbeitsstelle, Job →	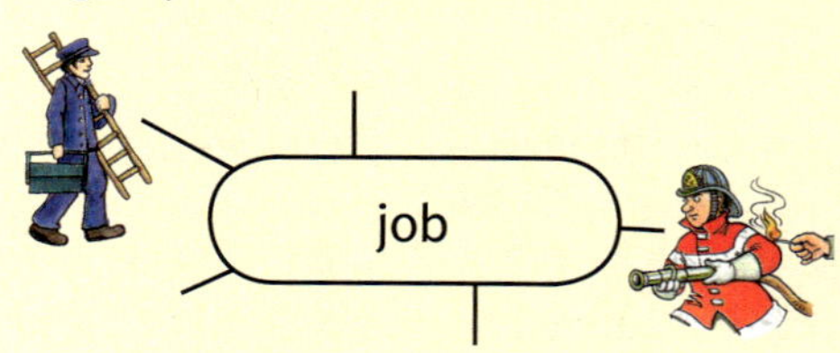
	to **enjoy** [ɪn'dʒɔɪ]	sich erfreuen, genießen	

Chats with Charlie

81	**umbrella** [ʌm'brelə]	Regenschirm	
	greenhouse ['gri:nhaʊs]	Gewächshaus →	We have a small *greenhouse* for tomatoes in our garden.
	storm [stɔ:m]	Sturm	

Story

82 rescue ['reskju:]	Rettung	
national ['næʃnl]	national →	Of a country.
stream [stri:m]	Bach →	A small river.
to **make sure** [meɪk 'ʃʊə]	sichergehen →	*Make sure* you've always got some money with you.
anorak ['ænəræk]	Anorak	
lip balm ['lɪp bɑ:m]	Lippenpflegestift	
fashion ['fæʃn]	Mode →	a *fashion* show 
stone [stəʊn]	Stein	
island ['aɪlənd]	Insel	
hard [hɑ:d]	hart, schwierig, stark →	Roger Federer hits the ball very *hard*. It's *hard* to play it back.
to **jump up** [dʒʌmp‿'ʌp]	hochspringen, aufspringen	
My God! [maɪ 'gɒd]	Mein Gott!	
83 to **disappear** [ˌdɪsə'pɪə]	verschwinden	

Moving about

to go	gehen	**to drive**	fahren
to go down	hinuntergehen	**to fly**	fliegen
to go in	hineingehen	**to ride**	fahren, reiten
to go out	(hin)ausgehen	**to run a race**	einen Wettlauf machen
to go over	hinübergehen	**to run away**	wegrennen
to go up	hinaufgehen	**to leave**	verlassen
to come	kommen	**to take home**	mit nach Hause nehmen
to come in	hereinkommen	**to arrive**	ankommen
to come over	herüberkommen	**to carry**	tragen
to get into	einsteigen	**to climb**	klettern
to get off	aussteigen	**to disappear**	verschwinden
to get out	aussteigen	**to escape**	flüchten, entkommen
to get up	aufstehen	**to follow**	folgen
to turn back	umkehren	**to jog**	joggen
to turn left/right	links/rechts abbiegen	**to skate**	Inlineskates fahren, skaten
to turn over	sich umdrehen	**to jump**	springen
to turn round	(sich) umdrehen	**to jump up**	hochspringen
to walk	gehen, laufen	**to move**	sich bewegen
to walk the dog	mit dem Hund spazieren gehen	**to visit**	besuchen

to **be trapped** [bi: 'træpt]	in der Falle sitzen	
to **be frightened (of)** [bi: 'fraɪtnd]	Angst haben (vor) →	Some people are *frightened of* big dogs.
to **rescue** ['reskju:]	retten →	rescue → *to rescue* 
service ['sɜ:vɪs]	Service, Dienst	
helicopter ['helɪˌkɒptə]	Helikopter, Hubschrauber	
to **get** [get]	werden	
half [hɑ:f]	halb	
to **wave** [weɪv]	winken, schwenken →	Emma *waved* at Sam out of the car window.

	evidence ['evɪdnts]	Beweis	
84	**end** [end]	Ende, Schluss	
85	to **go wrong** [gəʊ 'rɒŋ]	schief gehen →	wrong → *to go wrong*
	European [ˌjʊərə'piːən]	europäisch	

For my folder: Weather

Egal, wo man ist, alle Leute reden oft und gerne über das Wetter und du kannst jetzt auch auf Englisch mitreden. Schreibe alle Wetter-Wörter in deinen *folder*.

warm, hot, cold
sun – sunny
wind – windy
fog – foggy
...

Word game

Schreibe mit einem Freund/einer Freundin die folgenden Wörter auf Karten, die ihr in entsprechende Viererstapel sortiert. Jeder nimmt sich die Hälfte. Wer seine Viererreihen zuerst richtig alphabetisch geordnet hat, hat gewonnen.

past – put – print – packet
menu – meal – manager – maths
timetable – train – tomorrow – that
room – road – rice – rule
what – wear – white – watch
scone – science – school – scratch

BULLY
BURGER
BUS
BUSH
BUSY
BUTTER
BUY

Unit 7 A holiday in Ireland

Lerntipp: Eselsbrücken

Manches, was sich nur schwer behalten lässt, kannst du dir mit einer Eselsbrücke besser merken. Eselsbrücken helfen dir am besten, wenn du sie dir selbst oder mit Freunden/Freundinnen zusammen ausdenkst. Hier ein paar Beispiele:

- Du kannst dir nicht merken, ob du *to choose* mit einem oder zwei „o" schreibst? Vielleicht hilft es dir, dass *to choose* „auswählen" heißt. Beim Auswählen musst du dich zwischen zwei Sachen entscheiden, deshalb zwei „o".
- Du verwechselst die Fagewörter *where* und *who* nicht, wenn du daran denkst, dass in *where* die Antwort *here* schon drinsteckt.

88	**holiday(s)** ['hɒlədeɪ(z)]	Urlaub, Ferien	
	swap [swɒp]	Tausch	
	farmhouse ['fɑːmhaʊs]	Bauernhaus →	

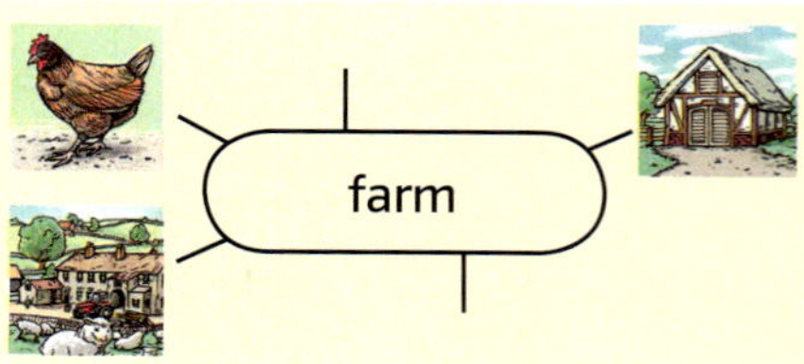

coast [kəʊst]	Küste	
barn [bɑːn]	Scheune	
table-tennis ['teɪbl,tenɪs]	Tischtennis →	tennis → *table tennis*
to **frighten away** [,fraɪtn‿ə'weɪ]	abschrecken →	frightened → *to frighten away*
probably ['prɒbəbli]	wahrscheinlich	
lots (of) ['lɒts‿əv]	viel/viele →	*lots of* = a lot of
sea [siː]	Meer →	! The *sea* = **die** See, nicht: der See.
to **fly** [flaɪ]	fliegen	
dump [dʌmp]	Dreckloch, Müllkippe	
none [nʌn]	keiner/keine →	no – no one – nothing – *none*
castle ['kɑːsl]	Schloss, Burg →	! Achtung! Das *t* in *castle* wird nicht gesprochen.
peace [piːs]	Friede	
quiet [kwaɪət]	Ruhe, Stille	
89 **city** ['sɪti]	Stadt, Großstadt	London is a *city*. 
to put down [pʊt 'daʊn]	auflegen *(Telefon)*; hinlegen, hinstellen	
airport ['eəpɔːt]	Flughafen →	Let's meet at the *airport*.

Language

90 to **iron** [aɪən]	bügeln	
journey ['dʒɜːni]	Reise, Fahrt →	It's a long *journey* from here to Berlin by car.
if [ɪf]	wenn, falls; ob	
to **lend**, **lent**, **lent** [lend, lent, lent]	leihen	
coat [kəʊt]	Mantel →	A *coat* is longer than an anorak.
leprechaun ['leprəkɔːn]	Gnom, Kobold	
Irish ['aɪrɪʃ]	irisch →	the *Irish* flag 
goblin ['gɒblɪn]	Kobold	
to **guard** [gɑːd]	bewachen	
pot [pɒt]	Topf	
gold [gəʊld]	Gold →	*Gold* is beautiful and expensive.
luggage ['lʌgɪdʒ]	Gepäck	
customs *(pl)* ['kʌstəmz]	Zoll	
departure [dɪ'pɑːtʃə]	Abflug, Abreise →	The time when a flight or train leaves.
desk [desk]	Schalter	
gate [geɪt]	Tor, Pforte; Gate →	When you go out of the garden, please close the *gate*.
envelope ['envələʊp]	Briefumschlag, Umschlag	
clear [klɪə]	klar →	If something is *clear*, you can understand it right away.
neighbour ['neɪbə]	Nachbar/Nachbarin →	Isn't our *neighbours'* house nice? 
burglar ['bɜːglə]	Einbrecher/Einbrecherin	
alarm [ə'lɑːm]	Alarm	
to **set**, **set**, **set** [set, set, set]	stellen, einstellen	

	adverb ['ædvɜ:b]	Adverb	
	adverb of manner [ˌædvɜ:b‿əv 'mænə]	Adverb der Art und Weise →	'Yesterday' is an adverb of time, and 'quickly' is an *adverb of manner*.
	to end in ['end‿ɪn]	enden auf	
91	**loud** [laʊd]	laut →	Don't sing too *loudly*.

Describing people

brave	tapfer, mutig	*alone*	allein
brilliant	fantastisch	*angry*	zornig, wütend
careful	vorsichtig	*awful*	schrecklich
clever	schlau, klug	*bad*	schlecht
cool	cool, klasse	*boring*	langweilig
different	anders	*dangerous*	gefährlich
excited	aufgeregt	*difficult*	schwierig
famous	berühmt, bekannt	*fierce*	wild
fantastic	großartig, toll	*gruesome*	grausig, schaurig
funny	komisch	*mad*	verrückt
good	gut	*nervous*	nervös
great	großartig, toll	*odd*	merkwürdig, seltsam
happy	glücklich, fröhlich	*scared*	ängstlich
important	wichtig	*scary*	unheimlich, gruselig
lucky	glücklich, fröhlich	*silly*	dumm, albern
nice	nett, schön	*spooky*	gespenstisch, gruselig
popular	beliebt, populär	*unhappy*	unglücklich

	wish [wɪʃ]	Wunsch	
	to come true [kʌm 'tru:]	wahr werden	
	to **win**, **won**, **won** [wɪn, wʌn, wʌn]	gewinnen, siegen →	He *won* the race.

Chats with Charlie

93	**cliff** [klɪf]	Klippe →	The *cliffs* on the Irish coast are great!

Story

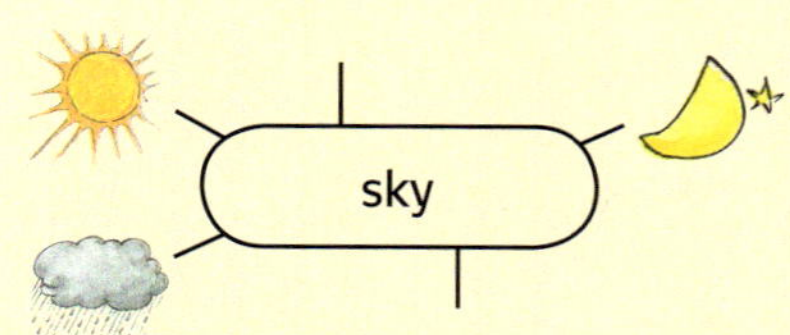

94	to go bump [gəʊ 'bʌmp]	rumsen	
	to **be asleep** [ˌbi:‿ə'sli:p]	schlafen	
	cloud [klaʊd]	Wolke	
	sky [skaɪ]	Himmel →	
	to **bang** [bæŋ]	schlagen, fest (an)klopfen	
	to **turn over** [ˌtɜ:n‿'əʊvə]	(sich) umdrehen	
	barn owl ['bɑ:n‿əʊl]	Schleiereule →	a *barn owl*
	to **hoot** [hu:t]	schreien, rufen *(Eule)*	
	to **get out of bed** [ˌget‿aʊt‿əv 'bed]	aufstehen	
	light [laɪt]	Licht	
	to **be on** [bi:‿'ɒn]	an sein, brennen *(Licht)* →	The light *is on*.

to **lean out** [li:n‿'aʊt]	(sich) hinauslehnen	
figure ['fɪgə]	Figur, Gestalt	
moon [mu:n]	Mond →	You can't see the *moon* tonight, there are clouds in the sky.
to **wake**, **woke**, **woken** [weɪk, wəʊk, 'wəʊkn]	(auf)wecken	

Unregelmäßige Verben

Mit dem present perfect *musst du eine dritte Form bei den unregelmäßigen Verben lernen, das so genannte* past participle. *Versuche einmal „rückwärts" zu lernen, indem du die Infinitive zu den* participles *findest.*

found	*made*	*brought*	*thrown*	*gone*	*sung*
left	*heard*	*told*	*given*	*done*	*drunk*
lost	*put*	*taken*	*written*	*been*	*stolen*
sent	*bought*	*eaten*	*come*	*seen*	*broken*

to **creak** [kri:k]	knarren, quietschen	
in fact [ɪn 'fækt]	in der Tat, genau genommen →	fact → *in fact*
soft [sɒft]	leise; weich, sanft	
sleepy ['sli:pi]	schläfrig, verschlafen →	He's *sleepy*. 
rubbish ['rʌbɪʃ]	Unsinn	
area ['eəriə]	Gebiet; Fläche	
at once [ət 'wʌnts]	sofort, plötzlich →	Sam! Come here *at once*!
95 **flash** [flæʃ]	Aufblinken, Blitzen	
to **press** [pres]	drücken, pressen	
button ['bʌtn]	Auslöser; Knopf →	It's easy to take a picture – just press the *button*.
to **put in** [pʊt‿'ɪn]	einsetzen	
battery ['bætri]	Batterie, Akku →	Your mobile won't work if the *battery* is old.
to **set off** [set‿'ɒf]	auslösen	
feeling ['fi:lɪŋ]	Gefühl →	to feel → *feeling*
scary ['skeəri]	unheimlich, gruselig →	to be scared → *scary*
middle ['mɪdl]	Mitte; Mittel- →	*middle* = centre
to think about ['θɪŋk‿əˌbaʊt]	nachdenken über, denken an	
to go off [gəʊ‿'ɒf]	losgehen *(Alarm)*	
beginning [bɪ'gɪnɪŋ]	Anfang, Beginn	
96 **surprising** [sə'praɪzɪŋ]	überraschend	
at the back [ət ðə 'bæk]	hinten, im hinteren Teil	
technical ['teknɪkl]	technisch	
97 to **turn left/right** [tɜ:n 'left/'raɪt]	links/rechts abbiegen →	The car is *turning right*. 

For my folder: Holiday

Du kennst jetzt schon eine Menge Ausdrücke, mit denen du über Urlaub und Reisen sprechen kannst. Schreibe sie in deinen *folder* und bilde Sätze damit. Du kannst auch versuchen, mit diesen Wörtern deinen letzten oder nächsten Urlaub zu beschreiben.

Reisen
helicopter, car, bus, …
England, Turkey, …
to fly, to drive, …
…

Word game

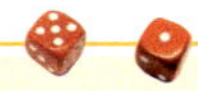

Weißt du wie *form* zu *fork* wird? Ganz einfach – indem du einen Buchstaben auswechselst. Aber wie wird aus *well* → *talk*? Versuche einfach immer wieder, einen Buchstaben zu ändern, um ein neues Wort zu bilden:
well → *wall* → *tall* → *talk*
Genauso kannst du bei den nebenstehenden Wörtern vorgehen.

mouse → ***horse***
time → ***rice***
past → ***mark***
easy → ***list***

Dictionary

In dieser alphabetischen Liste ist das Vokabular von *Orange Line 1* enthalten. Namen werden in einer gesonderten Liste am Ende des Vokabulars aufgelistet.
Das Zeichen ° bei einem Eintrag weist darauf hin, dass das Wort zum rezeptiven Wortschatz zählt.
Die mit * gekennzeichneten Verben sind unregelmäßig.
Wendungen, die aus mehreren Wörtern bestehen, werden meist unter mehreren Stichwörtern aufgeführt.
So ist z. B. *at home* unter *at* und *home* zu finden.
Die Fundstellen verweisen auf das erstmalige Vorkommen der Wörter, z. B.
about [ə'baʊt] über **IU3**, 40 kommt zum ersten Mal vor in Band I, Unit 3, Seite 40
colour ['kʌlə] Farbe **ILUA**, 24 kommt zum ersten Mal vor in Band I, Link-up A, Seite 24.
U = Unit, LU = Link-up, FA = Fakultativer Anhang (nur Namen)

A

a, an [ə; ən] ein/eine **I U1,** 10
a bit [ə 'bɪt] ein bisschen **I U2,** 35
a few [ə 'fju:] einige, ein paar **II U4,** 52
a lot [ə 'lɒt] viel **II U1,** 15
a lot of [ə 'lɒt‿əv] viel/viele, eine Menge **I U2,** 30
a week [ə 'wi:k] pro Woche, in der Woche **II U4,** 52
about [ə'baʊt] über **I U3,** 40
out and about ['aʊt‿nd‿ə'baʊt] unterwegs °**I U4,** 54
What about …? [wɒt‿ə'baʊt] Was ist mit …? Wie wäre es mit …? **I U2,** 30
What's the film about? [wɒts ðə 'fɪlm‿əˌbaʊt] Wovon handelt der Film? °**II U3,** 43
above [ə'bʌv] oben, über, oberhalb **II U5,** 70
accent ['æksnt] Akzent **II U3,** 36
accident ['æksɪdnt] Unfall **II U3,** 41
across [ə'krɒs] waagerecht *(im Kreuzworträtsel)* **II U3,** 42
to **act** [ækt] spielen *(Theater)* **I U7,** 90
action ['ækʃn] Handlung, Aktion °**I U6,** 81
activity [æk'tɪvəti] Aktivität °**I U7,** 91
actor ['æktə] Schauspieler **I U7,** 96
to **add** [æd] hinzufügen °**I U2,** 29
address [ə'dres] Adresse **I U5,** 70
adjective ['ædʒəktɪv] Adjektiv, Eigenschaftswort °**I U1,** 22
adventure [əd'ventʃə] Abenteuer **II U6,** 80
adverb ['ædvɜ:b] Adverb °**II U7,** 90
adverb of manner [ˌædvɜ:b‿əv 'mænə] Adverb der Art und Weise °**II U7,** 90
advice [əd'vaɪs] Rat, Ratschlag °**II U4,** 52
after ['ɑ:ftə] nach **I LUB,** 39
afternoon [ˌɑ:ftə'nu:n] Nachmittag **I U2,** 34
afternoon tea [ˌɑ:ftənu:n 'ti:] Nachmittagstee **I U7,** 94
in the afternoon [ˌɪn ði: ˌɑ:ftə'nu:n] nachmittags, am Nachmittag **I U3,** 47
again [ə'gen] wieder **I U3,** 48
ago [ə'gəʊ] vor *(zeitlich)* **II U2,** 26
air [eə] Luft **II U4,** 55
on the air [ˌɒn ði‿'eə] auf Sendung **II U4,** 55
airport ['eəpɔ:t] Flughafen **II U7,** 89
alarm [ə'lɑ:m] Alarm **II U7,** 90
alarm clock [ə'lɑ:m ˌklɒk] Wecker **I U5,** 75
all [ɔ:l] alle/alles; ganz **I U3,** 50
along [ə'lɒŋ] entlang **I U7,** 91
alphabet ['ælfəbet] Alphabet, Abc **I U1,** 15
alphabetical [ˌælfə'betɪkl] alphabetisch **I U6,** 88
already [ɔ:l'redi] schon **I U2,** 34
also ['ɔ:lsəʊ] auch **I U5,** 68
always ['ɔ:lweɪz] immer, ständig **I U1,** 16
American [ə'merɪkən] amerikanisch; Amerikaner/Amerikanerin **II U4,** 50
and [ænd] und **I U1,** 11
angry ['æŋgri] verärgert, böse **II U1,** 18
to be angry with [bi: 'æŋgri wɪð] böse sein auf **II U2,** 26
animal ['ænɪml] Tier **I U6,** 82
anorak ['ænəræk] Anorak **II U6,** 82
another [ə'nʌðə] noch ein/eine, ein anderer/eine andere/ein anderes **II U3,** 44
answer ['ɑ:ntsə] Antwort **I U4,** 58
to **answer** ['ɑ:ntsə] antworten, beantworten °**I LUA,** 24
any ['enɪ] irgendein, irgendwelche **II U4,** 54
anything ['eniθɪŋ] etwas, irgendetwas **I U5,** 66
apple ['æpl] Apfel **I U1,** 14
April ['eɪprl] April **I U5,** 70
area ['eəriə] Gebiet; Fläche **II U7,** 94
arena [ə'ri:nə] Arena, Stadion **II U2,** 22
arm [ɑ:m] Arm **II U3,** 40
around [ə'raʊnd] um … herum, umher **II U6,** 78
to **arrive** [ə'raɪv] ankommen **I U6,** 86
Art [ɑ:t] Kunst **II U1,** 10
as [æz; əz] als, wie **II U4,** 52
as … as [æz … æz; əz … əz] so … wie … **II U4,** 52
as long as [əz 'lɒŋ‿əz] solange **I U7,** 94
to **ask** [ɑ:sk] fragen **I U3,** 44
to ask for ['ɑ:sk fə] fragen nach, bitten um **I U4,** 60
*to be **asleep** [ˌbi:‿ə'sli:p] schlafen **II U7,** 94
assembly [ə'sembli] Versammlung, Morgenappell **II U1,** 10
shop **assistant** ['ʃɒp‿əˌsɪstnt] Verkäufer/Verkäuferin **II U5,** 67
at [æt; ət] in, auf, bei, an **I U1,** 10
at first [ət 'fɜ:st] zuerst, zunächst **II U6,** 80
at home [ət 'həʊm] zu Hause **I U2,** 26
at least [ət 'li:st] wenigstens, mindestens **I U6,** 87

at night [ət ˈnaɪt] nachts **II U3,** 47
at once [ət ˈwʌnts] sofort, plötzlich **II U7,** 94
at the back [ət ðə ˈbæk] hinten, im hinteren Teil °**II U7,** 96
at the moment [æt ðə ˈməʊmənt] im Augenblick, momentan **I U7,** 90
audition [ɔːˈdɪʃn] Vorsprechen, Vorsingen, Vortanzen **II U5,** 64
August [ˈɔːɡəst] August **I U5,** 70
aunt [ɑːnt] Tante **I U2,** 28
Australian [ɒsˈtreɪliən] australisch; Australier/Australierin **II U4,** 50
autograph [ˈɔːtəɡrɑːf] Autogramm **I U7,** 96
autumn [ˈɔːtəm] Herbst **I U6,** 79
away [əˈweɪ] weg **I U3,** 48
to run away [rʌn‿əˈweɪ] wegrennen **I U3,** 48

B

baby, babies *(pl)* [ˈbeɪbi; ˈbeɪbiz] Baby, Säugling **I U6,** 82
back [bæk] Rücken **II U3,** 41
at the back [ət ðə ˈbæk] hinten, im hinteren Teil °**II U7,** 96
back [bæk] zurück **I U3,** 42; Hinter-, rückwärtig **II U4,** 56
bad [bæd] schlecht **I U5,** 74
bad luck [ˌbæd ˈlʌk] Pech **I U4,** 63
badminton [ˈbædmɪntən] Badminton, Federball **I U3,** 40
bag [bæɡ] Tasche, Tüte **I U1,** 14
school bag [ˈskuːl bæɡ] Schultasche, Schulranzen **I U1,** 14
sleeping bag [ˈsliːpɪŋ ˌbæɡ] Schlafsack **I U6,** 84
ball [bɔːl] Ball **I U1,** 20
balloon [bəˈluːn] Luftballon °**I U5,** 71
banana [bəˈnɑːnə] Banane **II U1,** 15
to go bananas [ˌɡəʊ bəˈnɑːnəz] verrückt werden, durchdrehen **II U5,** 66
to **bang** [bæŋ] schlagen, fest (an)klopfen **II U7,** 94
piggy **bank** [ˈpɪɡi bæŋk] Sparschwein **II U2,** 23
burger **bar** [ˈbɜːɡə ˌbɑː] Fastfood-Restaurant **I U5,** 68
to **bark** [bɑːk] bellen **I U3,** 48
barn [bɑːn] Scheune **II U7,** 88
barn owl [ˈbɑːn‿əʊl] Schleiereule **II U7,** 94
basketball [ˈbɑːskɪtbɔːl] Basketball **I U3,** 40
bathroom [ˈbɑːθrʊm] Bad, Badezimmer **I LUA,** 24
battery [ˈbætri] Batterie, Akku **II U7,** 95
*to **be** [biː] sein **I U1,** 23
to be angry with [biː ˈæŋɡri wɪð] böse sein auf **II U2,** 26
to be asleep [ˌbiː‿əˈsliːp] schlafen **II U7,** 94
to be cold [biː ˈkəʊld] frieren **II U2,** 24
to be fed up [biː ˌfed‿ˈʌp] die Nase voll haben **I U2,** 34
to be frightened (of) [biː ˈfraɪtnd] Angst haben (vor) **II U6,** 83
to be fun [biː ˈfʌn] Spaß machen **I U3,** 43
to be good with … [biː ˈɡʊd wɪð] gut mit … umgehen können **I U2,** 34
to be in a hurry [biː‿ɪn‿ə ˈhʌri] es eilig haben **I U2,** 30
to be nuts about [biː ˌnʌts‿əˈbaʊt] verrückt nach … sein **II U1,** 18
to be on [biː‿ˈɒn] an der Reihe sein; im Gange sein, laufen **II U5,** 70; an sein, brennen *(Licht)* **II U7,** 94
to be pleased with [biː ˈpliːzd wɪð] zufrieden sein mit **I U6,** 87
to be right [biː ˈraɪt] Recht haben **II U4,** 56
to be trapped [biː ˈtræpt] in der Falle sitzen **II U6,** 83
to be upset [biː ʌpˈset] aufgeregt sein, bestürzt sein **II U3,** 44
to be worried [biː ˈwʌrid] besorgt sein, beunruhigt sein **I U6,** 87
bean [biːn] Bohne **II U4,** 54
beautiful [ˈbjuːtɪfl] schön, wunderschön **I U6,** 78
because [bɪˈkɒz] weil **I U2,** 30
bed [bed] Bett **I LUA,** 25
to get out of bed [ˌɡet‿aʊt‿əv ˈbed] aufstehen **II U7,** 94
bedroom [ˈbedrʊm] Schlafzimmer **I LUA,** 24
before [bɪˈfɔː] vor, bevor **I LUB,** 39
*to **begin** [bɪˈɡɪn] beginnen, anfangen **II U3,** 47
beginning [bɪˈɡɪnɪŋ] Anfang, Beginn °**II U7,** 95
behind [bɪˈhaɪnd] hinter **I U1,** 18
to **believe** [bɪˈliːv] glauben **II U1,** 18
bell [bel] Glocke, Klingel **II U2,** 24
The bell rings. [ðə ˈbel rɪŋz] Es klingelt. **II U4,** 50
beside [bɪˈsaɪd] neben, außer **II U1,** 18
best [best] beste/bester/bestes **II U1,** 14
*to **bet** [bet] wetten **II U1,** 14
better [ˈbetə] besser **II U4,** 50
between [bɪˈtwiːn] zwischen **I U7,** 90
big [bɪɡ] groß **I U1,** 12
bike [baɪk] Fahrrad **I LUB,** 38
by bike [baɪ ˈbaɪk] mit dem Fahrrad **I U4,** 57
bill [bɪl] Rechnung **II U4,** 55
bird [bɜːd] Vogel **II U4,** 59
birthday [ˈbɜːθdeɪ] Geburtstag **I U5,** 68
biscuit [ˈbɪskɪt] Keks **I U5,** 68
a **bit** [ə ˈbɪt] ein bisschen **I U2,** 35
black [blæk] schwarz **I LUA,** 24
blanket [ˈblæŋkɪt] (Woll-)Decke **II U6,** 74
wet blanket [wet ˈblæŋkɪt] Miesmacher/Miesmacherin **II U6,** 74
bloke [bləʊk] Typ, Kerl **I U7,** 96
blond [blɒnd] blond **II U2,** 28
*to **blow up** [bləʊ‿ˈʌp] aufblasen °**I U5,** 71
blue [bluː] blau **I LUA,** 24
board [bɔːd] Tafel, Wandtafel **I U1,** 18
body [ˈbɒdi] Körper °**II U3,** 41
book [bʊk] Buch **I U1,** 14
exercise book [ˈeksəsaɪz ˌbʊk] Heft, Übungsheft **I U1,** 14
rubber **boots** *(pl)* [ˌrʌbə ˈbuːts] Gummistiefel **II U6,** 74
bored [bɔːd] gelangweilt **II U2,** 24
boring [ˈbɔːrɪŋ] langweilig **I U1,** 20
to **borrow** [ˈbɒrəʊ] borgen, leihen **I U2,** 34
bottle [ˈbɒtl] Flasche **I U5,** 68
bowl [bəʊl] Schüssel **II U4,** 50
box, boxes *(pl)* [bɒks; ˈbɒksɪz] Kiste, Schachtel, Kasten **I U5,** 68
boy [bɔɪ] Junge **I U1,** 16
bread [bred] Brot **II U4,** 49
break [breɪk] Pause **II U1,** 12
*to **break** [breɪk] (zer)brechen, kaputtmachen **II U5,** 68
to **break-dance** [ˈbreɪkdɑːnts] Breakdance tanzen **I LUB,** 38
breakfast [ˈbrekfəst] Frühstück **I U3,** 44
bridge [brɪdʒ] Brücke **I LUC,** 52
brilliant [ˈbrɪljənt] toll, prima; leuchtend **II U5,** 70
*to **bring** [brɪŋ] bringen, mitbringen **I U3,** 43
to bring in [brɪŋ‿ˈɪn] hereinbringen, mitbringen °**I U7,** 93
broken [ˈbrəʊkn] kaputt, zerbrochen, gebrochen **I U6,** 84
brother [ˈbrʌðə] Bruder **I LUA,** 25

brown [braʊn] braun **I LUA,** 24
bully ['bʊli] Rabauke, jemand, der andere tyrannisiert **II U3,** 36
The bullies say they are sorry. [ðə ˌbʊliz seɪ ðeɪ ə 'sɒri] Die Rabauken sagen, dass es ihnen Leid tut. °**II U3,** 45
to **bully** ['bʊli] tyrannisieren **II U3,** 36
*to go **bump** [gəʊ 'bʌmp] rumsen °**II U7,** 94
burger ['bɜːgə] Hamburger **I U5,** 68
burger bar ['bɜːgə ˌbɑː] Fastfood-Restaurant **I U5,** 68
burglar ['bɜːglə] Einbrecher/Einbrecherin **II U7,** 90
bus, buses *(pl)* [bʌs; 'bʌsɪz] Bus **I LUC,** 52
bus stop ['bʌs ˌstɒp] Bushaltestelle **I LUC,** 52
on the bus [ˌɒn ðə 'bʌs] im Bus **II U1,** 18
bush [bʊʃ; 'bʊʃɪz] Busch, Strauch **I U6,** 86
busy ['bɪzi] beschäftigt, ausgefüllt **I U2,** 34
but [bʌt] aber **I U2,** 26
butter ['bʌtə] Butter **I U7,** 94
button ['bʌtn] Auslöser; Knopf **II U7,** 95
*to **buy** [baɪ] kaufen **I U5,** 66
by [baɪ] bis **II U6,** 78
by bike [baɪ 'baɪk] mit dem Fahrrad **I U4,** 57
bye [baɪ] tschüss **I U1,** 16

C

café ['kæfeɪ] Café **I U3,** 48
cafeteria [ˌkæfə'tɪəriə] Cafeteria **I U1,** 20
cake [keɪk] Kuchen **I U5,** 68
calendar ['kæləndə] Kalender **I U5,** 71
call [kɔːl] Anruf °**I U6,** 83
phone call ['fəʊn ˌkɔːl] (Telefon)anruf °**II U4,** 57
to **call** [kɔːl] rufen, anrufen, nennen **I U3,** 48
That's what I call .... [ˌðæts wɒt‿'aɪ ˌkɔːl] Das nenne ich .... **II U1,** 14
calm [kɑːm] ruhig **II U6,** 80
camera ['kæmrə] Kamera, Fotoapparat **II U5,** 62
camping ['kæmpɪŋ] Camping, Zelten **I U6,** 84
***can** [kæn] können, dürfen **I U1,** 19
cap [kæp] Kappe, Mütze **I U5,** 66
capital letter [ˌkæpɪtl 'letə] Großbuchstabe °**II U3,** 37
car [kɑː] Auto **I U3,** 49
card [kɑːd] Karte **I LUB,** 38
I don't **care.** [aɪ dəʊnt 'keə] Es ist mir egal. **II U4,** 58
careful ['keəfl] vorsichtig; sorgfältig **II U6,** 80
caretaker ['keəteɪkə] Hausmeister/Hausmeisterin **I U1,** 12
carrot ['kærət] Karotte, Mohrrübe **II U1,** 15
to **carry** ['kæri] tragen **I U6,** 80
pencil **case** ['pensl ˌkeɪs] Mäppchen **I U1,** 14
castle ['kɑːsl] Schloss, Burg **II U7,** 88
cat [kæt] Katze **I U2,** 26
*to **catch** [kætʃ] fangen °**II U3,** 45
CD [ˌsiː'diː] CD **I U5,** 69
CD player [ˌsiː'diː ˌpleɪə] CD-Spieler **II U4,** 56
Celsius (C) ['selsiəs] Celsius **II U6,** 78
centre ['sentə] Zentrum, Mittelpunkt **I LUC,** 52
information centre [ɪnfə'meɪʃn ˌsentə] Informationszentrum **I LUC,** 52
chain [tʃeɪn] Kette **II U3,** 40
chair [tʃeə] Stuhl **I U1,** 18
change [tʃeɪndʒ] Wechselgeld; Änderung **II U4,** 55
to **change** [tʃeɪndʒ] (ver)ändern, tauschen, wechseln **II U3,** 42
charity ['tʃærɪti] Wohltätigkeit, Wohltätigkeitsverein **I U7,** 90
chart [tʃɑːt] Schaubild, Diagramm °**II U4,** 51
chat [tʃæt] Geplauder, Unterhaltung **I U2,** 33
to **chat** [tʃæt] sich unterhalten **I U2,** 33
cheap [tʃiːp] billig **I U5,** 68
to **check** [tʃek] überprüfen **I U6,** 82
cheese [tʃiːz] Käse **I U5,** 68
chicken ['tʃɪkɪn] Huhn, Hähnchen **II U4,** 49
child, children *(pl)* [tʃaɪld; 'tʃɪldrɪn] Kind **I U2,** 26
only child ['əʊnli ˌtʃaɪld] Einzelkind **I U2,** 26
Chinese [tʃaɪ'niːz] chinesisch **II U4,** 49
chips *(pl)* [] Pommes frites **II U1,** 14
chocolate ['tʃɒklət] Schokolade **I U1,** 18
choice ['tʃɔɪs] Auswahl, Wahl °**II U1,** 21
*to **choose** [tʃuːz] wählen, auswählen **I U4,** 54
church [tʃɜːtʃ] Kirche **I LUC,** 52
cinema ['sɪnəmə] Kino **II U1,** 18
city ['sɪti] Stadt, Großstadt **II U7,** 89
to **clap** [klæp] klatschen **I U1,** 15
class [klɑːs] Schulklasse, Klasse **I U1,** 16; Kurs, Unterricht **II U1,** 18
classroom ['klɑːsrʊm] Klassenzimmer **I U1,** 16
to **clean** [kliːn] säubern, reinigen **II U3,** 40
clear [klɪə] klar **II U7,** 90
to **click** [klɪk] klicken **II U5,** 64
cliff [klɪf] Klippe **II U7,** 93
to **climb** ['klaɪm] klettern, steigen, besteigen **II U2,** 30
clock [klɒk] Uhr **I U4,** 54
alarm clock [ə'lɑːm ˌklɒk] Wecker **I U5,** 75
o'clock [ə'klɒk] Uhr *(Zeitangabe)* **I U3,** 40
to **close** [kləʊz] schließen, zumachen **I LUC,** 53
closed [kləʊzd] zu, geschlossen °**I U2,** 32
clothes *(pl)* [kləʊðs] Kleider, Kleidung **II U2,** 23
cloud [klaʊd] Wolke **II U7,** 94
cloudy ['klaʊdi] wolkig **II U6,** 78
club [klʌb] Klub, Verein, Arbeitsgemeinschaft **I LUB,** 39
clue [kluː] Hinweis **II U1,** 13
coast [kəʊst] Küste **II U7,** 88
coat [kəʊt] Mantel **II U7,** 90
coke [kəʊk] Cola **II U4,** 49
cold [kəʊld] kalt **I U4,** 62
to be cold [biː 'kəʊld] frieren **II U2,** 24
to **collect** [kə'lekt] sammeln **I LUB,** 38; abholen **II U5,** 71
colour ['kʌlə] Farbe **I LUA,** 24
*to **come** [kʌm] kommen **I U2,** 33
Come on. [kʌm‿'ɒn] Komm./Kommt. **I U2,** 35
to come in [kʌm‿'ɪn] hereinkommen **I U3,** 48
to come over [kʌm‿'əʊvə] herüberkommen **I U2,** 27
to come true [kʌm 'truː] wahr werden °**II U7,** 91
comic ['kɒmɪk] Comic, Comicheft **I LUB,** 38
comparative [kəm'pærətɪv] Komparativ **II U4,** 50
to **compare** [kəm'peə] vergleichen °**I U7,** 91
to **complete** [kəm'pliːt] vervollständigen °**I U4,** 54

English – German

computer [ˌkəm'pju:tə] Computer **I LUA,** 25
concert ['kɒnsət] Konzert **II U2,** 23
to **continue** [kən'tɪnju:] weitergehen, weitermachen °**II U2,** 27
cooking ['kʊkɪŋ] Kochen, Koch- **I U3,** 40
cool [ku:l] cool, prima **I U1,** 20
to **copy** ['kɒpi] abschreiben, kopieren **II U5,** 63
cornflakes ['kɔ:nfleɪks] Cornflakes **I U5,** 68
to **correct** [kə'rekt] korrigieren, verbessern °**I LUB,** 38
correct [kə'rekt] richtig, korrekt **II U1,** 10
corridor ['kɒrɪdɔ:] Gang, Flur, Korridor **I U7,** 96
*__could__ [kʊd] konnte/konnten **II U4,** 52
country, countries *(pl)* ['kʌntri; 'kʌntriz] Land **I U2,** 29
in the country [ˌɪn ðə 'kʌntri] auf dem Land **I U6,** 78
course [kɔ:s] Gang **II U4,** 49
of course [əv 'kɔ:s] natürlich, selbstverständlich **I U1,** 19
cousin ['kʌzn] Cousin/Cousine **I U2,** 28
cover ['kʌvə] Einband, Titelseite **II U5,** 64
cow [kaʊ] Kuh **I U6,** 82
crazy ['kreɪzi] verrückt **I U7,** 96
to drive crazy [draɪv 'kreɪzi] verrückt machen **II U5,** 71
to **creak** [kri:k] knarren, quietschen **II U7,** 94
ice-**cream** [aɪs 'kri:m] Eis, Eiscreme **I U7,** 92
cricket ['krɪkɪt] Kricket **I U7,** 92
crisp [krɪsp] Kartoffelchip **I U1,** 18
crossword (puzzle) ['krɒswɜ:d 'pʌzl] Kreuzworträtsel °**I U5,** 71
to **cry** [kraɪ] weinen; schreien, rufen **II U3,** 36
cupboard ['kʌbəd] Küchenschrank, Schrank **I U1,** 18
curry ['kʌri] Curry *(Gewürz oder Gericht)* **II U4,** 49
customs *(pl)* ['kʌstəmz] Zoll **II U7,** 90

D

dad [dæd] Papa, Vati **I LUA,** 25
to **dance** [dɑnts] tanzen **I U3,** 40
dangerous ['deɪndʒrəs] gefährlich **II U4,** 56
dark [dɑ:k] dunkel **I U2,** 34
date [deɪt] Datum **I U5,** 70
day [deɪ] Tag **I LUB,** 39
Have a nice day. [ˌhæv‿ə naɪs 'deɪ] Einen schönen Tag (noch). **II U4,** 55
one day [wʌn 'deɪ] eines Tages **II U3,** 36
sports day ['spɔ:ts deɪ] Sportfest **I U7,** 90
dear [dɪə] lieb **I U3,** 44
Dear [dɪə] Lieber … , Liebe … *(Anrede in Briefen)* **II U3,** 36
December [dɪ'sembə] Dezember **I U5,** 70
to **decide** [dɪ'saɪd] entscheiden **II U5,** 64
definition [ˌdefɪ'nɪʃn] Definition **II U1,** 20
degree (°) [dɪ'gri:] Grad **II U6,** 78
to **delete** [dɪ'li:t] löschen *(Text)* **II U5,** 63
department store [dɪ'pɑ:tmənt stɔ:] Kaufhaus **I LUC,** 52
departure [dɪ'pɑ:tʃə] Abflug, Abreise **II U7,** 90
to **describe** [dɪ'skraɪb] beschreiben °**I U7,** 92
desk [desk] Schreibtisch **I U1,** 18; Schalter **II U7,** 90
dessert [dɪ'zɜ:t] Dessert, Nachtisch **II U4,** 49
detective [dɪ'tektɪv] Detektiv/Detektivin **II U2,** 30
store detective ['stɔ: dɪˌtektɪv] Kaufhausdetektiv/Kaufhausdetektivin **II U2,** 30
dialogue ['daɪəlɒg] Gespräch °**I U3,** 42
dictionary ['dɪkʃnri] Wörterbuch °**II U3,** 46
diet [daɪət] Diät **II U4,** 52
to go on a diet [ˌgəʊ‿ɒn ə 'daɪət] eine Diät machen **II U4,** 52
different ['dɪfrnt] anders, verschieden **I U6,** 78
difficult ['dɪfɪklt] schwierig **II U1,** 13
digital ['dɪdʒɪtl] digital **II U5,** 62
dining room ['daɪnɪŋ rʊm] Esszimmer, Speisesaal **I LUA,** 24
dirty ['dɜ:ti] schmutzig **II U1,** 10
to **disappear** [ˌdɪsə'pɪə] verschwinden **II U6,** 83
disco ['dɪskəʊ] Disko **I U5,** 74
divorced from [dɪ'vɔ:st frəm] geschieden von **I U2,** 28
DJ [ˌdi:'dʒeɪ] DJ **I U2,** 33
*to **do** [du:] machen, tun **I U1,** 15
to do sports [du: 'spɔ:ts] Sport treiben **I U7,** 92
doctor ['dɒktə] Arzt/Ärztin **II U3,** 40
to see a doctor [si: ə 'dɒktə] zum Arzt gehen **II U4,** 52
dog [dɒg] Hund **I U2,** 27
dog-tired [ˌdɒg 'taɪəd] hundemüde **I U3,** 49
to walk the dog [wɔ:k ðə 'dɒg] mit dem Hund spazieren gehen **I U3,** 42
domino ['dɒmɪnəʊ] Dominospiel °**II U2,** 26
door [dɔ:] Tür **I U1,** 18
doorbell ['dɔ:bel] Türklingel **II U5,** 66
double ['dʌbl] Doppelgänger, das Doppelte **I U7,** 97
down [daʊn] senkrecht *(im Kreuzworträtsel)* °**II U3,** 42; (nach) unten, herunter, hinunter, nieder **II U2,** 30
Go down … . ['gəʊ daʊn] Geh … entlang. **I LUC,** 53
*to go down [gəʊ 'daʊn] hinuntergehen **II U2,** 30
to sit down [sɪt 'daʊn] sich setzen, sich hinsetzen **I U1,** 19
down under [daʊn‿'ʌndə] in Australien °**II U1,** 17
to **download** [ˌdaʊn'ləʊd] herunterladen **II U5,** 63
downstairs [daʊn'steəz] unten, im unteren Stock **I U2,** 27
drama ['drɑ:mə] Theater, Drama **I U3,** 40
*to **draw** [drɔ:] zeichnen **I LUB,** 38
dream [dri:m] Traum **I LUA,** 25
to **dress** [dres] sich anziehen **I U3,** 44
drink [drɪŋk] Getränk **I U7,** 95
*to **drink** [drɪŋk] trinken **I U5,** 75
*to **drive** [draɪv] fahren **I U6,** 86
to drive crazy [draɪv 'kreɪzi] verrückt machen **II U5,** 71
driver ['draɪvə] Fahrer/Fahrerin **I U4,** 54
to **drop** [drɒp] fallen, fallen lassen **II U1,** 18
drums *(pl)* [drʌmz] Schlagzeug **I U2,** 26
dump [dʌmp] Dreckloch, Müllkippe **II U7,** 88
DVD [ˌdi:vi:'di:] DVD **II U5,** 62
DVD player [di:vi:'di: 'pleɪə] DVD-Player **II U5,** 62
to **dye** [daɪ] färben **II U2,** 28

E

each [i:tʃ] jede/jeder/jedes °**I U6,** 87
each other [ˌi:tʃ‿'ʌðə] sich gegenseitig **II U1,** 19
ear [ɪə] Ohr **II U3,** 40
early ['ɜ:li] früh **I U3,** 46
east [i:st] Osten **I U4,** 54

easy ['i:zi] einfach, leicht **I U1,** 20
*to **eat** [i:t] essen, fressen **I U3,** 44
education [edʒʊ'keɪʃn] Erziehung, Bildung **II U1,** 10
Physical Education (PE) [ˌfɪzɪkl‿edʒʊ'keɪʃn] Sport *(Schulfach)* **II U1,** 10
Religious Education (RE) [rɪˌlɪdʒəs‿edʒʊ'keɪʃn] Religionsunterricht **II U1,** 12
egg [eg] Ei **I U5,** 68
elbow ['elbəʊ] Ellbogen **II U3,** 41
elephant ['elɪfənt] Elefant **I U7,** 96
else [els] sonst, noch **I U5,** 66
e-mail ['i:meɪl] E-Mail **I U3,** 44
embarrassing [ɪm'bærəsɪŋ] peinlich **II U2,** 26
empty ['empti] leer **II U1,** 18
end [end] Ende, Schluss **II U7,** 84
in the end [ɪn ði:‿'end] schließlich, zum Schluss **II U6,** 80
to **end** [end] enden **I U5,** 76
to end in ['end‿ɪn] enden auf °**II U7,** 90
ending ['endɪŋ] Ende, Schluss *(einer Geschichte)* °**II U1,** 19
enemy ['enəmi] Feind/Feindin **II U3,** 43
English ['ɪŋglɪʃ] englisch **I U1,** 11
to **enjoy** [ɪn'dʒɔɪ] sich erfreuen, genießen **II U6,** 80
envelope ['envələʊp] Briefumschlag, Umschlag **II U7,** 90
environment [ɪn'vaɪərnmənt] Umwelt, Umgebung **II U6,** 74
er [3:] äh °**I U1,** 12
erm [3:m] äh °**II U3,** 38
to **escape** [ɪ'skeɪp] flüchten, entkommen **II U6,** 78
etc. [ɪt'setrə] usw., et cetera **II U1,** 10
euro ['jʊərəʊ] Euro *(Währung)* **I U5,** 73
European [ˌjʊərə'pi:ən] europäisch °**II U6,** 85
even ['i:vn] selbst, sogar **I U7,** 90
evening ['i:vnɪŋ] Abend **I U3,** 47
in the evening [ˌɪn ði: 'i:vnɪŋ] abends, am Abend **I U3,** 47
that evening [ˌdæt‿'i:vnɪŋ] an diesem Abend **II U1,** 19
event [ɪ'vent] Veranstaltung, Ereignis **I U7,** 90
ever ['evə] jemals **II U5,** 66
every ['evri] jede/jeder/jedes **I U3,** 40
everything ['evriθɪŋ] alles **II U4,** 50
everywhere ['evriweə] überall **II U5,** 71
evidence ['evɪdnts] Beweis °**II U6,** 83
example ['ɪgzɑ:mpl] Beispiel °**I U1,** 13
exchange [ɪks'tʃeɪndʒ] Austausch, Tausch **I U7,** 94
excited [ɪk'saɪtɪd] aufgeregt **I U5,** 74
exciting [ɪk'saɪtɪŋ] spannend, aufregend **II U4,** 51
Excuse me! [ɪk'skju:z mi] Entschuldigung! **I U3,** 42
exercise ['eksəsaɪz] Übung, Aufgabe **I U1,** 19
exercise book ['eksəsaɪz ˌbʊk] Heft, Übungsheft **I U1,** 14
to **exercise** ['eksəsaɪz] üben, Sport machen **II U4,** 52
expensive [ɪk'spentsɪv] teuer **I U5,** 68
experiment [ɪk'sperɪmənt] Experiment, Versuch **II U1,** 13
to **explain** [ɪk'spleɪn] erklären, erläutern **II U5,** 64
eye [aɪ] Auge **I U2,** 35

F

face [feɪs] Gesicht **I U3,** 48
fact [fækt] Fakt, Tatsache **II U2,** 32
fact-file (on) ['fækt,faɪl] Datei mit Informationen (über) °**II U2,** 32
in fact [ɪn 'fækt] in der Tat, genau genommen **II U7,** 94
fair [feə] Messe, Jahrmarkt **I U7,** 90
summer fair ['sʌmə ˌfeə] Sommerfest **I U7,** 90
*to **fall** [fɔ:l] fallen, herunterfallen, hinfallen **II U2,** 26
to fall off [fɔ:l ɒf] herunterfallen **II U3,** 40
family ['fæmli] Familie **I LUA,** 25
family tree ['fæmli tri:] Familienstammbaum °**I U2,** 28
famous ['feɪməs] berühmt **I U4,** 54
fan [fæn] Fan **II U5,** 66
fantastic [fæn'tæstɪk] fantastisch, großartig **I U7,** 94
far [fɑ:] weit **II U6,** 78
farm [fɑ:m] Bauernhof, Farm **I U6,** 78
farmer ['fɑ:mə] Bauer/Bäuerin, Landwirt/Landwirtin **I U6,** 82
farmhouse ['fɑ:mhaʊs] Bauernhaus **II U7,** 88
fashion ['fæʃn] Mode **II U6,** 82
fast [fɑ:st] schnell **II U4,** 50
fast food [ˌfɑ:st 'fu:d] Schnellimbiss °**II U4,** 50
favourite ['feɪvrɪt] Lieblings- **I U1,** 12
February ['februri] Februar **I U5,** 70
*to **feed** [fi:d] füttern **I U6,** 80
to be fed up [bi: ˌfed‿'ʌp] die Nase voll haben **I U2,** 34
*to **feel** [fi:l] fühlen, sich fühlen **II U3,** 40
to feel sick [fi:l 'sɪk] Übelkeit verspüren **II U3,** 46
feeling ['fi:lɪŋ] Gefühl °**II U7,** 95
few [fju:] wenige **II U5,** 71
a few [ə 'fju:] einige, ein paar **II U4,** 52
field [fi:ld] Feld, Acker **I U6,** 88
sports field ['spɔ:ts fi:ld] Sportplatz **I U7,** 92
fierce [fɪəs] bösartig **II U5,** 70
figure ['fɪgə] Figur, Gestalt **II U7,** 94
to **fill** in [fɪl‿'ɪn] ausfüllen, einsetzen **II U5,** 64
film [fɪlm] Film **II U3,** 43
*to **find** [faɪnd] finden **I U3,** 48
to find out [faɪnd‿'aʊt] herausfinden **I U4,** 62
fine [faɪn] gut, in Ordnung, fein, schön **I U7,** 94
finger ['fɪŋgə] Finger **II U3,** 41
to **finish** ['fɪnɪʃ] beenden, erledigen, aufhören **I U2,** 34
fire [faɪə] Feuer, Brand **I U7,** 96
Where's the fire? [ˌweəz ðə 'faɪə] Wo brennt's denn? **I U7,** 96
first [f3:st] zuerst; erste/erster/erstes **I U4,** 54
at first [ət 'f3:st] zuerst; zunächst **II U6,** 80
fish, fish *(pl)* [fɪʃ] Fisch/Fische **I U6,** 78
to **fish** [fɪʃ] fischen, angeln **I U6,** 82
fishing ['fɪʃɪŋ] Angeln, Fischen **I U6,** 78
to **fit** [fɪt] passen **II U6,** 76
fit [fɪt] fit **II U4,** 52
flag [flæg] Flagge, Fahne **I U2,** 29
flash [flæʃ] Aufblinken, Blitzen **II U7,** 95
flash flood ['flæʃ ˌflʌd] flutartige Überschwemmung, Sintflut **II U6,** 74
flat [flæt] Wohnung **I U2,** 26
flight [flaɪt] Flug **II U2,** 23
flood [flʌd] Überschwemmung, Hochwasser **II U6,** 74
flash flood ['flæʃ ˌflʌd] flutartige Überschwemmung, Sintflut **II U6,** 74
floor [flɔ:] Fußboden **II U5,** 71
flower ['flaʊə] Blume **I U6,** 78
*to **fly** [flaɪ] fliegen **II U7,** 88
fog [fɒg] Nebel **II U6,** 78
foggy ['fɒgi] neblig **I U6,** 79
folder ['fəʊldə] Ordner, Mappe **I U4,** 60
to **follow** ['fɒləʊ] hinterhergehen, folgen, befolgen **I U7,** 96

following ['fɒləʊɪŋ] folgende/folgender/folgendes °**II U3,** 43
food [fu:d] Essen, Nahrung, Lebensmittel **I U7,** 95
fast food [ˌfɑ:st 'fu:d] Schnellimbiss °**II U4,** 50
foot, feet *(pl)* [fʊt; fi:t] Fuß **I U4,** 54
on foot [ɒn 'fʊt] zu Fuß **I U4,** 57
football ['fʊtbɔ:l] Fußball **I U1,** 12
for [fɔ:; fə] für **I U1,** 11; seit **II U5,** 69
for hours [fər‿'aʊəz] stundenlang **II U4,** 52
for supper [fə 'sʌpə] zum Abendessen **II U3,** 38
forecast ['fɔ:kɑ:st] Vorhersage **II U6,** 78
to **forecast** ['fɔ:kɑ:st] vorhersagen *(Wetter)* °**II U6,** 79
foreign ['fɒrɪn] fremd, ausländisch **II U1,** 10
*to **forget** [fə'get] vergessen **I U4,** 60
fork [fɔ:k] Gabel **II U4,** 50
form [fɔ:m] Form, Formular **II U5,** 64
long form ['lɒŋ fɔ:m] Langform °**I U1,** 16
free [fri:] frei **I U3,** 40
French [frentʃ] französisch **II U1,** 18
fresh [freʃ] frisch **II U4,** 54
Friday [fraɪdeɪ] Freitag **I LUB,** 39
friend [frend] Freund/Freundin **I U1,** 16
to **frighten** away [ˌfraɪtn‿ə'weɪ] abschrecken **II U7,** 88
*to be **frightened** (of) [bi: 'fraɪtnd] Angst haben (vor) **II U6,** 83
frightening ['fraɪtnɪŋ] schrecklich, furchtbar **II U6,** 80
from [frɒm] aus, von **I U1,** 10
divorced from [dɪ'vɔ:st frəm] geschieden von **I U2,** 28
Where are you from? [ˌweər‿ə jə 'frɒm] Woher kommst du? **I U1,** 11
in **front** of [ɪn 'frʌnt‿əv] vor **I U3,** 49
fruit [fru:t] Obst, Frucht **II U1,** 15
fun [fʌn] Spaß **I U3,** 41
Have fun! [ˌhæv 'fʌn] Viel Spaß! **I U6,** 82
to be fun [bi: 'fʌn] Spaß machen **I U3,** 43
to have fun [ˌhæv 'fʌn] Spaß haben, sich amüsieren **I U6,** 82
funeral ['fju:nrəl] Beerdigung **II U6,** 76
funny ['fʌni] komisch, lustig **I LUA,** 25
furniture ['fɜ:nɪtʃə] Möbel **I LUA,** 25

G

game [geɪm] Spiel **I U2,** 26
miming game ['maɪmɪŋ geɪm] Pantomime °**I U6,** 81
garden ['gɑ:dn] Garten **I U2,** 26
gate [geɪt] Tor, Pforte; Gate **II U7,** 90
g'day [gə'deɪ] Tag, hallo *(australische Begrüßung)* °**II U1,** 14
Geography [dʒi'ɒgrəfi] Geografie, Erdkunde **II U1,** 10
German ['dʒɜ:mən] deutsch; Deutscher/Deutsche **I U1,** 17
*to **get** [get] kommen, bekommen, besorgen **I U3,** 44; holen **II U2,** 26; werden **II U6,** 83
to get hungry [get 'hʌŋgri] Hunger bekommen **II U4,** 56
to get into [get‿'ɪntə] einsteigen in *(Auto)* **I U5,** 75
to get lost [get 'lɒst] verloren gehen, sich verirren **I U3,** 48
to get off [get‿'ɒf] aussteigen aus **I U4,** 59
to get onto [get‿'ɒntə] einsteigen *(Bus)* **II U1,** 19
to get out [get‿'aʊt] aussteigen **I U6,** 86
to get out of bed [ˌget‿aʊt‿əv 'bed] aufstehen **II U7,** 94
to get ready [get 'redi] sich vorbereiten **II U5,** 68
to get … right [get … 'raɪt] richtig machen **II U3,** 44
to get up [get‿'ʌp] aufstehen **I U3,** 44
to get … wrong [get … 'rɒŋ] falsch verstehen °**II U3,** 47; falsch machen **II U3,** 44
ghost [gəʊst] Geist, Gespenst **I U2,** 34
girl [gɜ:l] Mädchen **I U1,** 16
girlfriend ['gɜ:lfrend] Freundin *(in einer Paarbeziehung)* **II U3,** 39
*to **give** [gɪv] geben, schenken **I U4,** 60
to give … a dirty look [ˌgɪv‿ə dɜ:ti 'lʊk] einen vernichtenden Blick zuwerfen °**II U1,** 10
glass [glɑ:s] Glas **II U4,** 50
*to **go** [gəʊ] gehen **I U1,** 19
Go down … . ['gəʊ daʊn] Geh … entlang. **I LUC,** 53
Go left. [gəʊ 'left] Biege nach links ab. **I LUC,** 52
Go right. [gəʊ 'raɪt] Biege nach rechts ab. **I LUC,** 52
to go bananas [ˌgəʊ bə'nɑ:nəz] verrückt werden, durchdrehen **II U5,** 66
to go bump [gəʊ 'bʌmp] rumsen °**II U7,** 94
to go down [gəʊ 'daʊn] hinuntergehen, entlanggehen **II U2,** 30
to go in [gəʊ 'ɪn] hineingehen **II U2,** 26
to go + -ing [gəʊ] … gehen **II U4,** 52
to go off [gəʊ‿'ɒf] losgehen *(Alarm)* °**II U7,** 95
to go on a diet [ˌgəʊ‿ɒn ə 'daɪət] eine Diät machen **II U4,** 52
to go out [gəʊ‿'aʊt] (hin)ausgehen, erlöschen **II U3,** 38
to go over [gəʊ‿'əʊvə] hinübergehen **II U3,** 38
to go red [gəʊ 'red] rot werden **II U1,** 11
to go up [gəʊ‿'ʌp] hinaufgehen °**I U4,** 61
to go without [ˌgəʊ wɪ'ðaʊt] ohne … auskommen **II U4,** 52
to go wrong [gəʊ 'rɒŋ] schief gehen **II U6,** 85
goal [gəʊl] Tor, Ziel **I U1,** 12
goblin ['gɒblɪn] Kobold **II U7,** 90
My **God!** [maɪ 'gɒd] Mein Gott! **II U6,** 82
gold [gəʊld] Gold **II U7,** 90
good [gʊd] gut **I U1,** 16
Good grief! [gʊd 'gri:f] Du liebe Zeit! **II U2,** 28
Good luck! [ˌgʊd 'lʌk] Viel Glück! **I U4,** 63
Good morning! ['gʊd 'mɔ:nɪŋ] Guten Morgen! **I U1,** 16
I'm good at … [aɪm 'gʊd‿ət] ich bin gut in … **I U1,** 20
to be good with … [bi: 'gʊd wɪð] gut mit … umgehen können **I U2,** 34
to have a good time [ˌhæv‿ə gʊd 'taɪm] sich amüsieren **I U5,** 75
goodbye [gʊd'baɪ] auf Wiedersehen **I U1,** 19
grammar ['græmə] Grammatik °**II U1,** 16
grandad ['grændæd] Opa **I LUA,** 25
grandma ['grændmɑ:] Oma **I LUA,** 25
great [greɪt] großartig, toll **I U2,** 26
Greek [gri:k] griechisch; Grieche/Griechin **I U2,** 29
green [gri:n] grün **I LUA,** 24
greenhouse ['gri:nhaʊs] Gewächshaus **II U6,** 81
grid [grɪd] Gitter, Tabelle °**I U1,** 14

Good **grief!** [gʊd 'gri:f] Du liebe Zeit! **II U2,** 28
ground [graʊnd] Boden **II U2,** 26
group [gru:p] Gruppe **I U4,** 54
to **guard** [gɑ:d] bewachen **II U7,** 90
to **guess** [ges] raten, vermuten °**I U6,** 81
gym [dʒɪm] Turnhalle **I U3,** 40

H

hair [heə] Haar, Haare **II U2,** 28
hairdresser ['heəˌdresə] Friseur/Friseurin **II U2,** 28
half [hɑ:f] halb **II U6,** 83
half an hour [ˌhɑ:f‿ən‿'aʊə] eine halbe Stunde **II U2,** 26
half past (two) ['hɑ:f pɑ:st] halb (drei) **I U3,** 40
half-sister ['hɑ:fˌsɪstə] Halbschwester **I U2,** 26
hall [hɔ:l] Halle, Saal, Flur **I U3,** 40
ham [hæm] Schinken **II U4,** 49
hand [hænd] Hand **II U3,** 41
Hands off! [hændz‿'ɒf] Hände weg! **II U4,** 50
Hang on! ['hæŋ‿ɒn] Moment mal! Warte mal! **I U6,** 82
to **happen** ['hæpn] geschehen, passieren **I U6,** 86
happy ['hæpi] glücklich, froh **I U2,** 33
hard [hɑ:d] hart, schwierig, stark **II U6,** 82
hat [hæt] Hut **II U2,** 26
hate [heɪt] Hass **II U1,** 10
to **hate** [heɪt] hassen **II U1,** 10
*to **have** [hæv] haben **I U5,** 68
Have a nice day. [ˌhæv‿ə naɪs 'deɪ] Einen schönen Tag (noch). **II U4,** 55
Have fun! [ˌhæv 'fʌn] Viel Spaß! **I U6,** 82
I'm having .... [aɪm 'hævɪŋ] ich nehme .... **II U1,** 14
to have a good time [ˌhæv‿ə gʊd 'taɪm] sich amüsieren **I U5,** 75
to have a party [ˌhæv‿ə 'pɑ:ti] eine Party feiern **I U5,** 68
to have fun [ˌhæv 'fʌn] Spaß haben, sich amüsieren **I U6,** 82
to have got [hæv 'gɒt] besitzen, haben **I U2,** 30
to have supper [hæv 'sʌpə] zu Abend essen **I U3,** 44
to have to ['hæv tə] müssen **II U5,** 64
he [hi:] er **I U1,** 12
head [hed] Kopf **II U3,** 36
headphones *(pl)* ['hedfəʊnz] Kopfhörer **II U4,** 56
healthy ['helθi] gesund **II U4,** 50
*to **hear** [hɪə] hören **I U6,** 78
heating ['hi:tɪŋ] Heizung **II U6,** 78
heavy ['hevi] schwer **II U4,** 51
helicopter ['helɪˌkɒptə] Helikopter, Hubschrauber **II U6,** 83
Hello! [he'ləʊ] Hallo! **I U1,** 10
help [help] Hilfe **I U2,** 34
to **help** [help] helfen **I U2,** 34
helpful ['helpfəl] hilfreich **II U5,** 71
her [hɜ:] ihr/ihre; sie **I U2,** 26
here [hɪə] hier **I U1,** 12
Here you are! ['hɪə ju:‿ɑ:] Bitte schön! **I U1,** 20
hero, heroes *(pl)* ['hɪərəʊ; 'hɪərəʊz] Held **II U3,** 43
hey [heɪ] he °**I U1,** 16
Hi! [haɪ] Hi! **I U1,** 10
*to **hide** [haɪd] verstecken, sich verstecken **I U6,** 86
high [haɪ] hoch, groß **II U2,** 30
him [hɪm] ihn, ihm **I U4,** 60
his [hɪz] sein/seine **I LUA,** 25
History ['hɪstəri] Geschichte **II U1,** 10
*to **hit** [hɪt] schlagen, treffen **II U3,** 36
hobby, hobbies *(pl)* ['hɒbi; 'hɒbiz] Hobby **I LUB,** 38
hockey ['hɒki] Hockey **II U1,** 16
ice hockey ['aɪs ˌhɒki] Eishockey **II U2,** 23
holiday(s) ['hɒlədeɪ(z)] Urlaub, Ferien **II U7,** 88
home [həʊm] Zuhause, Heim; nach Hause **I U1,** 11
at home [ət 'həʊm] zu Hause **I U2,** 26
to take home [ˌteɪk 'həʊm] nach Hause bringen **I U2,** 35
homework ['həʊmwɜ:k] Hausaufgabe/Hausaufgaben **I U1,** 19
to **hoot** [hu:t] schreien, rufen *(Eule)* **II U7,** 94
to **hope** [həʊp] hoffen **I U5,** 72
horoscope ['hɒrəskəʊp] Horoskop **II U6,** 80
horrible ['hɒrəbl] schrecklich, furchtbar **II U2,** 24
horse [hɔ:s] Pferd **I LUB,** 38
hospital ['hɒspɪtl] Krankenhaus **II U3,** 36
hot [hɒt] heiß **I U6,** 79
hour ['aʊə] Stunde **I U2,** 34
hours ['aʊəz] Öffnungszeiten **I U4,** 62
for hours [fər‿'aʊəz] stundenlang **II U4,** 52
half an hour [ˌhɑ:f‿ən‿'aʊə] eine halbe Stunde **II U2,** 26
house [haʊs] Haus **I LUA,** 25
how [haʊ] wie **I U1,** 11
How are you? [ˌhaʊ‿'ɑ: ju:] Wie geht es dir/Ihnen/euch? **I U6,** 83
how many [haʊ 'meni] wie viele **I U5,** 68
How much are ... ? [ˌhaʊ 'mʌtʃ‿ɑ:] Wie viel kosten ... ? **I U5,** 66
How much is ... ? [ˌhaʊ 'mʌtʃ‿ɪz] Wie viel kostet ... ? **I U5,** 66
How old are you? [haʊ‿'əʊld‿ɑ: ju:] Wie alt bist du? **I U1,** 11
how to ... ['haʊ tə] wie man ... °**II U3,** 37
hundred ['hʌndrəd] hundert **II U2,** 23
hungry ['hʌŋgri] hungrig **II U1,** 14
to get hungry [get 'hʌŋgri] Hunger bekommen **II U4,** 56
*to be in a **hurry** [bi:‿ɪn‿ə 'hʌri] es eilig haben **I U2,** 30
Hurry up! [ˌhʌri‿'ʌp] Beeil dich! **I U2,** 30
*to **hurt** [hɜ:t] verletzen, weh tun **II U3,** 40

I

I [aɪ] ich **I U1,** 10
I'd like to [ˌaɪd 'laɪk tə] ich würde gern **II U2,** 22
I don't care. [aɪ dəʊnt 'keə] Es ist mir egal. **II U4,** 58
I'd rather [aɪd 'rɑ:ðə] ich würde lieber **II U2,** 22
I'm having .... [aɪm 'hævɪŋ] ich nehme .... **II U1,** 14
I'm scared. [aɪm 'skeəd] Ich habe Angst. **II U3,** 44
ice [aɪs] Eis **II U2,** 23
ice-cream [aɪs 'kri:m] Eis, Eiscreme **I U7,** 92
ice hockey ['aɪs ˌhɒki] Eishockey **II U2,** 23
ice rink ['aɪs rɪŋk] Eis-/Schlittschuhbahn **II U2,** 23
idea [aɪ'dɪə] Idee, Einfall **I LUB,** 33
idiot ['ɪdiət] Idiot, Dummkopf **I U1,** 21
if [ɪf] wenn, falls; ob **II U7,** 90
to **imagine** [ɪ'mædʒɪn] sich (etwas) vorstellen °**II U1,** 11
important [ɪm'pɔ:tnt] wichtig; einflussreich **II U6,** 74

English – German

impression [ɪm'preʃn] Eindruck °**II U4,** 57
in [ɪn] in, auf; herein **I U1,** 10
in fact [ɪn 'fækt] in der Tat, genau genommen **II U7,** 94
in front of [ɪn 'frʌnt‿əv] vor **I U3,** 49
in the end [ɪn ði:‿'end] schließlich, zum Schluss **II U6,** 80
Indian ['ɪndiən] indisch **II U4,** 49
information [ˌɪnfə'meɪʃn] Information/ Informationen **I LUC,** 52
information centre [ɪnfə'meɪʃn ˌsentə] Informationszentrum **I LUC,** 52
inside [ɪn'saɪd] innen, drin, nach drinnen **I U5,** 75
instruction [ɪn'strʌkʃn] Instruktion, Anweisung °**II U4,** 59
interested ['ɪntrəstɪd] interessiert **II U1,** 18
interesting ['ɪntrəstɪŋ] interessant **II U4,** 51
Internet ['ɪntənet] Internet **II U1,** 14
to surf the Internet [ˌsɜ:f ði‿'ɪntənet] im Internet surfen **II U1,** 14
interview ['ɪntəvju:] Interview **II U1,** 17
to **interview** ['ɪntəvju:] interviewen **II U1,** 17
into ['ɪntə] in; in ... hinein **I U3,** 44
to get into [get‿'ɪntə] einsteigen in *(Auto)* **I U5,** 75
introduction [ˌɪntrə'dʌkʃn] Einleitung °**II U4,** 55
invitation [ˌɪnvɪ'teɪʃn] Einladung **I U5,** 70
to **invite** [ɪn'vaɪt] einladen **I U5,** 68
Irish ['aɪrɪʃ] irisch **II U7,** 90
to **iron** [aɪən] bügeln **II U7,** 90
irregular [ɪ'regjələ] unregelmäßig °**II U2,** 26
island ['aɪlənd] Insel **II U6,** 82
it [ɪt] es **I U1,** 12
Italian [ɪ'tæliən] italienisch; Italiener/ Italienerin **I U2,** 29

J

jacket ['dʒækɪt] Jacke **I U6,** 86
jam [dʒæm] Marmelade **I U7,** 94
January ['dʒænjuri] Januar **I U5,** 70
jazz [dʒæz] Jazz **II U3,** 45
jealous (of) ['dʒeləs] eifersüchtig, neidisch (auf) **II U3,** 45
job [dʒɒb] Arbeitsstelle, Job **II U6,** 80
to **jog** [dʒɒg] joggen **II U4,** 52
joke [dʒəʊk] Witz **I U1,** 20
to **joke** [dʒəʊk] scherzen, Witze machen **I U6,** 82
journey ['dʒɜ:ni] Reise, Fahrt **II U7,** 90
judge [dʒʌdʒ] Richter, Kampfrichter **II U5,** 70
July [dʒʊ'laɪ] Juli **I U5,** 70
long **jump** ['lɒŋ ˌdʒʌmp] Weitsprung **I U7,** 90
to **jump** [dʒʌmp] springen **II U2,** 30
to jump up [dʒʌmp‿'ʌp] hochspringen, aufspringen **II U6,** 82
June [dʒu:n] Juni **I U5,** 70
just [dʒʌst] nur, gerade, einfach **I U2,** 30

K

kangaroo [ˌkæŋgər'u:] Känguru °**II U3,** 46
*to **keep** [ki:p] (be)halten **II U4,** 55
Keep out! [ki:p‿'aʊt] Eintritt verboten! **I U2,** 26
key [ki:] Schlüssel **II U5,** 67
to **kick** [kɪk] treten **I U5,** 74
kid [kɪd] Kind **I U3,** 44
kilo (kg) ['kɪləʊ] Kilo(gramm) **II U4,** 54
kind [kaɪnd] Art, Sorte °**II U4,** 50
PE **kit** [ˌpi:‿'i: kɪt] Sportzeug **II U1,** 10
kitchen ['kɪtʃɪn] Küche **I LUA,** 24
knee [ni:] Knie **II U3,** 41
knife, knives *(pl)* [naɪf; naɪvz] Messer **II U4,** 50
knight [naɪt] Ritter **II U2,** 22
knock [nɒk] Klopfen, Schlag **I U2,** 34
*to **know** [nəʊ] wissen, kennen **I U4,** 58

L

lab(oratory) [læb; lə'bɒrətri] Labor **II U2,** 23
lamb [læm] Lamm, Lammfleisch **II U4,** 49
land [lænd] Land **I LUB,** 38
language ['læŋgwɪdʒ] Sprache **I U2,** 29
lantern ['læntən] Laterne **I U7,** 90
laptop ['læptɒp] Laptop **I U2,** 34
large [lɑ:dʒ] groß, riesig **I U5,** 66
lassi ['lasɪ] Lassi *(Jogurtgetränk)* **II U4,** 49
last [lɑ:st] letzte/letzter/letztes **I U7,** 90
last night [lɑ:st 'naɪt] gestern Abend/ Nacht **II U3,** 37
late [leɪt] spät, zu spät, verspätet **I U1,** 16
later ['leɪtə] später **I U2,** 30
to **laugh** [lɑ:f] lachen **I U5,** 74
to laugh at ['lɑ:f‿ət] auslachen, sich lustig machen über **II U3,** 36
leader ['li:də] Führer/Führerin, Anführer/Anführerin **II U6,** 80
to **lean out** [li:n‿'aʊt] (sich) hinauslehnen **II U7,** 94
*to **learn** [lɜ:n] lernen **I U3,** 40; ; erfahren °**II U1,** 17
at **least** [ət 'li:st] wenigstens, mindestens **I U6,** 87
*to **leave** [li:v] lassen, verlassen, abfahren **I U3,** 43; ; (weg)gehen **II U1,** 18
left [left] linke/linker/linkes; links **I U4,** 55
Go left. [gəʊ 'left] Biege nach links ab. **I LUC,** 52
on the left [ɒn ðə 'left] links **I U2,** 28
to turn left/right [tɜ:n 'left/'raɪt] links/ rechts abbiegen **II U7,** 97
left [left] übrig **II U4,** 54
leg [leg] Bein **II U3,** 41
lemonade [ˌlemə'neɪd] Limonade **I U5,** 68
*to **lend** [lend] leihen **II U7,** 90
leprechaun ['leprəkɔ:n] Gnom, Kobold °**II U7,** 90
lesson ['lesn] Unterrichtsstunde **I U1,** 15
Let's . . . . [lets] Lasst uns . . . . **I U1,** 10
letter ['letə] Buchstabe, Brief **I U1,** 15
capital letter [ˌkæpɪtl 'letə] Großbuchstabe °**II U3,** 37
lettuce ['letɪs] Kopfsalat **II U4,** 54
life, lives *(pl)* [laɪf; laɪvz] Leben **II U3,** 42
light [laɪt] Licht **II U7,** 94
to **like** [laɪk] mögen, gern haben **I U3,** 44
I'd like to [ˌaɪd 'laɪk tə] ich würde gern **II U2,** 22
would like [wʊd 'laɪk] hätte gern, möchte gern **II U4,** 52
like [laɪk] wie **I U6,** 86
line [laɪn] Zeile, Text, Linie **I U3,** 43
lion ['laɪən] Löwe **II U5,** 68
lip balm ['lɪp bɑ:m] Lippenpflegestift **II U6,** 82
list [lɪst] Liste **I U5,** 68
to **listen** ['lɪsn] zuhören, anhören **I U1,** 11
little [lɪtl] klein **I U6,** 82
to **live** [lɪv] wohnen, leben **I U3,** 45
living room ['lɪvɪŋ rʊm] Wohnzimmer **I LUA,** 24
locker ['lɒkə] Schließfach **II U1,** 10
long [lɒŋ] lang **I U3,** 44

as long as [əz ˈlɒŋ‿əz] solange **I U7,** 94
long form [ˈlɒŋ fɔːm] Langform °**I U1,** 16
long jump [ˈlɒŋ ˌdʒʌmp] Weitsprung **I U7,** 90
look [lʊk] Blick, Aussehen **II U1,** 10
to give … a dirty look [ˌɡɪv‿ə dɜːti ˈlʊk] einen vernichtenden Blick zuwerfen °**II U1,** 10
to **look** [lʊk] sehen, schauen, aussehen **I U1,** 12
to look after [lʊk‿ˈɑːftə] sich kümmern um, aufpassen auf **II U1,** 14
to look at [ˈlʊk‿ət] ansehen **I U6,** 82
to look for [ˈlʊk fə] suchen **I U6,** 81
to look round [lʊk ˈraʊnd] sich umsehen **II U1,** 18
to look up [lʊk‿ˈʌp] (hin)aufschauen; nachschlagen **II U2,** 30
*to **lose** [luːz] verlieren **II U4,** 52
to get lost [ɡet ˈlɒst] verloren gehen, sich verirren **I U3,** 48
a **lot** [ə ˈlɒt] viel **II U1,** 15
a lot of [ə ˈlɒt‿əv] viel/viele, eine Menge **I U2,** 30
lots (of) [ˈlɒts‿əv] viel/viele **II U7,** 88
loud [laʊd] laut **II U7,** 91
love [lʌv] Herzliche Grüße *(am Briefende)*; Liebe **I U6,** 78
to **love** [lʌv] lieben, gern mögen **I U3,** 44
luck [lʌk] Glück **I U4,** 63
bad luck [ˌbæd ˈlʌk] Pech **I U4,** 63
Good luck! [ˌɡʊd ˈlʌk] Viel Glück! **I U4,** 63
lucky [ˈlʌki] glücklich **I U1,** 16
you're lucky [ˌjʊəˈlʌki] du hast Glück **I U1,** 16
luggage [ˈlʌɡɪdʒ] Gepäck **II U7,** 90
lunch [lʌntʃ] Mittagessen **I U1,** 18
lunchtime [ˈlʌntʃtaɪm] Mittag, Mittagszeit **I U1,** 19

M

mad [mæd] verrückt; wütend **II U1,** 18
magazine [mæɡəˈziːn] Zeitschrift, Magazin **I U2,** 33
main [meɪn] Haupt- °**II U4,** 49
*to **make** [meɪk] machen, tun **I U1,** 11
to make sure [meɪk ˈʃʊə] sichergehen **II U6,** 82
to make up [meɪk‿ˈʌp] erfinden, sich ausdenken **I U4,** 62
make-up [ˈmeɪkʌp] Make-up, Schminke **I U7,** 90
man, men *(pl)* [mæn; men] Mann **I U4,** 62
manager [ˈmænɪdʒə] Manager/ Managerin **I U2,** 26
adverb of **manner** [ˌædvɜːb‿əv ˈmænə] Adverb der Art und Weise °**II U7,** 90
many [ˈmeni] viele **I U5,** 68
how many [haʊ ˈmeni] wie viele **I U5,** 68
map [mæp] Stadtplan, Landkarte **I LUC,** 52
March [mɑːtʃ] März **I U5,** 70
mark [mɑːk] Fleck **I U2,** 30; ; Note *(in der Schule)* **II U3,** 44
to **mark** [mɑːk] markieren °**II U2,** 29
market [ˈmɑːkɪt] Markt **II U2,** 22
married to [ˈmærid tə] verheiratet mit **I U2,** 28
match [mætʃ] Spiel, Wettkampf **II U2,** 24
to **match** [mætʃ] zuordnen, zusammenfügen °**I U1,** 13
to match up [ˈmætʃ‿ʌp] zusammenfügen °**II U4,** 52
Maths [mæθs] Mathematik **II U1,** 10
***may** [meɪ] kann/könnte(n) vielleicht **II U4,** 55
May [meɪ] Mai **I U5,** 70
maybe [ˈmeɪbi] vielleicht **I U7,** 96
me [miː] mich, mir **I LUB,** 38
meal [miːl] Mahlzeit **II U4,** 52
*to **mean** [miːn] bedeuten, meinen **I U4,** 55
meaning [ˈmiːnɪŋ] Bedeutung °**I U7,** 98
media *(pl)* [ˈmiːdiə] Medien °**II U5,** 62
medium [ˈmiːdiəm] mittel **I U5,** 66
*to **meet** [miːt] treffen, sich treffen **I U3,** 45
meeting [ˈmiːtɪŋ] Treffen, Besprechung **II U1,** 12
menu [ˈmenjuː] Speisekarte, Menü **II U1,** 14
Meow! [miːˈaʊ] Miau! °**I U2,** 35
message [ˈmesɪdʒ] Nachricht **II U3,** 38
text message [ˈtekst ˌmesɪdʒ] SMS **I U6,** 80
mice *(pl)* [maɪs] Mäuse **I U3,** 45
microphone [ˈmaɪkrəfəʊn] Mikrofon **II U5,** 71
middle [ˈmɪdl] Mitte; Mittel- °**II U7,** 95
midnight [ˈmɪdnaɪt] Mitternacht **II U6,** 78
mile [maɪl] Meile *(brit. Längenmaß)* **II U6,** 74
milk [mɪlk] Milch **I U5,** 68
million [ˈmɪlɪən] Million **II U2,** 23
to **mime** [maɪm] pantomimisch darstellen °**I U6,** 81
miming game [ˈmaɪmɪŋ ɡeɪm] Pantomime °**I U6,** 81
mineral [ˈmɪnərəl] Mineral- **II U4,** 49 **II U4,** 49
minute [ˈmɪnɪt] Minute **I U4,** 64
to **miss** [mɪs] vermissen, fehlen; verpassen **II U6,** 76
to miss a turn [mɪs ə ˈtɜːn] einmal aussetzen °**II U6,** 79
Miss [mɪs] Frau *(Anrede)* **I U7,** 94
missing [ˈmɪsɪŋ] fehlend °**I U4,** 64
mobile [ˈməʊbaɪl] Handy, Mobiltelefon **I U1,** 11
moment [ˈməʊmənt] Moment, Augenblick **I U7,** 90
at the moment [ət ðə ˈməʊmənt] im Augenblick, momentan **I U7,** 90
Monday [ˈmʌndeɪ] Montag **I LUB,** 39
on Mondays [ɒn ˈmʌndeɪz] montags **I LUB,** 39
money [ˈmʌni] Geld **I U5,** 67
pocket money [ˈpɒkɪt ˌmʌni] Taschengeld **II U2,** 22
month [mʌnθ] Monat **I U5,** 70
moon [muːn] Mond **II U7,** 94
moor [mɔː] Hochmoor **II U6,** 74
more [mɔː] mehr **I U2,** 29
morning [ˈmɔːnɪŋ] Morgen, Vormittag **I U1,** 16
Good morning! [ˈɡʊd ˈmɔːnɪŋ] Guten Morgen! **I U1,** 16
in the morning [ˌɪn ðə ˈmɔːnɪŋ] morgens, am Morgen, vormittags **I U3,** 47
the next morning [ðə ˌnekst ˈmɔːnɪŋ] am nächsten Morgen **II U1,** 13
most [məʊst] das meiste, die meisten **I U3,** 44
mouse [maʊs] Maus **I U1,** 10
mouth [maʊθ] Mund **II U3,** 41
to **move** [muːv] (sich) bewegen; umziehen **II U6,** 78
MP3 [empiːˈθriː] MP3 **II U5,** 62
MP3 player [empiːˈθriː ˌpleɪə] MP3-Player **II U5,** 62
Mr [ˈmɪstə] Herr *(Anrede)* **I U1,** 12
Mrs [ˈmɪsɪz] Frau *(Anrede)* **I U1,** 12
much [mʌtʃ] viel **I U5,** 66
How much are … ? [ˌhaʊ ˈmʌtʃ‿ɑː] Wie viel kosten … ? **I U5,** 66
How much is … ? [ˌhaʊ ˈmʌtʃ‿ɪz] Wie viel kostet … ? **I U5,** 66

English – German

mum [mʌm] Mama, Mutti **I LUA,** 25
museum [mju:'zi:əm] Museum **I LUC,** 52
music ['mju:zɪk] Musik **I U2,** 34
*__must__ [mʌst] müssen **I U7,** 94
my [maɪ] mein/meine **I U1,** 10
My God! [maɪ 'gɒd] Mein Gott! **II U6,** 82
My name is .... [maɪ 'neɪm‿ɪz] Ich heiße .... **I U1,** 10

N

name [neɪm] Name **I U1,** 10
My name is .... [maɪ 'neɪm‿ɪz] Ich heiße .... **I U1,** 10
What's your name? [ˌwɒts jə 'neɪm] Wie heißt du?' **I U1,** 11
national ['næʃnl] national **II U6,** 82
near [nɪə] in der Nähe von, nahe **I LUC,** 53
to **need** [ni:d] brauchen, benötigen, müssen **II U1,** 21
neighbour ['neɪbə] Nachbar/Nachbarin **II U7,** 90
nervous ['nɜ:vəs] nervös, aufgeregt **II U5,** 71
never ['nevə] nie, niemals **I U3,** 44
new [nju:] neu **I U1,** 10
newsagent ['nju:sˌeɪdʒənt] Zeitschriftenhändler/ Zeitschriftenhändlerin **I LUC,** 52
next [nekst] nächste/nächster/ nächstes **I U5,** 69; als Nächstes °**II U1,** 19
next to ['nekst tə] neben **I U2,** 28
the next morning [ðə ˌnekst 'mɔ:nɪŋ] am nächsten Morgen **II U1,** 18
nice [naɪs] nett **I U1,** 12; ; schön **II U4,** 54
night [naɪt] Nacht **I U3,** 44
at night [ət 'naɪt] nachts **II U3,** 47
last night [lɑ:st 'naɪt] gestern Abend/Nacht **II U3,** 37
night nurse ['naɪt nɜ:s] Nachtschwester **I U3,** 47
no [nəʊ] nein, nicht; kein/keine **I U1,** 12
no one ['nəʊwʌn] niemand **II U2,** 30
noise [nɔɪz] Geräusch, Lärm **I U2,** 35
none [nʌn] keiner/keine **II U7,** 88
normal ['nɔ:ml] normal **I U3,** 44
north [nɔ:θ] Norden **I U4,** 55
nose [nəʊz] Nase **II U3,** 41
not [nɒt] nicht **I U1,** 16
not ... yet [jet] noch nicht **II U5,** 66
note [nəʊt] Notiz, Anmerkung **II U1,** 11
sick note ['sɪk ˌnəʊt] Krankmeldung **II U2,** 28
to take notes [teɪk 'nəʊts] sich Notizen machen °**II U4,** 55
nothing ['nʌθɪŋ] nichts **II U4,** 50
November [nəʊ'vembə] November **I U5,** 70
now [naʊ] jetzt, nun **I U1,** 20
right now [ˌraɪt 'naʊ] jetzt gleich, in diesem Augenblick **I U7,** 92
number ['nʌmbə] Nummer, Zahl **I U1,** 11
phone number ['fəʊn ˌnʌmbə] Telefonnummer **I U1,** 11
nurse [nɜ:s] Krankenschwester, Krankenpfleger **I U3,** 47
night nurse ['naɪt nɜ:s] Nachtschwester **I U3,** 47
*to be **nuts** about [bi: ˌnʌts‿ə'baʊt] verrückt nach ... sein **II U1,** 18

O

observatory [əb'zɜ:vətri] Observatorium, Sternwarte **I U5,** 73
October [ɒk'təʊbə] Oktober **I U5,** 70
odd one out [ɒd wʌn‿'aʊt] das nicht dazu passende (Wort) **II U5,** 72
of [ɒv; əv] von **I U2,** 26
of course [əv 'kɔ:s] natürlich, selbstverständlich **I U1,** 19
off [ɒf] herunter, ab, weg von **II U3,** 36
to get off [get‿'ɒf] aussteigen aus **I U4,** 59
to **offer** ['ɒfə] anbieten °**II U6,** 77
office ['ɒfɪs] Büro **II U2,** 31
often ['ɒfn] oft **I U3,** 44
oh [əʊ] oh °**I U1,** 12
OK [əʊ'keɪ] OK **I U1,** 12
is OK with us [ɪz‿əʊ'keɪ wɪð‿ʌs] ist uns recht **I U6,** 78
We're OK. [ˌwɪər‿əʊ'keɪ] Es geht uns gut. **I U6,** 83
old [əʊld] alt **I U1,** 11
How old are you? [haʊ‿'əʊld‿ɑ: ju:] Wie alt bist du? **I U1,** 11
on [ɒn] auf, an **I U1,** 14
on foot [ɒn 'fʊt] zu Fuß **I U4,** 57
on Mondays [ɒn 'mʌndeɪz] montags **I LUB,** 39
on the air [ˌɒn ði‿'eə] auf Sendung **II U4,** 55
on the bus [ˌɒn ðə 'bʌs] im Bus **II U1,** 18
on the left [ɒn ðə 'left] links **I U2,** 28
on the right [ɒn ðə 'raɪt] rechts **I U2,** 28
to be on [bi:‿'ɒn] an der Reihe sein; im Gange sein, laufen **II U5,** 70; an sein, brennen *(Licht)* **II U7,** 94
once [wʌnts] einmal, einst **II U3,** 36
at once [ət 'wʌnts] sofort, plötzlich **II U7,** 94
one day [wʌn 'deɪ] eines Tages **II U3,** 36
only ['əʊnli] nur, bloß, erst **I U2,** 26
only child ['əʊnli ˌtʃaɪld] Einzelkind **I U2,** 26
onto ['ɒntu:; 'ɒntə] auf ... hinauf **II U1,** 19
Oops! [u:ps] Huch! °**I U1,** 20
to **open** ['əʊpən] öffnen, aufmachen **I U1,** 19
open ['əʊpn] offen, geöffnet **II U2,** 23
opinion [ə'pɪnjən] Meinung °**II U4,** 51
opposite ['ɒpəzɪt] gegenüber °**II U4,** 49
or [ɔ:] oder **I U1,** 11
orange ['ɒrɪndʒ] Orange **II U4,** 54
order ['ɔ:də] Reihenfolge, Ordnung °**I U1,** 21
to **order** ['ɔ:də] bestellen **II U4,** 49
to **organize** ['ɔ:gənaɪz] organisieren **I U7,** 90
other ['ʌðə] andere/anderer/anderes **I U7,** 91
each other [ˌi:tʃ‿'ʌðə] sich gegenseitig **II U1,** 19
our ['aʊə] unser/unsere **I U2,** 26
out [aʊt] heraus, draußen, außerhalb **I U3,** 42
Keep out! [ki:p‿'aʊt] Eintritt verboten! **I U2,** 26
out and about ['aʊt‿nd‿ə'baʊt] unterwegs °**I U4,** 54
out of ['aʊt‿əv] aus ... heraus **I U3,** 49
to get out [get‿'aʊt] aussteigen **I U6,** 86
to sort out [sɔ:t‿'aʊt] klären, regeln *(ein Problem)* **I U2,** 30
to take out [teɪk‿'aʊt] herausnehmen **I U3,** 42
outside [aʊt'saɪd] außerhalb, draußen, nach draußen **I U2,** 30
oven ['ʌvn] Backofen **I U3,** 42
over ['əʊvə] über **I U2,** 26; vorbei, vorüber **II U5,** 70
over there [ˌəʊvə 'ðeə] da drüben **I U5,** 66
to come over [kʌm‿'əʊvə] herüberkommen **I U2,** 27
barn **owl** ['bɑ:n‿əʊl] Schleiereule **II U7,** 94

own [əʊn] eigener/eigene/eigenes **II U6,** 76
owner ['əʊnə] Besitzer/Besitzerin **II U5,** 71

P

to **pack** [pæk] packen **I U6,** 80
packet ['pækɪt] Päckchen, Paket **I U5,** 68
page [peɪdʒ] Seite **I U1,** 19
paint [peɪnt] Farbe **II U3,** 40
to **paint** [peɪnt] malen, anmalen **I U7,** 90
pair [peə] Paar °**I U1,** 22
to **panic** ['pænɪk] paniken, sich aufregen **II U5,** 70
panther ['pæntθə] Panter **II U2,** 25
parents ['peərənts] Eltern **I U2,** 26
park [pɑ:k] Park **I U3,** 40
part [pɑ:t] Teil **II U3,** 47; Rolle **II U5,** 70
partner ['pɑ:tnə] Partner/Partnerin **I U1,** 15
party ['pɑ:ti] Party, Feier **I U5,** 68
to have a party [ˌhæv‿ə 'pɑ:ti] eine Party feiern **I U5,** 68
to **pass** [pɑ:s] weitergeben, herüberreichen **II U1,** 18
past [pɑ:st] Vergangenheit **II U1,** 13
past [pɑ:st] vorbei, vorüber **I U7,** 97; nach *(Uhrzeit)* **II U1,** 12
half past (two) ['hɑ:f pɑ:st] halb (drei) **I U3,** 40
path [pɑ:θ] Pfad, Weg **II U4,** 56
PC [ˌpi:'si:] PC **II U5,** 63
pea [pi:] Erbse **II U4,** 54
peace [pi:s] Friede **II U7,** 88
pear [peə] Birne **II U4,** 54
pen [pen] Füller **I U1,** 14
pence *(pl)* [pents] Pence *(Währung)* **I U5,** 67
pencil ['pensl] Bleistift **I U1,** 14
pencil case ['pensl ˌkeɪs] Mäppchen **I U1,** 14
penknife, penknives *(pl)* ['pennaɪf; 'pennaɪvz] Taschenmesser **I U6,** 84
people ['pi:pl] Leute, Menschen **I U2,** 29
per [pɜ:] pro °**I LUA,** 24
person ['pɜ:sn] Person **II U3,** 42
phone [fəʊn] Telefon **I U1,** 11
phone call ['fəʊn ˌkɔ:l] (Telefon)anruf °**II U4,** 57
phone number ['fəʊn ˌnʌmbə] Telefonnummer **I U1,** 11
to **phone** [fəʊn] anrufen, telefonieren **I U2,** 33
photo ['fəʊtəʊ] Foto **II U5,** 64
phrase [freɪz] Redewendung, Ausdruck °**I U1,** 19
physical ['fɪzɪkl] physisch, körperlich **II U1,** 10
Physical Education (PE) [ˌfɪzɪkl‿edʒʊ'keɪʃn] Sport *(Schulfach)* **II U1,** 10
to **pick** [pɪk] pflücken, auswählen **I U6,** 78
to pick up [pɪk‿'ʌp] aufheben, abholen **II U1,** 18
picture ['pɪktʃə] Bild **I U1,** 14
to take pictures [teɪk 'pɪktʃəz] fotografieren, Fotos machen **II U5,** 62
pig [pɪg] Schwein **I U6,** 82
piggy bank ['pɪgi bæŋk] Sparschwein **II U2,** 23
pink [pɪŋk] pink, rosa **I LUA,** 24
pizza ['pi:tsə] Pizza **I U5,** 68
place [pleɪs] Platz, Stelle, Ort **I U2,** 26
plan [plæn] Plan **II U5,** 66
to **plan** [plæn] planen **II U4,** 52
plane [pleɪn] Flugzeug **II U2,** 23
plant [plɑ:nt] Pflanze **II U6,** 74
plate [pleɪt] Teller **II U4,** 50
play [pleɪ] Theaterstück, Spiel **I U7,** 90
to **play** [pleɪ] spielen **I U1,** 14
CD **player** [ˌsi:'di: ˌpleɪə] CD-Player **II U4,** 56
DVD **player** [ˌdi:vi:di: 'pleɪə] DVD-Player **II U5,** 62
playground ['pleɪgraʊnd] Schulhof, Spielplatz **I U1,** 18
please [pli:z] bitte **I U1,** 19
*to be **pleased** with [bi: 'pli:zd wɪð] zufrieden sein mit **I U6,** 87
plural ['plʊərl] Plural, Mehrzahl **I U6,** 83
pocket ['pɒkɪt] Hosen-/Jackentasche **II U2,** 22
pocket money ['pɒkɪt ˌmʌni] Taschengeld **II U2,** 22
point [pɔɪnt] Punkt **II U4,** 53
to **point** [pɔɪnt] zeigen °**I U1,** 18
police [pə'li:s] Polizei **I U6,** 87
policeman, policemen *(pl)* [pə'li:smən; pə'li:smen] Polizist **II U2,** 31
Polish ['pəʊlɪʃ] polnisch **I U2,** 29
polite [pə'laɪt] höflich **II U3,** 39
pony ['pəʊni] Pony **II U6,** 74
popular ['pɒpjələ] populär, beliebt **II U2,** 23
pork [pɔ:k] Schweinefleisch **II U4,** 49
postcard ['pəʊstkɑ:d] Postkarte **I U6,** 78
poster ['pəʊstə] Poster, Plakat **I U1,** 11
pot [pɒt] Topf **II U7,** 90
potato, potatoes *(pl)* [pə'teɪtəʊ] Kartoffel **II U4,** 54
pound (£) [paʊnd] Pfund *(Währung)* **I U5,** 66
pound (lb) [paʊnd] Pfund *(Gewicht)* **II U4,** 52
power ['paʊə] Kraft, Stärke, Macht **II U6,** 74
to **practise** ['præktɪs] üben, proben, praktizieren **II U5,** 66
present ['preznt] Geschenk **I U5,** 69; Gegenwart, Präsens °**II U2,** 26
to **present** [prɪ'zent] präsentieren °**II U6,** 79
president ['prezɪdnt] Präsident/ Präsidentin **II U3,** 43
to **press** [pres] drücken, pressen **II U7,** 95
price [praɪs] Preis **I U7,** 95
to **print** [prɪnt] drucken **II U5,** 64
probably ['prɒbəbli] wahrscheinlich **II U7,** 88
problem ['prɒbləm] Problem, Schwierigkeit **I U1,** 20
project ['prɒdʒekt] Projekt **I U2,** 34
promise ['prɒmɪs] Versprechen °**II U6,** 77
to **promise** ['prɒmɪs] versprechen **II U6,** 77
pudding ['pʊdɪŋ] Pudding; Nachtisch **II U4,** 49
to **pull** [pʊl] ziehen **II U4,** 57
pupil ['pju:pl] Schüler/Schülerin **I U1,** 10
purple ['pɜ:pl] lila, violett **I LUA,** 24
to **push** [pʊʃ] stoßen, schieben, drücken **II U3,** 36
*to **put** [pʊt] setzen, stellen, legen **I U3,** 42
to put down [pʊt 'daʊn] auflegen *(Telefon)*; hinlegen, hinstellen °**II U7,** 89
to put in [pʊt‿'ɪn] einsetzen **II U7,** 95
to put on [pʊt‿'ɒn] anziehen, aufsetzen **I U6,** 81; auftragen *(Make-up)* **II U5,** 71
to put up [pʊt‿'ʌp] aufstellen, aufbauen **I U6,** 84
puzzle ['pʌzl] Rätsel, Puzzle °**I U1,** 15
crossword (puzzle) ['krɒswɜ:d 'pʌzl] Kreuzworträtsel °**I U5,** 71

Q

quarter past ['kwɔ:tə pɑ:st] Viertel nach **I U3,** 42

quarter to ['kwɔ:tə tə] Viertel vor **I U3,** 42
queen [kwi:n] Königin **II U5,** 62
question ['kwestʃn] Frage **I U2,** 31
questionnaire [ˌkwestʃə'neə] Fragebogen °**II U4,** 53
quick [kwɪk] schnell **I U6,** 86
quiet [kwaɪət] Ruhe, Stille **II U7,** 88
quiet ['kwaɪət] ruhig, still, leise **I U6,** 78
quiz [kwɪz] Quiz, Rätsel °**I U1,** 13

R

race [reɪs] Wettlauf, Rennen **I U7,** 92
to run a race [ˌrʌn‿ə 'reɪs] einen Wettlauf machen **I U7,** 92
radio ['reɪdiəʊ] Radio **I U2,** 33
radio show ['reɪdiəʊ ˌʃəʊ] Radiosendung **I U2,** 33
rain [reɪn] Regen **II U6,** 78
to **rain** [reɪn] regnen **I U4,** 62
rainy ['reɪni] regnerisch, verregnet **I U6,** 79
rap [ræp] Rap **I U1,** 15
to **rap** [ræp] rappen **I U3,** 40
I'd **rather** [aɪd 'rɑ:ðə] ich würde lieber **II U2,** 22
to **reach** [ri:tʃ] erreichen **II U6,** 78
*to **read** [ri:d] lesen **I LUB,** 38
ready ['redi] fertig, bereit **II U4,** 50
to get ready [get 'redi] sich vorbereiten **II U5,** 68
real [rɪəl] echt, richtig, wirklich **II U3,** 38
really ['rɪəli] wirklich **I U2,** 34
recipe ['resɪpi:] Rezept **I U7,** 94
to **record** [rɪ'kɔ:d] aufnehmen; aufzeichnen **II U5,** 63
red [red] rot **I LUA,** 24
to go red [gəʊ red] rot werden **II U1,** 11
registration [ˌredʒɪ'streɪʃn] Registrierung, Erfassung **II U1,** 10
to **rehearse** [rɪ'hɜ:s] proben *(ein Theaterstück)* **I U7,** 90
religious [rɪ'lɪdʒəs] religiös **II U1,** 12
Religious Education (RE) [rɪˌlɪdʒəs‿edʒʊ'keɪʃn] Religionsunterricht **II U1,** 12
to **remember** [rɪ'membə] sich erinnern (an), sich merken **I U3,** 49
to **report** [rɪ'pɔ:t] berichten °**II U4,** 51
reporter [rɪ'pɔ:tə] Reporter/Reporterin **I U7,** 92
rescue ['reskju:] Rettung °**II U6,** 82
to **rescue** ['reskju:] retten **II U6,** 83
restaurant ['restrɒnt] Restaurant **II U4,** 55
revision [rɪ'vɪʒn] Wiederholung °**I U2,** 32
*to **rewrite** [ˌri:'raɪt] noch einmal schreiben °**II U4,** 58
rhyme [raɪm] Reim °**I LUA,** 25
rhyming ['raɪmɪŋ] (sich) reimend °**II U4,** 58
rice [raɪs] Reis **II U4,** 49
*to **ride** [raɪd] fahren, reiten **I LUB,** 38
right [raɪt] richtig, korrekt **I U1,** 13; rechter/rechte/rechtes; rechts **I U4,** 55
Go right. [gəʊ 'raɪt] Biege nach rechts ab. **I LUC,** 52
on the right [ɒn ðə 'raɪt] rechts **I U2,** 28
right away [raɪt‿ə'weɪ] sofort, gleich **II U4,** 57
right now [ˌraɪt 'naʊ] jetzt gleich, in diesem Augenblick **I U7,** 92
to be right [bi: 'raɪt] Recht haben **II U4,** 56
to get … right [get … 'raɪt] richtig machen **II U3,** 44
to turn left/right [tɜ:n 'left/'raɪt] links/rechts abbiegen **II U7,** 97
*to **ring** [rɪŋ] klingeln **I U5,** 75
The bell rings. [ðə 'bel rɪŋz] Es klingelt. **II U4,** 50
ice **rink** ['aɪs rɪŋk] Eis-/Schlittschuhbahn **II U2,** 23
*to **rise** [raɪz] steigen, wachsen, zunehmen **II U6,** 78
river ['rɪvə] Fluss **I LUC,** 52
road [rəʊd] Straße, Landstraße **I LUC,** 52
role [rəʊl] Rolle **II U1,** 10
roof [ru:f] Dach **I U2,** 26
room [ru:m; rʊm] Zimmer, Raum, Platz **I U1,** 16
dining room ['daɪnɪŋ rʊm] Esszimmer, Speisesaal **I LUA,** 24
living room ['lɪvɪŋ rʊm] Wohnzimmer **I LUA,** 24
RSVP [ˌɑ: es vi: 'pi:] um Antwort wird gebeten °**I U5,** 70
rubber ['rʌbə] Radiergummi **I U1,** 14
rubber boots (pl) [ˌrʌbə 'bu:ts] Gummistiefel **II U6,** 74
rubbish ['rʌbɪʃ] Abfall, Abfälle, Müll **I U6,** 84; Unsinn **II U7,** 94
rule [ru:l] Regel, Vorschrift **I U3,** 43
ruler ['ru:lə] Lineal **I U1,** 14
run [rʌn] Lauf **II U4,** 57
*to **run** [rʌn] rennen, laufen **I U3,** 48
to run a race [ˌrʌn‿ə 'reɪs] einen Wettlauf machen **I U7,** 92
to run away [rʌn‿ə'weɪ] wegrennen **I U3,** 48
runner ['rʌnə] Läufer/Läuferin **I U7,** 92
Russian ['rʌʃn] russisch; Russe/Russin **I U2,** 29

S

sad [sæd] traurig, bedauerlich **II U1,** 19
salad ['sæləd] Salat **II U4,** 49
same [seɪm] derselbe/dieselbe/dasselbe °**II U1,** 11
sandwich ['sænwɪdʒ] Sandwich, belegtes Brot **I U1,** 14
Saturday ['sætədeɪ] Samstag **I U2,** 34
sausage ['sɒsɪdʒ] Wurst, Würstchen **II U4,** 49
to **save** [seɪv] retten; sparen **II U6,** 80
*to **say** [seɪ] sagen, sprechen **I U1,** 11
It said … . [ɪt 'sed] Es lautete … . **II U2,** 30
What does it say? [ˌwɒt dʌz‿ɪt 'seɪ] Was steht da? **II U3,** 44
scared [skeəd] verängstigt **I U2,** 35
I'm scared. [aɪm 'skeəd] Ich habe Angst. **II U3,** 44
scary ['skeəri] unheimlich, gruselig **II U7,** 95
school [sku:l] Schule **I U1,** 10
school bag ['sku:l bæg] Schultasche, Schulranzen **I U1,** 14
Science ['saɪənts] Wissenschaft, Naturwissenschaft **II U1,** 10
scone [skɒn] Scone *(Gebäck)* **I U7,** 94
Scottish ['skɒtɪʃ] schottisch **II U3,** 36
sea [si:] Meer **II U7,** 88
season ['si:zn] Jahreszeit, Saison **I U6,** 79
seat [si:t] Sitz, Sitzplatz **II U2,** 23
second ['seknd] Sekunde **I U2,** 30
*to **see** [si:] sehen **I U2,** 33; ; besuchen **II U1,** 19
See you! ['si: jə] Bis dann! Bis … . **I U5,** 70
to see a doctor [si: ə 'dɒktə] zum Arzt gehen **II U4,** 52
*to **sell** [sel] verkaufen **I U7,** 90
*to **send** [send] schicken **I U6,** 80
to send in [send‿'ɪn] einschicken **II U5,** 64
sentence ['sentənts] Satz °**I U1,** 13

September [sep'tembə] September **I U5,** 70
service ['sɜ:vɪs] Service, Dienst **II U6,** 83
*to **set** [set] stellen, einstellen **II U7,** 90
to set off [set 'ɒf] auslösen **II U7,** 95
to set the table [ˌset ðə 'teɪbl] Tisch decken **II U4,** 50
she [ʃi:] sie **I U1,** 12
shed [ʃed] Schuppen **I U2,** 26
sheep, sheep *(pl)* [ʃi:p] Schaf/Schafe **I U6,** 78
shelf, shelves *(pl)* [ʃelf; ʃelvz] Regal, Regalbrett **I U2,** 30
ship [ʃɪp] Schiff **I U4,** 54
shirt [ʃɜ:t] Hemd **I U3,** 44
shoe [ʃu:] Schuh **I U1,** 12
shop [ʃɒp] Laden, Geschäft **I U2,** 26
shop assistant ['ʃɒp əˌsɪstnt] Verkäufer/Verkäuferin **II U5,** 67
sports shop ['spɔ:ts ʃɒp] Sportgeschäft **I U5,** 66
shopping ['ʃɒpɪŋ] Einkaufen, Einkauf **I U5,** 66
short [ʃɔ:t] kurz **I U4,** 55
shorts *(pl)* [ʃɔ:ts] Shorts, kurze Hose **II U1,** 10
***should** [ʃʊd] sollte/sollten **II U4,** 52
to **shout** [ʃaʊt] schreien, rufen **I U1,** 15
show [ʃəʊ] Show, Sendung, Schau **I U2,** 33
radio show ['reɪdiəʊ ˌʃəʊ] Radiosendung **I U2,** 33
*to **show** [ʃəʊ] zeigen **I U4,** 65
shower ['ʃaʊə] Regenguss; Dusche **II U6,** 74
to **shuffle** ['ʃʌfl] mischen **°II U6,** 79
shy [ʃaɪ] schüchtern **°II U3,** 46
sick [sɪk] krank **II U3,** 46
sick note ['sɪk ˌnəʊt] Krankmeldung **II U2,** 28
to feel sick [fi:l 'sɪk] Übelkeit verspüren **II U5,** 68
side [saɪd] Seite **°II U3,** 46
sign [saɪn] Schild, Zeichen **I U2,** 26
to **sign** [saɪn] unterschreiben **II U5,** 66
signal ['sɪgnl] Signal **II U2,** 26
silly ['sɪli] dumm; Dummkopf **II U1,** 11
*to **sing** [sɪŋ] singen **I U2,** 33
singer ['sɪŋə] Sänger/Sängerin **II U1,** 14
sister ['sɪstə] Schwester **I LUA,** 25
half-sister ['hɑ:fˌsɪstə] Halbschwester **I U2,** 26
*to **sit** [sɪt] sitzen **I U3,** 48
to sit down [sɪt 'daʊn] sich setzen, sich hinsetzen **I U1,** 19
to sit with ['sɪt wɪθ] sich setzen zu **I U5,** 74
to **skate** [skeɪt] Inlineskates fahren, skaten **I LUB,** 38
skateboard ['skeɪtbɔ:d] Skateboard **I U4,** 54
skates *(pl)* [skeɪts] Inlineskates **I U4,** 54
skill [skɪl] Fertigkeit; Geschick **°II U1,** 11
skirt [skɜ:t] Rock **II U1,** 10
sky [skaɪ] Himmel **II U7,** 94
*to **sleep** [sli:p] schlafen **I U3,** 46
sleeping bag ['sli:pɪŋ ˌbæg] Schlafsack **I U6,** 84
sleepy ['sli:pi] schläfrig, verschlafen **II U7,** 94
slow [sləʊ] langsam **I U2,** 34
small [smɔ:l] klein **I U2,** 26
to **smile** [smaɪl] lächeln **I U3,** 43
snack [snæk] Imbiss, Snack **II U4,** 55
snow [snəʊ] Schnee **II U6,** 79
to **snow** [snəʊ] schneien **II U6,** 79
snowy ['snəʊi] verschneit **I U6,** 79
so [səʊ] so, also, deshalb **I U2,** 26
soap [səʊp] Seifenoper, Seife **I U7,** 97
sofa ['səʊfə] Sofa, Couch **I LUA,** 25
soft [sɒft] leise; weich, sanft **II U7,** 94
some [sʌm] einige; etwas **II U1,** 13
someone ['sʌmwʌn] jemand **II U5,** 70
something ['sʌmθɪŋ] etwas **II U4,** 56
sometimes ['sʌmtaɪmz] manchmal **I U3,** 44
somewhere ['sʌmweə] irgendwo **II U4,** 57
song [sɒŋ] Lied **I U2,** 33
soon [su:n] bald **I U6,** 78
sorry ['sɒri] Tut mir Leid. Entschuldigung. **I U1,** 12
I'm sorry about … . [aɪm 'sɒri əˌbaʊt] Es tut mir Leid wegen … . **°II U3,** 39
The bullies say they are sorry. [ðə ˌbʊliz seɪ ðeɪ ə 'sɒri] Die Rabauken sagen, dass es ihnen Leid tut. **°II U3,** 45
to **sort** [sɔ:t] sortieren **°I U1,** 21
to sort out [sɔ:t 'aʊt] klären, regeln *(ein Problem)* **I U2,** 30
sound [saʊnd] Ton, Geräusch, Klang **I U6,** 85
soup [su:p] Suppe **II U1,** 15
sour ['saʊə] sauer **II U4,** 49
south [saʊθ] Süden **I U4,** 55
southwest [ˌsaʊθ'west] Südwesten **II U6,** 78
spaghetti [spə'geti] Spaghetti **II U1,** 13
*to **speak** [spi:k] sprechen **I U4,** 62
*to **spell** [spel] buchstabieren **I U4,** 60
spelling ['spelɪŋ] Orthographie, Rechtschreibung **°II U3,** 43
*to **spend** [spend] verbringen, ausgeben **I U6,** 83
spicy ['spaɪsi] würzig, pikant **II U4,** 49
sponge [spʌndʒ] Schwamm **I U7,** 90
spooky ['spu:ki] unheimlich **I U2,** 35
spoon [spu:n] Löffel **II U4,** 50
sport [spɔ:t] Sport **I U1,** 12
sports day ['spɔ:ts deɪ] Sportfest **I U7,** 90
sports field ['spɔ:ts fi:ld] Sportplatz **I U7,** 92
sports shop ['spɔ:ts ʃɒp] Sportgeschäft **I U5,** 66
to do sports [du: 'spɔ:ts] Sport treiben **I U7,** 92
spring [sprɪŋ] Frühling **I U6,** 78
stall [stɔ:l] Stand, Bude **I U7,** 90
stall holder ['stɔ:l ˌhəʊldə] Standbesitzer/Standbesitzerin **II U4,** 54
white elephant stall [ˌwaɪt 'elɪfənt stɔ:l] Trödelstand **I U7,** 96
star [stɑ:] Star; Stern **°II U5,** 63
word star ['wɜ:d stɑ:] Wortstern **°I U1,** 22
start [stɑ:t] Anfang, Beginn, Start **II U1,** 10
to **start** [stɑ:t] anfangen, starten **I U3,** 44
starter ['stɑ:tə] Vorspeise **II U4,** 49
station ['steɪʃn] Wache, Station, Bahnhof **I U6,** 87
to **stay** [steɪ] bleiben **I U4,** 60
to stay with ['steɪ wɪð] wohnen bei **I U6,** 78
*to **steal** [sti:l] stehlen **II U4,** 57
stepdad ['stepdæd] Stiefvater **I U2,** 26
stick [stɪk] Stock **II U2,** 26
still [stɪl] noch, immer noch **II U1,** 21
stomach ['stʌmək] Magen, Bauch **II U3,** 41
stone [stəʊn] Stein **II U6,** 82
stop [stɒp] Halt, Haltestelle **I LUC,** 52
bus stop ['bʌs ˌstɒp] Bushaltestelle **I LUC,** 52
to **stop** [stɒp] aufhören (mit), anhalten **I U3,** 42
to stop + -ing [stɒp] aufhören etw. zu tun **II U4,** 52
store [stɔ:] Kaufhaus, Geschäft, Laden **II U2,** 30
department store [dɪ'pɑ:tmənt stɔ:] Kaufhaus **I LUC,** 52
store detective ['stɔ: dɪˌtektɪv]

Kaufhausdetektiv/Kaufhausdetektivin **II U2,** 30
storm [stɔ:m] Sturm **II U6,** 81
stormy ['stɔ:mi] stürmisch **II U6,** 78
story ['stɔ:ri] Geschichte, Erzählung **I U1,** 21
strange [streɪndʒ] merkwürdig, seltsam **I U2,** 35
stream [stri:m] Bach **II U6,** 82
street [stri:t] Straße **I LUC,** 52
studio ['stju:diəʊ] Studio **I U2,** 33
to **study** ['stʌdi] studieren; lernen **II U6,** 74
stupid ['stju:pɪd] dumm, blöd **I U2,** 35
subject ['sʌbdʒɪkt] Schulfach; Thema **II U1,** 13
suddenly ['sʌdnli] plötzlich, auf einmal **I U2,** 35
suggestion [sə'dʒestʃn] Vorschlag, Anregung °**II U4,** 53
summer ['sʌmə] Sommer **I U6,** 79
summer fair ['sʌmə ˌfeə] Sommerfest **I U7,** 90
Sunday ['sʌndeɪ] Sonntag **I LUB,** 39
sunny ['sʌni] sonnig **I U6,** 79
suntan ['sʌntæn] Sonnenbräune **II U1,** 14
superlative [su:'pɜ:lətɪv] Superlativ **II U4,** 50
supermarket ['su:pəˌmɑ:kɪt] Supermarkt **I LUC,** 52
supper ['sʌpə] Abendessen **I U3,** 44
for supper [fə 'sʌpə] zum Abendessen **II U3,** 38
to have supper [hæv 'sʌpə] zu Abend essen **I U3,** 44
sure [ʃʊə] sicher **I U1,** 16
to make sure [meɪk 'ʃʊə] sichergehen **II U6,** 82
to **surf** [ˌsɜ:f] surfen, windsurfen **II U1,** 14
to surf the Internet [ˌsɜ:f ði‿'ɪntənet] im Internet surfen **II U1,** 14
surfing ['sɜ:fɪŋ] Wellenreiten, Surfen **II U1,** 14
surprised [sə'praɪzd] überrascht, erstaunt **II U1,** 18
surprising [sə'praɪzɪŋ] überraschend **II U7,** 96
survey ['sɜ:veɪ] Umfrage **I U4,** 56
swap [swɒp] Tausch **II U7,** 88
to **swap** [swɒp] tauschen **I LUB,** 38
sweatshirt ['swetʃɜ:t] Sweatshirt **II U1,** 10
sweet [swi:t] Bonbon, Süßigkeit **II U4,** 53
sweet [swi:t] süß **I LUA,** 24
*to **swim** [swɪm] schwimmen **I LUB,** 38
symbol ['sɪmbl] Symbol °**II U6,** 78

T

table ['teɪbl] Tisch **I U1,** 18
table-tennis ['teɪblˌtenɪs] Tischtennis **II U7,** 88
to set the table [ˌset ðə 'teɪbl] Tisch decken **II U4,** 50
*to **take** [teɪk] nehmen, mitnehmen, wegnehmen, bringen **I U3,** 42
to take home [ˌteɪk 'həʊm] nach Hause bringen **I U2,** 35
to take notes [teɪk 'nəʊts] sich Notizen machen °**II U4,** 55
to take out [teɪk‿'aʊt] herausnehmen **I U3,** 42
to take pictures [teɪk 'pɪktʃəz] fotografieren, Fotos machen **II U5,** 62
takeaway ['teɪkəweɪ] Restaurant mit Straßenverkauf; Essen zum Mitnehmen **II U4,** 48
to **talk** [tɔ:k] sprechen, reden **I U1,** 10
to talk to ['tɔ:k tə] sprechen mit, reden mit **II U2,** 28
tall [tɔ:l] groß, hoch **II U3,** 36
to **taste** [teɪst] schmecken **I U7,** 94
tasty ['teɪsti] schmackhaft **II U4,** 50
Pizza is tastier. ['pi:tsə ɪz ˌteɪstɪə] Pizza schmeckt besser. **II U4,** 50
tea [ti:] Tee, Abendessen **I U7,** 94
afternoon tea [ˌɑ:ftənu:n 'ti:] Nachmittagstee **I U7,** 94
*to **teach** [ti:tʃ] lehren **I LUB,** 38
teacher ['ti:tʃə] Lehrer/Lehrerin **I U1,** 12
team [ti:m] Mannschaft, Team **II U2,** 23
technical ['teknɪkl] technisch °**II U7,** 96
Technology [tek'nɒlədʒi] Technik **II U1,** 10
teen [ti:n] Jugendlicher/Jugendliche **II U6,** 80
*to **tell** [tel] erzählen, sagen **I U3,** 49
temperature ['temprətʃə] Temperatur **II U6,** 78
table-**tennis** ['teɪblˌtenɪs] Tischtennis **II U7,** 88
tent [tent] Zelt **I U6,** 84
term [tɜ:m] Trimester *(Einteilung des englischen Schuljahrs)* °**II U1,** 10
terrible ['terəbl] schrecklich, furchtbar **I U2,** 35
test [test] Test, Klassenarbeit **II U3,** 44
to **test** [test] testen, prüfen °**I U2,** 31
text [tekst] Text °**I U2,** 27
text message ['tekst ˌmesɪdʒ] SMS **I U6,** 80
than [ðæn] als **I U4,** 55
to **thank** [θæŋk] danken **I U4,** 60
thank you ['θæŋk‿ju:] danke **I U1,** 12
thanks [θæŋks] danke **II U2,** 26
that [ðæt] das, jenes **I U1,** 12
that (bad) ['ðæt bæd] so (schlimm) **II U2,** 24
that evening [ˌdæt‿'i:vnɪŋ] an diesem Abend **II U1,** 19
That's what I call .... [ˌðæts wɒt‿'aɪ ˌkɔ:l] Das nenne ich .... **II U1,** 14
that's why ['ðæts ˌwaɪ] deshalb **II U1,** 18
the [ðə; ði] der/die/das **I U1,** 11
their [ðeə] ihr/ihre **I U2,** 30
them [ðem] sie, ihnen **I U4,** 60
then [ðen] dann **I LUB,** 38
there [ðeə] dort, da **I U2,** 26
over there [ˌəʊvə 'ðeə] da drüben **I U5,** 66
there are [ðer‿'ɑ:] da sind, es gibt **I U2,** 32
there is [ðer‿'ɪz] da ist, es gibt **I U2,** 32
these [ði:z] diese, diese hier **I U6,** 84
they [ðeɪ] sie *(Mehrzahl)* **I U1,** 16
thing [θɪŋ] Sache, Ding **I U3,** 40
*to **think** [θɪŋk] denken **I U3,** 49; glauben **II U4,** 50
to think about ['θɪŋk‿əˌbaʊt] nachdenken über, denken an °**II U7,** 95
to think of ['θɪŋk‿əv] denken an °**II U3,** 39
third [θɜ:d] dritte/dritter/drittes **I U5,** 70
this [ðɪs] dies; diese/dieser/dieses **I U1,** 12
those [ðəʊz] diese dort, jene **I U6,** 84
thousand ['θaʊznd] tausend **II U2,** 23
through [θru:] durch **II U4,** 57
*to **throw** [θrəʊ] werfen **I U3,** 49
Thursday ['θɜ:zdeɪ] Donnerstag **I LUB,** 39
to **tick** [tɪk] abhaken °**II U5,** 65
ticket ['tɪkɪt] Ticket, Fahrschein, Eintrittskarte **I U7,** 90
tiger ['taɪgə] Tiger **I U2,** 26
time [taɪm] Zeit **I U2,** 30; ; Mal **II U1,** 18
to have a good time [ˌhæv‿ə gʊd 'taɪm] sich amüsieren **I U5,** 75
What's the time, please? [ˌwɒts ðə 'taɪm ˌpli:z] Wie viel Uhr ist es, bitte? **I U3,** 42

to **time** [taɪm] stoppen, die Zeit nehmen **I U7,** 92
timeline ['taɪmlaɪn] Zeitleiste °**I U4,** 63
timetable ['taɪmteɪbl] Stundenplan, Fahrplan **II U1,** 12
tiny ['taɪni] winzig **I LUA,** 25
tip [tɪp] Tipp **II U4,** 52
tired ['taɪəd] müde **II U3,** 38
dog-tired [ˌdɒg 'taɪəd] hundemüde **I U3,** 49
title ['taɪtl] Titel, Überschrift **II U3,** 42
to [tʊ; tə] zu, nach, bis **I U1,** 19
today [tə'deɪ] heute **I U2,** 29
toe [təʊ] Zeh **II U3,** 41
together [tə'geðə] zusammen, miteinander **I LUB,** 38
toilet ['tɔɪlɪt] Toilette **I U1,** 19
tomato, tomatoes *(pl)* [tə'mɑːtəʊ; tə'mɑːtəʊz] Tomate **I U5,** 68
tomorrow [tə'mɒrəʊ] morgen **II U1,** 18
tongue twister ['tʌŋ ˌtwɪstə] Zungenbrecher °**II U4,** 55
tonight [tə'naɪt] heute Abend, heute Nacht **I U6,** 84
too [tuː] auch **I U1,** 10; ; zu **I U5,** 66
topic ['tɒpɪk] Thema **I U2,** 33
torch, torches *(pl)* [tɔːtʃ; 'tɔːtʃɪz] Taschenlampe, Fackel **I U6,** 84
town [taʊn] Stadt **I U3,** 41
train [treɪn] Zug **I U4,** 54
transport ['træntspɔːt] Transport **I U4,** 57
*to be **trapped** [biː 'træpt] in der Falle sitzen **II U6,** 83
tree [triː] Baum **I U1,** 20
family tree ['fæmli triː] Familienstammbaum °**I U2,** 28
trick [trɪk] Trick, Streich **I U3,** 40
trip [trɪp] Ausflug, Reise **I U6,** 80
trouble [trʌbl] Schwierigkeiten, Ärger **I U2,** 30
trousers *(pl)* ['traʊzəz] Hose **II U1,** 10
true [truː] wahr **II U1,** 18
to come true [kʌm 'truː] wahr werden °**II U7,** 91
to **try** [traɪ] versuchen, probieren **II U1,** 10
T-shirt ['tiːʃɜːt] T-Shirt **I U2,** 30
tucker ['tʌkə] Essen *(australischer Ausdruck)* °**II U1,** 14
Tuesday ['tjuːzdeɪ] Dienstag **I LUB,** 39
tunnel ['tʌnl] Tunnel, Unterführung **I U4,** 54
Turkish ['tɜːkɪʃ] türkisch **I U2,** 29
It's your **turn.** [ɪts jɔː 'tɜːn] Du bist dran. **II U1,** 13
to **turn** back [tɜːn 'bæk] umkehren, zurückgehen **II U1,** 19
to turn left/right [tɜːn 'left/'raɪt] links/rechts abbiegen **II U7,** 97
to turn off [tɜːn‿'ɒf] abschalten, ausschalten **I U5,** 75
to turn over [ˌtɜːn‿'əʊvə] (sich) umdrehen **II U7,** 94
to turn round [ˌtɜːn 'raʊnd] (sich) umdrehen **II U1,** 18
TV [ˌtiː'viː] Fernsehen, Fernseher **I LUA,** 25

U

umbrella [ʌm'brelə] Regenschirm **II U6,** 81
uncle ['ʌŋkl] Onkel **I U2,** 28
under ['ʌndə] unter **I U1,** 18
to **underline** [ˌʌndə'laɪn] unterstreichen **II U1,** 18
underlined [ˌʌndə'laɪnd] unterstrichen °**I U7,** 98
*to **understand** [ˌʌndə'stænd] verstehen °**II U1,** 16
unhappy [ʌn'hæpi] unglücklich **I U2,** 33
unhealthy [ʌn'helθi] ungesund **II U4,** 53
uniform ['juːnɪfɔːm] Uniform **I U3,** 44
until [ʌn'tɪl; n'tɪl] bis **II U4,** 56
up [ʌp] auf, hinauf, oben **II U2,** 30
Hurry up! [ˌhʌri‿'ʌp] Beeil dich! **I U2,** 30
to get up [get‿'ʌp] aufstehen **I U3,** 44
to go up [gəʊ‿'ʌp] hinaufgehen °**I U4,** 61
to wake up [weɪk‿'ʌp] aufwecken, aufwachen **I U3,** 48
What's up? [ˌwɒts‿'ʌp] Was ist los? **I U1,** 16
to **update** [ʌp'deɪt] aktualisieren °**II U5,** 62
*to be **upset** [biː ʌp'set] aufgeregt sein, bestürzt sein **II U3,** 44
upstairs [ʌp'steəz] oben, im oberen Stock **I U2,** 27
us [ʌs] uns **I U4,** 60
use [juːs] Verwendung, Nutzung °**II U5,** 63
to **use** [juːz] benutzen, verwenden **I U4,** 54
usually ['juːʒli] normalerweise, gewöhnlich **II U4,** 53

V

van [væn] Lieferwagen **I U6,** 86
vegetable ['vedʒtəbl] Gemüse **II U1,** 15
verb [vɜːb] Verb °**II U1,** 20
very ['veri] sehr **I U1,** 20
video ['vɪdiəʊ] Video **I LUB,** 38
visit ['vɪzɪt] Besuch **I U7,** 94
to **visit** ['vɪzɪt] besuchen, besichtigen **I U4,** 54
visitor ['vɪzɪtə] Besucher/Besucherin **I U4,** 55
vocabulary [vəʊ'kæbjəlri] Wortschatz, Vokabular °**II U1,** 20
voice [vɔɪs] Stimme **II U2,** 31
volleyball ['vɒlibɔːl] Volleyball **I U3,** 40

W

to **wait** [weɪt] warten **I U5,** 69
to wait for ['weɪt fɔː] warten auf **I U6,** 86
waiter ['weɪtə] Kellner, Bedienung **II U4,** 55
*to **wake** [weɪk] (auf)wecken **II U7,** 94
to wake up [weɪk‿'ʌp] aufwecken, aufwachen **I U3,** 48
to **walk** [wɔːk] gehen, laufen **I U4,** 54
to walk the dog [wɔːk ðə 'dɒg] mit dem Hund spazieren gehen **I U3,** 42
wall [wɔːl] Wand, Mauer **I U1,** 18
wallet ['wɒlɪt] Brieftasche, Geldbeutel **II U4,** 56
to **want** (to) ['wɒnt tə] wollen, mögen **I U4,** 54
wardrobe ['wɔːdrəʊb] Kleiderschrank, Garderobe **I U2,** 30
warm [wɔːm] warm **II U2,** 25
to **wash** [wɒʃ] sich waschen, waschen **I U3,** 44
to **watch** [wɒtʃ] ansehen, beobachten **I LUB,** 38; ; achten auf **II U2,** 31
water ['wɔːtə] Wasser **I U5,** 68
to **wave** [weɪv] winken, schwenken **II U6,** 83
way [weɪ] Weg **I U3,** 42
He is on his way to … . [ˌhiː‿ɪz‿ɒn hɪz 'weɪ tə] Er ist auf dem Weg zu … . **I U3,** 42
we [wiː] wir **I U1,** 16
*to **wear** [weə] anhaben, tragen **I U3,** 45
weather ['weðə] Wetter **II U1,** 14
weatherman, weathermen *(pl)* ['weðəmæn; 'weðəmen] Meteorologe °**II U6,** 78

webcam ['webkæm] Webcam °**II U5,** 63
website ['websaɪt] Website, Internetauftritt **II U5,** 64
Wednesday ['wenzdeɪ] Mittwoch **I LUB,** 39
week [wi:k] Woche **I LUB,** 39
a week [ə 'wi:k] pro Woche, in der Woche **II U4,** 52
weekend [ˌwi:k'end] Wochenende **I U3,** 45
to **welcome** ['welkəm] willkommen heißen **I U7,** 90
You're **welcome.** [jʊə 'welkəm] Bitte sehr!, Gern geschehen! **I U1,** 19
well [wel] also, na ja, nun gut **I U2,** 29
west [west] Westen **I U4,** 54
wet [wet] nass **II U6,** 74
wet blanket [wet 'blæŋkɪt] Miesmacher/Miesmacherin **II U6,** 74
what [wɒt] welche/welcher/welches **I U1,** 11
What about …? [wɒt‿ə'baʊt] Was ist mit …? Wie wäre es mit …? **I U2,** 30
What a week! [ˌwɒt‿ə 'wi:k] Was für eine Woche! **II U2,** 22
What does it say? [ˌwɒt dʌz‿ɪt 'seɪ] Was steht da? **II U3,** 44
What's the film about? [wɒts ðə 'fɪlm‿əˌbaʊt] Wovon handelt der Film? °**II U3,** 43
What's the time, please? [ˌwɒts ðə 'taɪm ˌpli:z] Wie viel Uhr ist es, bitte? **I U3,** 42
What's up? [ˌwɒts‿'ʌp] Was ist los? **I U1,** 16
What's your name? [ˌwɒts jə 'neɪm] Wie heißt du? **I U1,** 11
when [wen] wenn, als; wann **I U2,** 33
where [weə] wo, wohin **I U1,** 11
Where are you from? [ˌweər‿ə jə 'frɒm] Woher kommst du? **I U1,** 11
Where's the fire? [ˌweəz ðə 'faɪə] Wo brennt's denn? **I U7,** 96
which [wɪtʃ] welche/welcher/welches **II U1,** 14
which [wɪtʃ] der/dem/den/die/das *(Relativpronomen)* **II U3,** 42
to **whisper** ['wɪspə] flüstern, zuflüstern **II U1,** 18
white [waɪt] weiß **I LUA,** 24
white elephant stall [ˌwaɪt 'elɪfənt stɔ:l] Trödelstand **I U7,** 96
who [hu:] wer, wem, wen **I U5,** 70; der/dem/den/die *(Relativpronomen)* **II U3,** 42
whose [hu:z] wessen **II U5,** 68
why [waɪ] warum **I U5,** 70
wicked ['wɪkɪd] großartig **II U5,** 70
wig [wɪg] Perücke **II U2,** 28
***will ('ll), won't** [wɪl; wəʊnt] werden *(futurisch)* **II U6,** 76
*to **win** [wɪn] gewinnen, siegen **II U7,** 91
wind [wɪnd] Wind **I U2,** 35
window ['wɪndəʊ] Fenster **I U1,** 18
windy ['wɪndi] windig **I U6,** 79
winter ['wɪntə] Winter **I U6,** 79
wish [wɪʃ] Wunsch °**II U7,** 91
with [wɪð] mit **I U1,** 14; ; bei **II U1,** 11
without [wɪ'ðaʊt] ohne **I U4,** 54
to go without [ˌgəʊ wɪ'ðaʊt] ohne … auskommen **II U4,** 52
wizard ['wɪzəd] Zauberer **II U5,** 69
woman, women *(pl)* ['wʊmən; 'wɪmɪn] Frau **I U4,** 62
Woof! [wʊf] Wau! °**I U2,** 27
word [wɜ:d] Wort **I U1,** 15
word star ['wɜ:d stɑ:] Wortstern °**I U1,** 22
work [wɜ:k] Arbeit **I U3,** 47
to **work** [wɜ:k] arbeiten, funktionieren **I U3,** 48
worksheet ['wɜ:kʃi:t] Arbeitsblatt **I U4,** 58
world [wɜ:ld] Erde, Welt °**II U6,** 74
*to be **worried** [bi: 'wʌrid] besorgt sein, beunruhigt sein **I U6,** 87
to **worry** ['wʌri] sich Sorgen machen **I U6,** 82; ; ängstigen, beunruhigen **II U3,** 45
worse [wɜ:s] schlimmer, schlechter **II U4,** 50
worst [wɜ:st] schlimmste/schlimmster/schlimmstes, schlechteste/schlechtester/schlechtestes **II U4,** 50
***would** like [wʊd 'laɪk] hätte gern, möchte gern **II U4,** 52
wow [waʊ] wow °**I U1,** 12
*to **write** [raɪt] schreiben **I U3,** 43
to write down ['raɪt ˌdaʊn] aufschreiben °**I LUB,** 38
wrong [rɒŋ] falsch **I U1,** 16
to get … wrong [get … 'rɒŋ] … falsch verstehen, falsch machen °**II U3,** 47
to go wrong [gəʊ 'rɒŋ] schief gehen **II U6,** 85

Y

year [jɪə] Jahr, Jahrgangsstufe **I U1,** 10
yellow ['jeləʊ] gelb **I LUA,** 24
yes [jes] ja **I U1,** 12
yesterday ['jestədeɪ] gestern **II U2,** 26
not … **yet** [jet] noch nicht **II U5,** 66
you [ju:; jə] dich, dir, Sie, Ihnen, euch **I LUB,** 38; ; du, ihr **I U1,** 11
Here you are! ['hɪə ju:‿ɑ:] Bitte schön! **I U1,** 20
thank you ['θæŋk‿ju:] danke **I U1,** 12
you're lucky [ˌjʊə'lʌki] du hast Glück **I U1,** 16
You're welcome. [jʊə 'welkəm] Bitte sehr!, Gern geschehen! **I U1,** 19
young [jʌŋ] jung **I U3,** 45
your [jɔ:] dein/deine, euer/eure, Ihr/Ihre **I U1,** 11
Yours [jɔ:z] Dein …/Deine …/Euer …/Eure … *(in Briefen)* **II U3,** 36
youth [ju:θ] Jugend **II U2,** 32

Z

zoo [zu:] Zoo, Tierpark **II U2,** 22
zookeeper ['zu:ki:pə] Tierpfleger/Tierpflegerin, Wärter/Wärterin **II U2,** 26

Boys' names

Angus ['æŋgəs] **II FA,** 103
Ben [ben] **I U2,** 27
Bob [bɒb] **I U6,** 78
Burt [bɜ:t] **II U4,** 55
Chandler ['tʃændlə] **II U3,** 37
Charlie ['tʃɑ:li] **I U2,** 33
Daniel ['dænjəl] **II U4,** 51
David ['deɪvɪd] **I U2,** 28
Derek ['derɪk] **II U4,** 51
Dicken ['dɪkn] **II FA,** 110
Douglas ['dʌgləs] **II FA,** 102
Eric ['erɪk] **I FA,** 102
Henry ['henri] **II FA,** 114
Jack [dʒæk] **I FA,** 102
Jake [dʒeɪk] **II U1,** 14
James [dʒeɪmz] **I U2,** 28
Jim [dʒɪm] **I U5,** 73
Jo [dʒəʊ] **I FA,** 105
Joey ['dʒəʊi] **II U3,** 37
John [dʒɒn] **I U4,** 57
Mark [mɑ:k] **I U4,** 61
Matt [mæt] **II U2,** 31
Nelson ['nelsn] **I U1,** 13
Patrick ['pætrɪk] **II U7,** 88
Paul [pɔ:l] **I U6,** 85
Pete [pi:t] **II U1,** 11

Peter [ˈpi:tə] **I U4,** 61
Phil [fɪl] **I U2,** 28
Richard [ˈrɪtʃəd] **I U2,** 27
Rob [rɒb] **I U2,** 26
Robert [ˈrɒbət] **II U4,** 51
Roger [ˈrɒdʒə] **II U3,** 36
Ross [rɒs] **II U3,** 37
Sam [sæm] **I U1,** 16
Steve [sti:v] **I U1,** 23
Ted [ted] **I U2,** 26
Terry [ˈteri] **I U1,** 10
Thomas [ˈtɒməs] **I LUA,** 25
Tim [tɪm] **I LUA,** 25
Todd [tɒd] **II U3,** 36
Tom [tɒm] **I U1,** 10
Tony [ˈtəʊni] **I LUA,** 25

Girls' names

Alison [ˈælɪsən] **II U5,** 67
Anna [ˈænə] **I U3,** 47
Debbie [ˈdebi] **II U3,** 36
Dorothy [ˈdɒrəθi] **II U5,** 68
Elena [ˈelɪnə] **I U2,** 28
Em [em] **II FA,** 114
Emma [ˈemə] **I U1,** 12
Farah [ˈfɑ:rə] **I U2,** 26
Fiona [fiˈəʊnə] **I U2,** 26
Glinda [ˈglɪndə] **II FA,** 114
Grace [greɪs] **I U2,** 26
Helen [ˈhelən] **II U7,** 88
Jade [dʒeɪd] **I U2,** 27
Jenny [ˈdʒeni] **I U4,** 57
Kate [keɪt] **I U4,** 57
Kath [kæθ] **I U6,** 78
Laura [ˈlɔ:rə] **II U1,** 11
Lisa [ˈli:sə] **I U1,** 10
Maria [məˈri:ə] **I U2,** 28
Mary [ˈmeəri] **I U4,** 57
Monica [ˈmɒnɪkə] **II U3,** 37
Nadine [neɪˈdi:n] **I U1,** 13
Nasreen [nʌsˈri:n] **I U2,** 26
Nicola [ˈnɪklə] **I FA,** 100
Nicole [nɪˈkəʊl] **II U3,** 36
Pat [pæt] **II U1,** 16
Phoebe [ˈfi:bi] **II U3,** 37
Rachel [ˈreɪtʃl] **II U3,** 37
Sally [ˈsæli] **I U6,** 85
Sarah [ˈseərə] **I U2,** 28
Stella [ˈstelə] **II FA,** 104
Sue [su:] **I U2,** 27
Susan [ˈsu:zn] **I U2,** 28
Suzanne [su:ˈzæn] **I U1,** 11
Tamara [təˈmɑ:rə] **I LUA,** 25
Tess [tes] **I U6,** 85
Tilly [ˈtɪli] **I LUA,** 25
Tina [ˈti:nə] **I LUA,** 25
Tracy [ˈtreɪsi] **I U2,** 28

Surnames

Bell [bel] **II U4,** 52
Black [blæk] **II U1,** 11
Bland [blænd] **II FA,** 108
Brook [brʊk] **I U1,** 12
Brown [braʊn] **II U1,** 11
Carter [ˈkɑ:tə] **I U1,** 12
Gruntle [ˈgrʌntl] **II FA,** 108
Gulch [gʌltʃ] **II FA,** 114
Howard [haʊəd] **II U1,** 14
Hunter [ˈhʌntə] **I U6,** 82
Jackson [ˈdʒæksn] **I U1,** 10
Lean [li:n] **I FA,** 104
Marco [ˈmɑ:kəʊ] **II U1,** 11
Martin [ˈmɑ:tɪn] **I FA,** 106
McArthur [məkˈɑ:θə] **II FA,** 102
Monte [ˈmɒnteɪ] **I U2,** 28
Muir [mjʊə] **II FA,** 103
Newman [ˈnju:mən] **I U1,** 12
O'Brien [əʊˈbraɪən] **II U7,** 88
Pilch [pɪltʃ] **I U2,** 28
Richards [ˈrɪtʃədz] **II U3,** 45
Rose [rəʊz] **I U4,** 60
Spencer [ˈspentsə] **I U2,** 28
Stavros [ˈstʌvrəs] **I U2,** 28
Taylor [ˈteɪlə] **I U1,** 10

Place names

America [əˈmerɪkə] **II U3,** 36
Australia [ɒsˈtreɪliə] Australien **II ZI,** 8
Bath [bɑ:θ] **I U6,** 79
Bow Church [ˌbəʊ ˈtʃɜ:tʃ] **I FA,** 108
Bristol [ˈbrɪstl] **I U1,** 12
Britain [ˈbrɪtn] **II FA,** 102
British Isles [ˌbrɪtɪʃ ˈaɪlz] Britische Inseln **II ZI,** 8
Camden [ˈkæmdən] **II ZI,** 8
Cornwall [ˈkɔ:nwɔ:l] **II U6,** 78
Cutty Sark Gardens [kʌti ˌsɑ:k ˈgɑ:dnz] **I U4,** 54
Devon [ˈdevn] **II U6,** 78
Dublin [ˈdʌblɪn] **II U7,** 88
England [ˈɪŋglənd] England **I U2,** 29
Exmoor [ˈeksmɔ:] **II ZI,** 8
Germany [ˈdʒɜ:məni] Deutschland **I U2,** 29
Glasgow [ˈglæzgəʊ] **II FA,** 102
Greece [gri:s] Griechenland **I U2,** 29
Greenwich [ˈgrenɪdʒ] **I U1,** 10
Hither Farm Road [ˌhɪðə fɑ:m ˈrəʊd] **I U2,** 26
Holburne Road [ˌhɒlbɜ:n ˈrəʊd] **I U2,** 26
Houses of Parliament [ˌhaʊzɪz‿əv ˈpɑ:ləmənt] **I FA,** 114
Ireland [ˈaɪələnd] **II U6,** 85
Isle of Dogs [ˌaɪl əv ˈdɒgz] **I U4,** 54
Istanbul [ˌɪstænˈbʊl] **I U1,** 13
Italy [ˈɪtəli] Italien **I U2,** 29
Kansas [ˈkænzəs] **II FA,** 114
Kilkenny [kɪlˈkeni] **II U7,** 93
King William Walk [kɪŋ ˈwɪljəm ˌwɔ:k] °**I U4,** 62
Limerick [ˈlɪmrɪk] **II ZI,** 8
Loch Ness [ˌlɒx ˈnes] **II ZI,** 8
London [ˈlʌndən] **I U1,** 10
Madrid [məˈdrɪd] **I U1,** 13
Moher [ˈməʊhə] **II U7,** 93
Nairobi [naɪˈrəʊbi] **I U1,** 13
Neston [ˈnestn] **I U6,** 78
New York [ˌnju: ˈjɔ:k] **I U4,** 55
Northern Ireland [ˌnɔ:ðn‿ˈaɪələnd] **II U7,** 89
Nottingham [ˈnɒtɪŋəm] **II U2,** 25
Paris [ˈpærɪs] **I U1,** 13
Park Row [ˌpɑ:k ˈrəʊ] **I U4,** 60
Perth [pɜ:θ] **II ZI,** 8
Poland [ˈpəʊlənd] Polen **I U2,** 29
Pond Road [ˌpɒnd ˈrəʊd] **I U2,** 27
Republic of Ireland [rɪˌpʌblɪk‿əv‿ˈaɪələnd] **II U7,** 88
Royal Observatory [ˌrɔɪəl əbˈzɜ:vətri] **I U4,** 55
Russia [ˈrʌʃə] Russland **I U2,** 29
Scilly Isles [ˈsɪli ˌaɪlz] **II U6,** 78
Scotland [ˈskɒtlənd] Schottland **II ZI,** 9
Shannon [ˈʃænən] **II U7,** 93
Sherwood Forest [ˌʃɜ:wʊd ˈfɒrɪst] **II FA,** 110
Tarr Steps [ˌtɑ: ˈsteps] **II U6,** 82
the **Thames** [temz] **I U4,** 54
Thomas Tallis School [ˌtɒməs tælɪs ˈsku:l] **I U1,** 10
Tokyo [ˈtəʊkiəʊ] **I U1,** 13
Turkey [ˈtɜ:ki] Türkei **I U2,** 29
Urquhart Castle [ˌɜ:kət ˈkɑ:sl] **II FA,** 102
Wales [weɪlz] Wales **II ZI,** 9
Wendover Road [ˌwendəʊvə ˈrəʊd] **I U5,** 70
Western Australia [ˌwestən ɒsˈtreɪliə] **II U1,** 14
Wildcroft [ˈwaɪldkrɒft] **I FA,** 100
Wiltshire [ˈwɪltʃə] **I U6,** 78

English – German

Other names

24-hour-clock [ˌtwenti fɔː aʊə ˈklɒk] **I U4,** 54
Alice Fitzwarren [ˈælis ˌfɪtsˈwɒrn] **I FA,** 108
Aquarius [əˈkweəriəs] Wassermann **II U6,** 80
Arena [əˈriːnə] **II U2,** 22
Barker [ˈbɑːkə] **I U2,** 27
Barny Forge [ˌbɑːni ˈfɔːdʒ] **I FA,** 108
Blacky [ˈblæki] **I FA,** 108
Boxing Day [ˈbɒksɪŋ ˌdeɪ] **I FA,** 114
Buckingham Palace [ˌbʌkɪŋəm ˈpælɪs] **°II U3,** 47
Burger Bonanza [ˌbɜːgə bəˈnænzə] **II U3,** 44
Charlie Smart [ˌtʃɑːli ˈsmɑːt] **I FA,** 108
Ching Ming [ˌtʃɪŋ ˈmɪŋ] **II U4,** 48
Cutty Sark [ˌkʌti ˈsɑːk] **I U4,** 54
Dick Whittington [ˌdɪk ˈwɪtɪŋtən] **I FA,** 108
Discman [ˈdɪskmən] Discman **I U2,** 30
DLR [ˌdiːˌelˈɑː] **I U4,** 55
Docklands Light Railway [ˈdɒkləndz ˌlaɪt ˈreɪlweɪ] **I U4,** 55
Drayton Hall [ˌdreɪtn ˈhɔːl] **I FA,** 101
Eastenders [ˌiːstˈendəz] **I U7,** 96
Flight Lab [ˈflaɪt ˌlæb] **II U2,** 23
Friar Tuck [ˌfraɪə ˈtʌk] **II FA,** 110
George Buckingham [ˌdʒɔːdʒ ˈbʌkɪŋəm] **I FA,** 108
GMT [ˈdʒiː em ˈtiː] **I U4,** 55
Greenwich Mean Time [ˌgrenɪdʒ ˈmiːn taɪm] **I U4,** 55
Guy Fawkes [ˌgaɪ ˈfɔːks] **I FA,** 114
Harrods [ˈhærədz] **II U2,** 23
Harry Potter [ˌhæri ˈpɒtə] **II U1,** 11
I spy with my little eye something beginning with .... [aɪ ˌspaɪ wɪð maɪ lɪtlˈaɪ sʌmθɪŋ bɪgɪnɪŋ wɪð] Ich sehe was, was du nicht siehst, das fängt mit ... an. **°I U2,** 32
James Bond [ˌdʒeɪmz ˈbɒnd] **I FA,** 104
Lady Ann Fitzwarren [ˌleɪdiˌæn fɪtsˈwɒrn] **I FA,** 108
Lantern Procession [ˈlæntən prəˈseʃn] **I U7,** 90
Little John [ˌlɪtl ˈdʒɒn] **II FA,** 110
London Knights [ˌlʌndən ˈnaɪts] **II U2,** 22
Maid Marian [ˌmeɪd ˈmæriən] **II FA,** 110
Mario's [ˈmæriəʊz] **I U5,** 68
Meridian Line [məˈrɪdiən ˈlaɪn] **I U4,** 54
MTV [ˌemtiːˈviː] **I U6,** 82
Napoleon [nəˈpəʊliən] **II U5,** 62
Nessie [ˈnesi] **II FA,** 103
Nottingham Panthers [ˌnɒtɪŋəm ˈpænθəz] **II U2,** 25
Oz [ɒz] **II FA,** 114
Queen Elizabeth [ˌkwiːnˌɪˈlɪzəbəθ] **I U5,** 73
Radio Active [ˌreɪdiəʊˈæktɪv] **I U2,** 33
Robbie Williams [ˌrɒbi ˈwɪljəmz] **II U1,** 14
Robin Hood [ˌrɒbɪn ˈhʊd] **II FA,** 110
Rover [ˈrəʊvə] **II U7,** 88
Shakespeare [ˈʃeɪkspɪə] **II U5,** 62
Shrove Tuesday [ˌʃrəʊv ˈtjuːzdeɪ] **I FA,** 115
Sissy Forge [ˌsɪsi ˈfɔːdʒ] **I FA,** 108
Spiderman [ˈspaɪdəmæn] **II U6,** 85
Stouty Burke [ˌstaʊti ˈbɜːk] **I FA,** 108
Supermouse [ˈsuːpəmaʊs] **II U2,** 33
Taj Mahal [ˌtɑːdʒ məˈhɑːl] **II U4,** 48
Thames Festival Lantern Procession [ˌtemz ˈfestɪvl ˈlæntən prəˈseʃn] **I U7,** 90
Tiger [ˈtaɪgə] **I U2,** 26
Tom and Jerry [ˌtɒmˌən ˈdʒeri] **I U3,** 46
Toto [ˈtəʊtəʊ] **II FA,** 114
Valentine [ˈvæləntaɪn] **II U6,** 85
White House [ˈwaɪt ˌhaʊs] **°II U3,** 43
Will Scarlet [ˌwɪl ˈskɑːlət] **II FA,** 110
Wizard of Oz [ˌwɪzəd əvˈɒz] **°II U5,** 64

A

ab off [ɒf]
Abc alphabet ['ælfəbet]
Abend evening ['i:vnɪŋ]
am Abend in the evening [ˌɪn ði: 'i:vnɪŋ]
an diesem Abend that evening [ˌdæt‿'i:vnɪŋ]
heute Abend this evening [ðɪs 'i:vnɪŋ]; tonight [tə'naɪt]
zu Abend essen to have supper [hæv 'sʌpə]
Abendessen supper ['sʌpə]; tea [ti:]
zum Abendessen for supper [fə 'sʌpə]
abends in the evening [ˌɪn ði: 'i:vnɪŋ]
Abenteuer adventure [əd'ventʃə]
aber but [bʌt]
abfahren to leave [li:v]
Abfall rubbish ['rʌbɪʃ]
Abfälle rubbish ['rʌbɪʃ]
Abflug departure [dɪ'pɑ:tʃə]
abholen to collect [kə'lekt]; to pick up [pɪk‿'ʌp]
abnehmen *(ein Kleidungsstück)* to take off [teɪk‿'ɒf]
Abreise departure [dɪ'pɑ:tʃə]
abschalten to turn off [tɜ:n‿'ɒf]
abschrecken to frighten away [ˌfraɪtn‿ə'weɪ]
abschreiben to copy ['kɒpi]
achten auf to watch [wɒtʃ]
Acker field [fi:ld]
Adresse address [ə'dres]
Akku battery ['bætri]
Akzent accent ['æksnt]
Alarm alarm [ə'lɑ:m]
alle/alles all [ɔ:l]
alles everything ['evriθɪŋ]
Alphabet alphabet ['ælfəbet]
alphabetisch alphabetical [ˌælfə'betɪkl]
als as [æz; əz]
als *(Vergleich)* than [ðæn]
als *(zeitlich)* when [wen]
also so [səʊ]; well [wel]
alt old [əʊld]
Alter age [eɪdʒ]
Amerikaner/Amerikanerin American [ə'merɪkən]; American [ə'merɪkən]
amerikanisch American [ə'merɪkən]; American [ə'merɪkən]
sich amüsieren to have a good time [ˌhæv‿ə gʊd 'taɪm]; to have fun [ˌhæv 'fʌn]
an at [æt; ət]; on [ɒn]
an sein to be on [bi:‿'ɒn]
andere/anderer/anderes other ['ʌðə]
ein anderer/eine andere/ein anderes another [ə'nʌðə]
ändern to change [tʃeɪndʒ]
anders different ['dɪfrnt]
Änderung change [tʃeɪndʒ]
Anfang start [stɑ:t]
anfangen to begin [bɪ'gɪn]; to start [stɑ:t]
Anführer/Anführerin leader ['li:də]
angeln to fish [fɪʃ]
Angeln fishing ['fɪʃɪŋ]
Angst haben (vor) to be frightened (of) [bi: 'fraɪtnd]
Angst machen to scare [skeə]
Ich habe **Angst.** I'm scared. [aɪm 'skeəd]
ängstigen to worry ['wʌri]
anhaben to wear [weə]
anhalten to stop [stɒp]
anhören to listen ['lɪsn]
fest **anklopfen** to bang [bæŋ]
ankommen to arrive [ə'raɪv]
anlächeln to smile at ['smaɪl‿ət]
anmalen to paint [peɪnt]
Anmerkung note [nəʊt]
Anorak anorak ['ænəræk]
anrufen to call [kɔ:l]; to phone [fəʊn]
ansehen to look at ['lʊk‿ət]; to watch [wɒtʃ]
sich ansehen to look at ['lʊk‿ət]
Antwort answer ['ɑ:ntsə]
anziehen to put on [pʊt‿'ɒn]
sich anziehen to dress [dres]
Apfel apple ['æpl]
Appetit appetite ['æpɪtaɪt]
April April ['eɪprl]
Arbeit work [wɜ:k]
arbeiten to work [wɜ:k]
Arbeitsblatt worksheet ['wɜ:kʃi:t]
Arbeitsgemeinschaft club [klʌb]
Arbeitsstelle job [dʒɒb]
Arena arena [ə'ri:nə]
Ärger trouble [trʌbl]
Arm arm [ɑ:m]
Arzt/Ärztin doctor ['dɒktə]
zum Arzt gehen to see a doctor [si: ə 'dɒktə]
auch also ['ɔ:lsəʊ]; too [tu:]
auf at [æt; ət]; in [ɪn]; on [ɒn]; up [ʌp]
auf dem Land in the country [ˌɪn ðə 'kʌntri]
auf einmal suddenly ['sʌdnli]
auf … hinauf onto ['ɒntu:; 'ɒntə]
auf Sendung on the air [ˌɒn ði‿'eə]
auf Wiedersehen goodbye [gʊd'baɪ]
aufbauen to put up [pʊt‿'ʌp]
Aufblinken flash [flæʃ]
Aufgabe exercise ['eksəsaɪz]
aufgeregt excited [ɪk'saɪtɪd]; nervous ['nɜ:vəs]
aufgeregt sein to be upset [bi: ʌp'set]
aufheben to pick up [pɪk‿'ʌp]
aufhören to finish ['fɪnɪʃ]; to stop [stɒp]
aufhören etw. zu tun to stop + -ing [stɒp]
aufhören mit to stop [stɒp]
aufmachen to open ['əʊpən]
aufnehmen to record [rɪ'kɔ:d]
aufpassen auf to look after [lʊk‿'ɑ:ftə]
sich **aufregen** to panic ['pænɪk]
aufregend exciting [ɪk'saɪtɪŋ]
aufschauen to look up [lʊk‿'ʌp]
aufsetzen to put on [pʊt‿'ɒn]
aufspringen to jump up [dʒʌmp‿'ʌp]
aufstehen to get out of bed [ˌget‿aʊt‿əv 'bed]; to get up [get‿'ʌp]
aufstellen to put up [pʊt‿'ʌp]
auftragen *(Make-up)* to put on [pʊt‿'ɒn]
aufwachen to wake up [weɪk‿'ʌp]
aufwecken to wake up [weɪk‿'ʌp]; to wake [weɪk]
aufzeichnen to record [rɪ'kɔ:d]
Auge eye [aɪ]
Augenblick moment ['məʊmənt]
im Augenblick at the moment [æt ðə 'məʊmənt]
in diesem Augenblick right now [ˌraɪt 'naʊ]
August August ['ɔ:gəst]
aus from [frɒm]
aus … heraus out of ['aʊt‿əv]
sich **ausdenken** to make up [meɪk‿'ʌp]
Ausflug trip [trɪp]
ausfüllen to fill in [fɪl‿'ɪn]
ausgeben to spend [spend]
ausgehen to go out [gəʊ‿'aʊt]
ohne … **auskommen** to go without [ˌgəʊ wɪ'ðaʊt]
auslachen to laugh at ['lɑ:f‿ət]
ausländisch foreign ['fɒrɪn]
auslösen *(Alarm)* to set off [set‿'ɒf]
Auslöser button ['bʌtn]
ausschalten to turn off [tɜ:n‿'ɒf]
aussehen to look [lʊk]
Aussehen look [lʊk]
außer beside [bɪ'saɪd]
außerhalb outside [aʊt'saɪd]
aussteigen to get out [get‿'aʊt]
aussteigen aus to get off [get‿'ɒf]

German – English

Austausch exchange [ɪks'tʃeɪndʒ]
Australier/Australierin Australian [ɒs'treɪliən]
australisch Australian [ɒs'treɪliən]
auswählen to choose [tʃu:z]
ausziehen *(ein Kleidungsstück)* to take off [teɪk‿'ɒf]
Auto car [kɑ:]
Autogramm autograph ['ɔ:təgrɑ:f]

B

Baby baby, babies *(pl)* ['beɪbi; 'beɪbiz]
Bach stream [stri:m]
Backofen oven ['ʌvn]
Badezimmer bathroom ['bɑ:θrʊm]
Badminton badminton ['bædmɪntən]
Bahnhof station ['steɪʃn]
bald soon [su:n]
Ball ball [bɔ:l]
Banane banana [bə'nɑ:nə]
Basketball basketball ['bɑ:skɪtbɔ:l]
Batterie battery ['bætri]
Bauch stomach ['stʌmək]
Bauer/Bäuerin farmer ['fɑ:mə]
Bauernhaus farmhouse ['fɑ:mhaʊs]
Bauernhof farm [fɑ:m]
Baum tree [tri:]
Beamter/Beamtin officer ['ɒfɪsə]
bedauerlich sad [sæd]
bedeuten to mean [mi:n]
Bedienung waiter ['weɪtə]
Beeil dich! Hurry up! [ˌhʌri‿'ʌp]
beenden to finish ['fɪnɪʃ]
Beerdigung funeral ['fju:nrəl]
befolgen to follow ['fɒləʊ]
Beginn start [stɑ:t]
beginnen to begin [bɪ'gɪn]
behalten to keep [ki:p]
bei at [æt; ət]; with [wɪð]
Beilage side dish ['saɪd ˌdɪʃ]
Bein leg [leg]
bekommen to get [get]
beliebt popular ['pɒpjələ]
bellen to bark [bɑ:k]
benötigen to need [ni:d]
benutzen to use [ju:z]
beobachten to watch [wɒtʃ]
bereit ready ['redi]
berühmt famous ['feɪməs]
beschäftigt busy ['bɪzi]
besichtigen to visit ['vɪzɪt]
besitzen to have got [hæv 'gɒt]
Besitzer/Besitzerin owner ['əʊnə]
besonders special ['speʃl]
besorgen to get [get]
besorgt sein to be worried [bi: 'wʌrid]
Besprechung meeting ['mi:tɪŋ]
besser better ['betə]
beste/bester/bestes best [best]
besteigen to climb ['klaɪm]
bestellen to order ['ɔ:də]
bestürzt sein to be upset [bi: ʌp'set]
Besuch visit ['vɪzɪt]
besuchen to see [si:]; to visit ['vɪzɪt]
Besucher/Besucherin visitor ['vɪzɪtə]
Bett bed [bed]
beunruhigen to worry ['wʌri]
beunruhigt sein to be worried [bi: 'wʌrid]
bevor before [bɪ'fɔ:]
bewachen to guard [gɑ:d]
bewegen to move [mu:v]
  sich bewegen to move [mu:v]
Bibliothek library ['laɪbri]
Bild picture ['pɪktʃə]
Bildung education [edʒʊ'keɪʃn]
billig cheap [tʃi:p]
Birne pear [peə]
bis to [tʊ; tə]; until [ʌn'tɪl; n'tɪl]
  Bis dann! See you! ['si: jə]
ein **bisschen** a bit [ə 'bɪt]
bitte please [pli:z]
  Bitte schön! Here you are! ['hɪə ju:‿ɑ:]
  Bitte sehr! You're welcome. [jʊə 'welkəm]
bitten um to ask for ['ɑ:sk fə]
blau blue [blu:]
bleiben to stay [steɪ]
Bleistift pencil ['pensl]
Blick look [lʊk]
  einen vernichtenden Blick zuwerfen to give … a dirty look [ˌgɪv‿ə 'dɜ:ti lʊk]
Blindenschrift Braille [breɪl]
Blitzen flash [flæʃ]
blöd stupid ['stju:pɪd]
blond blond [blɒnd]
bloß only ['əʊnli]
Blume flower ['flaʊə]
Boden ground [graʊnd]
Bohne bean [bi:n]
Bonbon sweet [swi:t]
borgen to borrow ['bɒrəʊ]
bösartig fierce [fɪəs]
böse angry ['æŋgri]
  böse sein auf to be angry with [bi: 'æŋgri wɪð]
Brand fire [faɪə]
brauchen to need [ni:d]
braun brown [braʊn]
Breakdance tanzen to break-dance ['breɪkdɑ:nts]
brechen to break [breɪk]
brennen *(Licht)* to be on [bi:‿'ɒn]
Brief letter ['letə]
Brieftasche wallet ['wɒlɪt]
Briefumschlag envelope ['envələʊp]
bringen to bring [brɪŋ]; to take [teɪk]
  nach Hause bringen to take home [ˌteɪk 'həʊm]
Brot bread [bred]
  belegtes Brot sandwich ['sænwɪdʒ]
Brücke bridge [brɪdʒ]
Bruder brother ['brʌðə]
Buch book [bʊk]
Bücherei library ['laɪbri]
Buchstabe letter ['letə]
buchstabieren to spell [spel]
Bude stall [stɔ:l]
bügeln to iron [aɪən]
Burg castle ['kɑ:sl]
Büro office ['ɒfɪs]
Bus bus, buses *(pl)* [bʌs; 'bʌsɪz]
  im Bus on the bus [ˌɒn ðə 'bʌs]
Busch bush [bʊʃ; 'bʊʃɪz]
Bushaltestelle bus stop ['bʌs ˌstɒp]
Butter butter ['bʌtə]

C

Café café ['kæfeɪ]
Cafeteria cafeteria [ˌkæfə'tɪəriə]
Camping camping ['kæmpɪŋ]
CD CD [ˌsi:'di:]
  CD-Player CD player [ˌsi:'di: ˌpleɪə]
Celsius Celsius (C) ['selsiəs]
chinesisch Chinese [tʃaɪ'ni:z]
Cola coke [kəʊk]
Comic comic ['kɒmɪk]
Comicheft comic ['kɒmɪk]
Computer computer [ˌkəm'pju:tə]
cool cool [ku:l]
Cornflakes cornflakes ['kɔ:nfleɪks]
Couch sofa ['səʊfə]
Cousin/Cousine cousin ['kʌzn]
Curry *(Gewürz oder Gericht)* curry ['kʌri]

D

da there [ðeə]
  da drüben over there [ˌəʊvə 'ðeə]
  da ist there is [ðer‿'ɪz]

da sind there are [ðer_'ɑ:]
Dach roof [ru:f]
danke thanks [θæŋks]; thank you ['θæŋk_ju:]
danken to thank [θæŋk]
dann then [ðen]
das the [ðə; ði]; that [ðæt]
Das nenne ich … . That's what I call … . [ˌðæts wɒt_'aɪ ˌkɔ:l]
Datum date [deɪt]
Decke blanket ['blæŋkɪt]
dein/deine your [jɔ:]
Dein … *(in Briefen)* Yours [jɔ:z]
Deine … *(in Briefen)* Yours [jɔ:z]
denken to think [θɪŋk]
der the [ðə; ði]
der/dem/den/die *(Relativpronomen)* who [hu:]
der/dem/den/die/das *(Relativpronomen)* which [wɪtʃ]
deshalb that's why ['ðæts ˌwaɪ]
Dessert dessert [dɪ'zɜ:t]
Detektiv/Detektivin detective [dɪ'tektɪv]
deutsch German ['dʒɜ:mən]
Deutscher/Deutsche German ['dʒɜ:mən]
Dezember December [dɪ'sembə]
Diät diet [daɪət]
eine Diät machen to go on a diet [ˌgəʊ_ɒn ə 'daɪət]
dich you [ju:; jə]
die the [ðə; ði]
Dienst service ['sɜ:vɪs]
Dienstag Tuesday ['tju:zdeɪ]
dies this [ðɪs]
diese these [ði:z]
diese/dieser/dieses this [ðɪs]
an diesem Abend that evening [ˌðæt_'i:vnɪŋ]
diese dort those [ðəʊz]
diese hier these [ði:z]
digital digital ['dɪdʒɪtl]
Ding thing [θɪŋ]
dir you [ju:; jə]
Disko disco ['dɪskəʊ]
DJ DJ [ˌdi:'dʒeɪ]
Donnerstag Thursday ['θɜ:zdeɪ]
Doppelgänger double ['dʌbl]
das **Doppelte** double ['dʌbl]
dort there [ðeə]
Drama drama ['drɑ:mə]
draußen outside [aʊt'saɪd]
Dreckloch dump [dʌmp]
drin inside [ɪn'saɪd]
dritte/dritter/drittes third [θɜ:d]
drücken to press [pres]; to push [pʊʃ]
drucken to print [prɪnt]
du you [ju:; jə]
Du bist dran. It's your turn. [ɪts jɔ: 'tɜ:n]
dumm silly ['sɪli]; stupid ['stju:pɪd]
Dummkopf idiot ['ɪdiət]; silly ['sɪli]
dunkel dark [dɑ:k]
durch through [θru:]
durchdrehen to go bananas [ˌgəʊ bə'nɑ:nəz]
dürfen can [kæn]
nicht dürfen mustn't ['mʌsnt]
Dusche shower ['ʃaʊə]
DVD DVD [ˌdi:vi:'di:]
DVD-Player DVD player [di:vi:'di: 'pleɪə]

E

echt real [rɪəl]
Es ist mir **egal.** I don't care. [aɪ dəʊnt 'keə]
Ehefrau wife, wives *(pl)* [waɪf, waɪvz]
Ei egg [eg]
eifersüchtig (auf) jealous (of) ['dʒeləs]
eigener/eigene/eigenes own [əʊn]
es **eilig haben** to be in a hurry [bi:_ɪn_ə 'hʌri]
ein/eine a, an [ə; ən]
ein paar a few [ə 'fju:]
einander each other [ˌi:tʃ_'ʌðə]
Einband cover ['kʌvə]
Einbrecher/Einbrecherin burglar ['bɜ:glə]
einfach easy ['i:zi]
Einfall idea [aɪ'dɪə]
einflussreich important [ɪm'pɔ:tnt]
einige a few [ə 'fju:]; some [sʌm]
Einkauf shopping ['ʃɒpɪŋ]
Einkaufen shopping ['ʃɒpɪŋ]
einladen to invite [ɪn'vaɪt]
Einladung invitation [ˌɪnvɪ'teɪʃn]
einmal once [wʌnts]
einschicken to send in [send_'ɪn]
einsetzen to put in [pʊt_'ɪn]
einst once [wʌnts]
einsteigen *(Bus)* to get onto [get_'ɒntə]
einsteigen in *(Auto)* to get into [get_'ɪntə]
einstellen to set [set]
Eintritt verboten! Keep out! [ki:p_'aʊt]
Eintrittskarte ticket ['tɪkɪt]
Einzelkind only child ['əʊnli ˌtʃaɪld]
Eis ice [aɪs]; ice-cream [aɪs 'kri:m]
Eisbahn ice rink ['aɪs rɪŋk]
Eiscreme ice-cream [aɪs 'kri:m]
Eishockey ice hockey ['aɪs ˌhɒki]
Elefant elephant ['elɪfənt]
Ellbogen elbow ['elbəʊ]
Eltern parents ['peərənts]
E-Mail e-mail ['i:meɪl]
enden to end [end]
englisch English ['ɪŋglɪʃ]
entkommen to escape [ɪ'skeɪp]
entlang along [ə'lɒŋ]
Geh … entlang. Go down … . ['gəʊ daʊn]
entlanggehen to go down [gəʊ 'daʊn]
entscheiden to decide [dɪ'saɪd]
Entschuldigung! Excuse me! [ɪk'skju:z mi]
er he [hi:]
Erbse pea [pi:]
Erdkunde Geography [dʒi'ɒgrəfi]
Ereignis event [ɪ'vent]
Erfassung registration [ˌredʒɪ'streɪʃn]
erfinden to make up [meɪk_'ʌp]
sich **erfreuen** to enjoy [ɪn'dʒɔɪ]
sich **erinnern (an)** to remember [rɪ'membə]
erklären to explain [ɪk'spleɪn]
erläutern to explain [ɪk'spleɪn]
erledigen to finish ['fɪnɪʃ]
erlöschen to go out [gəʊ 'aʊt]
erreichen to reach [ri:tʃ]
erschrecken to scare [skeə]
erst only ['əʊnli]
erstaunt surprised [sə'praɪzd]
erste/erster/erstes first [fɜ:st]
erzählen to tell [tel]
Erzählung story ['stɔ:ri]
Erziehung education [edʒʊ'keɪʃn]
es it [ɪt]
es gibt there are [ðer_'ɑ:]; there is [ðer_'ɪz]
Es lautete … . It said … . [ɪt 'sed]
essen to eat [i:t]
Essen food [fu:d]
Essen zum Mitnehmen takeaway ['teɪkəweɪ]
Esszimmer dining room ['daɪnɪŋ rʊm]
et cetera etc. [ɪt'setrə]
etwas anything ['eniθɪŋ]; some [sʌm]; something ['sʌmθɪŋ]
euch you [ju:; jə]
euer/eure your [jɔ:]
Euer … *(in Briefen)* Yours [jɔ:z]
Eure … *(in Briefen)* Yours [jɔ:z]
Euro *(Währung)* euro ['jʊərəʊ]
Experiment experiment [ɪk'sperɪmənt]

F

Fackel torch, torches *(pl)* [tɔ:tʃ; 'tɔ:tʃɪz]
Fahne flag [flæg]
fahren to drive [draɪv]; to ride [raɪd]
Fahrer/Fahrerin driver ['draɪvə]
Fahrplan timetable ['taɪmteɪbl]
Fahrrad bike [baɪk]
mit dem Fahrrad by bike [baɪ 'baɪk]
Fahrschein ticket ['tɪkɪt]
Fahrt journey ['dʒɜ:ni]
Fakt fact [fækt]
in der **Falle sitzen** to be trapped [bi: 'træpt]
fallen to fall [fɔ:l]; to drop [drɒp]
fallen lassen to drop [drɒp]
falls if [ɪf]
falsch wrong [rɒŋ]
Familie family ['fæmli]
Fan fan [fæn]
fangen to catch [kætʃ]
fantastisch fantastic [fæn'tæstɪk]
Farbe colour ['kʌlə]; paint [peɪnt]
färben to dye [daɪ]
Farm farm [fɑ:m]
fast nearly ['nɪəli]
Fastfood-Restaurant burger bar ['bɜ:gə ˌbɑ:]
faxen to fax [fæks]
Februar February ['februri]
Federball badminton ['bædmɪntən]
fehlen to miss [mɪs]
Fehler mistake [mɪ'steɪk]
Feier party ['pɑ:ti]
eine Party **feiern** to have a party [ˌhæv‿ə 'pɑ:ti]
fein fine [faɪn]
Feind/Feindin enemy ['enəmi]
Feld field [fi:ld]
Fell coat [kəʊt]
Fenster window ['wɪndəʊ]
Ferien holiday(s) ['hɒlədeɪ(z)]
Fernsehen TV [ˌti:'vi:]
Fernseher TV [ˌti:'vi:]
fertig ready ['redi]
Feuer fire [faɪə]
Figur figure ['fɪgə]
Film film [fɪlm]
finden to find [faɪnd]
Finger finger ['fɪŋgə]
Fisch/Fische fish, fish *(pl)* [fɪʃ]
fischen to fish [fɪʃ]
Fischen fishing ['fɪʃɪŋ]
fit fit [fɪt]
Fläche area ['eəriə]
Flagge flag [flæg]
Flasche bottle ['bɒtl]
Fleck mark [mɑ:k]
Fleisch meat [mi:t]
fliegen to fly [flaɪ]
flüchten to escape [ɪ'skeɪp]
Flug flight [flaɪt]
Flughafen airport ['eəpɔ:t]
Flugzeug plane [pleɪn]
Flur corridor ['kɒrɪdɔ:]; hall [hɔ:l]
Fluss river ['rɪvə]
flüstern to whisper ['wɪspə]
flutartige Überschwemmung flash flood ['flæʃ ˌflʌd]
folgen to follow ['fɒləʊ]
Form form [fɔ:m]
Formular form [fɔ:m]
Foto photo ['fəʊtəʊ]
Fotos machen to take pictures [teɪk 'pɪktʃəz]
Fotoapparat camera ['kæmrə]
Fotografie photo ['fəʊtəʊ]
fotografieren to take pictures [teɪk 'pɪktʃəz]
Frage question ['kwestʃn]
fragen to ask [ɑ:sk]
fragen nach to ask for ['ɑ:sk fə]
französisch French [frentʃ]
Frau *(Anrede)* Miss [mɪs]; Mrs ['mɪsɪz]
Frau woman, women *(pl)* ['wʊmən; 'wɪmɪn]
frei free [fri:]
Freitag Friday [fraɪdeɪ]
fremd foreign ['fɒrɪn]
fressen to eat [i:t]
Freund/Freundin friend [frend]
Freundin *(in einer Paarbeziehung)* girlfriend ['gɜ:lfrend]
Friede peace [pi:s]
frieren to be cold [bi: 'kəʊld]
frisch fresh [freʃ]
Friseur/Friseurin hairdresser ['heəˌdresə]
froh glad [glæd]; happy ['hæpi]
Frucht fruit [fru:t]
früh early ['ɜ:li]
Frühling spring [sprɪŋ]
Frühstück breakfast ['brekfəst]
fühlen to feel [fi:l]
sich fühlen to feel [fi:l]
Führer/Führerin leader ['li:də]
Füller pen [pen]
funktionieren to work [wɜ:k]
für for [fɔ:; fə]
furchtbar frightening ['fraɪtnɪŋ]; horrible ['hɒrəbl]; terrible ['terəbl]
Fuß foot, feet *(pl)* [fʊt; fi:t]
Fuß *(Längenmaß: 30,48 cm)* foot, feet *(pl)* [fʊt; fi:t]
zu Fuß on foot [ɒn 'fʊt]
Fußball football ['fʊtbɔ:l]
Fußboden floor [flɔ:]
füttern to feed [fi:d]

G

Gabel fork [fɔ:k]
Gang corridor ['kɒrɪdɔ:]
Gang *(Menü)* course [kɔ:s]
ganz all [ɔ:l]
Garderobe wardrobe ['wɔ:drəʊb]
Garten garden ['gɑ:dn]
Gate gate [geɪt]
geben to give [gɪv]
Gebiet area ['eəriə]
gebrochen broken ['brəʊkn]
Geburtstag birthday ['bɜ:θdeɪ]
gefährlich dangerous ['deɪndʒrəs]
sich **gegenseitig** each other [ˌi:tʃ‿'ʌðə]
gehen to go [gəʊ]; to leave [li:v]; to walk [wɔ:k]
… gehen to go + -ing [gəʊ]
Geh … entlang. Go down … . ['gəʊ daʊn]
Geist ghost [gəʊst]
gelangweilt bored [bɔ:d]
gelb yellow ['jeləʊ]
Geld money ['mʌni]
Geldbeutel wallet ['wɒlɪt]
Gemüse vegetable ['vedʒtəbl]
genau genommen in fact [ɪn 'fækt]
genießen to enjoy [ɪn'dʒɔɪ]
geöffnet open ['əʊpn]
Geografie Geography [dʒi'ɒgrəfi]
Gepäck luggage ['lʌgɪdʒ]
Geplauder chat [tʃæt]
Geräusch noise [nɔɪz]; sound [saʊnd]
Gern geschehen! You're welcome. [jʊə 'welkəm]
gern haben to like [laɪk]
gern mögen to love [lʌv]
Geschäft shop [ʃɒp]; store [stɔ:]
geschehen to happen ['hæpn]
Geschenk present ['preznt]
Geschichte History ['hɪstəri]; story ['stɔ:ri]
geschieden von divorced from [dɪ'vɔ:st frəm]
Gesicht face [feɪs]
Gespenst ghost [gəʊst]
Gestalt figure ['fɪgə]
gestern yesterday ['jestədeɪ]

gestern Abend last night [lɑ:st 'naɪt]
gestern Nacht last night [lɑ:st 'naɪt]
gesund healthy ['helθi]
Getränk drink [drɪŋk]
Gewächshaus greenhouse ['gri:nhaʊs]
Gewicht weight [weɪt]
gewinnen to win [wɪn]
gewöhnlich usually ['ju:ʒli]
Glas glass [glɑ:s]
glauben to believe [bɪ'li:v]; to think [θɪŋk]
gleich right away [raɪt‿ə'weɪ]
Glocke bell [bel]
Glück luck [lʌk]
du hast Glück you're lucky [jʊə'lʌki]
Viel Glück! Good luck! [ˌgʊd 'lʌk]
glücklich happy ['hæpi]; lucky ['lʌki]
Gold gold [gəʊld]
Mein Gott! My God! [maɪ 'gɒd]
Grad degree (°) [dɪ'gri:]
Grieche/Griechin Greek [gri:k]
griechisch Greek [gri:k]
groß big [bɪg]; large [lɑ:dʒ]; tall [tɔ:l]
großartig fantastic [fæn'tæstɪk]; great [greɪt]; wicked ['wɪkɪd]
Großstadt city ['sɪti]
grün green [gri:n]
Gruppe group [gru:p]
gruselig scary ['skeəri]
Gummistiefel rubber boots *(pl)* [ˌrʌbə 'bu:ts]
gut fine [faɪn]; good [gʊd]
Es geht uns gut. We're OK. [ˌwɪər‿əʊ'keɪ]
Guten Morgen! Good morning! ['gʊd 'mɔ:nɪŋ]
gut mit … umgehen können to be good with … [bi: 'gʊd wɪð]
ich bin gut in … I'm good at … [aɪm 'gʊd‿ət]

H

Haar, Haare hair [heə]
haben to have [hæv]; to have got [hæv 'gɒt]
Hähnchen chicken ['tʃɪkɪn]
halb half [hɑ:f]
eine halbe Stunde half an hour [ˌhɑ:f‿ən‿'aʊə]
halb (drei) half past (two) ['hɑ:f pɑ:st]
Halbschwester half-sister ['hɑ:fˌsɪstə]
Halle hall [hɔ:l]
Hallo! Hello! [he'ləʊ]
halten to hold [həʊld]; to keep [ki:p]
Haltestelle stop [stɒp]
Hand hand [hænd]
Hände weg! Hands off! [hændz‿'ɒf]
Handy mobile ['məʊbaɪl]
hart hard [hɑ:d]
Hass hate [heɪt]
hassen to hate [heɪt]
hätte gern would like [wʊd 'laɪk]
Haupt- main [meɪn]
Haus house [haʊs]
zu Hause at home [ət 'həʊm]
Hausaufgabe/Hausaufgaben homework ['həʊmwɜ:k]
Hausmeister/Hausmeisterin caretaker ['keəteɪkə]
Heft exercise book ['eksəsaɪz ˌbʊk]
Heim home [həʊm]
heiß hot [hɒt]
Ich **heiße** …. My name is …. [maɪ 'neɪm‿ɪz]
Heißluftballon hot air balloon [ˌhɒt 'eə bə'lu:n]
Heizung heating ['hi:tɪŋ]
Held hero, heroes *(pl)* ['hɪərəʊ; 'hɪərəʊz]
helfen to help [help]
Helikopter helicopter ['helɪˌkɒptə]
Hemd shirt [ʃɜ:t]
heraus out [aʊt]
herausfinden to find out [faɪnd‿'aʊt]
herausnehmen to take out [teɪk‿'aʊt]
Herbst autumn ['ɔ:təm]
herein in [ɪn]
hereinkommen to come in [kʌm‿'ɪn]
Herr *(Anrede)* Mr ['mɪstə]
herüberkommen to come over [kʌm‿'əʊvə]
herüberreichen to pass [pɑ:s]
um … **herum** around [ə'raʊnd]
herunter off [ɒf]
herunterfallen to fall [fɔ:l]; to fall, fell [fɔ:l; fel]; to fall off [fɔ:l ɒf]
herunterladen to download [ˌdaʊn'ləʊd]
Herzliche Grüße love [lʌv]
heute today [tə'deɪ]
heute Abend this evening [ðɪs 'i:vnɪŋ]; tonight [tə'naɪt]
heute Nacht tonight [tə'naɪt]
Hi! Hi! [haɪ]
hier here [hɪə]
Hilfe help [help]
hilfreich helpful ['helpfəl]
Himmel sky [skaɪ]
hinauf up [ʌp]
hinaufschauen to look up [lʊk‿'ʌp]
hinausgehen to go out [gəʊ‿'aʊt]
hinauslehnen to lean out [li:n‿'aʊt]
sich hinauslehnen to lean out [li:n‿'aʊt]
hineingehen to go in [gəʊ 'ɪn]
hinfallen to fall [fɔ:l]
sich **hinsetzen** to sit down [sɪt 'daʊn]
hinter behind [bɪ'haɪnd]
Hinter- back [bæk]
hinterhergehen to follow ['fɒləʊ]
hinübergehen to go over [gəʊ‿'əʊvə]
hinuntergehen to go down [gəʊ 'daʊn]
Hinweis clue [klu:]
Hobby hobby, hobbies *(pl)* ['hɒbi; 'hɒbiz]
hoch high [haɪ]; tall [tɔ:l]
Hochmoor moor [mɔ:]
hochspringen to jump up [dʒʌmp‿'ʌp]
Hochwasser flood [flʌd]
Hockey hockey ['hɒki]
hoffen to hope [həʊp]
höflich polite [pə'laɪt]
holen to get [get]
hören to hear [hɪə]
Horoskop horoscope ['hɒrəskəʊp]
Hose trousers *(pl)* ['traʊzəz]
kurze Hose shorts *(pl)* [ʃɔ:ts]
Hosentasche pocket ['pɒkɪt]
Hubschrauber helicopter ['helɪˌkɒptə]
Huhn chicken ['tʃɪkɪn]
Hund dog [dɒg]
mit dem Hund spazieren gehen to walk the dog [wɔ:k ðə 'dɒg]
hundemüde dog-tired [ˌdɒg 'taɪəd]
hundert hundred ['hʌndrəd]
Hunger bekommen to get hungry [get 'hʌŋgri]
hungrig hungry ['hʌŋgri]
Hut hat [hæt]

I

ich I [aɪ]
ich bin I'm [aɪm]
Ich hätte gern I'd like [aɪd 'laɪk]
Ich heiße …. My name is …. [maɪ 'neɪm‿ɪz]
Ich nehme …. I'm having …. [aɪm 'hævɪŋ]
ich würde gern I'd like to [ˌaɪd 'laɪk tə]
ich würde lieber I'd rather [aɪd 'rɑ:ðə]
Idee idea [aɪ'dɪə]
Idiot idiot ['ɪdɪət]

ihm him [hɪm]
ihn him [hɪm]
ihnen them [ðem]
Ihnen you [ju:; jə]
ihr you [ju:; jə]
ihr/ihre her [hɜ:]; its [ɪts]; their [ðeə]
Ihr/Ihre your [jɔ:]
im Gange sein to be on [bi:‿'ɒn]
Imbiss snack [snæk]
immer always ['ɔ:lweɪz]
immer noch still [stɪl]
in at [æt; ət]; in [ɪn]; into ['ɪntə]
in … hinein into ['ɪntə]
indisch Indian ['ɪndiən]
Information/Informationen information [ˌɪnfə'meɪʃn]
Informationszentrum information centre [ɪnfə'meɪʃn ˌsentə]
Inlineskates skates *(pl)* [skeɪts]
Inlineskates fahren to skate [skeɪt]
innen inside [ɪn'saɪd]
Insel island ['aɪlənd]
interessant interesting ['ɪntrəstɪŋ]
interessiert interested ['ɪntrəstɪd]
Internet Internet ['ɪntənet]
im Internet surfen to surf the Internet [ˌsɜ:f ði‿'ɪntənet]
Internetauftritt website ['websaɪt]
Interview interview ['ɪntəvju:]
interviewen to interview ['ɪntəvju:]
irgendein any ['enɪ]
irgendetwas anything ['eniθɪŋ]
irgendwelche any ['enɪ]
irgendwo somewhere ['sʌmweə]
irisch Irish ['aɪrɪʃ]
ist is [ɪz]
Italiener/Italienerin Italian [ɪ'tæliən]
italienisch Italian [ɪ'tæliən]

J

ja yes [jes]
Jacke jacket ['dʒækɪt]
Jackentasche pocket ['pɒkɪt]
Jahr year [jɪə]
Jahreszeit season ['si:zn]
Jahrgangsstufe year [jɪə]
Jahrmarkt fair [feə]
Januar January ['dʒænjuri]
Jazz jazz [dʒæz]
jede/jeder/jedes every ['evri]
jemals ever ['evə]
jemand someone ['sʌmwʌn]
jene those [ðəʊz]
jenes that [ðæt]
jetzt now [naʊ]
jetzt gleich right now [ˌraɪt 'naʊ]
Job job [dʒɒb]
joggen to jog [dʒɒg]
Jugend youth [ju:θ]
Jugendlicher/Jugendliche teen [ti:n]
Juli July [dʒʊ'laɪ]
Jumbojet jumbo jet [ˌdʒʌmbəʊ 'dʒet]
jung young [jʌŋ]
Junge boy [bɔɪ]
Juni June [dʒu:n]

K

Kalender calendar ['kæləndə]
kalt cold [kəʊld]
Kamera camera ['kæmrə]
Kampfrichter judge [dʒʌdʒ]
Kappe cap [kæp]
kaputt broken ['brəʊkn]
kaputtmachen to break [breɪk]
Kapuze hood [hʊd]
Karotte carrot ['kærət]
Karte card [kɑ:d]
Kartoffel potato, potatoes *(pl)* [pə'teɪtəʊ]
Kartoffelchip crisp [krɪsp]
Käse cheese [tʃi:z]
Kasten box, boxes *(pl)* [bɒks; 'bɒksɪz]
Katze cat [kæt]
kaufen to buy [baɪ]
Kaufhaus department store [dɪ'pɑ:tmənt stɔ:]; store [stɔ:]
Kaufhausdetektiv/Kaufhausdetektivin store detective ['stɔ: dɪˌtektɪv]
kein/keine no [nəʊ]
keiner/keine none [nʌn]
Keks biscuit ['bɪskɪt]
Kellner waiter ['weɪtə]
kennen to know [nəʊ]
Kerl bloke [bləʊk]
Kette chain [tʃeɪn]
kicken to kick [kɪk]
Kilo(gramm) kilo (kg) ['kɪləʊ]
Kind kid [kɪd]; child, children *(pl)* [tʃaɪld; 'tʃɪldrɪn]
Kino cinema ['sɪnəmə]
Kirche church [tʃɜ:tʃ]
Kiste box, boxes *(pl)* [bɒks; 'bɒksɪz]
Klang sound [saʊnd]
klar clear [klɪə]
klären *(ein Problem)* to sort out [sɔ:t‿'aʊt]
Klasse class [klɑ:s]
Klassenarbeit test [test]
Klassenzimmer classroom ['klɑ:srʊm]
klatschen to clap [klæp]
Kleider clothes *(pl)* []
Kleiderschrank wardrobe ['wɔ:drəʊb]
Kleidung clothes *(pl)* []
klein little [lɪtl]; small [smɔ:l]
klettern to climb ['klaɪm]
klicken to click [klɪk]
Klingel bell [bel]
klingeln to ring [rɪŋ]
Es klingelt. The bell rings. [ðə 'bel rɪŋz]
Klippe cliff [klɪf]
fest **klopfen** to bang [bæŋ]
Klopfen knock [nɒk]
Klub club [klʌb]
knarren to creak [kri:k]
Knie knee [ni:]
Knopf button ['bʌtn]
Kobold goblin ['gɒblɪn]
kochen to cook [kʊk]
Kochen cooking ['kʊkɪŋ]
komisch funny ['fʌni]
kommen to come [kʌm]; to get [get]
Komm./Kommt. Come on. [kʌm‿'ɒn]
Komparativ comparative [kəm'pærətɪv]
Königin queen [kwi:n]
können can [kæn]
kann/könnte(n) vielleicht may [meɪ]
konnte/konnten could [kʊd]
Konzert concert ['kɒnsət]
Kopf head [hed]
Kopfhörer headphones *(pl)* ['hedfəʊnz]
Kopfsalat lettuce ['letɪs]
kopieren to copy ['kɒpi]
körperlich physical ['fɪzɪkl]
korrekt correct [kə'rekt]; right [raɪt]
Korridor corridor ['kɒrɪdɔ:]
Kraft power ['paʊə]
krank sick [sɪk]
Krankenhaus hospital ['hɒspɪtl]
Krankenpfleger nurse [nɜ:s]
Krankenschwester nurse [nɜ:s]
Krankmeldung sick note ['sɪk ˌnəʊt]
kratzen to scratch [skrætʃ]
Kratzer scratch [skrætʃ]
Kricket cricket ['krɪkɪt]
Küche kitchen ['kɪtʃɪn]
Kuchen cake [keɪk]
Küchenschrank cupboard ['kʌbəd]
Kuh cow [kaʊ]
sich **kümmern um** to look after [lʊk‿'ɑ:ftə]
Kunst Art [ɑ:t]
Kurs class [klɑ:s]
kurz short [ʃɔ:t]
Küste coast [kəʊst]

L

Labor lab(oratory) [læb; lə'bɒrətri]
lächeln to smile [smaɪl]
lachen to laugh [lɑːf]
Laden shop [ʃɒp]; store [stɔː]
Lamm lamb [læm]
Lammfleisch lamb [læm]
Land country, countries *(pl)* ['kʌntri; 'kʌntriz]; land [lænd]
Landkarte map [mæp]
Landstraße road [rəʊd]
Landwirt/Landwirtin farmer ['fɑːmə]
lang long [lɒŋ]
langsam slow [sləʊ]
langweilig boring ['bɔːrɪŋ]
Laptop laptop ['læptɒp]
Lärm noise [nɔɪz]
lassen to leave [liːv]
Lasst uns .... Let's .... [lets]
Lassi *(Jogurtgetränk)* lassi ['lasɪ]
Laterne lantern ['læntən]
Lauf run [rʌn]
laufen to be on [biː‿'ɒn]; to run [rʌn]; to walk [wɔːk]
Läufer/Läuferin runner ['rʌnə]
laut loud [laʊd]
Es **lautete** .... It said .... [ɪt 'sed]
leben to live [lɪv]
Lebensmittel food [fuːd]
leer empty ['empti]
legen to put [pʊt]
lehren to teach [tiːtʃ]
Lehrer/Lehrerin teacher ['tiːtʃə]
leicht easy ['iːzi]
Tut mir **Leid.** sorry ['sɒri]
leihen to borrow ['bɒrəʊ]; to lend [lend]
leise quiet ['kwaɪət]; soft [sɒft]
lernen to learn [lɜːn]; to study ['stʌdi]
lesen to read [riːd]
letzte/letzter/letztes last [lɑːst]
leuchtend brilliant ['brɪljənt]
Leute people ['piːpl]
Licht light [laɪt]
lieb dear [dɪə]
Liebe love [lʌv]
Liebe ... *(Anrede in Briefen)* Dear [dɪə]
Lieber ... *(Anrede in Briefen)* Dear [dɪə]
lieben to love [lʌv]
ich würde **lieber** I'd rather [aɪd 'rɑːðə]
Lieblings- favourite ['feɪvrɪt]
Lied song [sɒŋ]
Lieferwagen van [væn]
lila purple ['pɜːpl]
Limonade lemonade [ˌlemə'neɪd]
Lineal ruler ['ruːlə]
Linie line [laɪn]
linke/linker/linkes left [left]
links left [left]; on the left [ɒn ðə 'left]
links abbiegen to turn left/right [tɜːn 'left/'raɪt]
Lippenpflegestift lip balm ['lɪp bɑːm]
Liste list [lɪst]
Löffel spoon [spuːn]
löschen *(Text)* to delete [dɪ'liːt]
Löwe lion ['laɪən]
Luft air [eə]
lustig funny ['fʌni]
sich lustig machen über to laugh at ['lɑːf‿ət]

M

machen to do [duː]; to make [meɪk]
eine Diät machen to go on a diet [ˌgəʊ‿ɒn ə 'daɪət]
sich gut machen to do OK [ˌduː‿əʊ'keɪ]
sich lustig machen über to laugh at ['lɑːf‿ət]
Spaß machen to be fun [biː 'fʌn]
Macht power ['paʊə]
Mädchen girl [gɜːl]
Magazin magazine [mægə'ziːn]
Magen stomach ['stʌmək]
Mahlzeit meal [miːl]
Mai May [meɪ]
Make-up make-up ['meɪkʌp]
Mal *(zeitlich)* time [taɪm]
malen to paint [peɪnt]
Mama mum [mʌm]
Manager/Managerin manager ['mænɪdʒə]
manchmal sometimes ['sʌmtaɪmz]
Mann man, men *(pl)* [mæn; men]
Mannschaft team [tiːm]
Mantel coat [kəʊt]
Mäppchen pencil case ['pensl ˌkeɪs]
Mappe folder ['fəʊldə]
Markt market ['mɑːkɪt]
Marmelade jam [dʒæm]
März March [mɑːtʃ]
Mathematik Maths [mæθs]
Mauer wall [wɔːl]
Maus mouse [maʊs]
Meer sea [siː]
mehr more [mɔː]
Mehrzahl plural ['plʊərl]
Meile *(brit. Längenmaß)* mile [maɪl]
mein/meine my [maɪ]
Mein Gott! My God! [maɪ 'gɒd]
das **meiste** most [məʊst]
die meisten most [məʊst]
eine **Menge** a lot of [ə 'lɒt‿əv]
Menschen people ['piːpl]
Menü menu ['menjuː]
sich **merken** to remember [rɪ'membə]
merkwürdig strange [streɪndʒ]
Messe fair [feə]
Messer knife, knives *(pl)* [naɪf; naɪvz]
mich me [miː]
Miesmacher/Miesmacherin wet blanket [wet 'blæŋkɪt]
Mikrofon microphone ['maɪkrəfəʊn]
Milch milk [mɪlk]
Million million ['mɪlɪən]
mindestens at least [ət 'liːst]
Mineral- mineral ['mɪnərəl]
Minestrone minestrone [ˌmɪnɪ'strəʊni]
Minute minute ['mɪnɪt]
mir me [miː]
mit with [wɪð]
mitbringen to bring [brɪŋ]
miteinander together [tə'geðə]
mitnehmen to take [teɪk]
Mittagessen lunch [lʌntʃ]
Mittagszeit lunchtime ['lʌntʃtaɪm]
mittel medium ['miːdiəm]
Mittelpunkt centre ['sentə]
Mitternacht midnight ['mɪdnaɪt]
Mittwoch Wednesday ['wenzdeɪ]
Möbel furniture ['fɜːnɪtʃə]
Mobiltelefon mobile ['məʊbaɪl]
möchte gern would like [wʊd 'laɪk]
Mode fashion ['fæʃn]
mögen to like [laɪk]
gern mögen to love [lʌv]
Mohrrübe carrot ['kærət]
Moment moment ['məʊmənt]
Moment mal! Hang on! ['hæŋ‿ɒn]
momentan at the moment [æt ðə 'məʊmənt]
Monat month [mʌnθ]
Mond moon [muːn]
Montag Monday ['mʌndeɪ]
montags on Mondays [ɒn 'mʌndeɪz]
morgen tomorrow [tə'mɒrəʊ]
Morgen morning ['mɔːnɪŋ]
am Morgen in the morning [ˌɪn ðə 'mɔːnɪŋ]
am nächsten Morgen the next morning [ðə ˌnekst 'mɔːnɪŋ]
Guten Morgen! Good morning! [ˌgʊd 'mɔːnɪŋ]

German – English

Morgenappell assembly [ə'sembli]
morgens in the morning [ˌɪn ðə 'mɔ:nɪŋ]
MP3 MP3 [empi:'θri:]
MP3-Player MP3 player [empi:'θri: ˌpleɪə]
müde tired ['taɪəd]
Müll rubbish ['rʌbɪʃ]
Müllkippe dump [dʌmp]
Mund mouth [maʊθ]
Museum museum [mju:'zi:əm]
Musik music ['mju:zɪk]
müssen must [mʌst]; to have to ['hæv tə]; to need [ni:d]
nicht müssen needn't ['ni:dnt]
Mutti mum [mʌm]
Mütze cap [kæp]

N

nach after ['ɑ:ftə]; to [tʊ; tə]
nach *(Uhrzeit)* past [pɑ:st]
nach draußen outside [aʊt'saɪd]
nach drinnen inside [ɪn'saɪd]
nach Hause home [həʊm]
nach Hause bringen to take home [ˌteɪk 'həʊm]
Nachbar/Nachbarin neighbour ['neɪbə]
Nachmittag afternoon [ˌɑ:ftə'nu:n]
am Nachmittag in the afternoon [ˌɪn ði: ˌɑ:ftə'nu:n]
nachmittags in the afternoon [ˌɪn ði: ˌɑ:ftə'nu:n]
Nachmittagstee afternoon tea [ˌɑ:ftənu:n 'ti:]
Nachricht message ['mesɪdʒ]
nachschlagen to look up [lʊk‿'ʌp]
nächste/nächster/nächstes next [nekst]
am nächsten Morgen the next morning [ðə ˌnekst 'mɔ:nɪŋ]
Nacht night [naɪt]
heute Nacht tonight [tə'naɪt]
nachts at night [ət 'naɪt]
Nachtisch dessert [dɪ'zɜ:t]; pudding ['pʊdɪŋ]
Nachtschwester night nurse ['naɪt nɜ:s]
nahe near [nɪə]
in der **Nähe von** near [nɪə]
Nahrung food [fu:d]
Name name [neɪm]
namens called [kɔ:ld]
Nase nose [nəʊz]
die Nase voll haben to be fed up [bi: ˌfed‿'ʌp]

nass wet [wet]
national national ['næʃnl]
natürlich of course [əv 'kɔ:s]
Naturwissenschaft Science ['saɪənts]
Nebel fog [fɒg]
neben beside [bɪ'saɪd]; next to ['nekst tə]
neblig foggy ['fɒgi]
nehmen to take [teɪk]
Ich nehme .... I'm having .... [aɪm 'hævɪŋ]
neidisch (auf) jealous (of) ['dʒeləs]
nein no [nəʊ]
nennen to call [kɔ:l]
Das nenne ich .... That's what I call .... [ˌðæts wɒt‿'aɪ ˌkɔ:l]
nervös nervous ['nɜ:vəs]
nett nice [naɪs]
neu new [nju:]
nicht no [nəʊ]; not [nɒt]
noch nicht not ... yet [jet]
nichts nothing ['nʌθɪŋ]
nie never ['nevə]
niemals never ['nevə]
niemand no one ['nəʊwʌn]
noch else [els]; still [stɪl]
noch ein/noch eine another [ə'nʌðə]
noch nicht not ... yet [jet]
Norden north [nɔ:θ]
normal normal ['nɔ:ml]
normalerweise usually ['ju:ʒli]
Note *(in der Schule)* mark [mɑ:k]
Notiz note [nəʊt]
November November [nəʊ'vembə]
Nudel noodle ['nu:dl]
Nummer number ['nʌmbə]
nun now [naʊ]
nur only ['əʊnli]

O

ob if [ɪf]
oben above [ə'bʌv]; up [ʌp]; upstairs [ʌp'steəz]
oberhalb above [ə'bʌv]
Observatorium observatory [əb'zɜ:vətri]
Obst fruit [fru:t]
oder or [ɔ:]
offen open ['əʊpn]
öffnen to open ['əʊpən]
Öffnungszeiten hours ['aʊəz]
oft often ['ɒfn]
ohne without [wɪ'ðaʊt]
ohne ... auskommen to go without [ˌgəʊ wɪ'ðaʊt]

ohnmächtig werden to faint [feɪnt]
Ohr ear [ɪə]
OK OK [əʊ'keɪ]
Oktober October [ɒk'təʊbə]
Oma grandma ['grændmɑ:]
Onkel uncle ['ʌŋkl]
Opa grandad ['grændæd]
Orange orange ['ɒrɪndʒ]
Ordner folder ['fəʊldə]
organisieren to organize ['ɔ:gənaɪz]
Ort place [pleɪs]
Osten east [i:st]

P

ein **paar** a few [ə 'fju:]
Päckchen packet ['pækɪt]
packen to pack [pæk]
Paket packet ['pækɪt]
paniken to panic ['pænɪk]
Panter panther ['pæntθə]
Papa dad [dæd]
Park park [pɑ:k]
Partner/Partnerin partner ['pɑ:tnə]
Party party ['pɑ:ti]
eine Party feiern to have a party [ˌhæv‿ə 'pɑ:ti]
passen to fit [fɪt]
das nicht dazu **passende (Wort)** odd one out [ɒd wʌn‿'aʊt]
Pause break [breɪk]
PC PC [ˌpi:'si:]
Pech bad luck [ˌbæd 'lʌk]
peinlich embarrassing [ɪm'bærəsɪŋ]
Pence *(Währung)* pence *(pl)* [pents]
Person person ['pɜ:sn]
Perücke wig [wɪg]
Pfad path [pɑ:θ]
Pferd horse [hɔ:s]
Pflanze plant [plɑ:nt]
pflücken to pick [pɪk]
Pforte gate [geɪt]
Pfund *(Währung)* pound (£) [paʊnd]
Pfund *(Gewicht)* pound (lb) [paʊnd]
physisch physical ['fɪzɪkl]
pikant spicy ['spaɪsi]
pink pink [pɪŋk]
Pizza pizza ['pi:tsə]
Plakat poster ['pəʊstə]
Plan plan [plæn]
planen to plan [plæn]
Platz place [pleɪs]; room [ru:m; rʊm]
plötzlich at once [ət 'wʌnts]; suddenly ['sʌdnli]
Plural plural ['plʊərl]

Polizei police [pə'li:s]
Polizist policeman, policemen *(pl)* [pə'li:smən; pə'li:smen]
polnisch Polish ['pəʊlɪʃ]
Pommes frites chips *(pl)* []
Pony pony ['pəʊni]
populär popular ['pɒpjələ]
Poster poster ['pəʊstə]
Postkarte postcard ['pəʊstkɑ:d]
praktizieren to practise ['præktɪs]
Präsident/Präsidentin president ['prezɪdnt]
Preis price [praɪs]
pressen to press [pres]
prima brilliant ['brɪljənt]; cool [ku:l]
proben to practise ['præktɪs]
proben *(ein Theaterstück)* to rehearse [rɪ'hɜ:s]
probieren to try [traɪ]
Problem problem ['prɒbləm]
Projekt project ['prɒdʒekt]
Pudding pudding ['pʊdɪŋ]
Punkt point [pɔɪnt]

Q

quietschen to creak [kri:k]

R

Rabauke (to) bully ['bʊli]
Radiergummi rubber ['rʌbə]
Radio radio ['reɪdiəʊ]
Radiosendung radio show ['reɪdiəʊ ˌʃəʊ]
Rap rap [ræp]
rappen to rap [ræp]
Raum room [ru:m; rʊm]
Rechnung bill [bɪl]
Recht haben to be right [bi: 'raɪt]
rechte/rechter/rechtes right [raɪt]
rechts on the right [ɒn ðə 'raɪt]; right [raɪt]
rechts abbiegen to turn left/right [tɜ:n 'left/'raɪt]
reden to talk [tɔ:k]
reden mit to talk to ['tɔ:k tə]
Regal shelf, shelves *(pl)* [ʃelf; ʃelvz]
Regalbrett shelf, shelves *(pl)* [ʃelf; ʃelvz]
Regel rule [ru:l]
regeln *(ein Problem)* to sort out [sɔ:t‿'aʊt]
Regen rain [reɪn]
Regenguss shower ['ʃaʊə]
Regenschirm umbrella [ʌm'brelə]
Registrierung registration [ˌredʒɪ'streɪʃn]
regnen to rain [reɪn]
regnerisch rainy ['reɪni]
reinigen to clean [kli:n]
Reis rice [raɪs]
Reise journey ['dʒɜ:ni]; trip [trɪp]
reiten to ride [raɪd]
Religionsunterricht Religious Education (RE) [rɪˌlɪdʒəs‿edʒʊ'keɪʃn]
religiös religious [rɪ'lɪdʒəs]
rennen to run [rʌn]
Rennen race [reɪs]
Reporter/Reporterin reporter [rɪ'pɔ:tə]
Restaurant restaurant ['restrɒnt]
Restaurant mit Straßenverkauf takeaway ['teɪkəweɪ]
retten to rescue ['reskju:]; to save [seɪv]
Rezept recipe ['resɪpi:]
Richter judge [dʒʌdʒ]
richtig correct [kə'rekt]; right [raɪt]
richtig machen to get … right [get … 'raɪt]
riesig large [lɑ:dʒ]
Ritter knight [naɪt]
Rock skirt [skɜ:t]
Rolle part [pɑ:t]; role [rəʊl]
rosa pink [pɪŋk]
rot red [red]
rot werden to go red [gəʊ 'red]
Rücken back [bæk]
rückwärtig back [bæk]
rufen to call [kɔ:l]; to cry [kraɪ]; to shout [ʃaʊt]
rufen *(Eule)* to hoot [hu:t]
Ruhe quiet [kwaɪət]
ruhig calm [kɑ:m]; quiet ['kwaɪət]
Russe/Russin Russian ['rʌʃn]
russisch Russian ['rʌʃn]

S

Saal hall [hɔ:l]
Sache thing [θɪŋ]
sagen to say [seɪ]; to tell [tel]
Saison season ['si:zn]
Salat salad ['sæləd]
sammeln to collect [kə'lekt]
Samstag Saturday ['sætədeɪ]
Sandwich sandwich ['sænwɪdʒ]
sanft soft [sɒft]
Sänger/Sängerin singer ['sɪŋə]
säubern to clean [kli:n]
sauer sour ['saʊə]
Säugling baby, babies *(pl)* ['beɪbi; 'beɪbiz]
Schachtel box, boxes *(pl)* [bɒks; 'bɒksɪz]
Schaf/Schafe sheep, sheep *(pl)* [ʃi:p]
Schalter desk [desk]
Schau show [ʃəʊ]
schauen to look [lʊk]
Schauspieler actor ['æktə]
schenken to give [gɪv]
scherzen to joke [dʒəʊk]
Scheune barn [bɑ:n]
schicken to send [send]
schieben to push [pʊʃ]
schief gehen to go wrong [gəʊ 'rɒŋ]
Schild sign [saɪn]
Schinken ham [hæm]; ham [hæm]
schlafen to be asleep [ˌbi:‿ə'sli:p]; to sleep [sli:p]
schläfrig sleepy ['sli:pi]
Schlafsack sleeping bag ['sli:pɪŋ ˌbæg]
Schlafzimmer bedroom ['bedrʊm]
Schlag knock [nɒk]
schlagen to bang [bæŋ]; to hit [hɪt]
Schlagzeug drums *(pl)* [drʌmz]
schlecht bad [bæd]
schlechter worse [wɜ:s]
schlechteste/schlechtester/schlechtestes worst [wɜ:st]
Schleiereule barn owl ['bɑ:n‿əʊl]
schließen to close [kləʊz]
Schließfach locker ['lɒkə]
schließlich in the end [ɪn ði:‿'end]
schlimmer worse [wɜ:s]
schlimmste/schlimmster/schlimmstes worst [wɜ:st]
Schlittschuhbahn ice rink ['aɪs rɪŋk]
Schloss castle ['kɑ:sl]
zum **Schluss** in the end [ɪn ði:‿'end]
Schlüssel key [ki:]
schmackhaft tasty ['teɪsti]
schmecken to taste [teɪst]
Pizza schmeckt besser. Pizza is tastier. ['pi:tsə ɪz ˌteɪstɪə]
Schminke make-up ['meɪkʌp]
schmutzig dirty ['dɜ:ti]
Schnee snow [snəʊ]
schneien to snow [snəʊ]
schnell fast [fɑ:st]; quick [kwɪk]
Schokolade chocolate ['tʃɒklət]
schön beautiful ['bju:tɪfl]; fine [faɪn]; nice [naɪs]
schon already [ɔ:l'redi]
schottisch Scottish ['skɒtɪʃ]

Schramme scratch [skrætʃ]
Schrank cupboard ['kʌbəd]
schrecklich frightening ['fraɪtnɪŋ]; horrible ['hɒrəbl]; terrible ['terəbl]
schreiben to write [raɪt]
Schreibtisch desk [desk]
schreien to cry [kraɪ]; to shout [ʃaʊt]
schreien *(Eule)* to hoot [hu:t]
Schuh shoe [ʃu:]
Schule school [sku:l]
Schüler/Schülerin pupil ['pju:pl]
Schulfach subject ['sʌbdʒɪkt]
Schulhof playground ['pleɪgraʊnd]
Schulklasse class [klɑ:s]
Schulleiter/Schulleiterin head teacher [ˌhed 'ti:tʃə]
Schulranzen school bag ['sku:l bæg]
Schultasche school bag ['sku:l bæg]
Schuppen shed [ʃed]
Schüssel bowl [bəʊl]
Schwamm sponge [spʌndʒ]
schwarz black [blæk]
Schwein pig [pɪg]
Schweinefleisch pork [pɔ:k]
schwenken to wave [weɪv]
schwer heavy ['hevi]
Schwester sister ['sɪstə]
schwierig difficult ['dɪfɪklt]; hard [hɑ:d]
Schwierigkeit problem ['prɒbləm]
schwimmen to swim [swɪm]
Scone *(Gebäck)* scone [skɒn]
sehen to look [lʊk]; to see [si:]
sehr very ['veri]
Seife soap [səʊp]
Seifenoper soap [səʊp]
sein to be [bi:]
an der Reihe sein to be on [bi:‿'ɒn]
an sein to be on [bi:‿'ɒn]
sein/seine his [hɪz]
seit for [fɔ:]; since [sɪnts]
seitdem since [sɪnts]
Seite page [peɪdʒ]
Sekunde second ['seknd]
selbstverständlich of course [əv 'kɔ:s]
seltsam strange [streɪndʒ]
Sendung show [ʃəʊ]
auf Sendung on the air [ˌɒn ði‿'eə]
September September [sep'tembə]
Service service ['sɜ:vɪs]
sich **setzen** to sit down [sɪt 'daʊn]
sich setzen zu to sit with ['sɪt wɪθ]
Shorts shorts *(pl)* [ʃɔ:ts]
Show show [ʃəʊ]
sicher sure [ʃʊə]
sichergehen to make sure [meɪk 'ʃʊə]
sie her [hɜ:]; she [ʃi:]
sie *(Mehrzahl)* they [ðeɪ]; them [ðem]
Sie you [ju:; jə]
siegen to win [wɪn]
Signal signal ['sɪgnl]
singen to sing [sɪŋ]
Sintflut flash flood ['flæʃ ˌflʌd]
Sitz seat [si:t]
sitzen to sit [sɪt]
in der Falle sitzen to be trapped [bi: 'træpt]
Sitzplatz seat [si:t]
Skateboard skateboard ['skeɪtbɔ:d]
skaten to skate [skeɪt]
SMS text message ['tekst ˌmesɪdʒ]
Snack snack [snæk]
so so [səʊ]
so … wie … as … as [æz … æz; əz … əz]
so (schlimm) that (bad) ['ðæt bæd]
Sofa sofa ['səʊfə]
sofort at once [ət 'wʌnts]; right away [raɪt‿ə'weɪ]
sogar even ['i:vn]
solange as long as [əz 'lɒŋ‿əz]
sollte/sollten should [ʃʊd]
Sommer summer ['sʌmə]
Sommerfest summer fair ['sʌmə ˌfeə]
Sonnenbräune suntan ['sʌntæn]
sonnig sunny ['sʌni]
Sonntag Sunday ['sʌndeɪ]
sonst else [els]
sich **Sorgen machen** to worry ['wʌri]
sorgfältig careful ['keəfl]
Spaghetti spaghetti [spə'geti]
spannend exciting [ɪk'saɪtɪŋ]
sparen to save [seɪv]
Sparschwein piggy bank ['pɪgi bæŋk]
Spaß fun [fʌn]
Spaß haben to have fun [ˌhæv 'fʌn]
Spaß machen to be fun [bi: 'fʌn]
Viel Spaß! Have fun! [ˌhæv 'fʌn]
spät late [leɪt]
später later ['leɪtə]
zu spät late [leɪt]
Speisekarte menu ['menju:]
Speisesaal dining room ['daɪnɪŋ rʊm]
speziell special ['speʃl]
Spiel game [geɪm]; match [mætʃ]; play [pleɪ]
spielen to play [pleɪ]
spielen *(Theater)* to act [ækt]
Spielplatz playground ['pleɪgraʊnd]
Sport sport [spɔ:t]
Sport *(Schulfach)* Physical Education (PE) [ˌfɪzɪkl‿edʒʊ'keɪʃn]
Sport machen to exercise ['eksəsaɪz]
Sport treiben to do sports [du: 'spɔ:ts]
Sportfest sports day ['spɔ:ts deɪ]
Sportgeschäft sports shop ['spɔ:ts ʃɒp]
Sportplatz sports field ['spɔ:ts fi:ld]
Sportzeug PE kit [ˌpi:‿'i: kɪt]
Sprache language ['læŋgwɪdʒ]
sprechen to say [seɪ]; to speak [spi:k]; to talk [tɔ:k]
sprechen mit to talk to ['tɔ:k tə]
springen to jump [dʒʌmp]
Stadion arena [ə'ri:nə]; stadium ['steɪdiəm]
Stadt city ['sɪti]; town [taʊn]
Stadtplan map [mæp]
Stand stall [stɔ:l]
Standbesitzer/Standbesitzerin stall holder ['stɔ:l ˌhəʊldə]
ständig always ['ɔ:lweɪz]
stark hard [hɑ:d]
Stärke power ['paʊə]
Start start [stɑ:t]
starten to start [stɑ:t]
Station station ['steɪʃn]
stehlen to steal [sti:l]
steigen to climb ['klaɪm]; to rise [raɪz]
Stein stone [stəʊn]
Stelle place [pleɪs]
stellen *(Uhr)* to set [set]
Sternwarte observatory [əb'zɜ:vətri]
Stiefvater stepdad ['stepdæd]
still quiet ['kwaɪət]
Stille quiet [kwaɪət]
Stimme voice [vɔɪs]
Stock stick [stɪk]
im oberen Stock upstairs [ʌp'steəz]
im unteren Stock downstairs [daʊn'steəz]
stoßen to bump [bʌmp]; to push [pʊʃ]
Straße road [rəʊd]; street [stri:t]
Strauch bush [bʊʃ; 'bʊʃɪz]
Streich trick [trɪk]
streng strict [strɪkt]
studieren to study ['stʌdi]
Studio studio ['stju:diəʊ]
Stuhl chair [tʃeə]
Stunde hour ['aʊə]
eine halbe Stunde half an hour [ˌhɑ:f‿ən‿'aʊə]
stundenlang for hours [fər‿'aʊəz]
Stundenplan timetable ['taɪmteɪbl]
Sturm storm [stɔ:m]
stürmisch stormy ['stɔ:mi]
suchen to look for ['lʊk fə]
Süden south [saʊθ]

Südwesten southwest [ˌsaʊθ'west]
Superlativ superlative [suː'pɜːlətɪv]
Supermarkt supermarket ['suːpəˌmɑːkɪt]
Suppe soup [suːp]
surfen to surf [sɜːf]
im Internet surfen to surf the Internet [ˌsɜːf ðiˌ'ɪntənet]
Surfen surfing ['sɜːfɪŋ]
süß sweet [swiːt]
Süßigkeit sweet [swiːt]
Sweatshirt sweatshirt ['swetʃɜːt]

T

Tafel board [bɔːd]
Tag day [deɪ]
Einen schönen Tag noch. Have a nice day. [ˌhævˌə naɪs 'deɪ]
eines Tages one day [wʌn 'deɪ]
Tagesgericht special [speʃl]
Tante aunt [ɑːnt]
tanzen to dance [dɑːnts]
Breakdance tanzen to break-dance ['breɪkdɑːnts]
Tasche bag [bæg]
Taschengeld pocket money ['pɒkɪt ˌmʌni]
Taschenlampe torch, torches *(pl)* [tɔːtʃ; 'tɔːtʃɪz]
Taschenmesser penknife, penknives *(pl)* ['pennaɪf; 'pennaɪvz]
Tasse cup [kʌp]
in der **Tat** in fact [ɪn 'fækt]
Tatsache fact [fækt]
Tausch exchange [ɪks'tʃeɪndʒ]; swap [swɒp]
tauschen to change [tʃeɪndʒ]; to swap [swɒp]
tausend thousand ['θaʊznd]
Team team [tiːm]
Technik Technology [tek'nɒlədʒi]
Tee tea [tiː]
Teil part [pɑːt]
telefaxen to fax [fæks]
Telefon phone [fəʊn]; telephone ['telɪfəʊn]
Telefonanruf phone call ['fəʊn ˌkɔːl]
telefonieren to phone [fəʊn]
Telefonnummer phone number ['fəʊn ˌnʌmbə]
Teller plate [pleɪt]
Temperatur temperature ['temprətʃə]
Test test [test]
teuer expensive [ɪk'spentsɪv]
Theaterstück play [pleɪ]
Thema subject ['sʌbdʒɪkt]; topic ['tɒpɪk]
Ticket ticket ['tɪkɪt]
Tier animal ['ænɪml]
Tierpark zoo [zuː]
Tierpfleger/Tierpflegerin zookeeper ['zuːkiːpə]
Tiger tiger ['taɪgə]
Tipp tip [tɪp]
Tisch table ['teɪbl]
Tisch decken to set the table [ˌset ðə 'teɪbl]
Tischtennis table-tennis ['teɪblˌtenɪs]
Titel title ['taɪtl]
Titelseite cover ['kʌvə]
Toilette toilet ['tɔɪlɪt]
toll brilliant ['brɪljənt]; great [greɪt]
Tomate tomato, tomatoes *(pl)* [tə'mɑːtəʊ; tə'mɑːtəʊz]
Ton sound [saʊnd]
Topf pot [pɒt]
Tor gate [geɪt]; goal [gəʊl]
tragen to carry ['kæri]
Transport transport ['træntspɔːt]
Traum dream [driːm]
traurig sad [sæd]
treffen to hit [hɪt]; to meet [miːt]
sich treffen to meet [miːt]
Treffen meeting ['miːtɪŋ]
treten to kick [kɪk]
Trick trick [trɪk]
trinken to drink [drɪŋk]
Trödelstand white elephant stall [ˌwaɪt 'elɪfənt stɔːl]
tschüss bye [baɪ]
T-Shirt T-shirt ['tiːʃɜːt]
tun to do [duː]; to make [meɪk]
Tunnel tunnel ['tʌnl]
Tür door [dɔː]
türkisch Turkish ['tɜːkɪʃ]
Türklingel doorbell ['dɔːbel]
Turnhalle gym [dʒɪm]
Tüte bag [bæg]
Typ bloke [bləʊk]
tyrannisieren (to) bully ['bʊli]

U

Übelkeit verspüren to feel sick [fiːl 'sɪk]
üben to exercise ['eksəsaɪz]; to practise ['præktɪs]
über above [ə'bʌv]; over ['əʊvə]; about [ə'baʊt]
überall everywhere ['evriweə]
überprüfen to check [tʃek]
überraschend surprising [sə'praɪzɪŋ]
überrascht surprised [sə'praɪzd]
Überschrift title ['taɪtl]
Überschwemmung flood [flʌd]
flutartige Überschwemmung flash flood ['flæʃ ˌflʌd]
übrig left [left]
Übung exercise ['eksəsaɪz]
Übungsheft exercise book ['eksəsaɪz ˌbʊk]
Uhr clock [klɒk]
Uhr *(Zeitangabe)* o'clock [ə'klɒk]
Wie viel Uhr ist es, bitte? What's the time, please? [ˌwɒts ðə 'taɪm ˌpliːz]
umdrehen to turn over [ˌtɜːnˌ'əʊvə]; to turn round [ˌtɜːn 'raʊnd]
sich umdrehen to turn over [ˌtɜːnˌ'əʊvə]; to turn round [ˌtɜːn 'raʊnd]
Umfrage survey ['sɜːveɪ]
Umgebung environment [ɪn'vaɪərnmənt]
umher around [ə'raʊnd]
umkehren to turn back [tɜːn 'bæk]
Umschlag envelope ['envələʊp]
sich **umsehen** to look round [lʊk 'raʊnd]
Umwelt environment [ɪn'vaɪərnmənt]
umziehen to move [muːv]
sich umziehen to change [tʃeɪndʒ]
und and [ænd]
Unfall accident ['æksɪdnt]
ungesund unhealthy [ʌn'helθi]
unglücklich unhappy [ʌn'hæpi]
unheimlich scary ['skeəri]; spooky ['spuːki]
Uniform uniform ['juːnɪfɔːm]
uns us [ʌs]
unser/unsere our ['aʊə]
Unsinn rubbish ['rʌbɪʃ]
unten downstairs [daʊn'steəz]
unter under ['ʌndə]
Unterführung tunnel ['tʌnl]
sich **unterhalten** to chat [tʃæt]
Unterhaltung chat [tʃæt]
Unterricht class [klɑːs]
unterrichten to teach [tiːtʃ]
Unterrichtsstunde lesson ['lesn]
unterschreiben to sign [saɪn]
unterstreichen to underline [ˌʌndə'laɪn]
Urlaub holiday(s) ['hɒlədeɪ(z)]
usw. etc. [ɪt'setrə]

V

Vati dad [dæd]
vegetarisch vegetarian [ˌvedʒɪ'teəriən]
verändern to change [tʃeɪndʒ]
verängstigt scared [skeəd]
Veranstaltung event [ɪ'vent]
verärgert angry ['æŋgri]
verbringen to spend [spend]
Verein club [klʌb]
Vergangenheit past [pɑ:st]
vergessen to forget [fə'get]
verheiratet mit married to ['mærid tə]
sich **verirren** to get lost [get 'lɒst]
verkaufen to sell [sel]
Verkäufer/Verkäuferin shop assistant ['ʃɒp‿əˌsɪstnt]
verlassen to leave [li:v]
verletzen to hurt [hɜ:t]
verlieren to lose [lu:z]
verloren gehen to get lost [get 'lɒst]
vermissen to miss [mɪs]
verpassen to miss [mɪs]
verregnet rainy ['reɪni]
verrückt crazy ['kreɪzi]; mad [mæd]
verrückt machen to drive crazy [draɪv 'kreɪzi]
verrückt nach … sein to be nuts about [bi: ˌnʌts‿ə'baʊt]
verrückt werden to go bananas [ˌgəʊ bə'nɑ:nəz]
Versammlung assembly [ə'sembli]
verschieden different ['dɪfrnt]
verschlafen sleepy ['sli:pi]
verschneit snowy ['snəʊi]
verschwinden to disappear [ˌdɪsə'pɪə]
verspätet late [leɪt]
versprechen to promise ['prɒmɪs]
verstecken to hide [haɪd]
sich verstecken to hide [haɪd]
Versuch experiment [ɪk'sperɪmənt]
versuchen to try [traɪ]
verwenden to use [ju:z]
Video video ['vɪdiəʊ]
viel a lot [ə 'lɒt]; much [mʌtʃ]
viele many ['meni]
viel/viele a lot of [ə 'lɒt‿əv]; lots (of) ['lɒts‿əv]
Viel Glück! Good luck! [ˌgʊd 'lʌk]
vielleicht maybe ['meɪbi]
Viertel nach quarter past ['kwɔ:tə pɑ:st]
Viertel vor quarter to ['kwɔ:tə tə]
violett purple ['pɜ:pl]
Vogel bird [bɜ:d]
Volleyball volleyball ['vɒlibɔ:l]
von from [frɒm]; of [ɒv; əv]
vor before [bɪ'fɔ:]; in front of [ɪn 'frʌnt‿əv]
vor *(zeitlich)* ago [ə'gəʊ]
vorbei over ['əʊvə]
sich **vorbereiten** to get ready [get 'redi]
Vorhersage *(Wetter)* forecast ['fɔ:kɑ:st]
Vormittag morning ['mɔ:nɪŋ]
vormittags in the morning [ˌɪn ðə 'mɔ:nɪŋ]
Vorschrift rule [ru:l]
vorsichtig careful ['keəfl]
Vorsingen audition [ɔ:'dɪʃn]
Vorspeise starter ['stɑ:tə]
Vorsprechen audition [ɔ:'dɪʃn]
Vortanzen audition [ɔ:'dɪʃn]
vorüber over ['əʊvə]

W

wachsen to rise [raɪz]
wählen to choose [tʃu:z]
wahr true [tru:]
während during ['djʊərɪŋ]
wahrscheinlich probably ['prɒbəbli]
Wand wall [wɔ:l]
Wandtafel board [bɔ:d]
wann when [wen]
warm warm [wɔ:m]
warten to wait [weɪt]
Warte mal! Hang on! ['hæŋ‿ɒn]
warten auf to wait for ['weɪt fɔ:]
Wärter/Wärterin zookeeper ['zu:ki:pə]
warum why [waɪ]
was what [wɒt]
Was ist los? What's up? [ˌwɒts‿'ʌp]; What's wrong? [ˌwɒts 'rɒŋ]
Was ist mit …? What about …? [wɒt‿ə'baʊt]
Was steht da? What does it say? [ˌwɒt dʌz‿ɪt 'seɪ]
waschen to wash [wɒʃ]
sich waschen to wash [wɒʃ]
Wasser water ['wɔ:tə]
Wassermann Aquarius [ə'kweəriəs]
Website website ['websaɪt]
Wechselgeld change [tʃeɪndʒ]
wechseln to change [tʃeɪndʒ]
wecken to wake [weɪk]
Wecker alarm clock [ə'lɑ:m ˌklɒk]
weg away [ə'weɪ]
Weg path [pɑ:θ]; way [weɪ]
Er ist auf dem Weg zu … . He is on his way to … . [ˌhi:‿ɪz‿ɒn hɪz 'weɪ tə]
wegen because of [bɪ'kɒz‿əv]
weggehen to leave [li:v]
wegnehmen to take [teɪk]
wegrennen to run away [rʌn‿ə'weɪ]
weh tun to hurt [hɜ:t]
weich soft [sɒft]
weil because [bɪ'kɒz]
weinen to cry [kraɪ]
weit far [fɑ:]
weitergeben to pass [pɑ:s]
Weitsprung long jump ['lɒŋ ˌdʒʌmp]
welche/welcher/welches what [wɒt]; which [wɪtʃ]
Wellenreiten surfing ['sɜ:fɪŋ]
wem who [hu:]
wen who [hu:]
wenige few [fju:]
wenigstens at least [ət 'li:st]
wenn if [ɪf]; when [wen]
wer who [hu:]
werden to get [get]
werden *(futurisch)* will ('ll), won't [wɪl; wəʊnt]
werfen to throw [θrəʊ]
wessen whose [hu:z]
Westen west [west]
wetten to bet [bet]
Wetter weather ['weðə]
Wettkampf match [mætʃ]
Wettlauf race [reɪs]
einen Wettlauf machen to run a race [ˌrʌn‿ə 'reɪs]
wichtig important [ɪm'pɔ:tnt]
wie *(Vergleich)* like [laɪk]
wie how [haʊ]
Wie alt bist du? How old are you? [haʊ‿'əʊld‿ɑ: ju:]
Wie findest du … ? What do you think of … ? [ˌwɒt du: ju: 'θɪŋk‿əv]
Wie geht es dir/Ihnen/euch? How are you? [ˌhaʊ‿'ɑ: ju:]
Wie heißt du? What's your name? [ˌwɒts jə 'neɪm]
wie viele how many [haʊ 'meni]
Wie viel kosten … ? How much are … ? [ˌhaʊ 'mʌtʃ‿ɑ:]
Wie viel kostet … ? How much is … ? [ˌhaʊ 'mʌtʃ‿ɪz]
Wie viel Uhr ist es, bitte? What's the time, please? [ˌwɒts ðə 'taɪm ˌpli:z]
Wie wäre es mit …? What about …? [wɒt‿ə'baʊt]
wieder again [ə'gen]
auf **Wiedersehen** goodbye [gʊd'baɪ]
willkommen heißen to welcome ['welkəm]
Wind wind [wɪnd]

windig windy ['wɪndi]
windsurfen to surf [sɜ:f]
winken to wave [weɪv]
Winter winter ['wɪntə]
winzig tiny ['taɪni]
wir we [wi:]
wirklich real [rɪəl]; really ['rɪəli]
wissen to know [nəʊ]
Wissenschaft Science ['saɪənts]
Witz joke [dʒəʊk]
Witze machen to joke [dʒəʊk]
wo where [weə]
Woche week [wi:k]
in der Woche a week [ə 'wi:k]
pro Woche a week [ə 'wi:k]
Wochenende weekend [ˌwi:k'end]
Woher kommst du? Where are you from? [ˌweər‿ə jə 'frɒm]
wohin where [weə]
Wohltätigkeit charity ['tʃærɪti]
Wohltätigkeitsverein charity ['tʃærɪti]
wohnen to live [lɪv]
wohnen bei to stay with ['steɪ wɪð]
Wohnung flat [flæt]
Wohnzimmer living room ['lɪvɪŋ rʊm]
Wolke cloud [klaʊd]
wolkig cloudy ['klaʊdi]
Wolldecke blanket ['blæŋkɪt]
wollen to want (to) ['wɒnt tə]
Wort word [wɜ:d]
wunderschön beautiful ['bju:tɪfl]
Wurst sausage ['sɒsɪdʒ]
Würstchen sausage ['sɒsɪdʒ]
würzig spicy ['spaɪsi]
wütend mad [mæd]

Z

Zahl number ['nʌmbə]
Zauberer wizard ['wɪzəd]
Zeh toe [təʊ]
Zeichen sign [saɪn]
zeichnen to draw [drɔ:]
zeigen to show [ʃəʊ]
Zeile line [laɪn]
Zeit time [taɪm]
Du liebe Zeit! Good grief! [gʊd 'gri:f]
Zeitalter age [eɪdʒ]
Zeitschrift magazine [mægə'zi:n]
Zeitschriftenhändler/ Zeitschriftenhändlerin newsagent ['nju:sˌeɪdʒənt]
Zeitung newspaper ['nju:sˌpeɪpə]
Zelt tent [tent]
Zelten camping ['kæmpɪŋ]
Zentrum centre ['sentə]
zerbrechen to break [breɪk]
zerbrochen broken ['brəʊkn]
zerkratzen to scratch [skrætʃ]
ziehen to pull [pʊl]
Ziel goal [gəʊl]
Zimmer room [ru:m; rʊm]
Zoll customs *(pl)* ['kʌstəmz]
Zoo zoo [zu:]
zu to [tʊ; tə]
zuerst at first [ət 'fɜ:st], first [fɜ:st]
zuflüstern to whisper ['wɪspə]
zufrieden sein mit to be pleased with [bi: 'pli:zd wɪð]
Zug train [treɪn]
Zuhause home [həʊm]
zuhören to listen ['lɪsn]
zumachen to close [kləʊz]
zunächst at first [ət 'fɜ:st]
zunehmen to rise [raɪz]; to rise, rose, risen [raɪz, rəʊz, rɪzn]
zurück back [bæk]
zurückgehen to turn back [tɜ:n 'bæk]
zusammen together [tə'geðə]
Zusatz extra ['ekstrə]
zusätzlich extra ['ekstrə]
zwischen between [bɪ'twi:n]

Place names

Australien Australia [ɒs'treɪliə]
Britische Inseln British Isles [ˌbrɪtɪʃ 'aɪlz]
Deutschland Germany ['dʒɜ:məni]
England England ['ɪŋglənd]
Griechenland Greece [gri:s]
Italien Italy ['ɪtəli]
Polen Poland ['pəʊlənd]
Russland Russia ['rʌʃə]
Schottland Scotland ['skɒtlənd]
Türkei Turkey ['tɜ:ki]
Wales Wales [weɪlz]

In the classroom

You

Problems

My pen has gone.	Mein Stift ist verschwunden.
Have you got a pen that I can borrow?	Hast du einen Stift für mich?
Sir, Tobias has taken my bag.	Herr …, Tobias hat meine Tasche genommen.
Miss, I've forgotten my PE kit.	Frau …, ich habe meine Sportsachen vergessen.
Should I ask … about the homework?	Soll ich … nach den Hausaufgaben fragen?
I don't understand this exercise.	Ich verstehe diese Übung nicht.
Wait, I'll help you.	Warte mal! Ich helfe dir.
I'll carry those books for you, Miss.	Ich trage Ihnen die Bücher, Frau … .
I'll get a note from my mum.	Ich werde Mutti um eine Entschuldigung bitten.

Questions

What are your subjects?	Was sind deine Fächer?
Who have you got for Maths/… ?	Wen habt ihr in Mathe/ … ?
When does the next lesson start?	Wann fängt die nächste Unterrichtsstunde an?
How do you say 'hello' in French/…?	Wie sagt man „Guten Tag" auf Französisch/… ?
What are we doing tomorrow?	Was machen wir morgen?
Will I need rubber boots/ … for Biology?	Brauche ich Gummistiefel/ … in Biologie?

Sorry!

I'm sorry about my homework/… .	Es tut mir Leid wegen meiner Hausaufgaben.
I'm sorry that I was late.	Es tut mir Leid, dass ich zu spät kam.

Your teacher

Instructions

This is … . He's/She's new.	Das hier ist … . Er/Sie ist neu.
Can you look after him/her, please?	Kannst du dich bitte um ihn/sie kümmern?
Make a 'grammar card'.	Stelle eine Grammatikkarte her.
Make notes.	Schreibt euch Notizen auf.
Take notes.	Macht euch Notizen.
Read the definitions.	Lest die Definitionen.
Look on the Internet for more information.	Sucht im Internet nach mehr Informationen.
Sort it out with him/her!	Kläre es mit ihm/ihr!
Don't send text messages in class.	Schickt keine SMS im Unterricht.
Fill in the forms, please.	Füllt bitte die Formulare aus.
Ask your parents to sign them.	Bittet eure Eltern, sie zu unterschreiben.

Questions

What subjects have you got after lunch?	Was habt ihr nach dem Mittagessen für Fächer?
Where is your book?	Wo ist dein Buch?
What have you done to your face?	Was hast du mit deinem Gesicht gemacht?
How did you do that?	Wie hast du das denn gemacht?
Can you find the mistakes?	Könnt ihr die Fehler entdecken?
What did I tell you yesterday?	Was habe ich gestern zu euch gesagt?

List of irregular verbs

to be [bi:]	was/were [wɒz/wɜ:]	been [bi:n]	sein
to begin [bɪ'gɪn]	began [bɪ'gæn]	begun [bɪ'gʌn]	beginnen, anfangen
to bet [bet]	bet [bet]	bet [bet]	wetten
to break [breɪk]	broke [brəʊk]	broken ['brəʊkn]	(zer)brechen; kaputtmachen
to bring [brɪŋ]	brought [brɔ:t]	brought [brɔ:t]	bringen, mitbringen
to buy [baɪ]	bought [bɔ:t]	bought [bɔ:t]	kaufen
to catch [kætʃ]	caught [kɔ:t]	caught [kɔ:t]	fangen
to choose [tʃu:z]	chose [tʃəʊz]	chosen ['tʃəʊzn]	wählen, auswählen
to come [kʌm]	came [keɪm]	come [kʌm]	kommen
to cut [kʌt]	cut [kʌt]	cut [kʌt]	schneiden
to do [du:]	did [dɪd]	done [dʌn]	machen, tun
to draw [drɔ:]	drew [dru:]	drawn [drɔ:n]	zeichnen
to drink [drɪŋk]	drank [dræŋk]	drunk [drʌŋk]	trinken
to drive [draɪv]	drove [drəʊv]	driven ['drɪvn]	fahren
to eat [i:t]	ate [et/eɪt]	eaten ['i:tn]	essen, fressen
to fall [fɔ:l]	fell [fel]	fallen ['fɔ:ln]	fallen, herunterfallen, hinfallen
to feed [fi:d]	fed [fed]	fed [fed]	füttern
to feel [fi:l]	felt [felt]	felt [felt]	fühlen, sich fühlen
to find [faɪnd]	found [faʊnd]	found [faʊnd]	finden
to fly [flaɪ]	flew [flu:]	flown [fləʊn]	fliegen
to forget [fə'get]	forgot [fə'gɒt]	forgotten [fə'gɒtn]	vergessen
to get [get]	got [gɒt]	got [gɒt]	kommen, bekommen; werden
to give [gɪv]	gave [geɪv]	given ['gɪvn]	geben, schenken
to go [gəʊ]	went [went]	gone [gɒn]	gehen
to hear [hɪə]	heard [hɜ:d]	heard [hɜ:d]	hören
to hide [haɪd]	hid [hɪd]	hidden ['hɪdn]	verstecken, sich verstecken
to hit [hɪt]	hit [hɪt]	hit [hɪt]	schlagen, treffen
to hurt [hɜ:t]	hurt [hɜ:t]	hurt [hɜ:t]	verletzen, weh tun
to keep [ki:p]	kept [kept]	kept [kept]	(be)halten
to know [nəʊ]	knew [nju:]	known [nəʊn]	wissen, kennen
to learn [lɜ:n]	learnt [lɜ:nt]	learnt [lɜ:nt]	lernen
to leave [li:v]	left [left]	left [left]	lassen, verlassen, abfahren
to lend [lend]	lent [lent]	lent [lent]	leihen
to lose [lu:z]	lost [lɒst]	lost [lɒst]	verlieren
to make [meɪk]	made [meɪd]	made [meɪd]	machen, tun
to mean [mi:n]	meant [ment]	meant [ment]	bedeuten, meinen
to meet [mi:t]	met [met]	met [met]	treffen, sich treffen
to put [pʊt]	put [pʊt]	put [pʊt]	setzen, stellen, legen
to read [ri:d]	read [red]	read [red]	lesen
to ride [raɪd]	rode [rəʊd]	ridden ['rɪdn]	fahren, reiten
to ring [rɪŋ]	rang [ræŋ]	rung[rʌŋ]	klingeln; anrufen
to rise [raɪz]	rose [rəʊz]	risen [rɪzn]	steigen, wachsen, zunehmen
to run [rʌn]	ran [ræn]	run [rʌn]	rennen, laufen
to say [seɪ]	said [sed]	said [sed]	sagen, sprechen
to see [si:]	saw [sɔ:]	seen [si:n]	sehen; besuchen
to sell [sel]	sold [səʊld]	sold [səʊld]	verkaufen
to send [send]	sent [sent]	sent [sent]	schicken
to set [set]	set [set]	set [set]	stellen, einstellen
to show [ʃəʊ]	showed [ʃəʊd]	shown [ʃəʊn]	zeigen
to sing [sɪŋ]	sang [sæŋ]	sung [sʌŋ]	singen
to sit [sɪt]	sat [sæt]	sat [sæt]	sitzen
to sleep [sli:p]	slept [slept]	slept [slept]	schlafen
to speak [spi:k]	spoke [spəʊk]	spoken ['spəʊkn]	sprechen
to spell [spel]	spelt [spelt]	spelt [spelt]	buchstabieren
to spend [spend]	spent [spent]	spent [spent]	verbringen, ausgeben
to steal [sti:l]	stole [stəʊl]	stolen ['stəʊln]	stehlen
to swim [swɪm]	swam [swæm]	swum [swʌm]	schwimmen
to take [teɪk]	took [tʊk]	taken ['teɪkn]	nehmen, mitnehmen, bringen
to teach [ti:tʃ]	taught [tɔ:t]	taught [tɔ:t]	lehren
to tell [tel]	told [təʊld]	told [təʊld]	erzählen, sagen
to think [θɪŋk]	thought [θɔ:t]	thought [θɔ:t]	denken, glauben
to throw [θrəʊ]	threw [θru:]	thrown [θrəʊn]	werfen
to understand [ˌʌndə'stænd]	understood [ˌʌndə'stʊd]	understood [ˌʌndə'stʊd]	verstehen
to wake [weɪk]	woke [wəʊk]	woken ['wəʊkn]	(auf)wecken
to wear [weə]	wore [wɔ:]	worn [wɔ:n]	anhaben, tragen
to win [wɪn]	won [wɒn]	won [wɒn]	gewinnen, siegen
to write [raɪt]	wrote [rəʊt]	written ['rɪtn]	schreiben

Lösungen

Check-out

Unit 1 Seite 21

1 The new boy

Hi, how are you? And how is Bristol? I must tell you about the new boy in our year. He's really nice! His name is Jake and he **comes** from Australia. His dad still **lives** there. His mum and his brother **live** near us, and he sometimes **takes** the bus home with me. They **don't wear** a uniform in his school in Australia, but they **get** a lot of homework. He **doesn't play** football, he **plays** hockey and after school he and his friends **go** surfing. He **says** it's great! I want to go there next year. But I **haven't got** the money.

2 Questions for the first day

1. Where do we get the bus?
2. How do we get to the sports hall?
3. When does lunchtime finish?
4. Who do we ask?
5. What do we need for gym?
6. Why does he say "G'day"?

3 There's a choice.

1. **Which** sports do you play: hockey, football or basketball?
2. **What** languages do you speak?
3. **What** English towns do you know?
4. **Which** English towns are in your book: Bristol, Bath or London?
5. **Which** languages do you learn at school: French, Italian or German?
6. **Which** animals have you got at home: cats, dogs or fish?
7. **What** sports do you like?
8. **What** animals do you like?

Unit 2 Seite 33

1 Jade's story

1. No, **he wasn't**, Jade. He was **really angry**.
2. No, **you weren't**, Jade. You were very happy **for one hour**.
3. Yes, **you were**, Jade. You were really hungry **after an hour**.
4. No, **they weren't**, Jade. They were **great**.
5. No, **it wasn't**. It was **difficult**.
6. No, **I wasn't**, Jade. I was very angry **with you**.

2 Barker's story

I waited outside with the other dogs. People **stopped** and **played** with us. One man **gave** me his sandwich! A little boy **talked** to me for fifteen minutes, but then he **went** inside. When the store **closed** and Lisa **came** out, I **was** really happy. I **jumped** up on her and then she and her friends **followed** me. I **walked** behind the store and **found** Terry.

3 Telling a story

Last Saturday Tom **watched** TV. He **saw** Supermouse. **The next day** he went to a shop.
He **bought** something to dye his hair. **Later** he **looked at** T-shirts. He **put on** a red T-shirt.
After that he **dyed** his hair. **An hour later** he **said**, "I look like Supermouse!" **Then** his mum **found** the bottle.
She **was** very angry. **That evening** she **shouted at** Tom. He **washed** his hair again.

Unit 3 Seite 47

1 Grandma got it wrong.

1. **I didn't try** a new game. I tried a new **trick**.
2. **They didn't push** me off the bike. **I fell off**.
3. **We didn't put** black paint on the bike. We put **yellow** paint on it.
4. **He didn't take** me to the school nurse. He took me to the **doctor's**.
5. **You didn't see** a horrible mark on his T-shirt. You saw a horrible mark on his **trousers**.
6. **I didn't feel** really happy. I felt really **terrible**.

2 Sam's accident

Emma: **Did you see** Terry yesterday?
Sam: **Yes, I did.**
Emma: **Did you go** to the park?
Sam: **No, we didn't.** Terry had homework.
Emma: **Did you take** your bike?
Sam: **No, I didn't.** I took my dad's bike.
Emma: **Did he give** it to you?
Sam: **No, he didn't.** I borrowed it.
Emma: **Did you do** some tricks?
Sam: **Yes, I did.** But I fell off.
Emma: Oh! **Did you break** your arm?
Sam: **No, I didn't.** But it still hurts.
Emma: **Did you go** to the doctor?
Sam: **Yes, I did.** I'm OK.

3 Guess who or what it is.

1. It's the name of a person **who** works in a hospital at night. – **A night nurse.**
2. It's the name of a game **which** begins with the letter 'h'. – **Hockey.**
3. It's the name of a place in London **which** has got a lot of animals. – **London Zoo.**
4. It's the name of a very famous woman **who** lives in Buckingham Palace. – **Queen Elizabeth.**
5. It's the name of a part of your arm **which** is between elbow and fingers. – **Hand.**

Unit 4 Seite 59

1 Comparing things

1. The vegetable curry is **spicy**. It is **spicier** than the fish curry but the lamb curry is **the spiciest**.
2. The ham sandwiches are **expensive**. They are **more expensive** than the cheese sandwiches. But the fish sandwiches are **the most expensive**.
3. Fish and chips are not **healthy** food. Are they **healthier** than cake? Salads and vegetables are **the healthiest** food.
4. Sam thinks salad is **boring** food. It's even **more boring** than soup. But vegetables are **the most boring** food.
5. The doctor thinks walking is **good**. But jogging is **better** and swimming is **the best** sport.
6. Terry's teacher says cakes are **bad** for you. Are they **worse** than sausages? She says burgers are **the worst** food for you.

2 In town

1. c 2. e 3. a 4. b 5. d

3 Have we got any tomatoes?

Terry's dad: I want to make **some** lunch for us, Terry. Have we got **any** tomatoes or **any** lettuce?
Terry: No, we haven't got **any** salad things.
Terry's dad: Oh, no! I must eat **some** vegetables today.
Terry: Well, we've got **some** carrots and **some** beans. You can make **some** vegetable burgers.
Terry's dad: But we haven't got **any** potatoes. I can't eat just burgers!
Terry: No, you're right. But there's **some** rice in the cupboard.

Unit 5 Seite 73

1 Saturday morning at the Taylors' house

2. **Jade's hands and face are** clean. **She has just washed them.**
3. **Breakfast is** ready. **Mr Taylor has just set** the table.
4. **Mrs Taylor is** hungry. **She has just jogged** in the park.
5. **Ben is** tired. **He has just turned off** the alarm clock.
6. **Lisa is** ready. **She has just put** on a sweatshirt.

2 On the phone

Emma: Hi, Lisa. **Have** you had breakfast yet?
Lisa: No, I **haven't**. But Dad **has** just told me it's ready.
Emma: **Has** he made breakfast this morning?
Lisa: Yes, he **has**. Mum **has** gone to the park.
Emma: **Has** she started her diet yet?
Lisa: No, she **hasn't**. She wants to start tomorrow.
Emma: Oh, **have** you asked your mum and dad about this evening yet?
Lisa: Yes, I **have**. It's OK. We can go to the cinema. But they **haven't** given me my pocket money yet.
Emma: Don't worry. Mum **has** just given me ten pounds.
Lisa: Great! I must go, Emma. Mum **has** just come in.

3 Steve's questions

1. **Who has taken my shoes?**
2. **Where have I left my book?**
3. **What has Mum put in my sandwich?**
4. **Where has the manager gone?**
5. **Who has drunk my water?**
6. **What has she written?**

Unit 6 Seite 85

1 Girls will be girls

Lisa: Hi, Emma. Have you got this week's "Star" magazine there?
Emma: No, Nasreen has got it at the moment. **I'll** go and get it from her.
Lisa: No, wait. **I'll** read something to you. It's my horoscope for next week.
Emma: OK, just a minute. **I'll** close the door, so Nasreen **won't** hear. OK. What does it say?
Lisa: It says, "Be really careful! Things **will** go wrong for you at the weekend. You**'ll** meet a new friend but he **won't** be very nice to you. You **won't** be very happy on Saturday."
Emma: So what's the big problem? Just don't go out with a boy on Saturday and you**'ll** be happy.

Lisa: But I want to go to *Spiderman III* with Peter tomorrow.
Emma: Lisa, it'**ll** be OK. Peter isn't a new friend. You've known him for weeks. And Martin and I **will** be there, too. But you **won't** tell Jake, I hope.

2 European weather
Italy: It will be hot and sunny. The temperature will be 28° to 30°.
Poland: It will be cold and windy. The temperature will be 5° to 10°.
Ireland: It will be rainy and warm. The temperature will be 24° to 25°.

3 Was the note right?
Go to the café at the station. **A young** mouse will **sit next to** your table. He **will order a lemonade**. He will give you **some flowers**. There **won't be any** money with it. He **will** smile, **and** he **will** ask you a question.

Unit 7 Seite 97

1 In town
1. You should always drive carefully when the roads are wet.
2. If you ride your bike crazily there will be an accident.
3. Ring your bell loudly before you go past people in the park.
4. Skate slowly when you are near old people.
5. You can play music quietly in the bus.
6. Give a sign correctly before you turn left or right.

2 Tom's week
a)

adjective	adverb of manner
angry	angrily
bad	badly
beautiful	beautifully
correct	correctly
quick	quickly

adjective	adverb of manner
excited	excitedly
healthy	healthily
hungry	hungrily
nervous	nervously
soft	softly

b) shout • run • sing • cook • dance • wait • watch • write • whisper • eat

2. Tom ran quickly.
3. Tom sang badly.
4. Tom cooked healthily.
5. Tom ate hungrily.
6. Tom danced beautifully.
7. Tom waited nervously.
8. Tom watched excitedly.
9. Tom wrote correctly.
10. Tom whispered softly.

3 Find the questions.
1. If it is sunny tomorrow, we **will go swimming in the river.**
2. If the plane is late, they **will wait in the café.**
3. If sheep come into the garden, the dog **will bark.**
4. If you go to Ireland, I hope you **will send us a postcard.**

Revision 1 Seite 34

1 Dave's free morning
1. At 6:00 Dave often feeds the cows. At 6:00 this morning he is sleeping.
2. At 8:00 Dave often takes vegetables to the market. At 8:00 this morning he is listening to music.
3. At 9:30 Dave often feeds the dogs. At 9:30 this morning he is having breakfast.
4. At 10:00 Dave often collects eggs. At 10:00 this morning he is checking his e-mails.
5. At 10:30 Dave often checks the sheep. At 10:30 this morning he is reading a magazine.
6. At 11:00 Dave often helps the farmer with the pigs. At 11:00 this morning he is phoning Mary.

2 A boring day
1. take; is raining
2. is wearing; wears; is
3. meet; play
4. is visiting; are having
5. makes; is making
6. wants; want
7. is taking; are making
8. makes; hates; is having

Seite 35

3 It was terrible
was; was; were; weren't; were; was; were; were; was; Were; wasn't; was; were; was; Wasn't; was; was

4 Super, Barker!

1. Where; was; was
2. Who; was; was
3. What; was; was
4. Where; were; were
5. Why; was; were; were; were
6. What; was; were
7. Where; was; was; was
8. Where; was; was
9. How; was; was

5 A letter from home

are; is; talk; started; met; is; did; gave; was; were; sit; is; came; thinks; asked; wear; laughed; are

Revision 2 Seite 60

1 Did you see Jake yesterday?

Did; didn't; didn't didn't; didn't; Didn't; didn't; Did; did; didn't; Did; did; didn't

2 A phone call from Mum!

a) 1. Why were you
2. Who did you meet
3. What did you do
4. Where did you find
5. How was
6. What did you write

b) a 2; b 5; c 6; d 3; e 1; f 4

3 A new plan

They didn't learn about money on Monday. They played computer games.
They didn't play football on Tuesday. They jogged in the park.
They didn't do experiments on Wednesday. They made a poster.
They didn't finish their project on Wednesday. They watched a video.
They didn't go on a class trip on Thursday. They told stories.
They didn't start Unit 4 on Thursday. They did exercises on a worksheet.
They didn't talk about problems on Friday. The acted role plays.

Seite 61

4 Pupils get fit.

most; more; best; healthier; better; more; best; more; cooler; worst; better; fit; easier; bad; worse; good; biggest

5 Happy birthday!

any; some; some; some; any; any; some; any; some; some; any; some; any; some; any; any; some

Revision 3 Seite 86

1 Things have changed.

has lived; has seen; have moved; have left; have gone; have changed; have taken; have put; has changed; have gone; has bought; has invited; has disappeared; has gone; have forgotten; have closed; have changed

2. Have they done it yet?

a) Have you and Ben made the beds yet? – Yes, we have.
Have you and Jade taken Barker out to the park yet? – No, we haven't.
Have you turned off the computer yet? – Yes, I have.
Has Jade put her games back in the cupboard yet? No, she hasn't.
Have you all eaten your supper yet? – Yes, we have.
Has Barker found my car keys yet? – No, he hasn't.

b) Ben hasn't finished his homework yet.
Lisa and Ben have made the beds.
Lisa and Jade haven't taken Barker out to the park yet.
Lisa has turned off the computer.
Jade hasn't put her games back in the cupboard yet.
All of them have eaten their supper.
Barker hasn't found her car keys yet.

3 Help!

already; yet; yet; ever; never; already; just; still; already; still

Seite 87

4 Visitors to Greenwich

a) 1. It will be cloudy and the temperature will rise to 23-26°C.
2. It will rain on Friday.
3. It will be sunny on Wednesday and on Thursday.
4. On Friday it will rain and the temperature will be 19-21°C.
5. No, you won't need an umbrella on Thursday because it will be sunny.
6. Yes, Thursday will be a good day for photos because it will be sunny.

b) On Monday it will be cloudy and there will be a storm. The temperature will be 18-20°C.
On Tuesday it will be foggy and the temperature will be 20°C.
On Wednesday it will be sunny and windy and the temperature will rise to 22-26°C.
On Thursday it will be sunny and the temperature will be 25°C.
On Friday it will be rainy and the temperature will be 19-21°C.
At the weekend it will be sunny and cloudy and the temperature will rise to 23-25°C.

5 Lisa's horoscope

You will meet a young man in the park.
Two boys will arrive.
They will have a football.
One boy will kick the ball.
It will go into the river.
You will run and get it.

6. Wait! I'll help you.

Text- und Bildquellen

Textquellen: S.43: Randy Newman © Walt Disney Music; S.46: PONS express Wörterbuch Englisch; S. 69: E.Y. Harburg © Leo Feist Inc.; S.81: Richard Davies, Roger Hodgson © Almo Music Corp./Delicate Music Ltd, Rondor Musikverlag GmbH, Berlin

Bildquellen: Umschlag: Klett-Archiv (Hacker); S.8: Fotosearch RF (Maps Resources); S.9: Mauritius (O'Brien); www.britain-onview.com; Corbis UK Limited; Getty Images (Stone); Getty Images RF (Digital Vision); Silvestris (Lothar Lenz); Getty Images; Cinetext; S.10: Klett-Archiv (Fletcher) (auch S.4); Klett-Archiv (Fletcher); Klett-Archiv (Hacker); Klett-Archiv (Hacker); S.11: Klett-Archiv (Hacker); Getty Images (Image Bank); Klett-Archiv (Fletcher); S.12: Klett-Archiv (Hacker); S.13: Avenue Images GmbH (Digital Vision); S.15: ZEFA (masterfile); S.17: Picture-Alliance (Glyn Genin) (auch S.4); Fotosearch RF (Digital Vision); S.19: Getty Images (Image Bank); S.22: Klett-Archiv (Hacker); Getty Images; Alamy Images RM (don jon red) (auch S.4); Alamy Images RM (Paul Panayiotou); Corbis (Sandro Vannini) (auch S.4); S.23: Getty Images; Alamy Images RM (Alex Segre); Alamy Images RF (RF); MEV; S.24: Klett-Archiv (Hacker); Getty Images (Image Bank); S.25: Klett-Archiv (Hacker); Bananastock RF (auch S.60); Klett-Archiv (Fletcher); Getty Images; S.26: AP; S.29: Corbis (Hulton-Deutsch Collection); Ingram Publishing; 3+6 creativ collection; MEV; 5+7 Corel Corporation; Getty Images RF (Eyewire); S.32: Picture-Alliance (epa Dempsey); Alamy Images RM (Mark Dyball); Alamy Images RM (Justin Kase); S.35: Fotosearch RF (PhotoDisc); S.36: ZEFA (Huber); Getty Images (Image Bank); S.37: 1+5 Getty Images (Stone); Bananastock RF; ZEFA (Grace); Fotosearch RF (Stockbyte); S.39: Bananastock RF; Klett-Archiv (Hacker); S.43: MEV (auch S.5); Avenue Images GmbH (Image Source); Avenue Images GmbH (Stockbyte Gold); S.44: Klett-Archiv (Hacker); Klett-Archiv (Hacker) (auch S.5); S.45: Klett-Archiv (Hacker); S.46: Advance Features (Dave Follows); S.48: 1,6,10+16 Alamy Images RM (foodfolio); Stockfood Photo Stock Agency (Cazals, Jean); Avenue Images GmbH (brandX-pictures); Alamy Images RM (Marie-Louise Avery); Avenue Images GmbH (Image Source); 7–9 Avenue Images GmbH (Ingram Publ. RF); 11+15 MEV; Getty Images RF (PhotoDisc); Corbis (RF); Stockfood Photo Stock Agency (Cimbal, Walter); S.49: Alamy Images RM (geophotos); Klett-Archiv (Hacker) (auch S.5); Avenue Images GmbH (Thinkstock RF); Alamy Images RM (Shout) (auch S.5); Stockfood Photo Stock Agency (Mewes); S.51: 1–3 Avenue Images GmbH (Ingram Publ. RF); S.52: Alamy Images RM (Pegaz); Mauritius (Stock Image); 3,5-6 MEV; Avenue Images GmbH (ImageshopRF); S.53: Getty Images (Stone); S.55: Getty Images (Photographer's Choice); S.58: Gert Elsner, Stuttgart; 2,5,6,8,10–13 MEV; Corel Corporation; 4+14 Klett-Archiv; Stockfood Photo Stock Agency (Pete Eising); Avenue Images GmbH (Ingram Publishing); 15+18 Alamy Images RM (foodfolio); Avenue Images GmbH (Ingram Publishing); Corbis UK Limited (rf); Stockfood Photo Stock Agency; S.61: Klett-Archiv (Fletcher); S.63: Getty Images (Image Bank); Bananastock RF; Getty Images (Taxi) (auch S.6); Avenue Images GmbH (PhotoDisc) (auch S.6); S.65: Avenue Images GmbH (PhotoAlto); S.69: The Moviestore Collection (auch S.7); The Moviestore Collection; S.72: Klett-Archiv; Avenue Images GmbH (Ingram Publishing); Silvestris (Otto Stadler); Anja Hofmeister, Malmsheim; Ingram Publishing; Reinhard-Tierfoto; S.74: Klett-Archiv (Aribert Jung); DigitalVision; Unbekannter Lieferant, Stuttgart; 4+5 Klett-Archiv (Hacker); S.75: Getty Images (Stone); Alamy Images RM (Agripicture/Peter De); Alamy Images RM (Worley design); Fotofinder (picturenews/Oliver A) (auch S.6); Klett-Archiv (Fletcher); S.77: Klett-Archiv (Hacker); Getty Images (Stone); S.81: Avenue Images GmbH (Corbis RF) (auch S.6); Getty Images (Stone +); S.83: Royal Air Force; S.84: Mauritius (Albinger); 2+4 MEV; Helga Lade; Helga Lade (P. Thompson); S.86: IdealHomes: Suburbia in Focus/www.ideal-homes.org.uk; Klett-Archiv (Hacker); S.87: Klett-Archiv (Fletcher); S.88: 1+4 Getty Images (Stone); ZEFA (Photo Company) (auch S.7); ZEFA (Haenel); S.89: Alamy Images RM (David Newham); 2+3 Alamy Images RF (RF); Avenue Images GmbH (Digital Vision); Avenue Images GmbH (PhotoDisc); S.90: 1–5 MEV; S.91: AKG (1FK-3469-F1997-1); Corel Corporation; Avenue Images GmbH (Comstock); Camp Beaumont Worthington House; Bananastock RF; Picture-Alliance; S.92: 1+7 Getty Images RF (Photodisc); MEV; Kessler-Medien; Klett-Archiv (Aribert Jung); Corbis UK Limited; Alamy Images RF (RF) (auch S.7); Martin Lüdecke, Marburg-Moischt; S.93: ullstein bild (Kohl); 2–4 Alamy Images RF (RF); S.95: Avenue Images GmbH (Image Source); S.96: Okapia; Mauritius (Sipa Image); Image 100 (RF); Bosch Sicherheitssysteme GmbH, Ottobrunn; 5,7-8 Alamy Images RF (RF); Mauritius (age fotostock); EKS-Red. S (Marion Köster); S.102: Picture-Alliance (Wöstmann); S.103: Bilderberg (Popper) (auch S.7); S.118: Alamy Images RF (RF Ashton); Getty Images (Stone/Paul Harris); S.119: Alamy Images RM (don jon red); Corbis (Jeremy Horner); Getty Images (taxi/Howard Kingsnorth); Alamy Images RM (Neil Setchfield); S.123: Picture-Alliance (PA/Gareth Copley); AP; Microsoft GmbH; Corbis (Mitchell Gerber).

Every effort has been made to trace the proper owners of the copyrighted material. However, in a few cases, this may have proved impossible despite repeated enquiries. The publishers would be glad to hear from any further copyright owners of material reproduced in this book.

Look at the map. In which of these countries is English the official language?

India | Brazil | the UK | Russia | China
Australia | South Africa | the United States

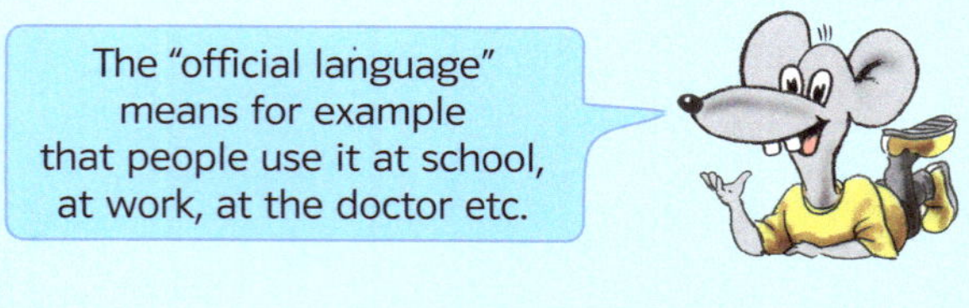

Did you know?

- More than 400 million people speak English as a first language.
- There are about 500,000 words in English.
- The main language on the Internet is English.